PROBLEMS & PROSPECTS OF THE NEGRO MOVEMENT

Edited by

RAYMOND J. MURPHY
University of California, Los Angeles

and

HOWARD ELINSON
Yale University

Wadsworth Publishing Company, Inc., Belmont, California

L. C. Cat. Card No.: 66–23085
Printed in the United States of America

Preface

The increasing importance of the civil rights movement and Negro political action in America has brought with it an urgency for informed public opinion. In the final analysis, the success or failure of the movement—and the direction it will take—will depend largely upon what the majority of the citizens think about the actions of the minority who are directly involved in the movement.

In selecting articles for this book from among the many high quality papers in the field, we have been guided primarily by the general relevance of each to the issues and problems at hand. Thus, we have avoided detailed treatments of specific historical events or communities and have excluded the older classics in the area of race relations and the large psychological literature on prejudice.

A second criterion has been the availability of the articles selected. We believe the basic justification of a book of readings is that it makes available important sources of information that are not otherwise readily available.

Given the length of the book, there is not an especially large number of readings. Particularly in the handling of a subject so complex, we feel it is important to give the readings of each topic thorough and extended treatment. Therefore, it was necessary to sacrifice sheer quantity for depth of meaning.

Although the editors have made their views apparent in the introductory material, the articles presented include the views of all the major forces that are active, and often conflicting, in the Negro movement.

The editors owe their greatest debt to the authors and publishers who have allowed their material to be reprinted in this collection of readings. We greatly appreciate their cooperation. Without the help of Mrs. Donna Katz, who provided excellent technical and clerical assistance, this book could not have been prepared. We also wish to thank Leonard Freedman for his expert editorial advice and assistance and Peter Orleans, Samuel Surace, and Charles Wright, colleagues in the Department of Sociology of UCLA, for their interest and helpful suggestions.

Raymond J. Murphy
Howard Elinson

WADSWORTH CONTINUING EDUCATION SERIES

Leonard Freedman, General Editor

Contents

PROBLEMS & PROSPECTS OF THE NEGRO MOVEMENT

Introduction

It does not take the perspicacity of a scholar or a researcher to discover that the American Negro is actively concerned with improving his opportunities and legal rights. Newspapers every day give us dramatic accounts of the efforts of a multitude of individuals and groups who are trying to correct present injustices and ensure eventual gains. The Negro movement is as much a reality of the 1960's as is the existence of man traveling in outer space. Yet, as familiar as the movement may be to millions of Americans, we suspect that the issues it has raised and the seemingly endless number of organizations it has spawned are perplexing to many. The purpose of this book is to give the reader some understanding of the American Negro's situation and of the different answers— or strategies—that have been proposed to improve it.

Many people date the origins of the Negro movement with the Supreme Court's 1954 decision on school desegregation. While such an event may give us a bench mark in the process of change, we must not overlook the fact that change is continuous. The current Negro movement cannot be interpreted merely as a response to legal decisions or any other particular events of the 1950's or '60's. It must be viewed against a background of broad secular developments in American society over a long period of time.

The increasing urbanism of the United States is one of the most important developments. The persistent stereotype of the Negro as a rural dweller tending fields of cotton may be picturesque, but it is inaccurate. In 1900, only 22.7 per cent of American Negroes lived in cities, as compared with 42.4 per cent of the whites. By 1960, 73.4 per cent of American Negroes had become urban dwellers, a somewhat higher proportion than whites (69.5 per cent). The most recent census shows not only that the majority of American Negroes live in cities but also that Negroes tend to be proportionately more concentrated in the largest metropolitan areas of the country than whites. Thirty per cent of all urban Negroes live in the 26 largest metropolitan centers of the United States today, while about 25 per cent of the white urbanites live in these large population centers. The same data reveal that Negroes have concentrated more in the central cities of large metropolitan areas than in the suburban areas.

The dramatic pace of the urban trend, particularly among Negroes, can be seen by comparing the census findings of 1960 with those of 1950. If we look at figures for "urbanized areas" and note the percentage of increase during the decade for white and nonwhite populations, we get a good idea of the magnitude of this population change. By "urbanized area" the Census Bureau means those cities of 50,000 population or over and their surrounding regions of dense population. In the decade 1950–1960, the nonwhite population of urbanized areas as a whole increased by 61.6 per cent, while the white population showed an increase of only 35.1 per cent.

A closely related demographic trend of similar importance is regional migration. Many of us think of American Negroes predominantly as residents of the South, as they were in the past. In 1910, 89 per cent of American Negroes did live in the South; but in 1960, only a little more than half of them, about 60 per cent, lived in the South. Figures on population increases in the South for whites and Negroes during the decade 1950–1960 show that whites increased by about 18 per cent, while Negroes showed only a 10.6 per cent gain. Figures for other regions of the country indicate the directions of Negro movement. States in the Pacific region had an increase of 38.6 per cent in their white population and nearly 90 per cent in Negro population during the decade. The East North Central states, including Ohio, Indiana, Illinois, Michigan, and Wisconsin, showed a percentage gain of 16.5 per cent for whites and 60 per cent for Negroes. In the Middle Atlantic states of New York, New Jersey, and Pennsylvania, whites increased 10.8 per cent while Negroes increased 48.5 per cent. Some of these growth differentials undoubtedly reflect differing birth rates of the white and Negro groups. However, it seems clear that migration accounted for the majority of these population changes.

It should be kept in mind that when discussing regional migration we have referred to *rates of increase* in population, not percentages of total population, white or Negro, at a particular time. For example, although the Negro population of the Pacific region increased at a much higher rate than the white population in 1960, the percentage of whites (91.1) in the total population of the area was far greater than that of Negroes (4.5). In sum, recent years have shown a migratory trend among Negroes from the South to other areas in the country, particularly the industrial regions of the West and North.

Concomitant with the migratory trends have been changes in the occupational structure; the status of the Negro has been changing rapidly from that of small-farm owner, operator, or sharecropper to that of urban laborer. In 1963, only 9.7 per cent of employed nonwhites were engaged in agricultural work, while a third were in semiskilled or unskilled urban occupations. A more detailed discussion of the current occupational position of Negroes and its implications for the future is in Part Two of this book.

We feel that these three major population shifts—increasing urbanization, migration to the Western and Northern industrial areas, and the changing occupational status—are the central processes underlying the tensions and problems of the Negro. They also help to explain the particular strategies advocated by spokesmen for the Negro cause and why the spokesmen so often disagree. However, other developments, both at home and abroad, should be mentioned.

Since World War II, major political developments in the "underdeveloped" areas of the world have had some effect on Negroes in the United States. The major colonial powers have granted independence or self-rule to many territories. At the same time, there has been an increase in the spirit of nationalism among many "colored" persons. While the majority of American Negroes may not feel a close sense of kinship with these peoples, it seems evident that they have noticed the rising aspirations of new nations in Africa and Asia. Comparisons with the frustrated ambitions and social injustices at home seem inevitable and probably lend support to the feeling that the time for action is now.

Also worth mentioning is the role of mass communication, which makes it obvious to the Negro that his problems of race are not local. The mass media also keep him well informed about what others have that he does not. Thus, the Negro may feel relatively more deprived, because he is exposed to a continuing bombardment of stimuli glorifying life in an affluent society. He has learned, too, that by effective use of the media he can dramatize his plight and influence public opinion. Although critics of "mass society" often decry the "leveling-down" effects of the mass media, we would suggest that the media also generate pressures toward a "leveling up" in standards of living and life styles.

Though there is general agreement that the major trends we have discussed are of great significance, there is considerable disagreement about how to proceed from these background factors to a more detailed analysis of the problems of the Negro. All observers agree that the Negro problem is not a single problem but a complex tangle of problems embracing the areas of education, housing, employment, and justice. But there is almost no agreement as to what is the relationship among the major problem areas. Neither of the two "traditional" ways of expressing the relationship is particularly satisfactory. The first is the search for a key. People have attempted to identify various factors as the basic key to the problem; all "key" arguments rest on the premise that a single factor is the cause and that others are mere effects. For example, it has been argued that the root of the Negro problem is inferior education: from inferior education stems lack of skills, which causes low-paying employment and high unemployment; these economic conditions cause high crime and inferior housing. The great shortcoming of the single-factor approach is that the alleged effects can always be shown to exert some causal influences. In this case, it can easily be shown that the inferiority of Negro education is partly a result of high unemployment and inadequate housing.

The second tradition is to throw up one's hands in despair at the confusion and complexity of the problem and retreat to an indiscriminate multicausal approach. This approach conceptualizes the problem of Negroes as a vicious circle. There are neither clear causes nor clear effects. Instead, all factors are said to "interact with each other." The fault in this approach is that, in avoiding a single-factor explanation, it tends to assess all factors as of equal or indeterminable significance.

Both approaches, single-factor and multifactor, derive their popularity more from their relative simplicity than from their validity. The alternative perspective—the one toward which this book of readings is oriented—cannot be stated either simply or precisely. Its basic premise is that factors interact but do not have equal causal significance because: (1) historical research will show some factors to precede others in time; (2) sociological analysis will show some factors to be more common, more forceful, or more significant in some other way.

Let us discuss, for example, the possible relationships between economic deprivation and inadequate housing. The monistic approach would argue that inadequate housing can be explained entirely in terms of economic deprivation. That is, if Negroes had more money and better jobs, they could afford better housing and would be able to "buy" the political power they need to remove discrimination in the housing field. The multicausal approach would argue that if Negroes had better housing they would have more stable family arrangements; children would do better in school, and school success would contribute to job advancements; better jobs, in turn, would bring better housing; and so forth.

Our analysis would indicate that economic deprivation is much more important than inadequate housing. However, it is not the necessary and sufficient cause of inadequate housing, nor is it so purely a "cause" that it is not affected by housing conditions. Clearly, economic oppression is an earlier and more universal fact of Negro life than is the particular housing problems Negroes now have. Further, the single factor that goes farthest to explain the housing conditions of Negroes is their inability to pay for adequate housing. Yet this does not complete the picture. It is also true, as Loren Miller shows in Part Two, that Negro housing is considerably worse than one could justify on mere economic grounds. For example, much of the housing in Harlem is markedly worse than housing that costs the same amount of money in white neighborhoods. Negroes do not live in Harlem merely because they cannot afford to live in white neighborhoods. Discrimination in housing is a problem even for Negroes who are well paid. As for the causal significance of housing conditions, that whole complex of conditions we can refer to as "ghetto life" results partly from poor-quality, segregated housing. The part segregation plays, however, is not equal with all the other pieces in the causal puzzle. It is smaller than the part played by high rates of unemployment and underemployment and the heavy concentration of Negroes in the lowest-paying occupations.

Thus, what we suggest is an analysis that weighs the relative causal significance of each factor while avoiding the pitfalls of the traditional single-cause and multicause approaches.

It should be made explicit that there is a direct and important relationship between one's assessment of causal factors and his commitments to programs and policy. The identification of a single cause is the prelude to a single-minded program. Conversely, the multifactor approach generally precedes a "do everything at once" policy. From a policy standpoint, neither of these views is satisfactory. It is difficult to justify an almost total disregard of housing or schools in order to concentrate on, perhaps, employment or political power. However, the resources of the civil rights movement are far too limited to justify a policy of equal effort in all areas. Tactical decisions must be made on the most important and most promising areas.

To reach the proper decisions, two distinct analyses must be made. First, some judgment must be made on the relative causal impact of each factor on the whole picture; the second part of this book is directed toward that problem. Second, the relative susceptibility of each factor to change and the likely outcomes of various strategies must be analyzed; the third part of the book is relevant for this. It is important not to confuse causal judgments with tactical judgments. Residential segregation provides a good case of the distinction. The concentration of Negroes in segregated neighborhoods is undoubtedly of great causal significance. However, the return from efforts to change housing patterns significantly is probably much smaller than returns on equivalent expenditures of effort in, for example, the area of education.

In making our selections from the vast quantity of available materials, we had to take some things for granted and to assess others as problematic. Here are the assumptions and problems that guided us in choosing.

ASSUMPTIONS

1. *The moral and legal basis of the Negro movement is not open to question.* While various strategies and proposals may raise serious questions of morality and law, the foundations of the civil rights movement are sound. This essential soundness derives from two sources: (a) The legitimacy of the legal and political bases is indisputable. By 1965, the civil rights movement rested not merely on the 1954 Supreme Court decision but also on unequivocal action by Congress and the President (1964 Civil Rights Bill, 1965 Voting Bill, President Johnson's moral and legal stand). (b) Polls of public opinion, national media, the clergy, and so forth, indicate the development in recent years of a national consensus, encompassing most groups, on the essential justness of most Negro demands. Some segments of society (such as a proportion of whites in the Deep South) are excluded from the consensus.

2. *Race and race relations are thoroughly social in their nature. They have no "essence" rooted in racial memories, human nature, or human biology.* It has become popular among some leaders, especially literary and religious ones (James Baldwin, Erskine Caldwell, William Stringfellow, Thomas Merton), to regard the problems of Negroes in America as basically metaphysical. Oddly, elements of both extreme pro-Negro and extreme anti-Negro forces have argued that the problem is one of the heart or soul and not readily amenable to what they regard as superficial social reforms. Their position rests on a mystical belief that race is a force so powerful that only other mystical soul-forces (love or repentance) can overcome it. Without denying the unfathomable depths

of racial feeling in many Americans, we have rejected the metaphysical approach. We view problems of race as subject to successful change by the most ordinary of means: well-conceived laws that are enforced, shrewd use of ordinary political power, rational innovations in the field of education. When these methods fail, it is not because of any eternity or spirituality of race but for one of three possible reasons: (a) insufficient power on the part of Negroes and their allies; (b) insufficient knowledge of the social mechanisms that create and sustain certain problems; (c) the impact of historical and social forces so great that no measures can be found which are equal to the goals.

PROBLEMS

There are two broad, unresolved and controversial issues which encompass almost all discussions about American race relations today:

1. *Is the situation of the American Negro an aberration or an integral element of American society?* Those who view it as an aberration imply that we can proceed with "business as usual" as long as we systematically include, rather than exclude, Negroes from the conduct of that business. Their assumption is that Negroes are no different from other minority groups. They have fared worse because they have not been treated like the other groups. According to this line of reasoning, the abolition of gross forms of segregation and discrimination should result in a course of development for the Negro similar to that experienced by the Irish, Jews, Italians, etc. Just as the American political and economic system has been able to accommodate these groups, it can also accommodate the Negro.

Those who view the plight of the Negro as an integral element of our society imply that "business as usual" means a grossly unequal position for Negroes. They believe the ordinary processes of American society cannot include Negroes adequately without undergoing basic changes. For example, as long as unemployment and underemployment remain high, Negroes will be economically disadvantaged. The present structure of the economy does not provide full employment. Thus, the question of Negro employment cannot be separated from larger questions involving economic planning and our rate of economic growth. Behind each problem of the Negro is a broader problem that arises from the nature of our most basic institutions. This position dismisses as irrelevant the experience of various immigrant groups. These groups rose in our system at a time when unskilled manual labor and small retail business played major roles. Negroes cannot, under any circumstances, be expected to follow a similar pattern in today's economy, which rests on advanced technical skills and large corporate enterprises.

Obviously, it will make a big difference to the Negro which of these views, or combination of them, the country chooses. The holders of each of these conflicting perspectives are committed to alternative versions of the history of the Negro, the nature of the present situation and appropriate policies for it, and their expectations for the future. The most important thing to be said about both views is that they are problematic. While it is unlikely that either one is totally correct, one view is probably closer to reality than the other.

2. *How much should "be done for Negroes" and how much should they do for themselves?* Since the days of Booker T. Washington, the notion of Negro self-help has been equated with the idea of Negroes "behaving themselves" while whites ignore their problems. As a reaction to this view, another inadequate version of the relationship between the races has come into prominence. It holds that the problems of American Negoes stem from hundreds of years of cruel, calculating, and profitable exploitation by whites. Since whites created "the Negro problem," the moral burden is on white people to right the injustices. Further, all moral considerations aside, only whites have the power to alter the situation. Since their economic and political strength even exceeds their great numerical majority, no Negro self-help can avail without massive help from the larger white society. Once white society puts its house in order, self-help will not be necessary, but self-interest will prompt Negroes to take advantage of opportunities as they open up.

Without denying the need for massive action by the society as a whole, one can argue that failure or success would depend largely on some version of self-help. However, Negroes will not take their opportunities unless there is a mass movement among them to convince them of both the possibility and the desirability of a "new way of life." The apathy, demoralization, and cynicism rooted in hundreds of years of repression cannot be changed from the outside. Further, as Ellison points out, despite the noble intentions of the view that puts all blame on the white man, this view denies the essential humanity of the Negro. It makes him a ball of putty, a totally passive man whose whole existence is one of reaction to whites. Certainly this is historically untrue. The Negro's church has been a positive force of his own—a creative and, at times, ingenious means of making the best of a hopeless situation. The civil rights movement itself is proof of the role Negroes can and do play in solving their own problems. However, thus far the movement has been turned outward. The achievement of major changes in white society requires the active quest for changes in Negro society that will bring Negroes to take full advantage of hard-won gains. For example, new techniques in education and the breaking down of school segegation must be coupled with action in the Negro community to convince parents and children of the value of education. At many junctures in the civil rights movement, these platitudes will pose bitter and painful problems. Given the limited resources of the movement, it may be necessary at times to choose between consolidation of gains through work within the Negro community and the battle for new gains through attack on the larger society.

THE FUTURE

The fact that American Negroes have made unquestionable gains in all areas since World War II may lull observers into an unwarranted sense of accomplishment. Many of the gains are satisfying only by comparison with a dismal past. For example, can we expect Negroes to be very excited about the right to vote—a right that has been a legal fiction for 100 years? While the vote is an instrument of magnificent power, it hardly fills one's life. The day-to-day problems of inferior jobs, schools, and housing loom very large beside the gains of recent years. It should also be noted that most of the gains are *absolute* rather than relative. As Miller shows, absolute gains have come simultaneously with comparative losses. Grossly put, Negroes are doing better than they used to, but whites are doing *much* better than *they* used to.

We wish to make clear the uncertainty of the Negro future. Americans are deeply attached to the idea of progress, but progress is by no means assured for the American Negro. A careful study of the available materials makes it possible to outline at least three possible prognoses. However, the picture is too ambiguous to argue strongly that any one is certain. The future, of course, is always affected by our expectations of it. Therefore, it seems worthwhile to consider these prophecies.

1. *Things will get worse for the American Negro—both absolutely and relatively.* Fear of economic reprisals combined with traditional apathy and cynicism will prove enormous barriers to the development of Negro political power even with the new Voting Rights Bill.

Massive "secular trends" in the economy will result in increased unemployment and underemployment among Negroes. Automation in both manufacturing and service industries will cut deeply into the Negroes' economic position.

Federal programs to help Negroes will be used to better advantage by poor whites, Puerto Ricans, and Mexican-Americans. These groups, which have fewer problems in their own communities and are not subject to nearly so much prejudice and discrimination as Negroes, will enjoy the bulk of jobs and housing available for people from low-income backgrounds.

2. *The Negro will continue to experience absolute improvement in his situation.* However, no relative gains *vis-à-vis* whites will be made, and some losses can be expected. The educational attainments, job levels, quality of housing, and income of Negroes will all improve. Nevertheless, whites will also continue to make dramatic gains in all these areas. Thus, while the "bottom of society" will be higher and more comfortable than it used to be, Negroes will still be at the bottom. It is hard to imagine that any amount of running will enable the Negro to catch up, since there is no chance that whites will slow down or stand still.

3. *There will be steady improvements in both the absolute and relative positions of Negroes.* Phenomenal increases in Negro voting in the South coupled with political hegemony in the major cities will make the Negroes a major political bloc. An alliance for mutual advantage will be entered into by Negroes, labor unions, poor whites, Puerto Ricans, and Mexican-Americans. This alliance will provide the political muscle to deal with automation and other causes of unemployment. Massive increases will occur in the level of activity by the federal government in all areas. This activity will bring gains in education, housing, and employment, enabling Negroes to catch up, at least in part. While whites will continue to make gains, their rate of advancement will be much slower because of the absence of federal programs in their behalf and because of the high level at which their advancement must begin. The adoption of rational testing programs in schools and industry will cause downward mobility for some whites. All these things will combine to decrease the size of the gap between Negroes and whites.

It is one of the great ironies of social science that the way in which people react to contradictory predictions will influence the future in some measure.

Part One
The Background: Opinions and Issues

      As the reader may have inferred from our introductory remarks, it is our view that the Negro's quest for greater equality and opportunities will require major structural changes in American society. We believe that problems of the American Negro are more than a matter of prejudice correctable by widespread attitudinal changes. Whatever merit "positive thoughts" may have for the individual, the recent acts of violence must serve to remind us that actions, not words, are the bench marks by which American Negroes chart the success of their 100-year quest. At the same time, deeds cannot be divorced from belief. The perceptions, hopes, and anxieties of a population serve to define the parameters of potential accomplishment, and thus represent an important part of the setting for the drama of the civil rights revolution. While the leaders of both white and Negro groups play the most important roles in shaping the scope and direction of the Negro drive for greater equality, the feelings of the "little" people cannot be ignored. Their general moods of optimism, fear, hostility, or indifference serve to influence the speed of change and the strategy used to effect the change. Public opinion serves as the radar of the congressional representative. In the arena of political struggle, it cannot be safely ignored.

Our discussion of the movement for equality and justice begins, then, with two pieces that summarize the results of the most comprehensive attempt to gauge the mood of the American nation during the 1960's —that conducted by the Louis Harris organization. The first article reports the attitudes of a cross section of American Negroes in 1965 and compares these recent opinions with those of a comparable group in 1963. It gives some idea of the direction of change in beliefs over two eventful years—in a period marked by riots, a presidential campaign, and the most comprehensive civil rights bill passed by Congress since the Civil War.

The second article summarizes the opinions of a national sample of whites with regard to equality of the Negro and their reactions to the efforts of those in the civil rights movement. It enables us to estimate the amount of resistance to change that can be expected in such areas as employment, housing, and social relationships. That attitudes in these areas are subject to rapid change is indicated in the most recent Harris poll, released in the fall of 1965. This survey shows that whites expressed more tolerance to the idea of having a Negro move next door to them (in 1963, 51% objected to a Negro neighbor; in 1965, only 37% indicated disapproval), and fewer negative feelings about working next to Negroes (17% objected in 1963 compared with 10% in 1965). The 1965 Harris survey also indicates a decline in acceptance of the traditional stereotype of the Negro as a shiftless, happy-go-lucky, unambitious person. Despite such increases in tolerance, however, the poll shows little change in feelings about intimate contact between the races. The vast majority of whites would object, for example, to having a close relative marry a Negro. Thus the relationship between verbal expressions of attitudes or knowledge on the one hand and actual behavior on the other remains complex. We suggest that the two attitudinal articles in this section be read as a unit that gives an overview of the pushes and resistances facing the civil rights movement in this stage of its development.

Many articles in this book point up the wide divergence of opinions among persons who share a concern for the Negro and his future. Questions of appropriate goals, strategies, priority of needs, etc., have become arenas for debate. The varieties of opinion, though interesting in themselves, are often more valuable for the underlying assumptions and ideologies of spokesmen within the general movement that they reveal. One area of contention—that of white responsibility—is revealed in the final articles of this section. The provocative article by Eric Hoffer takes a critical look at the Negro community and its efforts to achieve social and economic progress. Rather than focusing on the responsibilities that whites have to Negroes and the tasks that face us as a nation, Hoffer emphasizes the responsibilities Negroes have towards themselves. He relates many problems to the weaknesses and shortcomings of Negroes rather than to the failures and discriminatory practices of whites. While some will find his accusations unjust, every reader should be stimulated by the question he raises: How much should Negroes be expected to do to solve their own problems? In contrast with this piece by Hoffer, we call the reader's attention to the article in Section Three by Arthur I. Waskow. Waskow defends many of the "disruptive" aspects of the civil rights movement which Hoffer criticizes. His analysis emphasizes the positive functions of "creative disorder."

Another view of white responsibility is seen in the advocacy of compensation programs for Negroes. Advocates argue that since the Negro has been harshly and categorically disfavored for so long, he deserves categorical favoritism until Negroes begin to "catch up" with whites. There have been several serious and concrete proposals based on this line of reasoning. For example, it has been proposed that Negro applicants be given a point bonus on civil service exams comparable to the ten-point bonus often given veterans. In New York City, some civil rights officials have suggested that the admission requirement for Negroes in the city colleges be 5 percentage points lower than for whites. Whitney Young and Kyle Haselden ably discuss the relevant points on both sides of this thorny issue.

Newsweek Magazine
THE NEGRO IN AMERICA—1965

The revolt of the American Negro was born of two and a half centuries in chains and one of imperfect freedom. But it has been, from the beginning, a revolution of enduring, almost incredible hope. Its anthem speaks both its program and its faith: "We shall overcome someday."

Today, according to a *Newsweek* Poll by public-opinion analyst Louis Harris, Negroes are experiencing a fresh surge of hope. They feel heartened that their fighting faith has been doubly rewarded—by the passage of the Civil Rights Act of 1964 and by the landslide burial of its most prominent opponent, Barry Goldwater. Black America has no illusion that the millennium has arrived—and no intention of relaxing its fight for full equality. But Negroes do feel more certain than ever that they will indeed overcome—and that the "someday" of the song is tangibly nearer at hand.

The poll marks the second in-depth visit by Harris interviewers to the nation's Negro community. The first, nineteen months ago, produced the groundbreaking "Negro in America" survey (*Newsweek*, July 29, 1963)—a micrometer measurement of the breadth, the depth, and the direction of the civil-rights revolt in its first flood-tide summer. The follow-up took place in the fall and winter months of 1964: the ebb-tide days after the summer of the Civil Rights Act and the nomination of Barry Goldwater, the triple-lynching in Mississippi and the ghetto riots in the North. Interviewers—almost all Negroes—presented a wide-ranging battery of questions to a cross-sectional sample of 500 black Americans across the U.S.

Their findings:

■   Far from being an explosively frustrated mass, Negroes are, in the main, caught up by an exhilarating sense of progress. Southerners particularly have already seen the first palpable benefits of the rights law: the widespread disappearance of white-only signs from restaurants, hotels, motels, theaters, and public facilities. And Negroes on both sides of the Mason-Dixon line believe they will be still better off five years from now in the stickier, substantive areas of housing, schooling, and jobs.

■   As a tender of goodwill, the rights law has reaffirmed and deepened the Negro's faith in white America—and so did Goldwater's defeat. By acclamation, Lyndon Johnson—and his party—have cinched places in the pantheon of heroes of the revolt; Goldwater ranks second only to the Ku Klux Klan in its demonology. Congress has mended its good name, tarnished after years of inaction. Negroes still have mixed feelings about the white man generally—but they think he is getting better all the time, and they bank increasingly on him to meet them halfway.

■   Negroes are more deeply committed than ever to the strategy of nonviolence—and they are likely to be more selective in using militant tactics. The Northern riots gave them a bad scare. Moreover, the battles already won have strengthened the Negro's allegiance to his established,

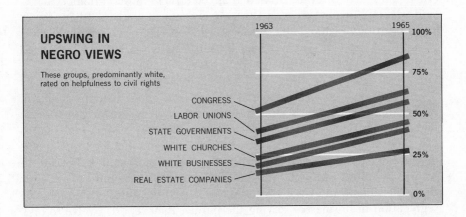

UPSWING IN NEGRO VIEWS

These groups, predominantly white, rated on helpfulness to civil rights

CONGRESS
LABOR UNIONS
STATE GOVERNMENTS
WHITE CHURCHES
WHITE BUSINESSES
REAL ESTATE COMPANIES

1963   1965   100%
75%
50%
25%
0%

middle-class, church-oriented leaders. He is turning sharply away from such tactics as pupil boycotts to win school integration—and such techniques as busing to implement it.

■   Yet the revolt is not over—far from it. Negroes have not backed down from their basic demands for an end to discrimination in all its forms—or from the majority view that the pace of progress is still too slow. They regard the trophies of two revolutionary summers, including the rights act, as promissory notes still to be paid in full. They are generally inclined now to believe that white America will honor these pledges. But they won't stop making demands.

WHITE MAN FIRST: And small wonder; the scars of color prejudice run too deep to be erased by an act of Congress. The constant in both Harris surveys was the vast majority of Negroes who could cite some painful, personal experience with discrimination. One in three said it bruised them worst on the job: "A white man will get hired before I will," said a 25-year-old Pittsburgh hospital worker. "I can't buy the things for my wife and kids that I should." One in ten mentioned schools: "I used to work for white people," a young South Carolina farm-store employee said. "I could see a third-grade child spell words a fifth- or sixth-grade Negro child could not." Some mentioned the private hurts of public segregation: "I went to the store to buy a coat, but I couldn't try it on because of my race." "I went South driving and was told to go to the back door when I stopped at a restaurant." "White people were unkind to me, called me 'nigger,' but I never paid it no mind—I just call it ignorance."

But none were so eloquent as those who could not quite say when and where discrimination had affected them most. "I do not know," said Samuel Murphy, an aged Durham, N.C., farm worker. "I have for 72 years been segregated." Mrs. Annie Pearl Hunt, 26, of Greenville, S.C., a former nurse, put it simply: "I have been mad when I could have been pleased. I have been sad when I could have been happy."

OPENING DOORS: Against such fatalism about being a Negro in white America, the gains already in hand—even the token gains—have had an electrifying impact. Many Southern Negroes haven't yet tried to use their newly won entree into the white man's hotels, motels, and restaurants. "I wasn't going there in the first place," said a 27-year-old woman in Mount Pleasant, S.C., and "I ain't going in the third place." But they still look on the Civil Rights Act as something akin to the repeal of segregation in businesses serving the public; they report, twelve to one, that it has already opened new doors to them. And, though only one Negro child in 50 is going to school with whites in the South, three Negro adults in five believe that chances for their youngsters to attend mixed classes have improved in the past year. That rosy view suggests that a little integration goes a long way with Negroes—provided their feeling of forward motion is not deflected or stalled by white resistance.

And it hasn't been so far. Across the nation, two Negroes in five say their work situation has improved in the past year, while one in four reports he has better housing. But roughly two-thirds believe their lot will get better still, across the board, in the next five years. Again, they see the Civil Rights Act as the key; they believe, 47 to one, that it will bring further progress not only in desegregating public accommodations but in schooling, employment, and voting.

For all that, their demands remain substantially unchanged. Their revolt remains a revolution of rising expectations; Negroes feel they have only begun to sample the fruits of integration and to share in the material well-being of middle-class white America. The rights act itself is still just a glowing promise. "We have a law, but will it be enforced?" a Philadelphia pensioner wondered—and one Negro in four agreed that its implementation is one of the top two or three problems confronting them today.

This is their agenda of unfinished business:

Jobs and wages remain the No. 1 issue for rank-and-file Negroes. They feel they are getting a better break in some fields, especially politics, civil-service, and schoolteaching. But the potential collision points remain: one Negro in six ranks skilled labor and white-collar work among the trades at which Negro job hunters are least likely to succeed.

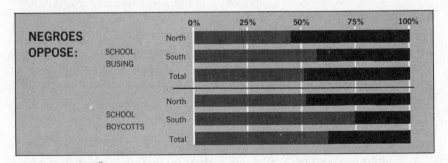

And Negroes want equal pay for equal work; three in five remain convinced that a white man will get better wages than a Negro doing the same job.

Education ranks a close second. By six to one, Negroes still want integrated schools. But the classroom integration to date, however limited, has helped persuade them in surprising numbers (60 per cent in the North, 47 per cent nationally) that their children are getting as good an education as whites. Northern Negroes now part company with some of their more militant local leaders on both tactics and aims. Significantly, they have switched from a 54-to-28 stance in favor of busing Negro children to white schools nineteen months ago to a 45-to-41 line-up against busing today. And they are 53 to 29 against school boycotts. "If we didn't demonstrate," said one boycott advocate, 30-year-old Rosetta Bray of Detroit, "the kids wouldn't get a chance to go to school with whites." But the majority view now is that education is too precious a commodity to be sacrificed even for a boycott of a single day. "The children need the education," said Mrs. Marie White, 25, a Chicago laborer's wife. "Get the education and then get up and fight."

Housing—perhaps the stickiest issue of all—has been relegated for now to the back burner. By an overwhelming 91 per cent, Negroes still cherish the American dream of a private home—preferably in a suburb or small town. And, by 64-to-18, they would still prefer racially mixed to all-Negro neighborhoods. "I'm not prejudiced," Mrs. White remarked. "If they can stand me, I can stand them." But in the year and seven months since the 1963 poll, integrated housing has run into stiffer white resistance than other Negro demands; fair-housing laws have been repealed or defeated by referendum in California and in several Northern cities. Today, housing ranks third behind jobs and education on the rank-and-file Negro priority list.

What has changed significantly is not the issues but the Negro's view of white America after the great symbolic victories of 1964. Nineteen months ago, Negroes looked on themselves as a lonely minority, fighting without much certainty of white support. Then, a majority thought that, at worst, the white man wanted to keep Negroes down—or, at best, simply didn't care. Only one in four believed that whites wanted to see Negroes get a better break. For a minority within the minority, doubt had turned to despair: one Negro in five either wasn't sure that the U.S. was worth fighting for—or was sure it wasn't.

BETTER ATTITUDES: Yet even then, a majority felt that white attitudes would improve—and now Negroes tend to believe that their trust has been rewarded. More than half think whites have changed for the better in the past year; nearly four in five believe their attitudes will improve still more by 1970. The number that doubted whether the U.S. was worth fighting for has been cut nearly in half.

And the number that believes whites want Negroes to get a better break has nearly doubled, from 25 to 44 per cent. James Ogden Jr., 25, a Detroit auto worker, still thinks that whites want to keep Negroes down—"because you're black, that's all"—and a young Philadelphia maintenance man remains unconvinced: "Why should they care? As long as we don't holler, they don't give a damn about me."

But now more feel that whites want to help. "When you look at it," said a 42-year-old San Diego transit worker, "a lot of them are working just as hard as the Negro for equal rights." Mrs. Helen Scott, 42, a widowed New Orleans beautician, remarked, "All white folk ain't against us. Some has a good heart." And a Los Angeles man added: "They fought for the civil-rights law."

But that was only part of the buoyant mood. More than ever, Negroes feel they have sorted their friends from their enemies—and their friends seem more numerous than they used to. They gave Barry Goldwater an 82-to-1 unfavorable rating. More than a fifth volunteered his name when asked to list the whites they disliked and distrusted most. ("Goldwater," said a 63-year-old Philadelphia woman, "is for whites and war.") But, with Goldwater's defeat, that list is increasingly restricted to the Deep South and the extreme right: the Ku Klux Klan (cited by 46 per cent), the white Citizens Councils (20 per cent), Alabama Gov. George C. Wallace (19 per cent), and the John Birch Society (8 per cent).

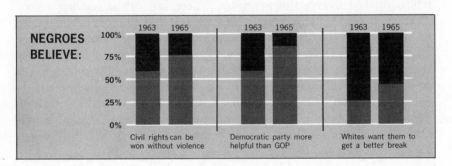

NEGROES BELIEVE:

Civil rights can be won without violence

Democratic party more helpful than GOP

Whites want them to get a better break

Lyndon Johnson, by contrast, gets an extraordinary 96-to-0 favorable job rating from Negroes—and a place, ahead of Bobby Kennedy, at the head of the class of whites most trusted by Negroes. The President owes that standing not only to his own commitment to civil rights but to his role as John F. Kennedy's legatee. "He's following Kennedy," a 65-year-old Philadelphia widow remarked. "Kennedy was a good man. He *liked* us." Today, Negroes clearly intend to stand wary watch on how well Mr. Johnson honors that commitment. But, for the moment, they have banked their political capital heavily—perhaps dangerously so for their own cause—with one man and, by an 87-to-1 landslide margin, one party.

GOODWILL FALLOUT: The passage of the Civil Rights Act in effect sustained the Negro's faith in the Presidency. More significantly, it redeemed his faith in Congress. In the 1963 poll, a bare 54 per cent thought Congress was doing more good than harm in the cause of civil rights. Now, its prestige rating has shot up to 85 per cent, on a par with the much-revered U.S. Supreme Court. And the fallout of goodwill has spread to other white institutions that seem to Negroes to have played some role in the drive for equality. Thus, their favorable rating for labor unions has gone up from 40 to 62 per cent; state governments, 35 to 56; local authorities, 30 to 49; white churches, 24 to 44; white businesses, 19 to 42, and even white real-estate companies, 16 to 27. In a year of spreading concession to Negro demands, even the white South suddenly seems more congenial to Negroes; nearly two-thirds of those who live there now say they wouldn't move North if they could.

And, by that optimistic view, how can violence be justified? In 1963, Negroes thought, three to one, that they could win without it; today, they believe by a doubly certain seven to one that they can and will overcome by nonviolent means. There are still dissenting voices. "You can't stand up and let someone else beat you down or sic their dogs on you or shoot you," a Detroit man said. "I believe what the Bible says: an eye for an eye and a tooth for a tooth." But Negroes now more than ever share the view of R. V. Edwards, 43, an Altus, Okla., cook: "If you kick a dog, he will bite you—but if you pet him, he will eventually make friends with you." Or Mrs. Eldora Basile, a 28-year-old New Orleans domestic: "We have come a long way without violence." Or the simple faith of a 52-year-old Los Angeles housewife: "We goin' win. Violence ain't goin' to be much."

OPEN WAR: The commitment to nonviolence has curiously little to do with raw considerations of power. Roughly half the Negroes believe they could win an open war with whites against 10-to-1 numerical odds, if it came to that. This is partly simple racial pride ("If violence breaks and the colored people know they have to fight, the whites will think there are ten Negroes to one white"), partly an article of faith ("The Lord will make a way for us since we have been treated as we have"), and partly the heartening feeling that many whites would take the Negro's side ("It's the white people helping us *now*").

The Negro tasted violence last summer in the chain-lightning series of riots that erupted in Harlem—and it was an unnerving, soul-bruising experience. They found reasons aplenty in the tindery atmosphere of the Northern ghettos. "Police brutality, restlessness, unemployment, and idleness and slum areas and segregation—they were just tired of it all," Mrs. Marie White summed up. Yet only one in five thought average Negro citizens were actually involved—and only one in 33 singled them out as ringleaders. Instead, they assigned the blame to young hoodlums and to extremists of both races: the Black Muslims, black nationalists, the Communists, the Klan, the Citizens Councils.

'BUSED AND SCORNED': One in five believed that the riots helped their cause. "The colored got tired of being kept down and 'bused and scorned," said Doris Lyles, 24, kitchen helper at Benedict College in Columbia, S.C. Some felt that even a riot is a valid protest demonstration: "They push us around," a Los Angeles woman said. "Now in the North we're pushing back." But two and a half times as many felt the riots were a real setback. "The whites," said a San Diego respondent, "have always taught that the Negroes are savages, and this gives them something to point a finger at and say, 'I told you so.'"

After the riots, Negroes, by a 49-to-34 margin, supported a leadership call for a moratorium on mass demonstrations during the election campaign. But the riot experience only tempered their militancy. More solidly than ever, Negroes support the leaders who have led the revolution thus far—the marching militants like Martin Luther King (94 per cent favorable) and CORE (70 per cent) as well as Establishment organizations like the NAACP (92 per cent) and the Urban League (60 per cent). More than ever, Southern Negroes distrust so-called "white moderates" who counsel them to go slow; more than ever, Northern Negroes look with respect—and even envy—on the persevering spirit of their Southern brethren. ("In the North we talk more," a Chicagoan said, "but the South are doing something about getting things done.")

APOSTLES OF DESPAIR: Negroes massively reject the racist counsels of the Muslims (by 64 to 5) as well as the claim of the Communists that no discrimination exists under their system (by 65 to 10). Yet those apostles of despair remain to goad the still-impatient majority—and to beckon the diminished but still alienated minority who feel that rioting is a good thing and that the Negro cannot win without violence.

Whatever the views of American Negroes, the price of a just peace remains for white America to determine. In the poll, Negroes pose the alternatives. More than one-fourth believed nineteen months ago—and nearly one-fifth still believe today—that the white man will come around only if he is forced to by Negro action. "Their consciences," says Mrs. Ann Jones, a Detroit nurse, "haven't bothered them in 100 years." But a 69 per cent majority—up 17 points since 1963—is now convinced that persuasion is the path of the revolution. "They have to come down to earth sometime," said Napoleon Parker Jr., 25, of Pittsburgh. "They will think that living under the same roof and getting along, it will be a better world for everybody."

William Brink
Louis Harris
WHAT WHITES THINK OF NEGROES

Eventually we will be healing a sore that has been open one hundred years.—A 68-year-old white woman in Virginia City, Nevada.

The Negro's attitude toward the white man is fundamentally simple: it is based on the desire for equality. But when the white man in America looks at the Negro he is torn by a conflict between his emotions and his intellect. His intellect tells him that the Negro has indeed suffered years of discrimination, directly contradicting the American creed of equality for all. But his emotions make him feel uneasy at the prospect of such equality for the Negro.

Newsweek conducted a special survey of whites to determine the extent of the gulf between the two races and the likelihood of bridging it. This poll confirmed many of the suspicions of Negroes about the negative feelings of whites—perhaps beyond even what many Negroes imagine.

In the course of interviews lasting over two hours each, some more than three, whites were asked how they felt about contact with Negroes and why. This question released a stream of uninhibited feeling about Negroes as people. The violent emotionalism of many comments was striking. A retired clerk from Inverness, Florida, declared, "They stink. In cafeterias here you go around and collect your food. Then niggers paw over your food and then you have to give them a tip to carry your tray. Big old dirty black paws pawing your food, then you've got to eat it." A 57-year-old hospital employee in Mobile, Alabama, said, "I couldn't stomach it if I thought I was eating after or beside a diseased Negro—which 90 per cent of them are. All this will lead to is social mixing. Their own kind don't keep a clean place."

The outpour was by no means limited to whites of the Deep

Reprinted from *The Negro Revolution in America* by William Brink and Louis Harris (New York: Simon and Schuster, 1964) by permission of Simon and Schuster, Inc. Copyright © 1963 by Newsweek, Inc.

Mr. Brink is a senior editor of *Newsweek Magazine,* and Mr. Harris is a political analyst and public-opinion researcher.

South. Mrs. Ethel Shuey, 62, of Palmyra, Pennsylvania, commented, "Their skin looks greasy and unclean." A 68-year-old woman in Rodney, Ohio, raised the specter of intermarriage, a white cry that was to be heard many times over: "Well, there's too much marrying colored. They are old, dirty things." Another elderly woman in Arkansas City, Kansas, pronounced, "You can smell them a mile away. They're just not our people." A 54-year-old housewife from Wyandotte, Michigan, qualified her feeling: "I don't mind them unless they are very dark or if they're very odorous." And a Washington, Pennsylvania, housewife, expressed the frequently mentioned aversion to personal contact: "I don't like to have to touch them. It just makes me squeamish. I know I shouldn't be that way but it still bothers me." A 56-year-old maintenance man for the Detroit, Michigan, highway department told this story: "There was a good Negro living around here and my little boy shook hands with him and then he turned his hand over and looked at it and the Negro said, 'It won't rub off on you.' I never forgot that. It's the idea of rubbing up against them. It won't rub off but it don't feel right, either."

The element of fear was evident in a number of responses. A woman in Baltimore, Maryland, again elderly, spelled out many of the details: "You don't know what they're going to do. You're leery. They carry razors, knives, rape women. You can't trust them. Don't know what they'll do. I'm scared of them." A young repairman in East Springfield, Massachusetts, said, "I feel as though I can't trust them. I think they'll start a fight. I might pick up some type of disease." A housewife from Cecil, Wisconsin, confessed, "I'm scared of them really." Silas Masters, 72, retired, of Palmetto, Florida, explained, "I don't like to use restrooms in those places where a darn nigger has been. It's venereal disease." A Baltimore housewife believed that "no matter how much you try to educate them or do for them, they still have the savage in them."

This wall of white emotion is the real enemy of the Negro revolution. The survey explored in detail the components of prejudice, both North and South. In addition, it sought to discover whether prejudice diminished with social contact.

A series of ten stereotypes about Negroes was set before the white people, who were then asked which statements they agreed with and which they rejected. Table 1 reports the results from the nationwide cross-section, from the South and from a special group of those who had had social contact with Negroes. This last group, 25 per cent of the total, proved throughout the survey to be the most sympathetic to the Negro and his cause.

While the white South accepts these stereotypes to a greater degree, it would be a vast error to conclude that the North is much different. Even those whites who have had social contact with Negroes share many of these feelings—some of them without even realizing it.

A 61-year-old resident of Alhambra, California, thought he was the epitome of tolerance: "They're human beings the same as the rest of us. Why should you feel uncomfortable with anyone not of the Caucasian race? I've even square danced with them." A rancher in Reno, Nevada, declared: "I have no racial prejudice. Took showers with star athletes—

TABLE 1. *White Stereotypes about Negroes*

Agree with statement:	NATIONWIDE %	SOUTH %	PREVIOUS SOCIAL CONTACT GROUP %
Negroes laugh a lot	68	81	79
Negroes tend to have less ambition	66	81	56
Negroes smell different	60	78	50
Negroes have looser morals	55	80	39
Negroes keep untidy homes	46	57	31
Negroes want to live off the handout	41	61	26
Negroes have less native intelligence	39	60	23
Negroes breed crime	35	46	21
Negroes are inferior to whites	31	51	15
Negroes care less for the family	31	49	22

went to school with them." Another Californian in his sixties, this one from San Diego, told where he would draw the line: "If you mean sexual intercourse, no. Shaking hands is O.K. Kissing, no thanks. But shaking hands, O.K." Mrs. Edward Schneider, 50, of Miami, Florida, declared that she worked with Negroes and didn't feel uncomfortable, but added, "The crummy ones do stink. They don't have to at all. I know they can take pills to avoid the odor they carry as a race. The better educated ones take pills and do not have that odor."

If views such as these comprised the total white attitude toward Negroes, then the only logical conclusion to draw would be that America is on the threshold of a bloody race war. But whites hold a whole roster of other beliefs that are in direct conflict with their emotions about Negroes as people. One is that Negroes have rights as citizens which must be guaranteed under the laws of the United States. Whites were asked about some of the Negro's demands:

TABLE 2. *The White View of Negro Rights*

Approve:	NATIONWIDE %	SOUTH %
Voting in elections	93	88
Unrestricted use of buses and trains	88	75
Job opportunities	88	80
Decent housing	82	76

The most startling figures in this table [2] are those that reflect Southern attitudes. Even in the South, a large majority of whites feel Negroes should be guaranteed these rights. What is more, sizable majorities of whites feel that further legislation is needed from Congress to strengthen Negro rights. On this question, however, Southern whites disagree sharply with white people elsewhere.

TABLE 3. *White Support for Civil-Rights Legislation*

	NATIONWIDE %	SOUTH %
Approve:		
Federal vote-enforcement law	57	31
Federal Fair Employment Practices law	62	40
Kennedy civil-rights bill	63	31
Public-accommodations bill	66	29

Comparison of these two tables [2 and 3] reveals an interesting anomaly: 88 per cent of the white Southerners believe that Negroes have the right to vote, but only 31 per cent favor legislation backing up that right. There is a similar though less striking contrast on the subject of jobs. Legislation seems to be the sticking point; all whites are more ready to approve other forms of Federal intervention for equal rights. Table 4 shows how they stand on the role played by the government since 1954.

TABLE 4. *Whites Assess Federal Action*

	NATIONWIDE %	SOUTH %
Approve:		
Eisenhower use of troops in Little Rock, Ark.	71	44
Kennedy use of troops at Oxford, Miss.	65	37
The original Supreme Court decision	64	35
Over-all role of Federal government in civil rights	64	35
Over-all role of Federal courts in civil rights	60	33

In the poll of whites, a deep and abiding sense of law and order came through powerfully. F. Arthur Cowen, 57, a commercial artist in Crestwood, Missouri, commented on the use of troops in Oxford: "It's a matter of upholding the law. It's a matter of principle." A laborer from Cromwell, Indiana, agreed: "That [sending troops to Little Rock] was the law. If one state gets by the law without obeying, why should I pay an income tax? Why should I obey the law? It's the same thing." To Arthur Jackson, 66, a real-estate broker in Breckenridge, Minnesota, the whole American system was on trial: "We can't do otherwise as a democracy. We have to practice what we preach to other nations." A Copley, Ohio, housewife saw government action as the only way out: "This situation has to be cleared up and if we can't do it through our government, how can we do it?" A Chicago laborer added, "If you leave it to the local government to start, it won't get done."

Over and over again, whites saw few alternatives under the American system other than to grant Negroes their rights. Alfred

Blanckaert, 69, a retired St. Louisan, said, "Federal laws are over state laws and one state can't tell the other part of the United States what to do. The big plantation owners don't want integration because of cheap labor. The Negroes are getting smart and want their rights. I don't approve all the Negroes do but don't approve of all the whites do either." Mrs. Mary Alice Beezley, 32, a housewife from Princeton, Indiana, saw any other course indefensible: "I feel that the Negro, although he's black, still has the red blood in him. He's human and he has as much right to the same rights as we have." Loree Donahue, 36, a San Diego, California, housewife, thought that if grownups stayed calm, the children would settle it: "I think that all should abide by the Supreme Court rule. The Negro didn't ask for his skin color. When parents keep their noses out, kids get along O.K. Kids kiss and make up. So older people cause all the trouble."

As their own words indicate, white people in America are not overjoyed about the necessity to support their Federal government in its efforts to insure Negro rights in reality. In fact, the majority (51 per cent) criticized the Kennedy Administration for its handling of the issue. And yet only a minority of whites could bring themselves to oppose specifically the steps their government had taken.

How do whites rationalize this acceptance of equality under the law with the personal aversions to Negroes so many of them apparently feel? Timing plays a part. By better than a 2 to 1 margin, whites feel that Negroes are moving too fast in their revolution. As an East Springfield, Massachusetts, housewife said, "They want everything in too short a time. They did nothing for too long a time, then a sudden uprising. They could have been doing these things all along. They can't be handed something for nothing. They have to earn it." A 45-year-old housewife in Milwaukee, Wisconsin, summed up the feeling this way: "It couldn't possibly be stopped now. But I think their leaders have urged them on too fast. A lot of them aren't ready to get all these things at one time."

By a 64–36 per cent count, whites feel Negroes are asking for more than they can possibly absorb. Minta Shumate, 28, a housewife in Crestwood, Missouri, said it for the majority: "Until the Negro wants to better educate himself and qualify for it, things aren't going to change overnight, even if the freedoms are guaranteed them. They will have to work for them." The methods of the revolution are just as disturbing to whites as its tempo. While Negroes feel demonstrations have been vital and effective most whites feel that the demonstrations have hurt the Negro cause. "A lot of it is show-off," thought a retired man in Palmyra, Pennsylvania. "They want to be seen, make a lot of noise." A 65-year-old widow from Macon, Georgia, made a judgment about the demonstration in her town: "I think locally it has hurt. They look like they are wild people out of the jungle and this is the way all Negroes are inside." A 23-year-old woman, also of Macon, thought the demonstrations "showed the brutality of them. Our maid says the young Negro boys have killed several old Negro men in their neighborhood. They took clubs and beat them to death out of meanness and it didn't even get in the newspapers." Joseph Brognano, 45, a laborer from Wampum, Pennsylvania, put it this way: "They just showed how they want to overrun the whites and tell them what to do. The nerve they have to buck whites. Now we won't trust them."

When asked in detail about the methods of the Negro revolution, whites went on record as 2 to 1 in opposition to the lunch-counter sit-ins, 4 to 3 against Negro willingness to go to jail voluntarily for their cause, 5 to 3 against picketing of stores and over 10 to 1 against the "lie-downs" in front of trucks on construction sites. However, by slim margins, whites do accept the general idea of demonstrating and think that the Negroes are justified in having conducted the march on Washington.

Sam Stump, 56, a retired farmer from Cromwell, Indiana, was typical in his reaction: "The march on Washington helped. It was like a calm voice there, telling what they wanted." A 65-year-old retired man from Bell, California, thought Negroes should slow down some, but added, "The Washington demonstration was remarkable. I don't think that many white people could have put it over that good." In Crestline, Ohio, Mrs. Mary Ogle was also enthusiastic: "It was very well organized —to have that many people and no violence." A. Gerard Patterson, 34, from Appleton, Wisconsin, saw positive results from the demonstrations: "After all, it's the squeaking wheel that gets the oil."

These very demonstrations appear to have driven home the whole point of the Negro protest. But the majority view of whites was clearly that the Negroes were pressing too hard, asking for too much. Whites have remarkably clear understanding of Negro demands. Table 5, drawn from volunteered comments, shows what whites think Negroes want:

TABLE 5. *What Whites Think Negroes Want*

	WHITES NATIONWIDE %
Equal treatment	41
Better jobs	14
Better education	11
Make America aware of their problem	8
Better housing	7
Dignity, respect, status	6
Publicity for the problem	6
Representation in government	5
Be able to go anywhere, do anything	2

There is a remarkable parallel between what whites think Negroes want and what Negroes themselves said they want.

Furthermore, there is widespread recognition among whites that Negroes are discriminated against. Fully 71 per cent of all whites in the country and even a majority of 56 per cent in the South acknowledged this fact. By better than 3 to 2, white people feel Negroes do not have job opportunities equal to whites. By a somewhat closer margin whites also believe Negro children receive an inferior education. And by almost 3 to 1, whites believe Negro housing is not nearly so good as that for whites.

Some whites recalled specific occasions when they had observed Negroes being discriminated against. Laurence Boyd, a laborer from Lake Zurich, Illinois, told this story: "We went to a restaurant with a colored guy who works with us and they wouldn't serve him. I thought this was a dirty, crying shame. Just cause he's black don't mean he ain't hungry. We all got up and left." A 49-year-old man from Dexter, Missouri, said, "They have been pushed down to lower-paying jobs and given the dirty jobs and I don't think that is right." William Reger, 25, a laborer from Cromwell, Indiana, gave his observation: "On TV you see it. Not getting served. No place to build where they want to. No chance to advance. They discriminate against Negroes in the services such as rank is concerned. I've only seen one colored officer in six years of service. This is all very wrong. Some are ten times smarter than whites but they have no chance."

In fact, when whites were asked how they thought it must feel to be discriminated against as a Negro, they bristled with indignation and even outrage at the thought of being treated like Negroes. "I think it would be hard on the morale," said Mrs. Donald Nei, 38, a housewife of Larwill, Indiana. "When we get some little minor snub, we are so upset. Imagine how it would be to live with discrimination all your life. It would take a mighty strong person to try to improve yourself." Mrs. Geraldine Gilbert, 45, of San Diego, California, put it this way: "It must be horrible. If it were me, there would be a terrible rage inside me. It would make me a mean, spiteful person and I'd be ready to do battle at any moment. I'd also treat anyone who suppressed me as dirt if I got the chance." In Detroit, Michigan, an office worker felt that "it would tend to make a person hate—which is serious." Cleveland Moffett, a 33-year-old New Yorker, was deeply indignant: "It makes a free-thinking person wince with rage to see the way Negroes are treated simply because they have dark skins." A 34-year-old housewife in Jonesboro, Tennessee, wasn't sure how it would feel to be a Negro discriminated against, but then had this afterthought: "I would feel like somebody without a country." Mrs. Ralph D. Sanders, 34, of Fayetteville, North Carolina, summed it all up for many mothers: "It must be horrible. From a

TABLE 6. *White Feeling about Contact with Negroes*

	NATIONWIDE %	SOUTH %	PREVIOUS SOCIAL CONTACT GROUP %
Would object to:			
Working next to a Negro on the job	17	31	8
Sitting next to a Negro at a lunch counter	20	50	4
Sitting next to a Negro on a bus	20	47	5
Sitting next to a Negro in a movie theater	23	54	6
Own children going to school with Negroes	23	55	9
Using same restroom as Negroes	24	56	9
Trying on same suit or dress that Negro had tried on in clothing store	32	57	16
Having own child bring Negro friend home to supper	41	76	16
Having Negro family as next-door neighbors	51	74	26
Close friend or relative marrying a Negro	84	91	70
Own teen-age daughter dating a Negro	90	97	80

mother's point of view, it must break their hearts to hear what the children are called and the way they are treated, and yet have to teach them that this is their way of life."

If whites are thus able to understand in human terms just what it means to be a Negro in America, how far are they willing to go toward integration? This is obviously a key question, and in large part American history of the next ten years will be written by the answer. The survey investigated the limits of white viability, from willingness to work side by side with a Negro to allowing a teen-age daughter to date a Negro boy. [See Table 6.]

It is immediately apparent from these results that the vast majority of white America is prepared to accept a great deal more contact with Negroes than has taken place up to now. The degree of Southern viability may come as a surprise. Nationwide, in view of the revulsion expressed by many earlier in this chapter, the over-all results testify to white willingness—grudging though it may be—to accommodate. But white America is not at all ready for social integration to the extent of dating and intermarriage. Even among those who have had social contact with Negroes, 70 per cent would object to a close friend or relative marrying a Negro and 80 per cent would be worried if their teen-age daughter dated a Negro. Some whites rationalized segregation in this area as former President Harry S Truman once did—all the way back to the Bible.

These results also indicate the likely areas of accommodation for the immediate future as well as the areas of sharp conflict.

Equal employment, which is also the number-one priority for Negroes, seems ripe for a breakthrough. Nearly nine out of every ten whites—including eight out of every ten Southerners—feel that Negroes have the right to equal jobs. What is more, as another question in the poll revealed, a majority all over the country do not fear that Negroes will take their jobs away. Significantly, a solid majority (62 per cent) of whites favor a Federal law enforcing an end to discrimination on the job. However, white people are equally adamant that there should *not* be a strict 10 per cent quota for Negroes in job hiring (rejected by over 4 to 1) or that Negroes should actually be given job preference over whites (turned down by a staggering 31 to 1 margin).

Part of the reason for whites' willingness to go along with an end to job discrimination is the highly positive experience of white people who have associated with Negroes on the job:

"You are there to get a job done, not to socialize. I don't mind working with them"—Mrs. Ralph Riddle, Dexter, Missouri.

"I've worked with colored girls. They were really on the ball, with good sense and efficient. Clean and neat, too"—a housewife, Mahwah, New Jersey.

"They were wonderful to me. I worked as a teacher and they were teachers. Because I was a substitute, I found them much better and kinder than many white teachers"—a 46-year-old woman in Alhambra, California.

"Color won't rub off. I work in the fire department, eat and sleep with a Negro. O.K., I'd say"—Robert Howard, 30, of Kokomo, Indiana.

"I used to sing and a Negro girl sang in my group. She was so clean and nice, I think I lost my prejudices"—a housewife in Tennessee.

"I have worked with them. I have worked with foreigners that I have minded more up north"—a 64-year-old laborer from Inverness, Florida.

"It is just like working with any other man. Heck, he's entitled to work"—Arvin Beaubien, 48-year-old laborer from Wyandotte, Michigan.

"He's just human. I've sewed for many of them, altering dresses, and they have always been clean, polite. I've never found any different odor about them either, though they do perspire a great deal"—a seamstress from Tacoma, Washington.

Education is another major area in which there appears to be a considerable amount of white willingness to go along with the Negro revolution, although the South registers a loud and determined "no" on this score. Better than seven out of ten whites would not mind their own children going to integrated schools, and an equal number reject the notion that the education of white children would suffer if both races go to school together. Finally, in reply to another question in the poll, fully three-quarters of all white people in America said they believed that school integration is inevitable. In fact, 57 per cent of the white South share this view.

The wife of a Rochester, New York, laborer explained her view on integrated education: "If my children started school with colored children they wouldn't even notice the difference. When they are young [color] does not matter to them." Mrs. Lenore Brucklacher, a minister's wife and mother of seven in Florence, South Dakota, said, "It is good for children to realize there are differences and yet we are all the same." A tobacco farmer's wife in Tennessee put it this way: "If they are good enough to go to school, they're good enough to go with my kids, I reckon." Another farmer's wife, in Larwill, Indiana, added, "There are some white children who could stand a little more training at home. The color of their skin isn't what makes them a decent companion for your children."

Whites may be receptive to the idea of integrated education, but they are not amenable to the next step, which is probably the only path to integrated schooling: whites and Negroes living in the same neighborhoods.

While 59 per cent of all whites in the country feel that integrated housing is on the way, 50 per cent say they would be upset if it happened where they live. However, those who now live in integrated neighborhoods report by better than 5 to 1 that they are not bothered by having Negroes live near them. This result should ease some of the fear that explosions are bound to occur in white neighborhoods now undergoing an influx of Negroes.

However, many whites who do not live near Negroes are highly doubtful that integrated housing will work. They think that when Negroes move in, whites move out. As a 73-year-old man in Detroit, Michigan, said, "If you get a block-buster,* most of the people get panicky and the homes are taken over entirely by Negroes." He went on to recall: "A brand-new school that was practically all white went practically all colored in twelve months in one area of the city." "Even if the whites did not move out," said State Senator James Slattery from Nevada, "the colored fellow would feel uncomfortable. Of course, the value of the property also goes 'way down." A widow in San Jose, California, harked back to what she thought of Negroes as people: "Negroes are their own worst enemy. [If they move in] the people that are for them will get disgusted and turn away." A housewife in Mobile, Alabama, agreed: "They are not capable of the general upkeep, maintenance and improvement of any home. This is why they are living in shacks."

To some whites, the idea of Negroes moving into their neighborhood evoked fighting words, such as those of a woman in Burnham,

---

* "A real-estate speculator who deliberately breaks a neighborhood color line by selling property to a Negro; this causes other white residents to move out, selling cheap, whereupon the block-buster buys up and sells at high profit."

Texas: "It ain't gonna happen right here. Maybe the edge of town. Nobody ain't gonna sell 'em no lots so as they can build. I tell you, nigger settlement here just ain't gonna be like whites."

But if one half of the white people, North and South, would be upset by integrated housing, the other half say they would not. For example, a 68-year-old laborer in St. Louis said simply, "They have the right to go anywhere they want to go." And a 51-year-old housewife in Hillsboro, Oregon, added, "They have earned people's respect and those who can afford the better homes are the nicer class, too." Thomas M. Brown, a laborer from Clay, Kentucky, saw it happening this way: "By the time they move in, we'll all be used to them being in better jobs."

A majority sensed that integrated housing is sure to come. Jerome Knuijt, 32, a science teacher in Lake Zurich, Illinois, said, "If this country is to exist, it's inevitable. And if one is intelligent, he doesn't fight the inevitable." Mr. Charles E. Drewett of Crestwood, Missouri, held the view, "There is an evolution we're going through. As Negroes get education, we will get educated with them. People are less biased than they were five, fifteen years ago."

In the bull's-eye areas of the revolution, jobs and education held out promise for steady progress. Housing, however, seems to be a sticking point. But is it really?

Some whites are sophisticated enough to perceive that for Negroes the right to integrate in housing is more important than the deed. Some of them also understand that there are Negroes who are reluctant to move into white neighborhoods. C. E. Matteson, retired, of Tucson, Arizona, said, "I do not feel that the Negro especially cares about living in white neighborhoods. But he doesn't want to be told he can't because of his color." Mrs. Audrey Klaeser, 42, of Milwaukee, Wisconsin, added, "They like to stay with their people. They wouldn't like to move in white neighborhoods any more than whites would want to move in theirs."

Does the oft-expressed revulsion of whites to Negroes, and their apparent resistance to accommodation, mean that the Negro's social revolt will end in a bloody clash? To some extent the very history of the United States argues differently. Time and again the American people have adapted to changing times, changing customs—and changing neighbors. This has happened with successive waves of immigration by the Irish, the Poles, the Italians and others.

Of course, there are obvious differences in the situation of the Negroes to argue against such optimism. Their color is different. A bitter war was fought in their name. They have been here far longer without achieving equality. And there are more of them to intensify conflict. But numbers can be a double-edged sword; for ultimate effectiveness in a democracy, numbers have counted in the past.

Furthermore, while some of the whites' emotions have vitiated their intellectual acceptance of equality for Negroes, other feelings are working in a different way. Many whites reported that their ministers were preaching that it is morally wrong to discriminate. According to the poll, whites feel by a 2 to 1 margin that the whole question of Negro rights is a moral issue. Mrs. Lucy J. Rittie, 84, of Cromwell, Indiana, said it thus: "Negroes are God's children and we want to do our best to accept them."

And Mrs. H. B. Kaszynski, 50, of Beaumont, Texas, added, "I don't know how you could be a Christian and feel better or superior to a colored person."

Eric Hoffer
THE NEGRO IS PREJUDICED AGAINST HIMSELF

The plight of the Negro in America is that he is a Negro first and only secondly an individual. Only when the Negro community as a whole does something that will win for it the admiration of the world will the Negro individual be completely himself. Another way of putting it is that the Negro in America needs pride—in his people, their achievements, their leaders—before he can attain self-respect. At present, individual achievement cannot cure the Negro's soul. No matter how manifest his superiority as an individual, he cannot savor "the unbought grace of life."

The predicament of the Negro in America, then, is that what he needs most is something he cannot give himself; something, moreover, which neither governments nor legislatures nor courts but only the Negro community as a whole can give him.

Despite the vehement protestations of Negro writers and intellectuals, the Negro is not the white man's problem. On the contrary, the white man is the Negro's chief problem. As things are now, the Negro is what the white man says he is—he knows himself only by white hearsay. That which corrodes the soul of the Negro is his monstrous inner agreement with the prevailing prejudice against him.

One begins to wonder whether the American Negro has the

From *The New York Times Magazine*, November 29, 1964. © 1964 by The New York Times Company. Reprinted by permission.

Eric Hoffer is a self-educated longshoreman of San Francisco. Author of *The True Believer,* he has written extensively on social movements and social change.

capacity to create a genuine community with organs for cooperation and self-help. You strain your ears in vain amid the present Negro clamor for a small voice saying: "Leave us alone and we will show you what we can do." If it be true that the only effective way to help the Negro is to help him help himself, then the Negro's aversion to, or perhaps incapacity for, a self-starting do-it-yourself way of life makes it questionable whether he can ever attain freedom and self-respect. One cannot think of another instance where a minority striving for equality has been so deficient in the capacity for mutual aid and co-operation.

The Negro leaders seem to have little faith in the character and potentialities of the Negro masses. Their words and acts are largely directed toward non-Negro America. They are not aware of the Negro masses as a reservoir of power and as an instrument of destiny. Almost invariably when a Negro makes his mark in whatever walk of life, his impulse is to escape the way of life, the mores and the atmosphere of the Negro people. He sees the Negro masses as a millstone hanging about his neck, pulling him down, and keeping him from rising to the heights of fortune and felicity. The well-off or educated Negro may use his fellow Negroes to enrich himself (in insurance, paper publishing, cosmetics) or to advance his career in the professions or in politics, but he will not lift a finger to lighten the burden of his people. Who ever hears of a rich Negro endowing a Negro school, hospital or church?

The leadership's lack of faith in the Negro masses is dictating the singular pattern of the Negro revolution. Its objectives, tactics and finances are not predicated on massive Negro backing. It is the nearest thing to a revolution by proxy: Its picket lines are manned largely by white men and women, the registration of Negro voters is done largely by white students, the drive for legislation is powered by white politicians and white liberals, and the money comes mainly from white pockets.

A cursory check among my Negro fellow longshoremen on the San Francisco waterfront (there are some 2,000 of them earning between $7,000 and $10,000 a year) showed that no one of those questioned has been asked to contribute to the Negro cause, and not one of them has come near a CORE picket line, whereas many white longshoremen receive requests for money from Negro organizations, and some of them, and their daughters, are passionately involved in CORE affairs. Whether it be legitimate or not to expect as much from the Negro as we expect from ourselves, it is clear that we can expect little from the Negro so long as he does not expect much from himself.

Since the revolution has no roots in the Negro masses, it cannot grow. It cannot engage in long-range programs which after a period of maturing may yield an abundance of striking results. It goes after immediate, showy objectives. It operates wholly in the present and takes no thought of the future.

In the past, wherever there were many wrongs to right, the one least capable of yielding palpable results was attacked first. (In early 19th-century England the abuses which called for remedy were many. There was unimaginable poverty among the masses, and a lack of protection by law of the weak, yet the attack which rallied all the reforming forces was directed against parliamentary corruption.) One has the feeling that the prospect of Negro equality would have been brighter had the first target been disfranchisement rather than segregation. But the Negro leaders, having no roots and no faith in the Negro masses, cannot wait for votes to yield results. They cannot heed Nkrumah's advice: "Seek ye first the political kingdom and all others shall be added unto it."

The questionable nature of the Negro revolution manifests itself in its choice of enemies. It wants an abundant supply of tame enemies— real enemies are too dangerous—and the way to come by tame enemies is to declare that your friends, the white liberals, are enemies because they are white. One can almost smell the psychological twist involved when a James Baldwin or a LeRoi Jones vilifies and baits white liberals who have championed the Negro's cause all their lives. So utterly convinced are Baldwin and Jones of the irremediable worthlessness of the Negro people that anyone who thinks well of the Negro must seem to them simple-minded or simply dishonest.

By a similar twist the Negro revolution tries to obtain tame substitutes for its only legitimate battleground. It has no stomach for Mississippi and Alabama, hence we find the head of CORE in San Francisco announcing to the world, from the steps of the San Francisco City Hall, that San Francisco is Mississippi. The Rev. Mr. Galamison from New York, who on that day happened to be in our city, amplified the statement by saying that San Francisco is worse than Mississippi. Even Martin Luther King is reported to have said that the Negro's real problem is in the North and not in the South. In short, the voice of the Negro revolution is telling us day in, day out, without hesitation and without qualifications, that it is we outside the South who are the Negro's real enemies; it is we who oppress him, exploit him and brutalize him.

How does this sound in our ears, and how do my kind of people react toward it?

The simple fact is that the people I have lived and worked with all my life, and who make up about 60 per cent of the population outside the South, have not the least feeling of guilt toward the Negro. The majority of us started to work for a living in our teens, and we have been poor all our lives. Most of us had only a rudimentary education. Our white skin has brought us no privileges and no favors. For more than 20 years I worked in the fields of California with Negroes, and now and then for Negro contractors. On the San Francisco waterfront, where I spent the next 20 years, there are as many black longshoremen as white.

My kind of people do not feel that the world owes us anything, or that we owe anybody—white, black or yellow—a damn thing. We believe that the Negro should have every right we have: the right to vote, the right to join any union open to us, the right to live, work, study and play anywhere he pleases. But he can have no special claims on us, and no valid grievances against us. He has certainly not done our work for us. Our hands are more gnarled and work-broken than his, and our faces more lined and worn. A hundred Baldwins could not convince me that the Negro longshoremen who come every morning to our hiring hall shouting, joshing, eating and drinking are haunted by bad dreams and memories of miserable childhoods; that they feel deprived, disabled, degraded, oppressed and humiliated. The drawn faces in the hall, the brooding backs and the sullen, hunched figures are not those of Negroes.

Equally absurd is the contention that the American Negro is alienated from America. Despite discrimination, the Negro actually seems more at home in this country than any other segment of the population. It is doubtful whether even the Negro intellectual could transplant himself and prosper. The white men who populated this continent, most of them lower peasants, were not of the type that transplant well. Their incurable homesickness not only made them perpetual wanderers but also gave them the feeling of being strangers on this planet; it drove them to impose their own man-made world on God's creation to a degree never attempted before, and undoubtedly contributed to America's unprecedented dynamism.

Even when it tries to be gentle, the voice of the Negro revolution grates on us and fills us with scorn. The Negro seems to say: "Lift me up in your arms. I am an abandoned and abused child. Adopt me as your favorite son. Feed me, clothe me, educate me, love and baby me. You must do it right away or I shall set your house on fire, or rot at your doorsteps and poison the air you breathe."

To sum up: The Negro revolution is a fraud. It has no faith in the character and potentialities of the Negro masses. It has no taste for real enemies, real battlegrounds and desperate situations. It wants cheap victories and the easy way.

A genuine mass movement does not shy away from desperate situations. It wants above all to prove the validity and potency of its faith, and this it can do only by acting against overwhelming odds, so that whatever it achieves partakes of the miraculous. Indeed, where there are no difficulties the true revolutionary will deliberately create them, and it often looks as if the chief function of his faith is to get the revolutionary out of difficulties he himself created.

I have said that the Negro outside the South can have no special claims on us, and no valid grievances against us. This does not mean that the Negro is not in real trouble and that he has no desperate problems which others do not have to face.

This country has always seemed good to me chiefly because, most of the time, I can be a human being first and only secondly something else—a workingman, an American, etc. It is not so with the Negro. His chief plight, as pointed out, is that in America he cannot be a human being first and only secondly a Negro. This is particularly galling to the Negro intellectual and to Negroes who have gotten ahead: No matter what and how much they have, they seem to lack the one thing they want most. There is no frustration greater than this.

Secondly, if every trace of discrimination were wiped away overnight, the Negro outside the South would still be in the throes of a soul-wrenching crisis, and we must know something of the nature of this crisis if we are to make sense of what is happening in the Negro ghettos. The Negro writer Ralph Ellison has pointed out that the American Negro is now undergoing a double drastic change. By merely stepping across the Mason-Dixon Line he steps from feudalism into the maelstrom of industrialism, and from legal subjection to legal equality. Now, in human affairs drastic change is almost always a convulsive and explosive process, and it matters not whether the change is for the better or the worse. The passage from slavery to freedom can be as charged with frustration and discontent as the passage from freedom to slavery.

We used to think that mass movements are the cause and instrument of drastic change. But the experience of the last several decades has shown us that revolutions and mass movements in general are actually by-products of change. Change comes first. Where things have not changed at all there is the least likelihood of revolution. According to Lincoln Steffens, "Heaven and hell are one place, and we all go there. To those who are prepared it is heaven; to those who are not fit and ready it is hell."

The fact is that we can never be fit and ready for that which is wholly new, and the unavoidable difficulties and irritations inherent in the adjustment to the new prepare the ground for the rise of mass movements. There is little doubt, for instance, that the national and social revolutions which racked the Occident during the past hundred years had as one of their chief causes the rapid transformation of millions of peasants into industrial workers. Similarly, the present rapid modernization of backward countries in Asia, Africa and Latin America is proceeding in an atmosphere of bedlam.

There is apparently in human nature a built-in resistance to change. Deep within us there is the conviction that we cannot really change; that we can adjust ourselves to the new only by getting out of our skins and becoming new men. Drastic change thus creates an estrangement from the self, and sets off a search for a new identity. There are any number of new identities one may assume, and any number of plays in which one may act, in such a crisis. One becomes a saint, a warrior, a member of a chosen people, a pioneer showing the way to the rest of mankind; and mass movements are often the means by which a population undergoing drastic change acquires a sense of rebirth and a new identity.

Mr. Ellison describes the fantastic forms which the groping for a new identity often assumes in the bedlam atmosphere of the Negro ghetto: "Life becomes a masquerade, exotic costumes are worn every day. Those who cannot afford to hire a horse wear riding habits; others who could not afford a hunting trip or who seldom attend sporting events carry shooting sticks."

It is part of the Negro's tragedy that his crisis of identity should occur at a time when automation is rapidly diminishing the opportunities for purposeful action and individual self-advancement open to common people. The millions of immigrants dumped on our shores prior to the First World War had to contend with a situation not unlike that which is now facing the Negro outside the South. They were torn from the warm communal existence of a small town or village somewhere in Europe and transferred almost overnight to the cold and dismal isolation of an individual existence. But they had a vast continent at their disposal and unlimited opportunities for self-advancement, and so these emigrants from stagnant small towns and villages in Europe plunged into the perpetual becoming of ceaseless action, tamed and mastered a continent in an incredibly short time, and the question of a conscious rebirth and a new identity did not come up.

With the present paucity of opportunities for fervent action it is doubtful whether the Negro could repeat the performance of past immigrants and adjust himself to a new existence as an individual on his own. He cannot cross alone the desert of transition and enter an individual promised land. Like the liberated ancient Israelites, he needs a genuine mass movement to enfold him, cover his nakedness of identity, guide and sustain him until he can stand on his own feet.

Moses wanted to accomplish a relatively simple thing: He wanted to transform the enslaved Hebrews into free men. One would think that all he had to do was to remove the Hebrews from their slavery, lead them out of Egypt, and things would take care of themselves. But being a genuine leader, Moses knew that you cannot turn slaves into free men by merely setting them free. He knew that the task of endowing the liberated slaves with a new identity and of immersing them in a new life required the employment of the most outlandish means. So he proceeded to create the fiction of a chosen people led by a mighty Jehovah to a promised land. The whole fabric of the Pentateuch—its theology, jurisprudence, pageantry and miracles—had for its chief purpose the creation of a new world and a new life, which are vital whenever human beings are subjected to a drastic change.

It is highly significant that the Hebrews needed a Moses to do it for them. Moses was not a Hebrew but an Egyptian. Indeed, he spoke Hebrew with so heavy an accent that he could not make himself understood, and he had to use the Hebrew Aaron, whom he adopted as a brother, as a mouthpiece. (The King James version says that Moses was "of slow speech," but the Hebrew words are *quad peh,* which means "heavy-mouthed.") Outsiders have often acted as the champions and saviors of oppressed groups.

One wonders how much of a handicap it is for the Negro that he cannot avail himself of such injections of wild energy from without. For it is abundantly clear that up to now the 20 million American Negroes have not been able to throw up a leader who could generate and sustain a genuine mass-movement spirit. Yet there is reason to suspect that were such a leader to rise his efforts to launch a full-fledged mass movement would be frustrated and defeated—not by the "unworthiness" of the Negro masses but because the spirit of America would work against him.

Up to now America has not been a good milieu for the rise of mass movements. What starts out here as a mass movement ends up as a racket, a cult or a corporation. Unlike those anywhere else, the masses in America have never despaired of the present and are not willing to sacrifice it for a new life and a new world. In this the American Negro, despite his handicaps, does not differ fundamentally from his fellow Americans. He has no extravagant dreams and visions, and no wild hopes. He cannot conceive of anything more grand and desirable than the life lived by a middle-class American.

Another way of putting it is that the American Negro minority is more American than minority. It cannot generate the alchemy of the soul which now and then enabled "the weak things of the world to confound the things which are mighty . . . and things which are not, to bring to nought things that are." It is questionable, therefore, whether it will be a mass movement that would cure the "nowhereness" and "nobodiness" of the Negro ghetto and lead the Negro out of his present crisis.

But what of Elijah Muhammad and the Black Muslim movement? Alone of all the Negro leaders Elijah Muhammad has a vivid awareness of the vital need of a new birth in any drastic human transformation, and he alone mastered the technique of staging a new identity. Bacon's dictum that you must change many things if you want to change one thing has particular application to drastic change. If the

Negro is to become a new man he must be stripped of his habits, attitudes, opinions, beliefs and even memories. He needs a new way of life: a new diet, a new way of dressing, a new purpose, even a new religion and a new name. The Black Muslim movement can point to many solid achievements. It has transformed idlers, criminals, junkies and drunkards into clean-living, purposeful human beings.

That Elijah Muhammad had to propound doctrines of breathtaking absurdity in order to implant a Puritan ethic and temper in Negro souls should come as no surprise to anyone aware of the fantastic quality of man's nature. Often in human affairs the simplest ends can be reached only by the most roundabout and outlandish means. It is worth remembering that what Elijah Muhammad is doing to the Negro is, in a sense, a recapitulation of what America had done to the immigrant from Europe: It stripped him of his traditions, habits, tastes, opinions and memories, and gave him a new diet, a new way of dressing, a new language and often a new name. The Frenchman Raoul de Roussy de Sales maintained that "to become an American is a process which resembles conversion. It is not so much a new country one adopts as a new creed."

The Black Muslim movement is equipping its converts for success in practical affairs, which means that it is equipping them for the successful pursuit of typical American careers. In doing this the Black Muslim movement is retracing an established pattern, namely, of mass movements serving as schools for effective American practicality.

The irresistible Americanization of mass movements militates against the nation of Islam becoming a movement of powerful sweep and drive. If Elijah Muhammad or his successor has vision, he will realize that the future of his movement lies not in America but in Africa. Traditional Islam is just now making considerable headway in the heart of Africa. It is conceivable that an Islamic heresy hatched by Negroes, preaching the primacy of the Negro race and coupled with American industrial know-how, could easily become an unequaled instrument for empire in Africa. If confined to America, the nation of Islam may eventually operate factories, department stores, banks, newspapers and farms, but the most it could aspire to would be a miniature Utah, with a mosque in its capital of New Mecca.

As to the other black nationalist groups that are springing up over the country, they are manifestations of the Negro's passion for alibis and the easy way. They are a plunge toward the impossible to escape the arduous effort required to attain the possible. As a black nationalist all you have to do is shoot your mouth off about the fire next time, and about grabbing six or seven Southern states, founding a Negro empire and breathing down the neck of a cornered, frightened white America. Your heart swells with heroic negritude, and you don't have to lift a finger to do a thing.

Finally, I cannot see how the American Negro can escape his crisis of identity by identifying himself, in the words of Martin Luther King, "with his black brothers of Africa and his brown and yellow brothers of Asia, South America and the Caribbean."

Assuming, as I must, that the American Negro is as American as I am, I cannot see at present in the whole of Asia, Africa and Latin America a single achievement, a single personality even, to inspire me with wholehearted admiration, to set my heart and mind on fire, and prompt me to identify myself with it. It is possible to see how a James Baldwin or a Malcolm X, lusting for a taste of power, can identify himself with a pseudo-intellectual dictator like Nkrumah. But it is inconceivable that a Negro longshoreman in San Francisco should swell with pride at the thought of a megalomaniac piecard who fancies himself a lord of creation.

Surely it should be the other way around: it is the American Negro who should demonstrate to the world what Negro energy, initiative, skill and guts can do, and serve as an object of identification for Negroes everywhere. It is to the American Negro that the new Negro nations of Africa should be able to turn when they want to build factories, dams and railroads, or create an army, or start an irrigation system and the like. Again one cannot help thinking that what a handful of Jews in Israel has done for the self-respect of Jews everywhere, and what they are doing to help new nations in Asia and Africa, should not be utterly beyond the reach of 20 million American Negroes who breathe the air we breathe and share in the work we do.

The question remains: what can the American Negro do to heal his soul and clothe himself with a desirable identity? As we have seen, he cannot look for a genuine mass movement to lead him out of the frustration of the Negro ghettos; he will certainly not allow a non-Negro Moses to lead him to a promised land, and he cannot attain self-respect by an identification with Negroes and negritude outside America. What, then, is left for him to do?

The only road left for the Negro is that of community-building— of creating vigorous Negro communities with organs of cooperation, self-improvement and self-defense. Whether he wills it or not, the Negro in America belongs to a distinct group, yet he is without the values and satisfactions which people usually obtain by joining a group. When we become members of a group we acquire a desirable identity, we derive faith and pride to bolster our confidence and self-esteem, and a sense of usefulness and worth by sharing in the efforts and the achievements of the group. Clearly, it is the Negro's chief task to convert this formless and purposeless group to which he is irrevocably bound into a genuine community capable of effort and achievement, and which can inspire its members with faith and hope.

Whereas the American mental climate is not favorable for the emergence of mass movements, it is ideal for the building of viable communities; the capacity for community-building is widely diffused. When we speak of the American as a skilled person we have in mind not only his technical but also his political and social skills.

Once, during the Great Depression, a construction company that had to build a road in the San Bernardino Mountains sent down two trucks to the Los Angeles skid row, and anyone who could climb onto the trucks was hired. When the trucks were full, the drivers put in the tailgates and drove off. They dumped us on the side of a hill in the San Bernardino Mountains, where we found bundles of supplies and equipment. The company had only one man on the spot.

We began to sort ourselves out: there were so many carpenters, electricians, mechanics, cooks, men who could handle bulldozers and jackhammers, and even foremen. We put up the tents and the cookshack, fixed latrines and a shower bath, cooked supper, and next morning went out to build the road. If we had to write a constitution we probably would have had someone who knew all the whereases and wherefores. We were a rotten branch, a shovelful of slime scooped off the pavement of skid row, yet we could have built America on the side of a hill in the San Bernardino Mountains.

When I speak of vigorous Negro communities, I do not mean Negro ghettos. You can have an effectively functioning Negro community even when its members live anywhere they please. What I have in mind is Negro centers, societies, agencies, loan associations, athletic clubs, discussion clubs and the like. You can see such communal organs functioning among the Jewish, Japanese, Chinese and other minorities.

My feeling is that right now the Negro in San Francisco, and probably elsewhere, is ripe for some grand cooperative effort in which he could take pride. It could be the building of a model Negro suburb, or a Negro hospital, a Negro theater, a Negro school for music and the dance, and even a model Negro trade school. You need dedicated men and women to mobilize and canalize abilities and money toward a cherished goal. It is being done in America every day by all sorts of people. Someone has to start these things—a single individual or a small group. In San Francisco the 2,000 affluent longshoremen could be such a group.

The healing of the Negro by community-building will be a slow process, and the end results, though a durable source of pride and solid satisfaction, will not be heavenly. There is no heaven on earth and no promised land waiting for the Negro around the corner. Only the rights and the burdens and the humdrum life of a run-of-the-mill American.

Whitney M. Young, Jr.
Kyle Haselden

SHOULD THERE BE "COMPENSATION" FOR NEGROES?

DOMESTIC MARSHALL PLAN

In 1948, by instituting the Marshall Plan to aid the war-torn countries of Europe, the United States took a step unparalleled in history. Recognizing the special need of the nations shattered by World War II, the people of this country committed some $17 billion in money, machines and technical aid to help our neighbors overseas to take their place again in the community of free nations.

This rightful action was in keeping with the long tradition of America's moral, political and economic credo. We have long given special, emergency aid to the oppressed, the sick, the handicapped and deprived. In recent years, we have seen this concept put into action through our aid—in employment, education, and welfare—to Hungarian and Cuban refugees. We see it annually carried out in the form of emergency help to "depressed" and "disaster" areas, suffering from joblessness or devastation by hurricanes, drought, and other misfortunes. The "G.I. Bill of Rights" after World War II was, in a sense, a recognition of the special need of our discharged veterans for education, housing, employment, and other benefits.

Recently, the National Urban League has attracted nationwide attention with its proposal for a temporary "more-than-equal" program of aid for Negro citizens. In the current drive for civil rights, with its demonstrations, marches, and sit-in's, this proposal has confused many white Americans. They ask: Is the Negro not to be satisfied by equality alone? Or, is he seeking, not equality, but preference? In the face of these

From *The New York Times Magazine,* October 6, 1963. © 1963 by The New York Times Company. Reprinted by permission.

The first article, "Domestic Marshall Plan," is by Whitney Young, executive director of the Urban League, a major civil rights leader, and frequent author on problems of the Negro movement.

Kyle Haselden expresses an opposing view in the second article, "Parity, Not Preference" (p. 49). Haselden is managing editor of *Christian Century* and author of *The Racial Problem in Christian Perspective* (1959).

questions, our history should teach us that what the Urban League proposes is not only directly in the American tradition, but has the arguments of racial justice, economic practicality, and morality—secular as well as religious—behind it.

On an economic level, the hard but simple fact—borne out by comparative statistics on unemployment, income, mortality rates, substandard housing, and education—is that the past of the Negro exists in the present. Citizens everywhere must realize that the effects of over three hundred years of oppression cannot be obliterated by doing business as usual. They must know, too, that in today's complex, technological society, a strong back and a will to succeed are no longer sufficient to break the bonds of deprivation, as was the case with minority groups in the past. For, in addition to the ordinary forces affecting one's way of life, the Negro's struggle into America's mainstream has been thwarted by the barriers of discrimination and denial based on the color of his skin.

The facts speak for themselves. Today, the average Negro family earns $3,233, as compared with $5,835 for the white family—a difference of 45 per cent. This gap has widened by two percentage points in the last decade alone. It has widened because the Negro started receiving too little, too late. More than 75 per cent of Negro workers are found in the three lowest occupational categories—service workers, semi-skilled workers, and unskilled and farm labor—the categories most affected by the geometric gowth of automation. These same categories include less than 39 per cent of white workers.

By the same token, one out of every six Negro dwellings is substandard, as compared with one in thirty-two white dwellings. One in every four Negro women with preschool children is working away from home. Of the school dropouts, 21 per cent are Negro; only 7 per cent of high-school graduates are Negroes. Unemployment rates for Negroes are from two and one-half to three times higher than those for white workers.

To overcome these conditions the National Urban League declares that the nation must undertake an immediate, dramatic, and tangible "crash program"—a domestic Marshall Plan—to close this intolerable economic, social, and educational gap, which separates the vast majority of Negro citizens from other Americans. Unless this is done, the results of the current heroic efforts in the civil-rights movement will be only an illusion, and the struggle will continue, with perhaps tragic consequences.

In its plea for such a domestic Marshall Plan, the Urban League is asking for a special effort, not for special privileges. This effort has been described as "preferential treatment," "indemnification," "special consideration," "compensatory activity." These are "scare" phrases that obscure the meaning of the proposal and go against the grain of our native sense of fair play.

We prefer that our recommendations be seen as necessary and just corrective measures that must be taken if equal opportunity is to have meaning. They are necessary, because only by such means can the majority of Negro citizens be prepared to assume the increased responsibilities that they will face in a more integrated society. They are just, because such an effort alone can repair the devastation wrought by generations of injustice, neglect, discrimination, and indifference based on race.

To put it another way, the scales of equal opportunity are now heavily weighted against the Negro and cannot be corrected in today's technological society simply by applying equal weights. For more than 300 years the white American has received special consideration, or "preferential treatment," if you will, over the Negro. What we ask now is that for a brief period there be a deliberate and massive effort to include the Negro citizen in the mainstream of American life. Furthermore, we are not asking for equal time; a major effort, honestly applied, need last only some ten years. This crash program must be a co-operative effort by all agencies, institutions, and individuals, public and private.

The elements of the crash program, or domestic Marshall Plan, would include:

Education. For the deprived child—Negro as well as white— provision for first-class schools, with the most modern facilities and the best and most experienced teachers. These are necessary to help him realize his potential and prepare him to take advantage of greater educational opportunity. Necessary also is intensified remedial instruction in the lower grades for culturally deprived and retarded pupils. Schools and colleges must find new ways to seek out Negro youths with undeveloped talents. Similarly, adult education programs must be expanded and geared to the needs of citizens lacking the basic literary and technical skills.

Employment. A planned effort to place *qualified* Negroes in all categories of employment, at all levels of responsibility. This would mean that employers would consciously seek to hire qualified Negro citizens and would intensify apprenticeship and training programs to prepare new Negro employees and upgrade those already employed. Labor unions, too, must make a conscientious effort to include Negroes in their membership and training programs.

Further, where Negroes have not been employed in the past at all levels, it is essential that there be conscious preferment to help them catch up. This does not mean the establishment of a quota system—an idea shunned by responsible Negro organizations and leaders. But, because we are faced with the hyprocrisy of "tokenism," where the presence of two or three Negro employees is passed off as integration, we are forced, during the transitional stages, to discuss numbers and categories. We demand, in all fairness, that the Negro not be expected to bear the brunt of unemployment.

Housing. Racial ghettos eliminated by providing genuine housing opportunities on the basis of need and financial ability. Programs of redevelopment and relocation, planned to provide both low-income housing and a racial diversity, are needed throughout our communities. This will require the active participation of real estate brokers as well as homeowners.

Health and Welfare. Public and private agencies seeking to provide the best personnel and facilities in low-income neighborhoods, and increased counseling services to troubled families. Here, particularly, the churches and schools must combine efforts to help Negro families develop a deeper sense of parental and community responsibility.

Finally, qualified Negro citizens should be sought and named to public and private boards and commissions, particularly those which shape employment, housing, education, and health and welfare policies. In achieving this objective, we would develop strong, responsible leadership within the Negro community. Also, we would prompt private foundations, business and government to reassess the extent and aims of their financial contributions to established Negro leadership and organizations.

The program outlined here has a simple, practical aim: to provide the Negro citizen with the leadership, education, jobs, and motivation that will permit him to help himself. It is not a plea to exempt him from the independence and initiative demanded by our free, competitive society. It makes practical economic sense as a measure to reduce unemployment and welfare costs and to increase our productivity and national income by including Negro citizens in the benefits of our rich society. President Kennedy's economic advisers estimated that our gross national product could be raised 2.5 per cent, were the Negro worker's earnings commensurate with the nation's average.

This program makes historical sense as a rehabilitation for the damage inflicted upon the Negro by generations of injustice and neglect. He, too, has given his blood, sweat, and tears to the building of our country; yet, where the labor and initiative of other minority groups have been rewarded by assimilation within the society, the black American has been isolated and rejected.

The domestic Marshall Plan has profound moral and religious justification. Our country is in dire jeopardy as long as it has within its body politic a socially and economically deprived group of citizens, whether they be actually enslaved or denied the full benefits of equality and freedom by an insidious economic and psychological slavery. In this sense, the crash programs that we propose are not an effort to impose the guilt and sins of a past generation on our present white community. This is an appeal for all Americans, working together, to rid present-day America of its sickening disease and its moral shame.

The Negro is in revolt today, not to change the fabric of our society or to seek a special place in it, but to enter into partnership in that society. It is a revolt with which every American should sympathize. Already a few educational and business institutions are working with intensified effort, special consideration, if you will, in solving this problem. We have the material and spiritual resources as a country to meet the challenge and accomplish the urgent task ahead. All we need is the will to act and the spirit of decency and sacrifice which abounds in our land.

PARITY, NOT PREFERENCE

An increasing number of Negro and white Americans agree that securing complete freedom and total equality for the Negro is this nation's No. 1 domestic issue and that justice for the deprived one-tenth of the nation's population is the end toward which the whole society should move speedily. Unanimous in this agreement, they nevertheless disagree as to the permissible and effective means to that end.

Varied in their temperaments, their religious convictions, their sense of what is prudent and practical, these Americans prefer one or another of the various strategies which seek racial justice. The options range from the doctrine of violent rebellion against white domination at one extreme to a patient yet active appeal to the nation's creeds, congresses, and courts at the other. Between these extremes fall various nonviolent strategies and schemes, each with its own supporters.

Unfortunately there are, in the ranks of men and women genuinely committed to racial justice, some who insist that unanimity of purpose requires uniformity of plan. They insist that whites and Negroes who share their objective also adopt their methods—however unruly, eccentric and impractical those methods—or accept vilification for Uncle Tomism. This absolutist, autocratic spirit believes that justice for the Negro is the ultimate criterion of all human action and that this end validates any means, whatever practicality or religious principle may dictate to the contrary.

This is a dangerous mood. It divides those who seek justice for Negroes; it alienates influential moderates unnecessarily; and, most serious, this authoritarian spirit lures the Negro into activities which corrupt his purpose and defeat his ultimate hope.

In the struggle for racial justice a technique is not valid simply because it annoys the white man or because it promises some temporary advantage to the Negro. It is valid only if it honors the moral ground on which the Negro makes his claim for justice, respects the right of all men to the same justice, preserves in the human relationship values which are equivalents of justice, and promotes rather than prevents the Negro's progress.

The idea of compensation, which has been suggested as a device to equalize competition between whites and Negroes, fails these crucial tests. By compensation—in the passive rather than the active sense—is meant compensation *for* the Negro rather than *by* the Negro. It has been proposed that the Negro cannot succeed in his search for freedom and equality unless there is an arbitrary—in fact, artificial—removal of the academic, cultural, and professional lag forced upon him by over two centuries of slavery and by another of exploitation. It is argued further that the Negroes' years of involuntary, payless servitude established a collectible claim against the descendants of those who enslaved and exploited him.

How can this debt be paid? The proposal is that the Negro be given preference in employment wherever a vacancy occurs, a premium in salary, and a quota system guaranteeing that one-tenth of all people hired by firms, professional enterprises, and industries be Negroes. Even though this proposal is obviously unfeasible, what shall we say of it as a theory?

Compensation must be rejected as an equalizer of competition between Negroes and whites for several reasons, all of which rest on the grounds to which the Negro appeals in his demand for freedom and equality.

First, compensation for Negroes is a subtle but pernicious form of racism. It requires that men be dealt with by society on the basis of race and color rather than on the basis of their humanity. It would therefore as a public policy legalize, deepen, and perpetuate the abominable racial cleavage which has ostracized and crippled the American Negro. Racism, whoever may be its temporary beneficiary, should be eliminated from the social order, not confirmed by it.

Second, preferential economic status for Negroes would penalize the living in a futile attempt to collect a debt owed by the dead. The twentieth-century white man is no more to blame for the fact that his ancestors bought and held slaves than are twentieth-century Negroes for the fact that some of their ancestors captured and sold slaves. This is the ironic tragedy of exploitation. It leaves with the descendants of the exploiters a guilt they cannot cancel and with the descendants of the exploited a debt they cannot collect.

Third, a scheme which gives Negroes preference in employment and a premium in salary would bestow on Negroes the debilitating social status which has for centuries cursed the initiative and enterprise of the white man in the South. Preferred status for the Negro, however much society may owe him a debt, will inevitably destroy in him the initiative and enterprise required of a minority people in a highly competitive society. Slavery corrupts ambition and self-reliance; so, too, does patronizing social status.

Fourth, compensation for Negroes would be unfair to other minorities handicapped by their history or by rapid social and industrial change—Puerto Ricans, Mexican-Americans, migrants of all races, Indians, coal miners, and others. Negroes are entirely right in demanding that they be hired, paid, and promoted on their merit and in boycotting those enterprises which discriminate on a racial basis. But they are not right in demanding an artificial scheme which is unworkable, racist, destructive of initiative, and unfair to other struggling Americans.

Our goal should be parity, not preferment, and there are three things we must do, none of them pleasant, none easy, if we are to attain it.

First, there must be a total, across-the-board desegregation of American society. Wherever the white man will not voluntarily surrender the psychic and material advantages of racial discrimination, the Negro must use the law, his power as a consumer, his increasing political leverage, and coercive nonviolent protests to assail and destroy the color structures of our society.

Equality of opportunity is an elemental civil right specifically declared in the sacred documents of the United States. Withholding that right from any people because of their race profanes every tenet in the political and religious creeds of the American people. Denying that right encumbers and humiliates twenty million American citizens. The first business of the nation is the total elimination of racial discrimination and its component, racial segregation.

Such liberation, however, would leave the Negro still handicapped by centuries of poor schooling and by his long exclusion from most trades and professions. A desegregated society would open to the Negro opportunities which are rightfully his and should be granted to him but for which centuries of neglect and abuse leave many of his race inadequately prepared. Even though all racial bars were removed, most Negroes could not, in a free and impartial society, compete on equal terms with most white people for jobs and preferments.

But this, as we have noted, is a handicap which Negroes share with another one-tenth of the population, whose competitive strength has also been sapped by an unfortunate history or by the entrapping eddies of industrial development.

Our second task, therefore, is to undertake a nationwide crash program for the education, training, and employment of the underprivileged, underdeveloped one-fifth of the nation, a domestic Point Four which would give to the employable a fair chance and to the unemployable qualifying education and training. Such a program would be based not on race but on need. Negroes would of course be the chief beneficiaries of an educational and economic crash program, because of the predominant number of deprived Negroes. But a domestic Point Four program aimed at the needs of *all* the nation's backward peoples would close rather than widen the nation's racial cleavage.

Finally, irritating as it may be, the fact might as well be faced that no immigrant or minority group has ever made its way into the mainstream of American life without studying and working harder and longer than the general population. This is the third task as it now confronts the Negro.

During their long pilgrimage through slavery and semislavery, most Negroes did not have an incentive for the kind of active self-compensation by which other minorities have climbed out of humiliating servitude into respected equality with other ethnic groups. Slavery and peonage do not generally encourage ambition. Even now the Negro must divert himself—his native abilities and his acquired skills, his initiative and enterprise, his devotion and endurance, his ablest leadership—from the pursuits followed by free men to the claiming of those dignities and opportunities which are the birthright of every American citizen. Yet the hard historical fact is that self-compensation is essential if he is to escape that social substratum into which a cruel history and an arrogant, avaricious white man have coerced him.

Along with several million Caucasian Americans, most Negroes need a lift from their government if they are to overcome the handicaps of a tragic history. More than that, however, Negroes need to throw off the white man's domination if they are to discover at last what they can do for themselves unencumbered in an open society.

Part Two
Problems

Attention in this section is focused on problems of a basic nature that are not likely to be solved soon or easily. Since we recognize that the majority of readers will be from urban areas in the North and West, we have excluded such problems as segregation in public accommodations or the denial of the vote in parts of the Deep South. The problems discussed in this section are certain to persist. They are extremely difficult to solve, and their complexities allow for a wide range of interpretations.

The first selection, from Drake and Cayton's classic study *Black Metropolis*, deals with the social and cultural context in which many of the problems facing the Negro movement must be seen: Northern, urban, lower-class Negro life. This investigation of Bronzeville, the Negro ghetto of Chicago, is the most comprehensive ethnographic account yet made of the urban life situation of the American Negro. Although it deals with the time between the Great Depression of the 1930's and the early period of World War II, much of its descriptive detail of life among those in the lower class is still relevant. Here one gets some understanding of the pressures, frustrations, pleasures, and values of this large group of underprivileged persons. When one considers that it is from these people that the Muslims and other "separatist" groups have worked the hardest to recruit members, the importance of knowing something about their cultural patterns becomes evident.

The article on the Negro family, excerpted from the controversial Department of Labor report *The Negro Family: The Case for National Action,* is said to have been written largely by Daniel Patrick Moynihan. It expresses alarm over the disintegration of family life among urban Negroes—especially lower-class Negroes in large cities. The report goes to great lengths to emphasize that the roots of the problems of the Negro family lie in the long history of slavery, segregation, and discrimination. The lack of employment opportunities for Negro men is cited as a paramount causal factor. Most important, however, is the conviction expressed in the report that the condition of the Negro family—caused by lack of opportunity—has itself become an important link in the causal processes that perpetuate the inequality of American Negroes. The consequences of family disintegration are cited. The most controversial aspect of the report is its insistence that the problems of the family must be attacked directly. The report argues that despite the significance of unemployment as a cause of family disintegration, equal employment opportunities will not restore the integrity of the Negro family. In fact, it says, family disintegration and its consequences sharply curtail Negroes' ability to take advantage of whatever opportunities are open to them. This section on the Negro family should be kept in view while reading the following sections in order to grasp the subtle interplay between the subculture of the lower-class Negro and the conditions external to the Negro community to which that subculture must respond.

The readings dealing with specific problem areas begin with employment, because in many ways it is at the core of the Negro's difficulties. Many of the injustices and inadequacies in housing, education, and so forth can be traced to the persistent failure of Negroes to find stable and rewarding employment. The article by Herbert Hill lays bare the patterns of discrimination in employment. Hill shows that job discrimination is rooted not only in the practices of employers but also in the history and current patterns of labor unions—especially the old-line craft unions.

Herman Miller presents a broad view of the past, present, and probable-future role of the Negro in the labor force. His careful analysis of Negro occupational statistics provides a sobering and, at times, discouraging alternative to glib promises of "continued progress."

The selection from the *Manpower Report of the President* outlines the demographic setting of the American Negro in the post-World-War-II period. Of special concern here are the facts about Negro employment and the social factors that influence the amount and level of employment in the society. In our experience, many discussions and arguments concerning the accomplishments and demands of the Negro population have been marked by a singular lack of facts. This article provides the basis for a more informed discussion, and while it is true that facts are subject to more than one interpretation, their existence helps to keep the limits of conversation within the bounds of credibility. We, therefore, urge the reader to study this material carefully and to consult it for guidance in judging the opinions of those caught up emotionally in the issues generated by the events of the day.

De facto school segregation is the first subject discussed in the section on education. *Time Magazine* presents the data it collected in major Northern cities. The data show that despite the absence of a tradition of legal school segregation, most Negro children in the North, like their counterparts in the South, attend schools that are predominantly Negro.

Charles Silberman's analysis is based on the easily demonstrated premise that the Negro ghetto school is not only separate but also shockingly unequal to white schools. He probes into the nature of the public schools and the complexities of Negro life for the roots of this inequality and presents strong grounds for regarding conventional educational reforms as inadequate. Silberman proposes massive and costly programs to combat cultural deprivation at all age levels—from the earliest years of childhood through maturity.

The passages from Benjamin Bloom's provocative book *Stability and Change in Human Characteristics* summarize research literature from a number of disciplines on the significance of early environment as a factor in determining measurable intelligence and educational achievement. Especially noteworthy is the conclusion that a shift from an extremely deprived environment to an extremely stimulating one could result in a change of twenty points in I.Q. The author emphasizes, however, that such an improvement in I.Q. can be expected *only* if the environmental change occurs early in life—especially before the age of five. His findings indicate that the gap in I.Q. between the races widens with increasing age. After the first few grades, the average distance between Negroes and whites is significantly large and grows steadily.

These data obviously have implications of the utmost seriousness for various plans for school integration. One can hardly ignore the fact that the integration of, for example, a predominantly white and a predominantly Negro high school, involves not only racial integration, but also the mixing of two groups of decidedly different average ability. The fact that the differences are traceable to social, rather than racial, causes provides little aid or comfort to the students, parents, and school officials who must deal with these problems in a practical way. The picture is further complicated by the fact that, despite the great differences in measures of central tendency—average scores—there is a large overlap. There are always many Negro students whose scores are superior to the average white score. Similarly, there are significant numbers of white students whose scores are below the Negro average. Large-scale racial integration would mix two groups of unequal average ability; integration based on ability would send a relatively small number of whites to Negro schools and a relatively small number of Negroes to white schools. Obviously, there are no easy solutions.

The final article on education describes the reactions of the white residents to a community plan to end *de facto* segregation by the regrouping of school children. Here, Kurt and Gladys Lang show that when people face changes in their traditional life styles, they do not react as a unified group. Rather, such individual considerations as socioeconomic status, cosmopolitanism, and mobility affect one's feelings about integration. The article reminds us that although many profess liberal attitudes with respect to the Negro, the real test comes when personal involvement enters the picture.

Loren Miller surveys the history and forms of segregation and discrimination in housing. Miller, who is a judge, analyzes the roles played by the law and by various governmental agencies in the establishment of the prevalent patterns of segregation in housing.

Glazer and Moynihan discuss the special problems of the Negro ghetto and where the ghetto fits in the broader picture of ethnically-based neighborhoods in American cities. Although their discussion centers on the specific problems of New York City, most of these problems exist, in a generally similar form, in most Northern cities. The authors' general discussion of the nature of ethnic neighborhoods and their place in American life provides a most appropriate context for the discussion of Negro housing problems.

Many discussions of the race problem turn, eventually, to the issues of crime and violence. During the 1964 Presidential campaign, many citizens seemed to view the race and crime problems as one and the same. Thomas Pettigrew gives a detailed analysis of Negro-American crime. His summary of research on this matter is as close as one could come in limited space to a definitive treatment of the topic.

Allen Grimshaw is concerned with the specific problem of violence in race riots and related disturbances. He identifies the major types of racial violence and discusses the causes, with special attention to the significance of the ecological patterns and processes of cities.

In most of the racial disturbances in recent years, Negroes have charged that police brutality is a major factor. The article by the United States Commission on Civil Rights presents a series of case examples of alleged brutality in its examination of the charge. It concludes that brutality does represent a serious problem and suggests some of its causes. While most of the examples cited in this report are from the South, charges of brutality are extremely common in Northern cities also. We suggest that the charges in these urban ghettos stem from acts of harassment and discourtesy by the police as well as from physical brutality. While the number of verified cases of brutality may be relatively small, the charge has great symbolic significance in the Negro community.

Although the problem of urban race riots has attracted increased interest in recent years, we are still far from an adequate understanding of them. In the final selection on crime and violence, Editor Murphy pinpoints some questions raised by the Los Angeles riot of 1965.

We conclude the section on problems with several selections on the topics of assimilation and identity. Assimilation and identity are only problematic for an ethnic group if the dominant group gives its members opportunities to participate fully in the dominant life. The exclusion of the Negro from most aspects of white American life in the past meant that assimilation was not a meaningful issue for most Negroes. However, as opportunities for varying degrees of participation in the dominant culture have opened up for the Negro, the nature of Negro identity and the range of possible relationships between Negroes and whites have become topics for serious concern and attention.

Milton Gordon's piece provides a comprehensive analytic framework within which the multiple dimensions of acculturation, integration, and assimilation can be discussed. He also provides generalizations about the patterns of various other ethnic groups in this area. His paper will prove useful in analyzing the status of Negroes in the broader context of the place held by other racial, linguistic, national, and religious minorities in America.

Ralph Ellison's autobiographical view of the nature of Negro subculture and one form of Negro identity is a testimony in favor of full and equal participation for Negroes. He argues against a thoroughgoing process of amalgamation that would eliminate all the distinctive attributes of Negro culture, identity, and style, many of which are uniquely positive.

E. U. Essien-Udom's reflections, based on his research on the Black Muslims, raise the possibility that the Negro needs and wants an identity and existence farther separated from the life of white America than Ellison envisages. Essien-Udom suggests that the Black Muslim movement points to a life and identity for American Negroes in which African heritage and association with the new African nations might play a large role. His observations pose the possibility that some Negroes will find more satisfaction and meaning in seeing themselves as "black men" or "Africans" than as American Negroes with the emphasis on "American."

Norman Podhoretz offers a personal memoir from the perspective of a white liberal. He sees the solution of the American race problem in complete assimilation and, as far as possible, biological amalgamation. His views are in sharp contrast to Ellison and Essien-Udom, who, in different ways, call for the preservation and extension of a distinct Negro subculture and identity. Podhoretz is disturbed by many things he sees as the consequence of Negro separateness. He expresses a conviction that the disappearance of the Negroes' problems is intricately linked to the disappearance of Negroes as a distinct social entity in American life.

E. Franklin Frazier summarizes the growth of the Negro urban middle class and characterizes its cultural propensities. Frazier takes no dispassionate view of Negro "society." He is sharply critical of the superficiality of members of this class in their efforts to better themselves and of their failure to speak and work for the Negro masses. Although this view does not present a balanced picture of the middle class, it seems important for two reasons: (1) It portrays the cultural responses and expressions of those in the Negro community who have enjoyed some measure of economic success but lack broader acceptance into the larger society because of their racial ancestry. (2) It raises the issue of leadership responsibility among the more successful members of the Negro community—an issue that has become a focal point among those involved with strategies and goals of the Negro movement.

The Setting

St. Clair Drake
Horace R. Cayton

THE WORLD OF
THE URBAN LOWER-CLASS NEGRO

LOWER CLASS: SEX AND FAMILY

DEPENDENT MEN AND FORCEFUL WOMEN: Since Reconstruction days, America has stereotyped Negro lower-class men as "lazy" and "shiftless." This stereotype has been reinforced in our generation by the "Amos and Andy" and "Stepin Fetchit" characterizations of radio and screen. Side by side with this portrait is another conception of Negro lower-class men as "healthy bucks" who can stand the heat of blast furnaces and the weight of cotton bales and who can do the back-breaking work of farm and city. The latter picture is much closer to the truth, for when lower-class men can get jobs they work, as even a casual examination of the census or relief records will reveal. Historically,

From *Black Metropolis: A Study of Negro Life in a Northern City*, copyright, 1945, by St. Clair Drake and Horace Cayton. Reprinted by permission of Harcourt, Brace & World, Inc.

Mr. Drake is Professor of Sociology and Director of the African Studies Program, Roosevelt University. He was formerly Chairman of the Department of Sociology, University College of Ghana. Mr. Cayton is a sociologist with long experience in research on the Negro. He is author of *Long Old Road*, an autobiography, and co-author of *Black Workers and the New Unions*.

however, in Bronzeville as elsewhere in America, Negro men have suffered from irregularity of employment and from actual unemployment more than any other segment of America's lower class. They are the last to be hired and the first to be fired from the common labor jobs and servant jobs which they usually hold. In the cotton country, the fruits of labor are seldom realized in the form of cash, though the man may work the year around. Negroes have not been allowed to compete freely for the better jobs.

During slavery the master supported his Negro families. Since slavery, Negro men have never been able, in the mass, to obtain good jobs long enough to build a solid economic base for family support. Those who through the years have been able to accumulate something have formed the backbone of the Negro middle class. There has never been sufficient economic opportunity, however, to permit the mass of Negro workers to acquire the material goods—housing, furniture, clothing, savings—for laying the basis for a middle-class way of life. This lack of economic opportunity, coupled with denial of access to even a grade-school education, resulted very early in a peculiar pattern of restless wandering on the part of Negro men.

This notorious and widespread wandering has been primarily a search for better or supplementary jobs. Thousands of share-croppers have traditionally left their wives and children at home while they went to the cities or the lumber and turpentine camps during "laying-by time" to gain a supplementary income. Many of them never came back to the subordination of the cotton fields. Thousands flocked north during the Great Migration and through the Fat Years and the Lean. They are still coming. Some sent for their wives and sweethearts. Many didn't. Beginning with economic necessity, this pattern has become a custom which runs on its own steam. A wanderer's life is an exciting life.[1]

The roving of masses of Negro men has been an important factor, during the eighty years since slavery, in preventing the formation of stable, conventional, family units. It has shifted the responsibility for the maintenance of household units to the women of the lower class.

The economic weakness of Negro men was not confined to the plantation, however. In the southern cities and towns the masses of Negro men, ill paid and irregularly employed, have never succeeded in becoming the steady providers for their families. It has always been their wives and girl friends who, working as servants in white families, have "brought home the butter in the bag." Thus, both husband and children come to look to their women as the ultimate source of support. Even in

---

[1] E. Franklin Frazier, *The Negro Family in the United States,* University of Chicago, 1939, Chapter XIII, "Roving Men and Homeless Women."

Bronzeville during the last phases of the Depression, when hundreds of lower-class Negro men had WPA jobs, it was often the women who, through illegal and surreptitious employment as domestic servants, had the only ready cash for food, recreation, and clothes. Negro lower-class women almost always hold the purse strings.

Lower-class men are thus in a weak economic position *vis-à-vis* their women and children. Male control loosened, the woman becomes the dominant figure. Since she pays the piper, she usually feels justified in calling the tune. But while lower-class men are in a weak economic position, they are in a strategic position otherwise. Negro lower-class women, like all women, have their affectional and sexual needs. Being predominantly working women of limited education, unable to spend time or money in "prettifying" themselves, they cannot hope to get husbands from the middle and upper classes. They also face the sexual competition of the most attractive lower-class girls who can get men to support them, and of the prostitutes and semi-prostitutes. In a sense, therefore, most lower-class women have to take love on male terms. The men, on the other hand, are strongly tempted to take advantage of such a situation and to trade love for a living. The net result is an attitude of suspicion toward men blended with a woman's natural desire to be loved for herself alone.

It is no accident that Bronzeville's barbershop wags during the Depression used to say that the Negro National Anthem was "I Can't Give You Anything But Love, Baby." It is likewise no accident that one of the most popular juke-box songs was a woman's command: "Why don't you do right like other men do? Get outa here—get me some money, too."

The emotional dilemmas that arise from this awkward situation have developed a pattern of defensive hardness among lower-class Negro women alternating with moods of lavish tenderness; have developed, too, a glorification of emotional "independence" which is always belied by the facts. The men, insecure in their economic power, tend to exalt their sexual prowess. They cultivate an attitude of "love 'em and leave 'em." The women's pose is, "I'll let him love me (and I'll love him) until he doesn't act right. Then I'll kick him out."

Thus, an old southern pattern is intensified and strengthened in Bronzeville. Unstable common-law marriages of relatively short duration alternate with periods of bitter disillusionment on the women's part. The end result is often a "widow" and her children, caused either by a husband's desertion or by a wife's impetuous dismissal of him.

About three out of every five lower-class men and women in Bronzeville claim to be married. Census-takers do not ask to see marriage certificates, so the figure includes numerous common-law marriages.

(Bronzeville's lower class has brought with it from the South a certain unconcern with the formalities of law and church as related to marriage.) Over half of the unmarried women claim to have been married at some period of their lives. The bulk of these have listed themselves as "widowed"—a term which Bronzeville's lower-class women use to include "desertion." Only one woman in five listed herself as single, and this term, too, probably includes some wives who have been deserted. The desertion rate is very high among the Negro lower class throughout the United States.

About forty out of every hundred lower-class women in Bronzeville before the war were "available" in the sense that they did not have husbands. About the same proportion of men were "available." Nearly all of these men, however, report themselves as "single," even though in many cases they may have been previously married.[2] The bulk of the "available" women, on the other hand, admit having once had some sort of "unfortunate" family life. Individuals from the ranks of the "sixty per cent married" are continuously dropping into the ranks of the "forty per cent available," and vice versa. Family tensions arising within the framework of the lower-class family are usually dissolved with violence, through arguing, fighting, and as a last resort, separation. While much of the instability of the family is due to desertion on the part of the males, a not inconsiderable proportion is due to the eviction of males by women who have decided not to "put up with foolishness" any longer.

One high school girl cited an instance where a husband finally wandered off after several years of internecine strife:

> My mother and father have been separated for two years. I don't miss my father at all. He was so unpleasant that I was glad to see him leave. He gambled and drank and didn't provide for the family. We had to go on relief because of the way he acted, so I hope I never see him again. He abused Mother, too. My mother has had a very hard life. She married young and he started mistreating her right after I was born—I'm the oldest; and he made her life so miserable that she had to leave him any number of times. But she always went back on account of us.

Sometimes a desertion is accompanied by a vindictive stealing of the other partner's personal effects, as in the case of a woman who reported that she had fought continually with her husband:

> One night he started an argument with me, and told me if I didn't treat him right I would not ever have the chance to treat him any way again. I wondered what he meant when he said that; I was

[2] Over half of the 2,000 unattached Negro men who sought aid from the shelters for transient men in Chicago during the Depression admitted that they had been married.

afraid that he meant to kill me. It looked like I slept sounder than ever that night, for while I was sleeping he got up, packed all of his things and the best silks I had and left. I haven't seen him from that day unto this.

Another lower-class woman on the West Side came to Chicago with her husband, worked in a box factory ten years, and gave Saturday night parties to increase her income. After saving a large sum of money, she quit her job. The husband ordered her back to work and a razor altercation ensued, after which he ran away. He soon returned, and she agreed to go back to work! A few days later he absconded with all her savings. When he came back six years later she had another husband. The woman insists that when she discovered the loss of the money she got drunk and stayed drunk for eighteen days. (Desertions by wives under similar circumstances are not unknown, and in several cases a husband accused his wife of leaving with all of his savings.)

A family may also be broken by the enforced absence of the husband for a time. Thus the twenty-five-year-old woman quoted below lived with her parents, sister, brother-in-law, and niece. She had been separated for a year.

> He wouldn't do right and I worked to help him until I had to go to the hospital to have my baby. When I came out I left him, and he got in trouble and went to jail for twenty years. He didn't care enough about me to come out to County [hospital] to see me, and I all but died.

In this case, she and her mother and her father were all on relief; the brother-in-law worked, and he and his wife paid the entire rent and half the coal bill. Cases are frequent of daughters who have come back to live with their parents after a separation or desertion.

A GOOD OLD MAN DON'T LIVE SWEET: Despite the instability and apparent disorder of sex and family relations, Bronzeville's lower class has its own standards for a "good" husband or a "good" wife. Lower-class women don't expect much from their husbands in terms of either complete sexual fidelity or economic security. Like most women in America they fantasy about romantic love and the ideal husband who has a steady job, brings his money home, and makes possible a life of leisure and comfort. In reality, however, a lower-class woman thinks she has a "good old man" if he will work when he can and if he does not spend all his money on gambling and drinking. If he does "run with other women," he will guard against emotional attachments and absolutely will not lavish his money on other women. A "good old man" may perhaps slap or curse his "old woman" if he's angry; he definitely will not "beat on her all the time" when he's sober, and will not endanger her life when drunk. If they have children, he will make some effort to feed and clothe them, and give them gifts. And, if she is to remain with him, she expects him to "satisfy" her sexually.

Inevitably, many a lower-class man tries to "live sweet" by depending entirely on a woman to provide him with money and clothes in exchange for companionship. But a woman who "pimps a man" is considered something of a "sucker" by other women. Although such "lucky men" may be looked upon with some envy by their fellows, it is generally considered unfair to "live on a woman." A "good old man don't live sweet."

A "good old woman" is sexually satisfying, will not "run around with other men," and will be loyal to her "old man" in arguments or fights. She'll divide up whatever money she garners from work or relief. If she's not a workingwoman, she'll keep other men out of the house during the day and will have supper ready on time when her husband gets home.[3] She will not try to "dog her husband around," nor will she be too demanding in terms of clothes and money. When the going gets too tough, she won't run off with another man or run home to her folks. Nor will she throw her husband into the street. And most important of all: she will not give his money to other men.

There is a good deal of tolerance for deviations from the pattern, but if a husband or wife flagrantly and too violently misbehaves, the spouse will issue the walking papers or else pack up and leave. Some couples manage to stick it out and maintain a stable, unbroken home, but this is not the typical lower-class pattern.[4]

SHE JUST AIN'T GOT THE STUFF IN HER TO BE A GOOD WOMAN! Often family fights and desertions result from breaking the "code." A case with many elements of a typical situation is cited below. Here a man has been arrested for beating his wife, and insists that he will never live with her again:

[3] This business of not having supper ready when the old man gets home was a frequent source of conflict in lower-class households during the Depression. The wives of men who worked on the WPA often took "day's work" to supplement the family income or spent time at the policy stations hoping for a lucky hit. When these activities interfered with the prompt preparation of meals, there was likely to be an explosion. The lower-class man seemed to view such "excuses" with suspicion, especially if the woman had no money to show in evidence. And even if she could show some money, how could he be sure where it came from? The atmosphere of mutual suspicion that characterizes lower-class family life is a dominant part of the *ethos* of Bronzeville.

[4] This generalization is based on the high desertion rate as well as on samplings within typical lower-class neighborhoods. In the study of the relatively stable West Side, for instance, over half the homes were broken, and in at least a third of the remaining families one partner had been previously married.

I work for a junk yard. I'm the night watchman and I don't get home until seven o'clock in the daytime. I'm tired and I go to bed. Well, I woke up and called my wife one day; she wasn't home, so I dressed and went out looking for her. I found her at her friend's house with two other men. When I walked in on the four of them, there was a bottle of whisky on the table. I asked her what she was doing there. She looked at me and said, "What do you think I'm doing?"

We began to argue and a rap came to the door. A young man said, "Is this the place that ordered the beer?" My wife said, "Yes, bring it in." She gave him a dollar bill and the boy was going to give her some change. She said, "It's on John"—meaning me. I got mad and I punched her. I chased the two men out and I grabbed her again. I told her to put her clothes on and get home. She was half drunk and she took a long time to get ready.

When we got down in front of the house she began to call me dirty names. I hit her on the face and she fell. She began to bleed, but I didn't care. I was so mad I could've killed her. Soon the police came, and here I am.

That woman where she was—she ain't no friend of mine; she is a no-good bum, and I told my wife not to go up there. Who does she think she is, spending my money on other men! . . . This is the first trouble I had and the last. I won't live with a woman like that.

When asked if he planned a divorce he answered: "No, sir; I'll just go my way and tell her to go hers. I'm through with her. I should've known she was no good. She just ain't got the stuff in her to be a good woman." John didn't know why he had ever married her: "I've been asking myself that question quite a few times. I got a good job; I'll get me a good wife the next time."

The interviewer said: "That will be bigamy. They can send you to jail for a thing like that."

"I don't care what they do to me—I'm through with that bitch forever."

Wild Children

Most of Bronzeville lies within those areas of Chicago which the sociologists call "delinquency areas." Wherever neighborhoods have begun to "go down"—where there are waste tracts of land, dilapidated buildings, railroad sidings—here are the "delinquency areas," regardless of what nationality or race lives there. Yet, Negroes show an unusually high delinquency rate.

In 1930, 20 out of every hundred boys hailed before the juvenile court were colored boys. The rates for girls were almost as high. The Depression made a chronic condition acute. Parents were without money to give children for the shows, the dances, and the "zoot suits" which lower-class adolescent status required. There were few odd jobs. Purse-snatching became general in lower-class areas and even on main thoroughfares. Occasionally, too, a gang of youngsters would crowd some other child who had a little money into a doorway and rob him—at knife-point. Studies of delinquents show that their behavior is partly "rational" (e.g., desire to get money for a show) and partly the search for a thrill or excitement.

Bronzeville's wild children were not so numerous as the frightened upper and middle class thought, but there were enough of them roaming the streets during the Depression, stealing, fighting, and molesting pedestrians, to cause everyone—including lower-class parents —to talk about the "youth problem." Much more prevalent were the thousands of lower-class young men who were never arrested as delinquents but who skirted the borderline of crime. These were the "cats" who, clad in "zoot-suits," stood around and "jived" the women. "Sexual delinquency" was probably more widespread than petty thievery and violence.

Babies without Fathers

Between 1928 and 1933 about 25,000 Negro babies were born in Chicago, and of these more than 2,000 were illegitimate.[5] The greater number of these "babies without fathers" were born of young lower-class mothers, most of whom had been in the city less than five years. Such an "accident" rarely happens to girls in other social classes, or even to lower-class girls wise in the ways of the city. When it does happen to one of the latter, however, she is not "disgraced." Her friends may perhaps gossip about her, and her parents, if religious, will grieve over their daughter's sin; but she will hardly lose her friends, male or female, and will probably continue her activities in any organizations to which she belongs. The lower class, unlike the middle and the upper, not only tolerates illegitimacy, but actually seems almost indifferent toward it. As the illegitimate child grows up, it does not ordinarily suffer marked embarrassment or encounter many taunts.

This attitude toward illegitimacy is imported from the South, where on the plantations the masses of the Negro people have historically considered a child a welcome gift, another "hand" to help make a crop. It is only in the cities that children become "handicaps," and illegitimate ones, liabilities.

During the Depression years, a lower-class mother in Bronzeville

[5] From 10 to 15 per cent of all Negro maternity cases at the Cook County Hospital between 1923 and 1928 were unmarried mothers. Virtually all of these were lower-class cases, since women of higher status do not go to the county hospital to have their babies delivered. (See E. Franklin Frazier, *The Negro Family in Chicago*, University of Chicago, 1932, pp. 179–83.)

with illegitimate children usually made an adjustment in one of the following ways:

a. She would live with her parents and contribute to the support of the joint family.

b. In a family without a male head, the mother would care for the illegitimate child while the daughter worked to support all three. If no work was available, relief provided for the family unit.

c. She would rent a room for herself and the child, and depend upon relief for support.

d. She would find a "boy friend" to support herself and the child.

One young woman with a three-year-old baby, commenting on this last arrangement, said: "I haven't got no husband. The boy was supposed to marry me, but he never did. I've got a new boy friend. He drives a cab and comes over here every day nearly."

Occasionally a woman with an illegitimate child is even fortunate enough to find a boy friend who may marry her, as in the case of this woman who detailed the circumstances of her two "slips":

> I was working, and he would meet me after work. I tried to avoid him but I couldn't. My mother told me fellows liked girls that were easy and not to have anything to do with him. I thought he was after my money. He was very nice to me. He would take me out and buy me anything I wanted to eat. He never gave me any money. One Sunday he met me after work and took me out and I didn't get home until Monday morning. We went from one tavern to another. He finally took me to a hotel. I was seventeen then, and he is the first man that I ever had. . . . The other baby's father wasn't any good either. Mother said that when I made one mistake, I shouldn't have made another one. I didn't know I would get caught so easily. What can you do? A woman has to have somebody. . . . I didn't love either of the children's daddies, but I love this man I go with now. We are engaged. He is crazy about the kids.

The girls' stories of these Bronzeville accidents usually follow the conventional boy-meets-girl pattern. Lucy, for instance, was living at home. Her boy-friend took the initiative:

> He used to stand on the corner of 49th Street, and when we girls would get out of school he and several other boys would follow us. So I liked him and I thought he liked me. He never would come out here to see me. I would meet him at another girl's home and we would go to shows. . . . He told me he loved me and asked me to go with him to a girl friend of his. I finally agreed to go with him. We went out there. The lady rented rooms. So he got a room, we went in, and he told me he wanted to be with me. I protested but he

finally out-talked me. . . . I was then at a stage where I could not help myself; something just seemed to hold me in a spell. . . . I told him if anything happened to me he would have to marry me. He agreed. After that we had frequent dates. I just fell in love with him. I told him that Mother was very much upset, and I begged him to marry me. He told me he didn't want to marry. He said he couldn't swear the baby was his, so I began to hate him. He just left the city. I don't want him any more.

Since hundreds of Bronzeville's lower-class girls are "on their own" at an early age, the locale of their seduction is often their own kitchenettes:

> I met him through a girl friend of mine he used to go with. So one day he carried me to work and when I got out of his car I offered to pay him and he wouldn't take it. The next day he came around to my house and I gave him dinner. While we were eating he asked me if he could go with me. He said he and my friend had quit and he liked me, but I would have to stop all these men from hanging around me, that he didn't want anyone around where he went. The next night was my night off, and he called and said he would be over and didn't want anyone here when he got here, that he would be a little late— to have him something good to eat. So I fixed him a real good supper that night, and it was almost one o'clock when he got here. I was up with my gown on and he knocked on the door. I opened it and he wanted to know what I was doing up so late. I told him I was mad because he had waited so late to come and the supper was cold. He kissed me and said that was all right. Then he told me he had a dream about me the night before and I was as naked as when I was born. I said, "Oh, that's a bad dream." He said, "No, it's a good dream" . . . and I got in a family way that night.

Though there is nothing distinctive about the way in which Bronzeville's babies without fathers originate, the attitudes of the mothers toward their own behavior is characteristically lower-class. Since lower-class men do not necessarily refuse to live with or even marry a girl who has had an illegitimate child, a girl has not necessarily "ruined herself." One woman, now married to a man who is not the child's father, said: "I had Petey before I was married. I was going to let his father marry me, but I didn't like him so well." Other women who have never married sometimes express both guilt and irritation, as in the case of a woman who shouted at an interviewer: "I ain't never had no husband. Haven't you heard of women having babies without a husband? Maybe I didn't want to get married."

One occasionally finds an older woman who has not only never married, but who boasts of the fact. The woman quoted below, though an extreme case, represents a type sometimes found in Bronzeville. A migrant from South Carolina, she exemplifies a pattern once widespread in the South but rare in Bronzeville—a woman with a large family of illegitimate children by a number of different men:

> I've been here eleven years, soon will be, and wouldn't be any place else I know of now. I was twenty-six years old when I came here. I didn't know where I was going when I came, but I had heard about Chicago and always said I was going up the country when I was older. None of my five children are whole sisters and brothers. One of my boys really has good blood in him—he is a white man's child and as bright as you are. He is really good-looking, even if I do say so. . . . Jack lived with me two years before he died. . . . No, we didn't live together all the time. I used to live on the place where I worked all the time, and when I had a day off I'd spend the night with him. I'm living with a boy friend now. He wants to marry, but I don't want to be bothered. I've been my boss too long now. I go and come and do what I want to do. I can't see when I can have anyone bossing me around now. . . . You see, I love the h— out of him, but I don't need anybody to just love. If he can't help me or pay me, I can't use him. I can love anywhere. . . . Sometimes I think of putting my kids in a home some place. It is so hard on me to work and come home to see my children, but I'd hate for them to leave me.

Most of Bronzeville's lower-class girls are neither "unspoiled children of Nature" nor defiant social rebels. They are aware of the fact that the church-centered lower class and the entire middle-class world does not approve of babies without fathers. Members of the more stable lower-class families express frequent verbal disapproval. Some of the other lower-class women, too, are responsive to the censure of the church people on their own class level and of the entire middle-class world. But the lower class does not make a grave social or moral issue of illegitimacy. Though a baby without a father may be an inconvenience to a lower-class mother, and most certainly a handicap to upward social mobility, the mother is not ostracized and the child is not ordinarily ridiculed. The interviewers on the Cayton-Warner Research reported several cases in which the mother felt that living with a man other than the child's father was more reprehensible than having an illegitimate child. One such woman was ashamed to move her new boy friend into her home, although she thought he would "do more" for her if she lived with him; but she'll starve, she says, before she'll let her illegitimate daughter see her do anything wrong! She wants to send the child to the country where "she can grow up educated and be able to do more than scrub floors and wash clothes."

The high illegitimacy rate in Bronzeville is sometimes cited as evidence of the "immorality" of Negroes, and the particularly high rate within the lower class as evidence of the special "immorality" of that class. Lower-class Negroes are quick to counter with the assertion that white people and higher-status Negroes "do everything they're big enough to do, but they don't have the babies." There is some element of truth in this if "immorality" means premarital or extramarital sex-relations. Babies without fathers are primarily the consequence of ignorance concerning birth-control and of a lack of concern for middle-class proprieties and "front." The prevalence of illegitimacy among the lower class is also a reflection of the incomplete urbanization of the rural southern migrants; for, as E. Franklin Frazier has suggested, illegitimacy in the rural South is not the social disaster it is considered in the cities, but "where the rural folkways concerning unmarried motherhood are in conflict with the legal requirements of the city, the persistence of these folkways in the urban environment will create social problems."

It's Hard to Keep Girls Straight

As a rule, lower-class parents do not approve of abortions— "murdering" babies they call it. If a girl is pregnant, they feel that she should "have the baby" and that the father (if they can find him) should contribute to its support. They seldom insist, however, that he marry the girl to "give the child a name" or to save their daughter's honor. The child may or may not assume its father's name. The daughter when able usually goes to work (or during the Depression, applied for relief). Older members of the family or relatives and friends help to care for the baby. Despite this acceptance of illegitimate children as "acts of God," parents do consider them unfortunate accidents. One West Side father hopes that his daughter won't have "bad luck," because "so many of the other girls have babies and have to get married." Yet he says, "If she has one, I don't want her to marry the boy unless she wants to." Another father has been wondering whether his eleven-year-old daughter is going to "come up with a baby" because it's so hard to keep girls straight "over here." But he is not going to insist that she marry if she does have a child.

A middle-aged husband, a migrant from North Carolina, wants to take his children "back South" to raise them because "I don't want no children of mine to be like the children I see on the streets nowadays." He proceeds to describe "girls fourteen or fifteen carrying babies when they ought to be carrying books," and concludes bitterly, "People waste a lot of money trying to make something out of these little whores!" Another father has already sent his two daughters to Florida, because "Chicago is no place to raise girls if you want them to be something when they grow up." But such decisions are rare even among the respectable lower class.

Lower-class parents who have the ambition to "make something" out of their girls may be atypical, but they are bitterly articulate:

> That's one reason so many of our girls don't even get through high school. They get knocked up and have a baby before they are in their teens good. And the boys all want to be pimps and gangsters, so they quit school and buy clothes to look sharp.

One lower-class mother approves of her daughter's desire to be a stenographer because it will give her a chance to get a nice man for a husband. (Her oldest son was in the county jail at the time for disorderly conduct.) Her fears are revealed by her comment that

> you can't raise a girl right over here . . . This is a rotten neighborhood. . . . By the time they are fifteen they are no good. The boys are the same way. It's because the parents don't care and the schools don't teach them anything. If she'll only listen to me I'm sure she won't come up with a baby.

"Listening" does not mean learning the use of contraceptives—it means hearing a lecture on "staying away from men." But such parents often have daughters who don't "listen," like this girl who has already had one baby:

> I don't want to hurt Mother again. She provokes me. I am very much upset about all of it. We were always taught the right way. It's no fault of Mother's. I must say my mother has always been a real mother ever since our father died. . . . I'm sorry for all of it, but I really think Mother should not be so hard on me. I love the baby and Mother loves it too, but I'll never let another man get me like that. I'll do anything to make Mother forget. We still go to church. I feel so ashamed among my chums, but I guess it will be over. I promised I will go back to school and forget the past and be a good girl.

THE WORLD OF THE LOWER CLASS

The physical "world" of Bronzeville's lower class is the world of store-front churches, second-hand clothing stores, taverns, cheap movies, commercial dance halls, dilapidated houses, and overcrowded kitchenettes. Its people are the large masses of the poorly schooled and the economically insecure who cluster in the "worst" areas or nestle in the interstices of middle-class communities. The lower-class world is complex. Basic to it is a large group of disorganized and broken families, whose style of life differs from that of the other social classes, but who are by no means "criminal" except so far as the children swell the ranks of the delinquents, or the elders occasionally run afoul of the law for minor misdemeanors. Existing side by side with these people is a smaller, more stable group made up of "church folks" and those families (church and non-church) who are trying to "advance themselves." In close contact with both these groups are the denizens of the underworld—the pimps and prostitutes, the thieves and pickpockets, the dope addicts and reefer smokers, the professional gamblers, cutthroats, and murderers. The lines separating these three basic groups are fluid and shifting, and a given household may incorporate individuals of all three types, since, restricted by low incomes and inadequate housing, the so-called "respectable" lowers find it impossible to seal themselves off from "shady" neighbors among whom they find themselves. The "church folks," despite their verbal protests, must live in close contact with the world of "Sin."

The world of the lower class is a public world; contacts are casual and direct with a minimum of formality. It is also a neat and compact world; mobility is quick and easy with dime jitneys always at hand and most places of congregation within walking distance. Conversation and rumor flow continuously—about policy, "politics," sports, and sex. Arguments (often on the "race problem"), while chronically short on fact, are animated and interesting. Emotional satisfactions in such situations are immediate. Physical gratifications are direct. There are status-bearers within this realm, but they are not the civic leaders and intellectuals. They are, rather, the "policy kings"; sportsmen, black and white; the clever preachers and politicians; legendary "tough guys"; and the good fighters and roisterers.

Lower-class people will *publicly* drink and play cards in places where people of higher status would lose their "reputations"—in the rear of poolrooms, in the backrooms of taverns, in "buffet-flats," and sometimes on street corners and in alleys. They will "dance on the dime" and "grind" around the juke-box in taverns and joints, or "cut a rug" at the larger public dance halls. They will "clown" on a street corner or in public parks. It is this *public* behavior that outrages the sensibilities of Bronzeville's "dicties." "It gives The Race a bad name," they are quick to announce.

These centers of lower-class congregation and festivity often become points of contact between the purveyors of pleasure "on the illegit" and their clientele—casual prostitutes, bootleggers, reefer peddlers, "pimps," and "freaks." Some of these places are merely "fronts" and "blinds" for the organized underworld.

THE UNDERWORLD: Policy is technically "on the illegit," but it is a protected business. Prostitution, bootlegging, "freak shows," "reefer dens," and "pads," however, must operate as an "underworld." They, too, are protected, but liquor, dope, and women are too "hot" for an open political "fix." Money passes, but in a very guarded fashion, and usually it is small change—to the cop on the beat or to the minor ward politicians. The big-shot politicians play the game safe.[6]

The primary institutions of the underworld are the tougher taverns, the reefer pads, the gambling dens, the liquor joints, and the call-houses and buffet-flats where professional prostitutes cater to the trade in an organized fashion.

Much of the petty gambling, bootlegging, and prostitution, however, is carried on in apartment houses, particularly in kitchenette buildings whose owners and superintendents make little or no effort to control the tenants' activities. The denizens of the underworld operate on a much wider scale, and may be found drumming up business in cabarets, more or less respectable dance halls, and—in the case of prostitutes—on the streets.

Religion and the Church

There are about 500 policy stations in Bronzeville, 80 poolrooms, 200 taverns, and scores of buffet-flats and dives. But there are also about 500 churches, at least 300 of these being located in definitely lower-class neighborhoods. The evening hours of Bronzeville's lower-class areas are noisy with the cacophony of both hymns and blues, gospel songs and "low-down" music. It is obvious that some people in Bronzeville take their pleasure by "making a joyful noise unto the Lord." This complex that we have just described is to them "The World of Sin," and they claim to live "in it, but not of it."

The church-oriented segment of the lower class is important because it represents an element of stability in a disordered milieu. The church world is a women's world, for less than a third of the lower-class church members are men. These lower-class church women are, on the whole, an influence for stable family relations within their social strata. As they phrase it, they are often "unequally yoked together" with men who are "sinners" and whose "sin" is reflected in a devotion to gambling, extra-marital sex relations, and "big-timing." "Respectable lowers"—male and female—are usually "church people," but they are a decided minority within the large lower class. The Negro "dicties" and the larger white world view lower-class religion with amused condescension. To some lower-class people, however, identification with the church is

---

[6] "On the illegit"—illegal.
"Reefers"—marijuana cigarettes.
"Reefer pad"—hangout for smokers of marijuana cigarettes.
"Freak shows"—pornographic exhibitions by sexual perverts.
"Pads"—houses of assignation where dope is available.

considered the "better" alternative of a forced option: complete personal disorganization or "serving the Lord.". . .

Interviews with a score of preachers in intimate contact with the lower class, as well as observation of families affiliated with lower-class churches, seem to indicate that where *both* heads of a family are "church people" the unit tends to have a pattern similar to that of the middle class. Most of the members of lower-class churches, however, are women married to husbands who are "unchurched" or women who have been deserted or divorced. In the latter case, sexual affairs outside of marriage, while frowned upon, do not ordinarily result in social ostracism so long as they do not involve open scandals or public fights. The influence of the church on lower-class sex and family life seems to be confined to moderating public brawling and to creating a group of women who try to make their children "respectable" and encourage them to assume a middle-class family pattern even though they themselves, due to "weakness of the flesh" or bitter experiences with men, do not maintain stable family relations. Children of such families are often torn between affection for a parent and contempt or disgust for the family behavior pattern. It is probable that juvenile delinquency is closely related to such conflicts. There are, of course, numerous lower-class women whose lives are so completely organized around the church and religion or middle-class ideology that sexual "delinquency" would never occur. . . .

The Communion of the Saints

Bronzeville's lower-class churches are sustained by what the ministers like to call "the faithful few." Probably less than 10,000 people (two-thirds of them women) form the core of Bronzeville's lower-class church life. These are the people who attend Sunday services regularly, who go to prayer meetings and special services, who contribute faithfully to the numerous collections, and spark-plug the rallies and financial drives. They beg and canvass and see that the preachers are housed and fed. Their lives revolve around religion and the church, and their emotional needs seem to be met primarily by active participation in the worship ceremonies.

Prayer meetings and communion services are the more significant experiences in their common life, and such services are highly charged with emotion. They involve group singing, individual prayers, and "testifying." On the occasions when the "true believers" relate their conversion experiences, they usually couch them in certain traditional phrases similar to the following:

> I remember the day and the hour when Christ spoke peace to my soul. He took my feet outa the miry clay and placed them on solid ground. He put a new song in my mouth.

They also recite their "trials and tribulations," sometimes weeping as they tell how they've been " 'buked and 'bused and scorned." They confess, too, that they haven't always been able to "live clean," and end by "telling their determination":

> I'm still pressing on up the King's Highway and I want you all to pray for me that I may grow stronger and stronger.

In such services individuals also express themselves in prayer. Lower-class church people look with scorn upon "book prayers," for praying is an art, and a person who can lead his fellows to the throne of grace with originality and eloquence gains high prestige. Praying sometimes becomes a collective ritual characterized by a sort of weird beauty. Rhythmic moans from the congregation, interjections of *Amen, Praise the Lord,* and *Hallelujah* encourage the intercessor, and prayers may be punctuated with the tapping of feet. Though each person makes up his own prayer, there is a common stock of striking phrases and images which are combined and recombined throughout the Negro lower-class religious world. The following generalized prayer includes phrases that may be heard in any place where the faithful meet to pray:[7]

> O Lord, we come this morning knee-bowed and body bent before thy throne of grace. We come this morning, Lord, like empty pitchers before a full fountain, realizing that many who are better by nature than we are by practice have passed into the great beyond, and yet you have allowed us, your humble servants, to plod along just a few days longer here in this waste-howling wilderness. We thank thee, Lord, that when we 'woke this morning, our bed was not a cooling board, and our sheet was not a winding shroud.[8] We are not gathered here for form or fashion or for an outside show unto the world, but we come in our humble way to serve thee. We bring no merit of our own, and are nothing but filthy rags in thy sight. We thank thee, Lord, that we are clothed in our right mind and are not racked upon a bed of pain. Bless the sick and the afflicted and those who are absent through no fault of their own. And when I've done prayed my

[7] Prayers of this type are often heard in churches which are not stratified as lower-class. When dealing with church rituals "lower-class" in Bronzeville almost becomes synonymous with "old-fashioned" or "southern" and in modern southern communities, or a generation ago everywhere, such prayers were common in colored Baptist or Methodist churches of *all* status levels. Therefore, an elderly person or an "old-fashioned" person in a Bronzeville middle-class congregation may pray in a manner which is *typical* of Chicago's lower-class congregations. A congregation cannot be stratified by any single item such as type of prayers or sermons. It is the total configuration of the ceremonies that counts.

[8] A member of one small store-front church utilized some of these phrases in a variant form, expressing satisfaction that "when God woke me up this morning my bed was not my cooling board, my four walls were not the grave walls, and my cover was not my winding sheet."

last prayer and done sung my last song; when I'm done climbing the rough side of the mountain; when I come down to tread the steep and prickly banks of Jordan, meet me with thy rod and staff and bear me safely over to the other side. All these things we ask in Jesus' name, world without end, *Amen*.

Revolt against Heaven

Bronzeville is in revolt against Heaven, and the rebellion centers in the lower class. It is reflected in continuous vitriolic attacks upon preachers and church members. It is a part of the general secularization of life in the urban, industrial society. In most cases, however, it is not a frank and open atheism. It is not even an attack upon the church *per se*, for Bronzeville's lower class seems to still feel that it ought to be religious. Rather, it takes the form of a protest against the alleged cupidity and hypocrisy of church functionaries and devotees.

The preachers bear the brunt of the attacks, and comments on ministers are sometimes violent. This was especially true during the Lean Years, when statements involving charges of clerical greed were commonplace:

> The Bible says we should not bring the price of a dog into the House of God, but these damn preachers don't care how the money is gotten; they take it.

> The average pastor is not studying the needs of his race. He's studying the ways to get more money out of people. He gives the little children cans to beg pennies with and has the older children give plays. He has the sisters and brothers go broke on rally days.

> Every time you see them [the preachers], they want money.

> I don't go to church. I need what the church needs—that's money.

> These preachers are sickening. They want you to work and bring them all of the money. That's worse than policy. They'll collect for their own benefit and then come around last for the sick collection. See, they know you've already given all your money. . . .

The most important factor in weakening the influence of the churches is the centripetal pull of the urban milieu. There is a bewildering diversity of denominations and of types of churches within a denomination. The movies, ball games, social clubs, and policy stations offer competing forms of participation and throw doubt on all absolute conceptions of sin. The group controls of the small town are absent. The prosperous "wicked" are a perpetual challenge to the "poor saints." "Take the world and give me Jesus" may be the essence of the old-time religion. "What do I get out of it?" is Bronzeville's persistent query.

When the Old Gods Go

In the face of this wide range of alternative interests, religion ceases to be the focus of lower-class life. The vast majority organize their behavior around "good-timing," fixing their attention on the cheaper forms of commercial recreation and gearing the rhythm of their daily life to the policy drawings. Some cling to the church as a subsidiary center of interest. Others drop their church connections entirely and become completely secularized except for fleeting moments of reverie or remorse.

Within the lower class are some individuals, however, who assume a pattern of serious secular interests. These are of four main types: (1) participation in "racial" movements; (2) identification with the Communist movement; (3) participation in trade union activities; (4) striving to "get ahead" in the traditional fashion of saving money, acquiring a middle-class consumption pattern, trying to get more education, and participating in ward politics. Occasionally an energetic or ambitious person may incorporate all these interests or shift from one to the other. Sometimes the individual may become a well-known "leader" on the lower level, and in specific crisis situations may attract a temporary following from the unorganized and undisciplined masses.

BRONZEVILLE 1961*

The Black Belt has grown enormously in size, and thousands of Negroes are now living in fine apartment buildings and in relatively new, attractive homes vacated during the last ten years by white people who were "getting ahead" (and who symbolized the fact by increasing the physical distance between themselves and Negroes). With money in the bank and G.I. and F.H.A. loans available, Bronzeville's home owners have been lavishing attention upon their newly acquired properties, partly because of intrinsic satisfaction in so doing, pride of possession, and also because it is part of the ritual of "advancing the race." They feel impelled to stamp out the stereotype that "Negroes always run neighborhoods down."

Even the older parts of the Black Belt have a new look. Extensive slum-clearance and rebuilding have changed the face of the Black Belt's northern section while "elbow grease," paint and grass, storm windows and flowers, have eliminated much of the drab, run-down, depression look of yesteryears. But unkempt neighborhoods and litter-laden alleys and streets have by no means disappeared; and Bronzeville's *masses* are

* From *Black Metropolis: A Study of Negro Life in a Northern City* (revised and enlarged edition), Volume II. Copyright © 1962 by St. Clair Drake and Horace R. Cayton. Reprinted by permission of Harper & Row, Publishers, Inc.

still piled up on top of each other in cramped quarters to a greater extent than in any other part of Midwest Metropolis. To them the Black Ghetto has become a gilded ghetto, but a ghetto all the same. . . .

Slum clearance and urban redevelopment programs have wiped out the concentrated cluster of lower-class institutions and scattered the population. But as a sub-culture, the "World of the Lower Class" still exists. Store-front churches flourish, but illiterate and semi-literate individuals who feel that they are "called to preach" find it increasingly difficult to rent stores, since run-down business streets are being eliminated by slum clearance, and low-cost housing projects make no provision for such spiritual entrepreneurs. There has been a substantial increase, however, in the number of conventional churches catering to lower-class religious tastes. . . . New churches appealing to recent immigrants from the South are now far more popular than either of these two. Churches still constitute a center of stability amid the constant flux and disorder of the world of the lower class. . . .

Within the disorganized segment of the lower class are the highly publicized unwed and deserted mothers, some of whom draw a regular income from welfare sources, as well as the women and men who have formed loose and shifting common-law alliances; the recalcitrant and sometimes violent school children; the teen-age gangsters; the dope users and pushers; and the small hard core of habitual criminals.

Urban renewal tends to make the entire city more aware of Bronzeville's *lumpen-proletariat,* for as the slums are cleared, and the physical locus of the lower class is shattered, individuals and families are forced to scatter into middle-class neighborhoods and onto the margins of these areas, since public "relocation housing" has never kept pace with demolition. Enterprising realtors in middle-class neighborhoods are always ready to convert houses and apartment buildings in order to accommodate new tenants in crowded discomfort, while the most marginal families huddle in dilapidated buildings awaiting demolition within clearance areas. An occasional tragedy, as when a firetrap burns or a baby is bitten by a rat, excites a spate of excited newspaper comment and sometimes an exposé. . . .

The lower-class churches do not speak to the condition of the disorganized masses and very few brands are snatched from the burning despite continuous praying and singing, preaching and revivals.

In recent years new "Black Gods of the Metropolis" have appeared. "The Leader and Teacher, the Honorable Elijah Mohammed, who was taught by the God whose proper name is Allah" has bought a Jewish synagogue near the University of Chicago and converted it into Mr. Mohammed's Temple No. 2, with its affiliated University of Islam. Here (and through his newspaper and over the radio), he exhorts the "so-called Negroes" to repudiate the white man's religion, to cast off the names inherited from slavery, to eschew pork, drinking, smoking, and gambling, and to help "build a Nation in this Wilderness of North America." He encourages his followers to go into business; but the attempts of the Muslims to erect a business center in a new Negro middle-class neighborhood created such vigorous opposition that the venture was blocked. (The "Moors" were operating in Chicago as early as the 20's, but it is only since the Second World War that Black Muslims have attracted a substantial following.) The female faithful in their colorful pseudo-Arabic gowns and the fanatical males, including the judo-trained Fruit of Islam, can fill the Chicago Stadium at nationwide conventions of the Black Muslims, but the number of people in Bronzeville who have actually joined the movement would hardly fill the auditoriums of the two largest Baptist churches. The rise of the Black Muslims is one index to the deep resentment among lower-class Negoes, but is no more likely to have a significant impact upon Bronzeville than did the Communist Party during the Depression years. Neither the Christian churches nor Mr. Mohammed are able to influence that large segment of the lower-class whose resentment is expressed in apathy, cynicism and aggression, and whose primary mode of escape is through "having a good time." . . .

From the Black Muslim's point of view, Negroes should deliberately accept segregation. They assert that Negroes of all social classes are losing their self-respect by pursuing an integrationist will-o'-the-wisp. The Muslims continuously assail Martin Luther King, the Freedom Riders, the NAACP, and the Urban League, and call for the building of a Black Nation upon land to be secured from the government as compensation for back wages "stolen" during several centuries of slavery. One member writes:

> There are at least three things that we must do in order to lift the heel of Satan (i.e., the white man) from our necks and that is to, one, separate our people from the Caucasian race, which means putting an end to integration; second, return the white man's religion of Christianity which is the mental chain that is rusting and destroying our people's minds; and third, we must come together—this means dissoving our very foolish and false class system. Doctors, professors, lawyers, college students, mothers and fathers, the young and old, should take up the banner of Islam and build a righteous nation on this earth.

Most Negroes reject the Muslim's racism and separatism while admiring their militancy and successful business enterprises.

During the 1960's there has been a marked increase of interest in Africa among the people of Black Metropolis—a fascination with the rise of the new African states, coupled with some resentment over the fact that special treatment is reserved for African diplomats so that they are less subject to discrimination. At the upper and upper-middle-class levels this interest is reflected in occasional parties for prominent African visitors, in vacation trips to Africa by the few who can afford it, by investment in a few African business projects, and by the frequent programming of lectures and discussions about Africa before church groups and clubs.[9] At lower status levels there is considerable vicarious identification with leaders like Jomo Kenyatta and Lumumba, who symbolize violent assault upon the ramparts of white supremacy. Yet, Bronzeville rejects neo-Garveyism with its Back-to-Africa emphasis as decisively as it rejects Mr. Mohammed's "Nation in This Wilderness.". . .

Negroes in Bronzeville are very much Americans. And this means, too, that if the masses are driven too far they are likely to fight back, despite their sometimes seemingly indifferent reactions to discrimination and segregation. A potential for future violence within Black Metropolis exists that should not and cannot be ignored.

[9] In 1955, one group of lower-middle-class men revived the Ancient Order of Ethiopia, a lodge which once existed in Chicago and which had as one of its stated goals "to bring to the world the ancient achievements, grandeur and glory of a lost culture—the Ethiopian." Negro History Week is celebrated annually by speeches and concerts under the auspices of an organization called the Afro-American Heritage Foundation. But very few individuals are involved in these groups. The members of the Ethiopian World Federation also meet regularly to discuss their plans for emigration to the Emperor's domains.

United States
Department of Labor

THE NEGRO AMERICAN FAMILY

At the heart of the deterioration of the fabric of Negro society is the deterioration of the Negro family.

It is the fundamental source of the weakness of the Negro community at the present time.

There is probably no single fact of Negro American life so little understood by whites. The Negro situation is commonly perceived by

Reprinted from *The Negro Family: The Case for National Action* by the Office of Policy Planning and Research, United States Department of Labor (U.S. Government Printing Office, March 1965).

whites in terms of the visible manifestations of discrimination and poverty, in part because Nego protest is directed against such obstacles, and in part, no doubt, because these are facts which involve the actions and attitudes of the white community as well. It is more difficult, however, for whites to perceive the effect that three centuries of exploitation have had on the fabric of Negro society itself. Here the consequences of the historic injustices done to Negro Americans are silent and hidden from view. But here is where the true injury has occurred: unless this damage is repaired, all the effort to end discrimination and poverty and injustice will come to little.

The role of the family in shaping character and ability is so pervasive as to be easily overlooked. The family is the basic social unit of American life; it is the basic socializing unit. By and large, adult conduct in society is learned as a child.

A fundamental insight of psychoanalytic theory, for example, is that the child learns a way of looking at life in his early years through which all later experience is viewed and which profoundly shapes his adult conduct.

It may be hazarded that the reason family structure does not loom larger in public discussion of social issues is that people tend to assume that the nature of family life is about the same throughout American society. The mass media and the development of suburbia have created an image of the American family as a highly standardized phenomenon. It is therefore easy to assume that whatever it is that makes for differences among individuals or groups of individuals, it is not a different family structure.

There is much truth to this; as with any other nation, Americans are producing a recognizable family system. But that process is not completed by any means. There are still, for example, important differences in family patterns surviving from the age of the great European migration to the United States, and these variations account for notable differences in the progress and assimilation of various ethnic and religious groups.[1] A number of immigrant groups were characterized by unusually strong family bonds; these groups have characteristically progressed more rapidly than others.

But there is one truly great discontinuity in family structure in the United States at the present time: that between the white world in general and that of the Negro American.

The white family has achieved a high degree of stability and is maintaining that stability.

By contrast, the family structure of lower class Negroes is highly unstable, and in many urban centers is approaching complete breakdown.

There is considerable evidence that the Negro community is in fact dividing between a stable middle-class group that is steadily growing stronger and more successful, and an increasingly disorganized and disadvantaged lower-class group. There are indications, for example, that the middle-class Negro family puts a higher premium on family stability and the conserving of family resources than does the white middle-class family.[2] The discussion of this paper is not, obviously, directed to the first group excepting as it is affected by the experiences of the second—an important exception.

There are two points to be noted in this context.

First, the emergence and increasing visibility of a Negro middle class may beguile the nation into supposing that the circumstances of the remainder of the Negro community are equally prosperous, whereas just the opposite is true at present, and is likely to continue so.

Second, the lumping of all Negroes together in one statistical measurement very probably conceals the extent of the disorganization among the lower-class group. If conditions are improving for one and deteriorating for the other, the resultant statistical averages might show no change. Further, the statistics on the Negro family and most other subjects treated in this paper refer only to a specific point in time. They are a vertical measure of the situation at a given moment. They do not measure the experience of individuals over time. Thus the average monthly unemployment rate for Negro males for 1964 is recorded as 9 percent. But *during* 1964, some 29 percent of Negro males were unemployed at one time or another. Similarly, for example, if 36 percent of Negro children are living in broken homes *at any specific moment,* it is likely that a far higher proportion of Negro children find themselves in that situation *at one time or another* in their lives.

Nearly a Quarter of Urban Negro Marriages Are Dissolved

Nearly a quarter of Negro women living in cities who have ever married are divorced, separated, or are living apart from their husbands.

The rates are highest in the urban Northeast where 26 percent of Negro women ever married are either divorced, separated, or have their husbands absent.

On the urban frontier, the proportion of husbands absent is even higher. In New York City in 1960, it was 30.2 percent, *not* including divorces.

Among ever-married nonwhite women in the nation, the proportion with husbands present *declined* in *every* age group over the decade 1950–60, as follows:

AGE	PERCENT WITH HUSBANDS PRESENT	
	1950	1960
15–19 years	77.8	72.5
20–24 years	76.7	74.2
25–29 years	76.1	73.4
30–34 years	74.9	72.0
35–39 years	73.1	70.7
40–44 years	68.9	68.2

Although similar declines occurred among white females, the proportion of white husbands present never dropped below 90 percent except for the first and last age group.[3]

Nearly One-Quarter of Negro Births Are Now Illegitimate

Both white and Negro illegitimacy rates have been increasing, although from dramatically different bases. The white rate was 2 percent in 1940; it was 3.07 percent in 1963. In that period, the Negro rate went from 16.8 percent to 23.6 percent.

The number of illegitimate children per 1,000 live births increased by 11 among whites in the period 1940–63, but by 68 among nonwhites. There are, of course, limits to the dependability of these statistics. There are almost certainly a considerable number of Negro children who, although technically illegitimate, are in fact the offspring of stable unions. On the other hand, it may be assumed that many births that are in fact illegitimate are recorded otherwise. Probably the two opposite effects cancel each other out.

On the urban frontier, the nonwhite illegitimacy rates are usually higher than the national average, and the increase of late has been drastic.

In the District of Columbia, the illegitimacy rate for nonwhites grew from 21.8 percent in 1950, to 29.5 percent in 1964.

A similar picture of disintegating Negro marriages emerges from the divorce statistics. Divorces have increased of late for both whites and nonwhites, but at a much greater rate for the latter. In 1940 both groups had a divorce rate of 2.2 percent. By 1964 the white rate had risen to 3.6 percent, but the nonwhite rate had reached 5.1 percent—40 percent greater than the formerly equal white rate.

Almost One-Fourth of Negro Families Are Headed by Females

As a direct result of this high rate of divorce, separation, and desertion, a very large percent of Negro families are headed by females. While the percentage of such families among whites has been dropping since 1940, it has been rising among Negroes.

The percent of nonwhite families headed by a female is more than double the percent for whites. Fatherless nonwhite families increased by a sixth between 1950 and 1960, but held constant for white families.

It has been estimated that only a minority of Negro children reach the age of 18 having lived all their lives with both their parents.

Once again, this measure of family disorganization is found to be diminishing among white families and increasing among Negro families.

The Breakdown of the Negro Family Has Led to a Startling Increase in Welfare Dependency

The majority of Negro children receive public assistance under the AFDC program at one point or another in their childhood.

At present, 14 percent of Negro children are receiving AFDC assistance, as against 2 percent of white children. Eight percent of white children receive such assistance at some time, as against 56 percent of nonwhites, according to an extrapolation based on HEW data. (Let it be noted, however, that out of a total of 1.8 million nonwhite illegitimate children in the nation in 1961, 1.3 million were *not* receiving aid under the AFDC program, although a substantial number have, or will, receive aid at some time in their lives.)

Again, the situation may be said to be worsening. The AFDC program, deriving from the long established Mothers' Aid programs, was established in 1935 principally to care for widows and orphans, although the legislation covered all children in homes deprived of parental support because one or both of their parents are absent or incapacitated.

In the beginning, the number of AFDC families in which the father was absent because of desertion was less than a third of the total. Today it is two-thirds. HEW estimates "that between two-thirds and three-fourths of the 50 percent increase from 1948 to 1955 in the number of absent-father families receiving ADC may be explained by an increase in broken homes in the population."[4]

A 1960 study of Aid to Dependent Children in Cook County, Ill.,[5] stated:

> The "typical" ADC mother in Cook County was married and had children by her husband, who deserted; his whereabouts are unknown, and he does not contribute to the support of his children. She is not free to remarry and has had an illegitimate child since her husband left. (Almost 90 percent of the ADC families are Negro.)[5]

The steady expansion of this welfare program, as of public assistance programs in general, can be taken as a measure of the steady disintegration of the Negro family structure over the past generation in the United States.

REFERENCES

1. NATHAN GLAZER and DANIEL PATRICK MOYNIHAN, *Beyond the Melting Pot* (Cambridge: MIT Press and Harvard University Press, 1963), pp. 290–291.

2. E. FRANKLIN FRAZIER, *Black Bourgeoisie* (New York: Collier Books, 1962).

3. Furnished by Dr. Margaret Bright, in a communication on January 20, 1965.

4. MAURINE MCKEANY, *The Absent Father and Public Policy in the Program of Aid to Dependent Children* (Berkeley: University of California Press, 1960), p. 3.

5. "Facts, Fallacies and Future: A Study of the Aid to Dependent Children of Cook County, Illinois" (New York: Greenleigh Associates, Inc., 1960), p. 5.

Employment

Herbert Hill

RACIAL INEQUALITY IN EMPLOYMENT: THE PATTERNS OF DISCRIMINATION

Optimistic assumptions regarding the Negro's progress in American society must be re-examined in the light of the Negro's current economic plight. The great mass of Negroes, especially in the urban centers, are locked in a permanent condition of poverty. This includes the long-term unemployed as well as the working poor, who know only a marginal economic existence and who increasingly are forced into the ranks of the unemployed.

THE UNEMPLOYMENT CRISIS

The Negro community throughout the United States is today experiencing a crisis of unemployment. Negroes now constitute a very large part of the hard-core, permanently unemployed group in American

Reprinted from *The Annals of the American Academy of Political and Social Science* (January 1965) by permission.

Mr. Hill is Labor Secretary of the National Association for the Advancement of Colored People and a member of the faculty of the New School for Social Research, New York. He is author of *Citizen's Guide to Desegregation*.

society. In Northern industrial centers one out of every three Negro workers was unemployed for varying lengths of time between 1958 and 1963, and a very high proportion exhausted all of their unemployment compensation benefits. More than 50 per cent of all the unskilled Negro workers in the country have been unemployed for substantial periods since 1958. Furthermore, it is evident that the unskilled Negro worker, forty-five years of age and over, who has lost his job, will never again work at productive gainful employment.

Of great significance is the fact that, since 1951, the differential in the average income of Negro and white workers has been increasing. By December of 1951, the Negro median wage was approaching 57 per cent of the white workers' average income. Since that time, however, the gap between the income of white and Negro workers has been growing steadily greater. In Michigan, for example, the ratio of average Negro income to white income dropped from 87 per cent in 1949 to 76 per cent in 1958, and has continuously deteriorated since that time.[1]

During the period of 1960–1961 in Chicago, Negroes, who constitute 20 per cent of the total labor force, were 43 per cent of Chicago's unemployed. This does not include the significant number of Negroes who, in Chicago, as elsewhere, have dropped out of the labor force and, therefore, are no longer counted among the unemployed.

During 1960–1961, white males in Chicago between the ages of 25 and 44 had an unemployment rate of only 2.2 per cent—minimal unemployment; however, in the Negro ghetto in Chicago, and in other urban industrial centers, unemployment has become a way of life. In thirty-one all-Negro census tracts, the unemployment rate was over 15 per cent, while only three white census tracts have a ratio that high. Labor force projections indicate that there will be 450,000 more workers in Chicago's metropolitan area in 1970 than there were in 1960. More than one-third of these will be Negro. Yet the trend of employment potentiality indicates that only 150,000 new positions will be created by 1970. The future holds only the prospect of increasing long-term unemployment for the Negro wage earner.[2]

As a result of automation and other technological changes in the economy, unskilled and semiskilled job occupations are disappearing at the rate of 35,000 a week or nearly two million a year. It is in these job classifications that there has been a disproportionate displacement of Negro workers.

The economic well-being of the entire Negro community is

[1] Herman P. Miller, *Rich Man, Poor Man* (New York: Thomas Y. Crowell, 1964), p. 88.

[2] Harold Baron, "Negro Unemployment—A Case Study," *New University Thought*, Vol. 3, No. 2 (September–October, 1963), p. 43.

directly and adversely affected by the generations of enforced overcon-
centration of Negro wage earners in the unskilled and menial job
classifications in the industrial economy. A continuation of this pattern
will cause even greater crises in the years to come unless fundamental
and rapid changes take place in the occupational characteristics and
mobility of Negro labor in the United States. In March of 1964, the
United States Department of Labor announced that Negroes constitute
20.6 per cent of the nation's unemployed, although Negroes comprise
only 10 per cent of the population. To quote the *New York Times,*
"Umemployment of these proportions were it general, would be a
national catastrophe."

Months before the 1964 summer racial disturbances in New York
City, a report was made public by Dr. Kenneth Clark, a well-known
psychologist on the faculty of the City College of New York and Director
of the Northside Clinic, a psychiatric center in Harlem.

This 615-page study known as the HARYOU report, sponsored
by Harlem Youth Opportunities Unlimited (HARYOU), a research
program jointly financed by United States government and New York
City funds, was conducted for over eighteen months by a staff directed
by Dr. Clark and was released under the subtitle: "A Study of the
Consequences of Powerlessness and a Blueprint for Change." This highly
significant report documented in great detail the pattern of life in Harlem
and described the Negro's status in the nation's largest segregated
community.

This report notes that unemployment in Harlem is more than
double the unemployment rate in the rest of the city, that median income
of Harlem residents is less than 60 per cent of the city's median, that even
for those who work, "the menial and unrewarding nature of the employment of most of the Negro men and women living in this ghetto
can only mean a marginal subsistence for their families."

In relation to future prospects for Negro employment, the report
indicates that almost half of all Negro workers in New York City are
concentrated in "dead end" jobs—in occupational classifications that will
be eliminated as a result of technological innovation—and that Negro
wage earners in large numbers are prevented from developing new
employment skills. The Study warns "that the unemployment situation
among Negro youth in Central Harlem is explosive," and notes an
increasing "movement towards jobs of an even more menial and marginal
nature." Dr. Clark's conclusions were confirmed by United States
government figures which revealed that 26 per cent of male Negro youths
were unemployed during July of 1964. The jobless rate among Negro
male youth for all of 1963 was 25.4 per cent, nearly twice as high as the
figure among their white counterparts.

THE NEGRO IN THE SOUTH

There can be no doubt that in the Southern states there exists a rigid and systematic pattern of employment discrimination based on race. Industrial management and organized labor, as well as state agencies and the federal government, are responsible for the continued existence of the pattern of racial job discrimination. An immense industrial development has been taking place in the southeastern states since the end of World War II, but a most disturbing aspect of the rapid growth of manufacturing facilities in the South has been the serious inability of the Negro worker to register significant employment gains in the new Southern industrial economy.

Investigations indicate that in the textile industry, still the basic manufacturing industry of the South, Negroes are in a most marginal position. According to state government figures, the number of textile workers employed in South Carolina was 48,000 in 1918 and 122,000 in 1960, while the percentage of Negroes in the textile labor force fell from 9 per cent to 4.7 per cent over this period. On July 6, 1961, the National Association for the Advancement of Colored People filed an extensive series of complaints against major textile manufacturing companies with the President's Committee on Equal Employment Opportunity. Three years later there is little change in the racial occupational pattern in the Southern textile industry. Negroes remain concentrated in menial and unskilled classifications and comprise about 2 per cent of the work force.

The Committee has very limited powers in carrying out the purpose of Executive Order 10925, which requires equal employment opportunities by all contractors doing business with the United States government. Its impotence becomes evident when confronted by the powerful financial and political forces in control of the textile industry.

On April 6, 1962, in an appraisal of the first year of operation of the President's Committee on Equal Employment Opportunity the NAACP stated:

> The administration has relied for favorable publicity on a superficial approach called "Plans for Progress." The so-called "Plans for Progress"—voluntary agreements entered into by a few large corporations—may yield high returns in press notices but only superficial and token results for Negro workers in new job opportunities. The "Plans for Progress" have not produced the large scale job opportunities for Negro workers that have been so long denied them. It is our experience that major U.S. Government contractors operating vast multi-plant enterprises regard the signing of a "Plan for Progress" as a way of securing immunity from real compliance with the antidiscrimination provision of their government contract.

In January 1963, the Southern Regional Council[3] confirmed the judgment of the NAACP regarding voluntary compliance and concluded with the following statement regarding the operation of the "Plans for Progress" in the Atlanta area:

> Most contractors felt—and readily stated—that the Plan was not applicable to them. A few said it would become applicable when the hiring of a Negro would be advantageous, i.e., when the Negro market demanded it. Some did not even know of the existence of the "Plans for Progress" while others who knew, and who did employ a few Negro janitors or porters on their staffs, felt they were thereby upholding the object of the Plan. To sum up, indications are that the interpretation of the voluntary and affirmative provisions of the program is being left to the individual signers themselves.

In heavy industry, the gains of Negro labor throughout the Southern states are most limited. Negro employment is negligible in such major industrial operations as the General Motors plants in Atlanta and Doraville, Georgia, and the Ford Motor Company plants in Atlanta, Memphis, Norfolk, and Dallas. The employment study made by the United States Commission on Civil Rights confirms our opinion that very little progress has been made by the Southern Negro in heavy industry. The Commission's findings are summarized in part in its published report as follows:

> This Commission's investigations in three cities—Atlanta, Baltimore and Detroit—and a Commission hearing in Detroit revealed that in most industries studied, patterns of Negro employment by Federal contractors conformed to local industrial employment patterns. In Atlanta, the two automobile assembly plants contacted employed no Negroes in assembly operations. Except for one driver of an inside power truck, all Negro employees observed were in janitorial work—sweeping, mopping, carrying away trash. Lack of qualified applicants cannot account for the absence of Negroes from automotive assembly jobs in Atlanta. Wage rates are relatively high for the locality and the jobs are in great demand. The work is at most semi-skilled and educational requirements are extremely low.[4]

A major problem for Negro workers in Southern industry is the operation of separate racial seniority lines in collective bargaining agreements entered into by management and labor unions. Investigations of the status of Negro workers in pulp and papermaking operations, in

[3] Southern Regional Council, *Plans for Progress: Atlanta Survey*, January 1963.

[4] U.S. Commission on Civil Rights, *Employment, 1961*, Report No. 3, pp. 65–66.

chemical and oil refining, in steel and tobacco manufacturing, as well as in other important sectors of the Southern industrial economy, clearly indicate that Negroes are usually hired exclusively in classifications designated as "common laborer" or "yard labor" or "nonoperating department" or "maintenance department." These are the euphemisms for the segregated all-Negro labor departments established by the separate racial promotional lines in many labor-management contracts throughout Southern industry. As a result of these discriminatory provisions, white persons are initially hired into production or skilled craft occupations which are completely closed to Negro workers. The Negro worker who is hired as a laborer in the "maintenance department" or "yard labor department" is denied seniority and promotional rights into desirable production classifications and is also denied admission into apprentice and other training programs. In these situations Negro seniority rights are operative only within certain all-Negro departments, and Negro workers therefore have an extremely limited job mobility. Thus Donald Dewey, of Columbia University, reports that most Southerners believe that their economy is divided into "white" and "Negro" jobs.[5] The North Carolina Advisory Committee to the United States Commission on Civil Rights reports that, "North Carolina in common with states of its region, has traditions which more or less automatically assign Negroes to menial or unskilled positions."[6]

The pulp and papermaking industry is one of the fastest growing manufacturing industries in the South. Company management and the trade unions which have jurisdiction in this important Southern industry are responsible for a rigid pattern of discriminatory practices including separate racial promotional lines in union contracts which limit Negro workers to menial, unskilled job classifications at low pay and which violate their basic seniority rights. The two dominant unions in this industry are the United Papermakers' and Paperworkers' Union and the International Brotherhood of Pulp, Sulphite and Paper Mill Workers' Union, both affiliated with the AFL-CIO. In virtually every paper mill in the South where they hold collective bargaining agreements, these two unions operate segregated locals and include discriminatory provisions in their union contracts. A compelling example of the operation of segregated locals with separate racial seniority lines is to be found at the large manufacturing plant of the Union Bag-Camp Paper Corporation in

[5] Donald Dewey, "Negro Employment in Southern Industry," *Journal of Political Economy*, LX (August 1952), pp. 279–293.

[6] *Equal Protection of the Laws in North Carolina: Report of the North Carolina Advisory Committee to the United States Commission on Civil Rights*, 1962, Washington, D.C., p. 87.

Savannah, where thousands of persons are employed. This plant has the largest single industrial payroll in Savannah.

The tobacco industry is important in the Southern industrial economy, and here, too, we find a pattern of separate racial seniority lines in virtually all collective bargaining agreements between the major tobacco manufacturing companies and the Tobacco Workers International Union, AFL-CIO. In one of the largest manufacturing plants, that of the Liggett & Myers Tobacco Company in Durham, North Carolina, colored workers are employed in unskilled and janitorial jobs with limited seniority rights operative only in all-Negro designated classifications. Investigations made by the NAACP indicate that in this tobacco manufacturing plant, as in so many others, Negroes are initially hired only as sweepers, janitors, and toilet attendants and are promoted exclusively within the limited "Negro" seniority line of progression.

Negro railway workers throughout the South are the victims of a traditional policy of job discrimination as a result of collusion between railway management and railroad labor unions. In St. Petersburg, the Atlantic Coast Line Railroad, and, in Memphis, the St. Louis-San Francisco Railroad Company, for example, have entered into agreements with the Brotherhood of Railroad Trainmen to deny qualified Negro railway workers opportunities for promotion and advancement. These are typical of similar practices elsewhere.

The Brotherhood of Railroad Trainmen, an AFL-CIO affiliate, removed the "Caucasian Only" clause from its constitution in 1959. However, this was apparently for public relations purposes only, as the union continues in most cities to exclude qualified Negro railroad employees. Frequently, in collusion with management, Negro brakemen are classified as "porters" and then refused membership in the union under the pretext of their being outside its jurisdiction. This, however, does not prevent the Trainmen's Union from negotiating wages and other conditions of employment for these so-called "porters" who have no representation in the collective bargaining unit.

STATE EMPLOYMENT SERVICES

Another extremely serious problem confronting Negro workers is the discriminatory practices of state employment services whose operation, in Southern states, is characterized by a pattern of racial segregation and discrimination. These states include Alabama, Florida, Georgia, Louisiana, Mississippi, North Carolina, South Carolina, and, partially, Virginia and Tennessee. Job orders are racially designated, and job referrals are made on the basis of race. Major industrial corporations operating with federal government contracts cannot possibly be in compliance with the President's Executive Order banning employment discrimination where such contractors in the South are using the facilities of the state employment services. The United States government is completely responsible for providing the operating costs of all state employment services. Federal funds are disbursed by the Department of Labor, which administers the Federal-State Employment Services program. It obviously makes no sense for the Administration to issue executive orders banning employment discrimination by government contractors while agencies of the federal government subsidize such discriminatory practices. The NAACP has repeatedly called upon the United States Department of Labor to take decisive action to eliminate the pattern of discrimination and segregation in the operation of state employment services.

FEDERAL SUPPORT OF DISCRIMINATION

Even in the North, the operation of the state employment services represents a serious problem to Negro workers. The state employment services receive funds and awards from the federal government based to a very large degree on the number of gross placements made during the year. This inevitably places operating personnel in the position of responding to arbitrary and discriminatory job requirements in referring workers for jobs and in selecting them for admission into training facilities. A further problem is the usual tacit assumption by local employment service personnel that there are "white" jobs and "colored" jobs. This is a result of the prevailing hiring pattern in many localities and the reluctance of state employment services to innovate changes in the established racial patterns.

Because the colored worker is extremely vulnerable to long-term unemployment as a result of the combined factors of racial discrimination and technological change, Negro workers more than any other group in the work force qualify for training under the Federal Manpower Development and Training Act. However, investigations made by the NAACP clearly indicate that Negroes, with some few exceptions, are being limited to programs that simply perpetuate the traditional concentration of Negroes in menial and unskilled jobs. Thus, in Portland, Oregon, there was an all-Negro training program for hotel waiters, and in Pensacola, Florida, there were all-Negro programs for chambermaids and waitresses. In Birmingham, Alabama, there are all-white training programs in electronics and arc welding, but Negroes are limited to training as laundry-machine operators and shirt-pressers. In Beaufort, South Carolina, there is a training program for Negro waiters, while in Greenville, South Carolina, there is an all-white program for general machine and tool machine workers. The *Courier-Journal*, Louisville, Kentucky, December 11, 1962, in a news report headlined "200 Retrainees Can't Get Jobs" states: "One course was held for Negro clerk-stenographers but it developed that employers in that area wanted only white clerical help."

On May 3, 1963, Clarence Mitchell, director of the NAACP Washington Bureau, in a strongly worded letter to Representative Carl D. Perkins, chairman of the General Subcommittee on Education of the House Committee on Education and Labor, protested against the racial practices of Manpower Development and Training Act (MDTA) programs. The Association requested the correction of policies which force Negroes to be shunted into training programs for "chambermaids, shirt pressers, service station attendants, waiters and waitresses." Although expressing support for the MDTA general program, the NAACP statement condemned practices "which foster racial segregation and also continue to promote the antiquated idea that the kitchen is the only place for colored wage-earners."

In addition to the pattern of racial segregation in the training programs conducted under the Manpower Development and Training Act in Alabama, Georgia, Mississippi, South Carolina, and other Southern states, reports from Northern communities indicate that because of the statutory requirement that there shall be "reasonable expectation of employment" as a basis for entry into training programs, unemployed low-skilled Negro workers are very frequently screened out of admission into desirable programs for skilled craft training. The consequences of the Manpower Development and Training Act for Negroes have been no training or segregated training or training for the lowest and least desirable job classifications. A continuation of this pattern will simply extend and deepen the job gap between white and Negro workers.

The Department of Health, Education, and Welfare each year distributes fifty-five millions of dollars of federal funds for education under the Smith-Hughes Act; a very large part of this is given to vocational training programs in which Negroes are totally excluded or limited to unequal segregated facilities. Vocational and trade schools in the Southern states receive a substantial part of these federal funds, but in most Southern urban areas where there has been a tremendous growth of manufacturing operations, we find that the limited programs offered in Negro vocational schools are obsolete in terms of modern industrial technology. Thus, while white students in vocational schools are preparing for advanced technology in electronics and for the automotive and aero-space industries, Negroes are limited to "home economics" and other traditional service occupations, and here also the federal government has a direct responsibility for helping to perpetuate the pattern that makes the Negro worker an unskilled worker and most vulnerable to large-scale permanent unemployment.

APPRENTICESHIP AND VOCATIONAL TRAINING

For every 100 skilled workers that the nation had in 1955, it will need 122 in 1965 and 145 in 1975. However, all the available data clearly indicate that the nation's apprenticeship programs, as well as other training programs, are not even turning out enough new craftsmen to replace those who retire. Automation and other technological changes in the economy have greatly increased the demand for skilled workers, and, currently, the large appropriations for national defense also significantly increase the demand for skilled workers and technicians. It is now clear that in the next decade the entire American economy will be faced with a serious crisis because of the lack of skilled manpower.

A major factor contributing to the irrational, wasteful, and socially harmful operation of the nation's apprenticeship and vocational training programs is the color discrimination and racial exclusion which characterize training programs in major sectors of the economy in the North as well as the South. Discrimination in job-training programs is also greatly responsible for the very high rate of Negro unemployment.

For many occupations the only way a worker can be recognized as qualified for employment is to successfully complete apprenticeship training programs. This is true for the printing trades, among machinists and metal workers, in the various crafts in the building and construction trades industry, and many others.

Studies such as that made by the New York State Commission Against Discrimination,[7] as well as by the National Association for the Advancement of Colored People, clearly indicate that no significant advances have been made by Negroes in those craft union apprenticeship training programs which have historically excluded nonwhites. An examination of the available data makes it evident that less than one per cent of the apprentices in the building and construction industry throughout the United States are Negro. In the ten-year period, 1950–1960, in the State of New York, the increase of Negro participation in building trades apprenticeship programs rose from 1.5 per cent to 2 per cent.

[7] New York State Commission Against Discrimination, *Apprentices, Skilled Craftsmen and the Negro: An Analysis* (New York, 1960); Herbert Hill, *The Negro Wage-Earner and Apprenticeship Training Programs* (New York; National Association for the Advancement of Colored People, 1960).

Open access to plumbing and pipe-fitting apprenticeship controlled by the Plumbers Union is a very rare experience for young Negroes in the North as well as the South. Similarly, Negro youths are excluded from apprenticeship programs controlled by the Sheet Metal Workers Union, the International Brotherhood of Electrical Workers, the Lathers and Plasterers Union, the Boilermakers, the Structural Iron Workers Union, and from other important craft unions operating in the construction industry.

Almost equally exclusive are the printing trades unions. In a survey made by the National Association for the Advancement of Colored People of the seven major New York City newspapers in 1962, we find that, with the exclusion of building services and maintenance personnel, less than one per cent of those employed on the major New York newspapers are Negro. Virtually all of the Negroes employed on these newspapers are in the "white collar" jurisdiction of the New York Newspaper Guild.

It is estimated that in New York City less than one half of one per cent of those currently employed in the newspaper crafts outside the Guild's jurisdiction are Negroes. This includes printing pressmen, compositors, photo-engravers, stereotypers, paper-handlers, mailers, and delivery drivers. As far as apprenticeship training for these crafts is concerned, we have been unable to detect a single instance where Negroes have been recently admitted into a training program in the newspaper crafts in the City of New York or in other major cities in the United States.

In the study entitled *Made in New York: Case Studies in Metropolitan Manufacturing*, published by Harvard University in 1959, we are told that

> Negro and Puerto Rican women who are on the lower rungs of the city's economic ladder have become important in the New York garment industry, but they work mainly in the more established branches and with few exceptions . . . they do not become highly skilled tailor system workers on dresses or "cloaks." As a result a shortage of skilled sewing machine operators is developing.

In most of these programs the role of the labor union is decisive because the trade union usually determines who is admitted into the training program and, therefore, who is admitted into the union membership.

Labor unions also exercise control over apprenticeship programs through hiring hall procedures in de facto closed shop situations. In these circumstances, craft unions have the power either to promote or to prevent the admission of individuals or of an entire class of persons. By means of a variety of formal and informal controls, craft unions are frequently the decisive factor in the recruitment process in many apprenticeship programs and often directly prevent Negro youth from becoming skilled craft workers via the established route of apprenticeship.

On the level of the small shop and local union, the tradition of racial discrimination has now become deeply institutionalized. A form of caste psychology impels many workers to regard their own positions as "white man's jobs," to which no Negro should aspire. These workers, and often their union leaders, regard jobs in their industries as a kind of private privilege, to be accorded and denied by them as they see fit. Often Negroes are not alone in being barred from such unions which have much of the character of the medieval guild, but Negroes as a group suffer the most from these practices. On the local level, the tradition which sustains discrimination is to be found among skilled workers in heavy industry as well as in the craft occupations, and in the North almost as commonly as in the South.

The Bureau of Apprenticeship and Training of the United States Department of Labor, in giving certification to an apprenticeship program, provides the legal basis for public subsidies to apprenticeship programs. The federal government, through grants-in-aid from the United States Office of Education of the Department of Health, Education, and Welfare, provides funds which subsidize apprenticeship training programs in many states. The federal government, therefore, is directly subsidizing discrimination in the skilled trades whenever a trade union or employer excludes Negroes and members of other minority groups from admission into a registered apprenticeship training program.

THE RACIAL PRACTICES OF ORGANIZED LABOR

The Report on Employment[8] of the United States Commission on Civil Rights indicated the significant extent of discrimination within organized labor, and stated that the "efforts of the AFL-CIO have proved to be largely ineffective" in curbing discrimination and that the impact of union discrimination, especially in skilled craft occupations, was a basic factor in contributing to the concentration of Negroes in menial, unskilled jobs in industry, their virtual exclusion from construction and machinist crafts, and accounted for the extreme vulnerability of Negro labor to long-term unemployment both of a cyclical and structural nature. The report urged passage of federal legislation for prohibiting discrimination by unions and stressed the inability of the AFL-CIO to

[8] United States Commission on Civil Rights, *Report on Employment*, Washington, D.C., 1961.

take action on its own initiative against the broad pattern of union racist practices.

The course of events in the past decade, and especially since the merger of the AF of L with the CIO in 1955, clearly indicates that the social consciousness of the industrial unions with their sensitivity to the problems of the Negro wage earner has now all but totally vanished. Instead, trade unions are responding like other conservative institutions in American society to the intensified demands of the Negro for full equality. A significant indication of this conservatism was the refusal of the AFL-CIO Executive Council to support the August 28, 1963, March on Washington, the greatest Negro demonstration in the nation's history.[9]

Dr. Kenneth Clark, writing in the HARYOU report, states:

> The status of Negroes in the power councils of organized labor in New York City is most tenuous, if not nonexistent. The persistent pattern of racial discrimination in various unions, including some which still enjoy the reputation of being liberal, reflects the essential powerlessness of Negroes to affect the conditions of their livelihood. HARYOU's difficulty in finding a suitable representative of labor for its Board of Directors highlighted the fact that there is no Negro who occupies a primary power position in organized labor in New York City. There are a few Negroes who are constantly referred to as representatives of labor, but upon careful examination it is found that these Negroes, for the most part, hold their positions at the pleasure of more powerful white bosses or leaders. Even in those unions where the bulk of all of the workers are Negroes and Puerto Ricans, the top overt or covert leadership is almost always white. There is evidence that under these circumstances the union leaders are not always above entering into sweetheart contracts, or other types of conspiracies with the bosses, to the disadvantage of the Negro and Puerto Rican workers.[*]

Even some unions which boast of a "liberal" past are under attack for discriminatory racial practices now that large numbers of Negroes have entered their jurisdiction. On April 4, 1961, a complaint was filed by Ernest Holmes, a Negro worker, against the International Ladies' Garment Workers Union (ILGWU) with the New York State Commission for Human Rights, the agency that administers the state's fair employment practices statutes. The ILGWU was accused of discriminatory practices involving Negro workers. Later investigations revealed that nonwhites in the New York garment industry were concentrated in

---

[9] For a discussion of trade union racial practices see Herbert Hill, "Labor Unions and the Negro," *Commentary* (December 1959), pp. 479–488; "Racism Within Organized Labor," *The Journal of Negro Education, 1961*, No. 2, pp. 109–118; and "Has Organized Labor Failed the Negro Worker?" *The Negro Digest* (May 1962), pp. 41–49.

the lowest-paid job classifications with very little job mobility, because, with some few exceptions, they were denied admission into the union's skilled craft locals, that the virtually all-Negro and Puerto Rican "push boys" unit known as 60A is in practice a "jim crow" auxiliary, and that not a single Negro was an International Union officer, or on the 23-man executive board, or permitted to serve in any significant leadership position.[10]

On May 18, 1963, in the case of Ernest Holmes, the ILGWU entered into a stipulation with the State Commission for Human Rights in which the Union agreed to admit Mr. Holmes into the Cutter's union, Local 10 of the ILGWU, to assist him in seeking employment, and to arrange for additional training as an apprentice cutter.

This is what the State Commission had ordered the ILGWU to do a year before when a finding of "probable cause" was issued by the investigating commissioner. The *New York Times,* July 2, 1962, in a report headlined "Union Told to Get Job For a Negro," stated:

> A garment cutters' union has been ordered by the State Commission for Human Rights to arrange for employment of a Negro at union rates commensurate with his skill and to admit the Negro into union membership if his work is satisfactory.

The *Times* story also states:

> With regard to the union, the decision found that "the evidence raises serious doubt as to its good faith to comply with the State Law Against Discrimination in the matter of his complaint; and that there was 'probable cause' to credit the allegations of the complaint."

On September 14, 1962, Ruperto Ruiz, Investigating Commissioner, New York State Commission for Human Rights, in a letter to Emil Schlesinger, attorney for Local 10, stated that the Commission had

> repeatedly requested and for a period of eight months tried to obtain data pertinent to a resolution of the charges of discrimination against Amalgamated Ladies Garment Cutters Union—Local 10. These efforts were unsuccessful. The failure of representatives of that local to co-operate in the investigation despite their promises to do so left me no alternative but to find "probable cause to credit the allegations of the complaint."

It is of some significance to note that this was not the first encounter by the ILGWU with the New York State anti-discrimination

[10] See *Congressional Record—House,* January 31, 1963, pp. 1496–1499 (Testimony of Herbert Hill on Racial Practices of ILGWU). See also Herbert Hill, "The ILGWU—Fact and Fiction," *New Politics,* 1962, No. 2, pp. 7–27.

agency. Eighteen years ago the ILGWU entered into an agreement with the New York State Commission Against Discrimination—the predecessor to the State Commission for Human Rights—that it would not bar Negroes, Spanish-speaking, or other persons from membership in the all-Italian locals (*Elsie Hunter* v. *Agnes Sullivan Dress Shop*, September 4, 1946). After the Commission called the union's attention to relevant portions of the State antidiscrimination law and informed the ILGWU that the existence of nationality locals was a violation of the statute, a conference was held on January 22, 1947, at the offices of the State Commission Against Discrimination in New York City. Frederick Umhey, executive secretary of the ILGWU, represented the Union, and Commissioner Caroline K. Simon, the State Commission.

This was an action brought by a Negro member of Local 22, International Ladies' Garment Workers Union, who was barred from higher paying jobs controlled by Local 89, an Italian local. The charge was dismissed after the union agreed to eliminate such exclusion practices. Today, eighteen years later, not a single Negro or Spanish-speaking person holds membership in the two Italian locals which have control of some of the highest paying jobs in the industry, and no action has been taken to comply with the state law forbidding such practices.

Currently, the Negro worker is confronted not with a trade union movement that is a force for social change, but, on the contrary, with a national labor organization that has become a very conservative and highly bureaucratized institution, defending the *status quo* which is now directly attacked by the Negro in virtually every area of American life.

Many trade unions lag behind the progress made by other institutions in the community. In East St. Louis, Illinois, and Tulsa, Oklahoma, for example, Negro children attend integrated schools during the day, but their parents attend segregated union meetings at night, if they are admitted into labor unions at all. Recently A. Philip Randolph, president of the Brotherhood of Sleeping Car Porters, called "for a crusade to desegregate the Southern AFL-CIO State Conventions and City Central bodies" and stated that "this is a problem probably not less significant or difficult than the desegregation of public schools in the South."

There is a deep distrust among many Negro wage earners and others within the Negro community toward trade unions. It is a distrust well founded in experience. For today, as in the past, there is a profound disparity between the public image presented by the national AFL-CIO and the day-to-day realities as experienced by many Negro workers. This is true in the North as well as the South. There are few exceptions, especially in the mass production industries where, historically, there has been a large concentration of Negro workers and in some unions such as the United Automobile Workers (UAW), the United Packinghouse Workers (UPW), and the National Maritime Union (NMU) where there is an ideological sensitivity to the "Negro question."

But for the Negro in major areas of the economy, in the building and construction trades, in the railroad industry, among the Seafarers and the Boilermakers and the oil and chemical workers and machinists, in pulp, tobacco, and paper manufacturing, in metal working, in the printing trades, and in many other industries highly unionized for a long period of time, trade union practices are characterized by a broad pattern of discrimination and segregation.

AFL-CIO affiliated unions engage in four basic categories of discriminatory racial practices. They are: exclusion of Negroes from membership, segregated locals, separate seniority lines in collective bargaining agreements, and refusal to admit qualified Negroes into apprenticeship training programs controlled by unions.

The Brotherhood of Railway and Steamship Clerks which operates many segregated local lodges in Northern as well as Southern cities is among the important international unions responsible for a broad pattern of segregation.

The United Brotherhood of Carpenters and Joiners, for over a half-century, has been among the most important of all the building trades unions, and, with very few exceptions, organizes Negroes and whites into separate locals insofar as it permits Negroes to join the union at all. In the South there seems to be no exception to this rule, and it is most often followed in Northern cities as well. In Memphis and Chicago, for example, Negro carpenters in segregated local unions found that members of the white locals refused to work on the same job with them.

The white locals are in control of the union hiring hall, and, because of frequent arrangements with municipal and county political machines, all hiring for major public as well as private construction projects is done through the "lily-white" union hiring hall. Quite frequently Negroes are excluded altogether from work in white neighborhoods. This means that Negro carpenters are restricted to marginal maintenance and repair work within the Negro community and that they seldom are permitted to work on the larger construction projects. The same practices are true for other building-trades unions in many cities throughout the country.

Discriminatory racial practices by trade unions are not simply isolated or occasional expressions of local bias against colored workers, but rather, as the record indicates, a continuation of the institutionalized pattern of anti-Negro employment practices that is traditional in important sectors of the American economy.

The pattern of union responsibility for job discrimination against

Negroes is not limited to any one area of the country or to some few industries or union jurisdictions, but involves many labor organizations in a wide variety of occupations in manufacturing and construction on the railroads and in the maritime trades. An example of this is the Seafarers International Union (SIU) which operates union-controlled hiring halls on Great Lakes ports such as Duluth, Chicago, Detroit, Buffalo, and Cleveland. As a systematic practice this union will dispatch Negro workers for menial jobs only as "mess boys" and cooks in the galley departments of ships operating under SIU collective bargaining agreements. Over the years Negro members of the Seafarers International Union have repeatedly protested this practice, but to no avail, as the union continues discriminatory job assignments in its hiring halls.

On occasion one or two Negroes have been admitted into an all-white local union as token compliance within a state or municipal fair employment practice law, as with the International Brotherhood of Electrical Workers in Cleveland, the Bricklayers Union in Milwaukee, and the Railway Clerks Union in Minneapolis, but this is essentially a limited and strategic adjustment to community pressure and represents very dubious "progress."

Certainly the token admission of a few Negroes into an electrical workers union in Cleveland or Washington, D.C., can no more be regarded as integration than can the token admission of two or three Negro children into a Southern public school. There are also several instances where unions have removed the "lily-white" exclusion clause from their constitutions as public relations gestures only, but continue to exclude Negroes from membership by tacit consent.

As long as union membership remains a condition of employment in many trades and crafts and Negroes are barred from union membership solely because of their color, then trade union discrimination is the decisive factor in determining whether Negro workers in a given industry shall have an opportunity to earn a living for themselves and their families. This is especially true in the printing trades, the construction industry, and other occupations where labor unions exercise a high degree of control over access to employment.

THE NEED FOR A FEDERAL FAIR EMPLOYMENT PRACTICES LAW

The operation of state and municipal fair employment practices commissions is absolutely no substitute for a strong federal fair employment practices law.[11] With one or two exceptions, state and municipal

---

[11] For an analysis of State FEPC laws, see Herbert Hill, "Twenty Years of State Fair Employment Practice Laws: A Critical Analysis," *Buffalo Law Review*, Vol. 13 (Autumn 1964), pp. 22–69.

fair employment practices commissions are drastically limited in their effectiveness by inadequate funds and inadequate staff. Most of these agencies are simply complaint-taking bureaus that often take years to resolve an individual complaint received from an aggrieved citizen. We know that, in practice, only a very small fraction of all individuals who are the victims of employment discrimination because of race or religion ever file complaints with state or municipal commissions; therefore, because of the complexities in eliminating discriminatory employment practices, the fundamental approach must be towards the initiation of affirmative action based upon the over-all pattern of employment discrimination. In addition, one must note the unfortunate inability of state and municipal fair employment practices commissions to eliminate discriminatory racial practices in many important areas of the active job market. Among these is the building and construction trades industry. The pattern of discrimination in this important sector of the economy was extensively studied for the New York State Advisory Committee to the United States Commission on Civil Rights by Dr. Donald F. Shaughnessy of Columbia University.[12]

The construction industry represents a segment of the economy which is not declining. General contractors and the employers associations believe that there is a severe shortage of both residential and nonresidential construction in New York City and other major urban centers. New York, with twice the population of Chicago, has over four times the need for office space. Data indicates that the construction demand is growing.

Dr. Donald Shaughnessy has pointed out that the fear of unemployment by construction workers must be set aside due to reliable estimates of forthcoming construction activity. New construction was scheduled to increase by 57 per cent between 1960 and 1964, and to double between 1970 and 1975, according to Commerce Department estimates. The volume of construction and new repairs is also expected to grow. Thus the skilled manpower necessary in 1970 will be 35 per cent above the present labor supply.

The *Wall Street Journal*, April 10, 1964, in a front page story, states: "Booming construction activity will provide strong support this year for the nation's economy." The report concludes by noting that "the general contractors who build highways, housing, office structures, and utility facilities generally agree they will have record volume." Although this industry is expanding, Negro workers have not been able to enter into the construction crafts. This occurs because, as Shaughnessy notes:

[12] D. F. Shaughnessy, "A Survey of Discrimination in the Building Trades Industry," New York City, April 1963. Dr. Shaughnessy's study was the basis for the "Report of the New York Advisory Committee to the U.S. Commission on Civil Rights" (August 1963).

"The economic characteristics of the industry have created a condition wherein the decision making power is concentrated in the local union."

It is the economic structure of the building industry which concentrates in the local unions the power to decide who obtains employment and who gets admitted to the craft. The men who are engaged in construction work are recruited from labor pools controlled exclusively by the various unions in the craft jurisdictions of building trades. The union is the sole employment agency, and the men who appear on the jobs are those whom the union has referred to the job site. Contractors are thus completely dependent upon local unions for their labor supply. This factor further increases the power of local craft unions to control the employment process.

A. H. Raskin in discussing this pattern writes that these practices go

> far beyond the issue of discrimination. It brings into challenge the sub rosa closed shop arrangements many unions of skilled craftsmen have managed to retain, even though these have technically been illegal since the passage of the Taft-Hartley Act seventeen years ago.[13]

Rather than admit Negro members, the unions frequently encourage the use of out-of-town labor. Based upon direct interviews, Shaughnessy found that commuters travel as much as 120 miles per day from Connecticut and elsewhere to find steady employment in New York, when the available local union membership supply is exhausted. But local sources of skilled Negro manpower are deliberately ignored. During the spring and summer of 1963, there were approximately 1,200 plumbers with "travelling cards" from other cities working in New York City.

Thus, the New York State Advisory Committee of the United States Commission on Civil Rights stated in its 1963 report that

> The building trades unions continue to maintain an effective shortage of labor. One way that shortage is preserved in the face of continuing high demand is the use of commuters like those from Bridgeport who represent an auxiliary source of manpower that can be cut off at any time.

Out-of-town construction workers commute over a hundred miles daily to jobs in New York City, while local Negroes and Puerto Ricans are denied employment and entry to union-controlled jobs and apprenticeship programs.

In the physical reshaping of New York City, as in other urban centers, there has been a tremendous increase in the rate of residential

---

[13] A. H. Raskin, "Civil Rights: The Law and the Unions," *The Reporter*, Vol. 31. No. 4, September 10, 1964, p. 26.

and nonresidential construction. Virtually all new construction work in New York City is performed by union labor operating under collective bargaining agreements with building trade unions that make contractors entirely dependent upon union-controlled hiring halls as the exclusive source of labor supply. With rare exceptions these union hiring halls are "lily-white" in New York and throughout the nation.[14]

During the summer of 1963, thousands of persons demonstrated at several public construction sites in New York City against the racial practices of the AFL-CIO building trades unions. The rights they were seeking through these demonstrations are nonnegotiable legal rights that exist at the federal level—Executive Orders 10925 and 11114; at the state level—New York Law Against Discrimination, Section 296 and the New York Public Works Law, Section 220-e; and at the city level—New York City Administrative Code, Section 343–8.01.

Despite repeated documentation and disclosures of discrimination in the construction industry by the United States Commission on Civil Rights, the Mayor's Action Panel, the New York City Commission on Human Rights, and the New York State Commission for Human Rights, as well as reports from the NAACP and the Urban League, public officials have refused, apparently for political reasons, to enforce these laws.

The state of Pennsylvania has had a fair employment practices law since 1955, and Philadelphia has had a municipal fair employment practices statute since 1948. However, at the present time there is a widespread pattern of Negro exclusion from the major building trades craft unions in the Philadelphia area, where there are vast construction projects. The Philadelphia *Tribune*, in its issue of February 12, 1962, stated: "Philadelphia labor unions have fostered a pattern of racial discrimination that is unsurpassed even in the Deep South." Mass demonstrations by civil rights organizations against the racial practices of building trade unions have also occurred in Philadelphia, Cleveland, Pittsburgh, Los Angeles, Newark, New Jersey, and other cities.

As is evident, the pattern of Negro exclusion from the major AFL-CIO building trades unions continues unabated even in cities and states where there has long been a fair employment practices law. This is significant as it indicates the serious inability of such agencies to reach the skilled craft occupations that are characterized by a pattern of discrimination and expanding job opportunities. Thus, today in the United States there are more Negroes with Ph.D. degrees than there are Negroes who are licensed plumbers or licensed electricians.

[14] See, *A Report of the New York Advisory Committee of the U.S. Commission on Civil Rights,* August 1963.

Year after year, thousands of nonwhite students graduate from vocational high schools in the major urban centers of the nation, but after satisfactorily completing their courses of study in a variety of craft skills, young Negro workers ready to enter the labor market are denied employment opportunities in the printing industry, among machinists, or in building and construction trades and are forced to take low-paying menial or unskilled jobs if they are to work at all. Many of them are forced completely to abandon hope for work in the craft for which they were trained. Is it any wonder that there are many school drop-outs each year among Negro youth in vocational training schools, who soon enough learn the realities of the racial practices of craft unions in New York City, Chicago, Philadelphia, and elsewhere and express their feeling of futility by leaving school at an early age?

Adoption of a federal fair employment practices law that would decisively intervene in breaking the national pattern of Negro exclusion in the building trades, the printing industry, the metal crafts, and other skilled occupations would have a significant effect in reducing the rate of school drop-outs among minority-group youth.

The Negro is now making the same demands upon organized labor that are being made upon all other institutions in American society, and it is certain that the attacks upon racism within trade unions will proceed with the same intensity as against other organizations that impose restrictions based on race and color.

In January 1961, the NAACP released a documented study entitled "Racism Within Organized Labor: A Report of Five Years of the AFL-CIO." This report concluded that during the five years which have passed since the AFL-CIO merger, there has been no systematic or co-ordinated effort by the Labor Federation to eliminate racism within local unions where anti-Negro practices are traditional. The NAACP report gave a detailed series of examples of the wide variety of anti-Negro practices and indicated the urgent need for action by the Federation's leadership.

The NAACP report received widespread public attention and was immediately attacked by spokesmen for the AFL-CIO but strongly defended by Negro trade unionists and by A. Philip Randolph—President of the Brotherhood of Sleeping Car Porters and conspicuously the only Negro Vice-President of the AFL-CIO—who stated that the NAACP survey was "factual and accurate," and "unquestionably a significant and useful document for those concerned with making organized labor the democratic force it should be." Randolph told a conference of Negro trade unionists:

We in the Negro American Labour Council can without reservation state that the basic statements are true and sound; the delegates of the

Brotherhood of Sleeping Car Porters have presented these facts to convention after convention of the AFL for a quarter of a century.

Randolph later presented to the Executive Council of the Federation, detailed charges of anti-Negro practices together with specific recommendations to eliminate discrimination and segregation within affiliated international and local unions. The response of the AFL-CIO Executive Council was to censure Randolph and to reject his proposals.

Because the NAACP has now concluded, on the basis of the factual record, that the national AFL-CIO and its affiliated international unions are either unable or unwilling to move decisively against racist elements and to eliminate widespread anti-Negro practices, the Association is attempting to develop a new body of labor law on behalf of Negro workers.

This effort involves the federal courts as well as the National Labor Relations Board (NLRB). On February 4, 1964, an NLRB trial examiner ruled that Negroes who are required by their unions to join racially segregated locals and to work under union contracts that discriminate can have those unions found guilty of unfair labor practices.

This ruling involving the AFL-CIO International Longshoreman's Association in Brownsville, Texas, represented an important step forward in the Negro workers' long fight against racial discrimination by trade unions. On July 2, 1964, the National Labor Relations Board in a historic decision ruled that racial discrimination by labor unions is an unfair labor practice and that unions may lose their certification as the collective bargaining agent as a result of such practices.

The charges of discrimination were filed on behalf of members of the all-Negro Local 2 of the Independent Metal Workers Union. In 1962, when Ivory Davis, a Negro member of Local 2, was denied admission to a company-sponsored apprenticeship training course, the white local (Local 1) refused to process his grievance. At the request of Local 2, the National Association for the Advancement of Colored People entered the case on October 4, 1962, and filed a motion with the National Labor Relations Board asking that Local 1's certification be rescinded. The NAACP also asked that this motion be consolidated with unfair labor practices proceedings previously instituted by the National Labor Relations Board against Local 1.

For the first time in the Board's history, it has ruled that racial discrimination by a union in membership practices—such as exclusion or segregation of Negroes—is a violation of the duty of fair representation under Section 9(a) of the National Labor Relations Act. In this case involving Negro workers at the Hughes Tool Company in Houston, Texas, a new principle in administrative labor law was established that will have far-reaching consequences if sustained by the federal courts.

The NAACP has other cases pending in state and federal district courts and with the NLRB in an effort to eliminate discriminatory practices within organized labor and by employers. The intent of these cases is to establish a new legal standard of responsibility for trade unions to represent all workers within their jurisdiction fairly and equitably and without regard to considerations of race and color. New cases will be initiated in state and federal courts in addition to further complaints before the NLRB on behalf of aggrieved Negro workers in the near future.

The civil rights issue has emerged as the central question confronting the entire American society. It is evident that the AFL-CIO and all other institutions will be judged by the Negro on the basis of their actual day-to-day performance and not on the exercise of empty ritual.

Negroes may be winning the broad legal and social struggles for equality in the United States, but they are losing the battle for equal employment opportunity and economic justice. At the present time, the historic civil rights gains won by Negroes in the past twenty years are in danger of being destroyed by the growing crisis of unemployment and underemployment that directly affects the well-being of the entire Negro community and leads to acute social dislocation and despair.

The emergence of a large "underclass" of the Negro unemployed, the growth of a permanent Black lumpenproletariat, might very well alter the character of the Negro civil rights movement—a movement that in the past has operated in the classic tradition of protest and reform—and thus lead to developments that have the gravest implication for the whole of American society.

Herman P. Miller

PROGRESS AND PROSPECTS
FOR THE NEGRO WORKER

Much as I am delighted to contribute an article for publication in this distinguished magazine, I feel obligated to warn the reader that I am no expert on Negro affairs. My only qualification for writing this article is that I have spent more years than I care to count at the Census

Reprinted from the February 1965 issue of *Challenge, The Magazine of Economic Affairs;* 475 Fifth Avenue, New York, N.Y. 10017.

Mr. Miller is an economist for the Bureau of the Census and author of *Rich Man, Poor Man.*

Bureau where many of the basic statistics about Negro life are collected.

I have decided, therefore, to focus on the general area of employment because this is a subject of vital importance to the Negro and, also, it is one for which there is a vast storehouse of statistical data. The particular aspect of the problem that I intend to explore is the change in the occupational distribution of whites and Negroes during the past 50 years. Census information on this subject goes back to 1910. Thanks to the efforts of the Conservation of Human Resources Project at Columbia University and the work of other research organizations in this field, we are now beginning to supplant impressionistic judgments with scholarly evaluations.

In any discussion of white and Negro differentials over time it is important to distinguish between *absolute* and *relative* changes. Although this distinction is very important, it is often overlooked. If you think about the problem for a minute, the difference between absolute and relative changes will appear quite obvious and you will recognize its importance. There has been a general upgrading of occupational skills for both whites and Negroes as the American economy has moved from agriculture and become more complex and industrialized. As a result, Negroes who were once highly concentrated in sharecropping and farm labor have now moved up to unskilled and semiskilled factory jobs. Appreciable numbers have even moved into white-collar employment. This change has raised the skills of the Negro labor force, it has increased their productivity and it is in large measure responsible for the vast improvement in their levels of living. If we take what is perhaps the single most important aspect of life that we attempt to measure, namely life expectancy itself, we find that the Negro infant born in 1960 could expect to live 21 years longer than his mother born in 1920. This represents a gain of nearly 50 per cent in life expectancy in a relatively brief span of 40 years. Not only are Negroes living longer, but they are also living far better than ever before. Negro housing, for example, may still leave much to be desired; but the proportion living in dilapidated homes was cut in half between 1950 and 1960. The real incomes of Negroes have also shown a remarkable rise. Between 1940 and 1960 the wages and salaries of the average male Negro worker rose from about $1,000 to about $3,000, both figures measured in terms of 1960 dollars. In other words, there was a threefold increase in Negro purchasing power during this period.

I could go on and on citing the gains that have been made by Negoes in recent years. It would not take very long, however, before you would begin to wonder why I fail to mention that there has been a parallel upgrading of jobs and levels of living for white workers as well. Here, of course we get to the *relative* aspects of the problem. It is not enough to know how much or how fast the lot of the Negro is improving.

The critical question in many minds, particularly for Negroes and their leaders, is whether the relative upward movement has been as great for Negroes as for whites. Sometimes this focus on relative position blinds critics to the fact that there has been an improvement in absolute status. For example, Tom Kahn, who was Bayard Rustin's assistant in organizing the March on Washington, recently wrote, "It takes a lot of running to stand still on the treadmill of this technologically advancing society. When you know you're running hard and everyone tells you that you're moving at a fast clip, and yet the scenery around you remains the same, the most appropriate word to describe your reactions is . . . frustration." Yet, the fact is that the Negro has not been standing still and the scenery around him has been changing most dramatically. He has had tremendous increases in life expectancy, purchasing power, levels of living, occupational classification, educational attainment, and significant improvements in many other aspects of life for which objective measures are available. The only reason many Negroes feel they are standing still is that the whites, too, have had these gains and in many areas the gap between the whites and Negroes does not appear to be narrowing. It is on these aspects of the problem that I will concentrate today. How has Negro employment changed over the past 50 years? How has it changed relative to the whites? What are the prospects for a narrowing of white-Negro differentials in employment?

By 1910 the white labor force had already completed much of the transition from agriculture to industry. In the census taken in that year, only one-fourth of the white workers were employed in farming; another one-fourth worked in white-collar jobs; and the remaining one-half were more or less equally divided among craftsmen, factory operatives, and nonfarm laborers or service workers. In that same year, 1910, the Negro labor force was split 50–50 between farming and nonfarm work. The farmers were, of course, largely Southern sharecroppers or laborers working and living under the most miserable conditions, even by contemporary standards. Those who were not working as farmers were employed largely as service workers (i.e., domestics, waiters, bootblacks and similar jobs) and as nonfarm laborers largely on railroads and construction gangs. Relatively few (only five per cent) had even risen to the point of semiskilled factory work, and even fewer (only three per cent) worked as craftsmen or as white-collar workers.

The next 50 years witnessed a dramatic movement out of agriculture for both whites and Negroes. This movement, by the way, must soon grind to a halt for the very simple reason that we are running out of farmers to be moved. At present, only about seven per cent of the white workers are farmers as compared with 28 per cent at the turn of the century. The biggest increase is, of course, in white-collar work. Nearly one out of two white workers is now employed in a white-collar job. At the turn of the century, only one out of four white workers were in this category.

The shift away from farming was even more dramatic for Negroes than for whites. As I mentioned earlier, in 1910 one-half of the Negro workers were employed in farming; in 1960 this proportion dropped to only one-tenth. The frequent cry of some economists for greater mobility as a solution to rural poverty has certainly been heeded by the Negro. He has shown tremendous mobility and energy in search of economic opportunity, often against overwhelming odds. The displacement of Negroes from farming has largely been absorbed by the manual and service trades. At present, about one-third of the Negroes are service workers; another one-third are nonfarm laborers or semiskilled factory workers; and the remaining 20 per cent are craftsmen or white-collar workers. Until about 1940 the occupational shift for Negroes was almost exclusively from farming into employment as domestics, factory hands and laborers. In recent years, opportunities in white-collar employment have been growing in importance.

A close examination of the decennial census data provides better insight than we have ever had before of the way in which the transformation of the Negro labor force took place. In each decade, as new industries and occupations developed, it was the white worker who moved in first.

According to one analysis by Prof. Dale L. Hiestand of Columbia University (*Economic Growth and Employment Opportunities for Minorities*), "white workers capture the newly growing fields in which labor resources are scarce, pay levels are good, prospects for advancement are bright, the technology is most advanced, and working conditions the most modern." They leave in their wake jobs in the older industries which become less desirable because the pay is not as good, nor are the prospects for advancement. Moreover, many of the jobs left behind by the whites were in industries dominated by an old technology, which when replaced, would be likely to require reduced manpower needs. Thus, in every decade, the newest and best opportunities available to the Negroes were often quite vulnerable. The jobs deserted by the whites were invariably better than the ones in which Negroes were employed at the time. They were, nonetheless, not the jobs with the bright futures. This pattern of occupational change is, as we shall soon see, of great significance in assessing the prospects of the Negro for narrowing the occupational gap between himself and the whites. It suggests that if the Negro is ever to approach occupational equality with the whites, he must seek out and somehow gain admittance to the "frontier area of occupational expansion." If he continues to get only those jobs that the white has left over, he may never bridge the occupational gap. Indeed, some would argue that if the Negro follows the traditional pattern of occupational mobility, he may find himself in a tighter and tighter job squeeze because the employment that would have normally been handed down to him is being automated out of existence.

It must be granted on the basis of the empirical evidence that the absolute position of the Negro worker, with respect to employment, has improved considerably in the past 50 years. The problem to which we shall now turn is an examination of the extent to which the relative gap between whites and Negroes has changed. In the work previously referred to, Prof. Hiestand of Columbia University constructed an occupational index which permits this type of comparison to be made. He first separated the white and Negro workers for each year into seven occupational groups: professional, managerial, clerical and sales, skilled, semiskilled, unskilled laborers, and agriculture. A weight was then assigned to each occupation that was roughly indicative of the relative earning power for that kind of work. The actual weights used were the median incomes reported in the 1950 Census for workers who were employed throughout the year. A weighted index for each year was then constructed by multiplying the proportion of workers in each occupation by the weight and summing the results for all seven occupation groups. This operation was performed separately for white and Negro men and women. The ratio of the Negro to the white index which was computed for each year shows the relative occupational position of Negroes to whites.

In the case of men, the index shows no significant change between 1910 and 1940. There was some slight improvement in the relative occupational position of Negro men during the past 20 years, but this is entirely due to their movement out of the South. Indexes which have been constructed on a state-by-state basis show that there were very few significant changes in the occupational distribution of Negro males relative to whites in the past 20 years.

The relative occupational distribution of Negro women relative to whites was about the same in 1940 as it was in 1910. As in the case of the males, there appears to have been some improvement in the relative occupational position of Negro women during the past 20 years, but this change may also be primarily due to their movement out of the South, with its very limited opportunities for Negro employment, rather than to any general upgrading of the kinds of jobs open to Negroes. The weight of the evidence, therefore, is strongly in support of the view that although there has been considerable occupational improvement for Negro workers during the past 50 years in an *absolute* sense, the position of Negroes relative to whites has not changed much.

Having established these facts, we may now turn to an examination of their meaning, particularly with respect to assessing their significance for future trends in Negro employment. Here we must tread with care because, as so many forecasters have discovered to their regret, past is not necessarily prologue. The Roman Emperor Constantius made a law forbidding "anyone to consult a soothsayer, a mathematician or a forecaster. . . . May curiosity to foretell the future be silenced forever," proclaimed the emperor. So be it; but I doubt very much that even the penalty of death dampened the enthusiasm of forecasters in ancient Rome. There is even less hope of stopping them today when so many economists and statisticians have been driven to earn their living by this vicious practice.

The weight of the statistical evidence is that the fate of the Negro worker is very much tied in with the fate of the economy as a whole. During previous periods of vigorous economic growth, white workers moved ahead very rapidly and Negro workers followed in their wake, generally picking up the jobs that were left behind. There was some movement of Negroes into the expanding areas of the economy, but the numbers were small relative to the total. Both groups moved ahead more or less proportionately as a result of the job opportunities made available by the process of growth. It is difficult to say at this point in time whether this pattern would continue if we were once again to enter on an extended period of vigorous economic growth. Of course, one might say that we are now going through such a period, having experienced growth rates in our national product of about five per cent for the past three years. Although these growth rates are considerably in excess of our long-run national average, they are associated with painfully high unemployment rates for Negro workers, suggesting that there is a shortage of job opportunities. The evidence, however, is by no means conclusive. There are many who would argue that it is still too soon to judge whether a more rapidly growing economy can provide full employment for Negroes (without inflation) despite the elimination of hundreds of thousands of unskilled and semiskilled jobs they formerly manned. The point has been made that it may take several years of vigorous growth to absorb the manpower slack that developed during the slow years since 1957. Moreover, the blind forces of the economy may have to be helped along by manpower training programs which will fit the Negro (and the displaced white workers) for new types of work.

It is understandably of great importance to the Negro not only to improve his situation, but also to narrow the gap between himself and the whites. This feeling must not be ascribed to any special perversity on the part of the Negro worker. Rather, it is a reflection of a prevalent attitude in our society which has long been recognized by economists and taken into account by them in explaining economic behavior. The British economist, Pigou, described the matter rather well around the turn of the century when he wrote that "men do not desire to be rich, but to be richer than other men."

What is the likelihood that the Negro will, in fact, be able to narrow the occupational gap between himself and the whites? This question is difficult to answer. The one thing that seems clear from the data is that the gap will not be narrowed if the traditional patterns of occupational change are maintained. In order to catch up with the whites, Negro workers will have to be propelled into promising new jobs in new industries instead of drifting into the old jobs in the dying industries, as they have done in the past. This change will come about for Negroes only if two conditions are met. They must obtain the education and training required for the new jobs, and the barriers to their entry into the better paying fields must be lowered. The prospects that both of these conditions will be met in the near future are not very good. It is unrealistic to talk about bridging the occupational gap in the modern world when one-fourth of the Negro youth in their early twenties have not gone beyond the eighth grade and over half have not completed high school. There is not much that people with so little education can be trained to do in our complex economy.

Even if the Negro showed more interest in education than the above figures imply, there is little evidence that society is willing to make the huge investments in education and training that are required if the Negro is ever to be able to compete on equal terms with the white in the labor market. Most attempts to provide effective school integration have met with hostility and "foot-dragging." Even in the prosperous North there has been more lip service than action in the improvement of the quality of education in deprived areas. Finally, we come to just plain discrimination, which may be the hardest of all obstacles to overcome because it is so deeply imbedded in our culture. We sometimes forget that about 60 per cent of the Negroes still live in the South, and according to any reasonable assumptions regarding rates of out-migration, nearly half of them will still be in that region by 1980. In view of the intensity of feeling that has been manifested by the Southern whites on racial matters, it is hard to believe that Negroes in this region will receive to any great extent either the training they need or the opportunity to move into the more promising jobs. In view of these and many other factors, I see little reason to be optimistic about the possibility of narrowing the occupational gap between the races in the foreseeable future. There are, however, offsetting forces which provide some hope.

At present, there is probably less discrimination against Negroes than at any previous time in our history. It is also likely that discrimination will tend to decrease with time because of the strong pressures being exerted by the federal government. These efforts should create new opportunities for Negro employment in federal, state and local governments, in private companies doing contract work for the federal government, and in other companies that will be under social pressure to liberalize their employment practices.

At the same time that the prospects for Negroes to obtain skilled employment have been increasing, the attitudes of the Negro leaders have been undergoing a change. In the past, the civil rights movement focused attention largely on efforts designed to publicize the plight of the Negro and to promote integration. This emphasis led to the March on Washington, demonstrations, sit-ins, picketing, and other activities that were instrumental in promoting passage of the civil rights and antipoverty legislation. Partly as a result of this success, but also because the Negro leadership may feel that the end of the line has been reached with this kind of effort, attention is now shifting to the fight for better jobs, education and housing, with only secondary emphasis on integration. This attitude was clearly expressed by Bayard Rustin when he said recently, "We have got to lift the school problem from integration to that of quality schools; which has to include, we say, integration secondarily." Implicit in a remark such as this is recognition of the importance of developing the skills and qualities that are needed by Negro workers in order to take full advantage of the job opportunities that may arise. As Nathan Glazer has pointed out very effectively in a recent article in *Commentary* magazine, the legislative gains that have been made by Negroes in the past few years make it possible and perhaps even necessary for contemporary leaders of the civil rights movement to return to the fundamental policies outlined by Booker T. Washington at the turn of the century. According to Glazer, Booker T. Washington "saw that the Negro had been denuded by slavery of the qualities necessary for building an independent and satisfying life. Primarily what concerned him . . . was the devaluation of work produced by slavery, for he felt that independent and productive work was the basis of racial respect. But Washington also assumed that the Negroes, as they gained in education and income, would be enfranchised and would be able to play a major role in politics and in the shaping of their own fate. He fought desperately against the movement to disenfranchise Negroes in the South in the 1890's. When this movement succeeded, and Jim Crow began to fasten its bonds on the Negro people, he was left with half a program. The other half became the program of 'protest.'" Glazer then goes on to state that "we now have a situation which corresponds . . . to the one Booker T. Washington first saw as his major task, the building up of the economic and social foundations of the Negro community."

The point is that so long as the Negro could see no reasonable prospect for advancement beyond the most menial jobs, he was behaving more or less rationally in assigning a low value to education, saving and the other fruitful avenues to advancement. Limited opportunities for employment in the professional fields forced Negroes to concentrate on those areas where there was a Negro market for their services—preaching, teaching and social work. Because of their concentration in these low-paid fields, the average Negro college graduate, even today, can expect to earn less over a lifetime than the white who does not go beyond the eighth grade.

In view of facts such as these, who could argue with the young school dropout who might feel what James Baldwin has expressed so well in the following words: "It is not to be wondered at that if . . . studying is going to prepare him only to be a porter or an elevator boy—or his teacher—well, then, to hell with it."

But we now have a chance to change all of this. Whether in fact we will depends upon two things: the extent to which our society opens up and takes the Negro in as a full-fledged participating member; and the extent to which the Negro is prepared to move in should the opportunities present themselves. Only time will tell whether or not we can succeed in getting both of these forces to move in the right direction at the right time.

United States
Department of Labor

THE EMPLOYMENT OF NEGROES: SOME DEMOGRAPHIC CONSIDERATIONS

The post war years have witnessed substantial progress in the economic and social status of Negroes. During the past decade, for example, the median educational attainment of nonwhite workers has advanced from 7.6 to 9.6 years of schooling and the number of them who are high school graduates has almost doubled—a startling development and an indication of the small number of graduates at the beginning of

Reprinted from the *Manpower Report of the President* and *A Report on Manpower Requirements, Resources, Utilization, and Training* by the United States Department of Labor (Washington, D.C.: U.S. Government Printing Office, 1964).

the period. There has been a growth in the proportion of nonwhites in professional, operative, and clerical jobs and a concomitant decrease in the percentage employed as private household workers and as laborers. The proportion owning their own homes has risen, and the median value of their homes has more than doubled. These developments reflect the fact that the median wage and salary income of men in this group rose from $2,038 in 1952 to $3,023 in 1962, while family income increased from $2,338 to $3,330.

The notable advances in Negro civil rights, education, occupational distribution, housing, and earnings have led to a widespread assumption that the economic gap between them and the white population of the country is consistently narrowing. Such an assumption ignores the economic progress of the white population which has been even more rapid than that of the Negro in the past decade. As a result, the differences between the two racial groups have not only failed to narrow but have actually widened in such major areas as housing, income, and unemployment. Only in education is the gap narrowing, and the full rewards of this development have yet to be reaped.

In 1963 there were more than 22 million nonwhites in the United States, most of whom were Negroes. Nonwhites comprised 11.7 per cent of the population, 11 per cent of the labor force, and 21 per cent of the unemployed. These stark figures serve to dramatize the disadvantaged status of Negro workers, for their disproportionately high rate of unemployment is essentially the climax of all the discriminatory forces shaping the lives of Negroes, not only in employment but in the whole complex of social institutions that determine opportunities for workers and their role in the labor force. Perhaps most crucial to the economic situation of the Negro community has been the enforced isolation from the mainstream of American life, its institutions and its aspirations.

Today, despite the advances that have been made by Negroes, the majority are born into impoverished families; live in substandard housing in the Negro ghettos, southern or northern; obtain an inferior education and less years of schooling than whites; have little opportunity for apprenticeship or other vocational training in skilled occupations; are employed in semiskilled or unskilled jobs, frequently in declining occupations and industries; are paid less than whites for the same work; and are subject to a much higher rate of unemployment than white persons.

In 1962 there were an estimated 20 million Negroes in the United States. Their proportion in the population has been growing since 1930 as a result of their higher birth rate. The benefits of improved sanitation, more extensive medical care, and other public health programs reached the Negro population later than they did the majority of whites. In 1963 the median age was 22 for nonwhites, more than 7 years below that of whites. Fourteen per cent of the population under 20 were nonwhites.

For almost a century the Negro population has been migrating from the South, a movement that accelerated after World War I and became ever more rapid after World War II. In the 1950's 1.5 million Negroes left the South, approximately 70 per cent of them going to the industrialized Middle Atlantic and East North Central States while another 24 per cent went to California. As a result of the long-term migration of Negroes, only 60 per cent now live in the South, where they account for one-fifth of the population. While the migrations encompassed Negroes of all ages, the rate of net outmigration from the Southern States was notably highest among the young.

The movement of Negroes both to other regions and within the South has been from the farms to the cities, a trend hastened by the dramatic reduction in farm jobs over the past decade. By 1960, 73 per cent of the Negro population was living in cities, as compared with 70 per cent of the white population.

One-fifth of the total Negro population in the United States lives in a half dozen northern and western cities—New York, Chicago, Philadelphia, Detroit, Washington, and Los Angeles. In Chicago 23 per cent of the population is Negro; in New York City, 14 per cent; in Philadelphia, 27 per cent; and in the District of Columbia, 55 per cent. Southern cities have even greater concentrations of Negroes than most northern cities. In Birmingham, Atlanta, and New Orleans, Negroes constitute approximately 40 per cent of all inhabitants.

Because of discrimination in housing and low-income levels, most of the Negro population live in neighborhoods with few white residents. For example, in 1960 two-thirds of the Chicago Negro population resided in 125 tracts in which 90 per cent or more of the population was Negro. A fourth of these lived in 33 tracts which had no white residents.

The unemployment rate for nonwhite men was more than twice that of white men in 1963 and this was true in all age groups but the youngest. Nonwhite married men and heads of families were especially disadvantaged; they had an unemployment rate of almost 7 per cent, as contrasted with 3 per cent for the comparable white group. This situation is one reason why so many Negro married women work even when they have young children.

The difference in unemployment rates between whites and nonwhites is not quite as great among women as among men. Nevertheless, unemployment was almost twice as frequent among nonwhite as white women in 1963, with the differential very wide in the youngest age groups but narrowing in the older ones.

In recent years the unemployment rate for nonwhite youth has been so excessive as to constitute a major social problem. One out of every four 14- to 19-year-old nonwhite boys in the labor force was unemployed in 1963. And the unemployment rate was still higher (33 per cent) among nonwhite girls. Even in the 20- to 24-year age group, 16 per cent of the men and 19 per cent of the women workers were unemployed. The unemployment rates for white girls in both age groups were less than half, and those for white boys about half or a little better, than the comparable figures for nonwhites. Moreover, rates of unemployment for young nonwhites, both high school graduates and dropouts, remain relatively high even after they have been out of school several years, but unemployment drops sharply among white graduates and dropouts as they gain experience.

Although the higher rate of unemployment for nonwhites in part results from their concentration in the less-skilled blue-collar and service occupations, it is notable that in every occupation their rate of unemployment exceeds that of white workers. Furthermore, the difference tends to be relatively greater in the occupations with higher skill demands—such as clerical and sales workers, and craftsmen and foremen—than in the less-skilled ones as, for example, farm laborers and foremen, and nonfarm laborers. While the Negro has advanced slowly into the more skilled occupations, where unemployment is a lesser hazard than in the unskilled ones, he is obviously hired reluctantly into these occupations and is the first to be discharged from them, perhaps in part because of his lower seniority.

Long-term unemployment is also more prevalent among nonwhites than whites. In 1963, on the average, about a third of all unemployed nonwhites were without work for 15 or more weeks, as compared with 25 per cent of the unemployed white workers. About 18 per cent of unemployed nonwhites were jobless for more than half a year, as contrasted with 12 per cent of the whites.

Additionally, nonwhite workers experience more part-time employment than whites. One out of every ten working in nonfarm industries was on a part-time basis because of slack work and other economic factors—three times the proportion of white workers. Involuntary part-time employment moreover, has been increasing among nonwhites but has not become more extensive among whites.

Since Negro workers tend to suffer more severe unemployment in both incidence and duration, the unemployment insurance system is often of great assistance to them. However, because workers in this group tend to have extended periods of unemployment, they face greater difficulty in building a work record of sufficient covered employment to qualify for unemployment insurance. Also because these workers tend to suffer longer duration of unemployment, they would more often exhaust their entitlement to benefits. Many Negroes are in jobs not covered by the unemployment insurance system, and none of its benefits are available to them.

The social implications of Negro unemployment can be fully appreciated only in the context of its concentration in large urban centers, and specifically in the Negro areas of those cities to which Negro workers from the South have flocked in the hope of improving their economic status. For example, 41 per cent of Negro men in one census tract in Detroit, wholly populated by Negroes, were jobless in 1960; in certain census tracts in Chicago, Los Angeles, and Baltimore—where 90 per cent or more of the inhabitants were Negro—the rates ranged from 24 per cent to 36 per cent. If youth unemployment is as much above the overall average in these neighborhoods as in the Nation generally, the situation is indeed charged with social dynamite.

Unemployment Rates by Color, Sex, and Age, 1963

SEX AND AGE	WHITE	NONWHITE
Male	4.7	10.6
14 to 19 years	14.2	25.4
20 to 24 years	7.8	15.6
25 to 34 years	3.9	9.5
35 to 44 years	2.9	8.0
45 to 54 years	3.3	7.1
55 years and over	4.1	8.0
Female	5.8	11.3
14 to 19 years	13.6	33.1
20 to 24 years	7.4	18.8
25 to 34 years	5.8	11.7
35 to 44 years	4.6	8.2
45 to 54 years	3.9	6.1
55 years and over	3.4	4.6

Some recent breakthroughs in Negro employment opportunities have been achieved and hold out the promise of substantial future improvement in their employment situation. However, the Negro labor force continues to a great extent to be barred by inadequate education and training from sharing fully in the Nation's economic life. Negroes continue to experience a rate of unemployment more than twice as high as that of whites. They suffer a substantially higher rate of long-term unemployment as well. Even more significant, the differential between white and nonwhite unemployment rates has widened during the postwar period. From 1947 to 1953, the unemployment rate for nonwhite workers averaged 71 per cent greater than for white workers. This differential has risen to an average of 112 per cent in the past decade. The relatively depressed condition of the Negro employment situation shown by these higher unemployment rates also appears to have been reflected in a declining participation of nonwhite men in the labor force.

A more rapid rate of growth in the economy and a general increase in employment opportunities would undoubtedly reduce unemployment among Negroes. However, it is unlikely that any real solution to the problem can be anticipated unless there is an increase in the educational levels of Negroes, unless training and retraining programs are expanded and are oriented especially toward the problems of deficient education and lack of skill and, above all, unless there is a general acceptance of the doctrine of equality of opportunity.

Unemployment Rate for Nonwhite Workers as Per Cent of Rate for White Workers, 1947–63

YEAR	UNEMPLOYMENT RATE		NONWHITE RATE AS PER CENT OF WHITE
	WHITE	NONWHITE	
1947	3.3	5.4	164
1948	3.2	5.2	163
1949	5.2	8.2	158
1950	4.6	8.5	185
1951	2.8	4.8	171
1952	2.4	4.6	192
1953	2.3	4.1	178
1954	4.5	8.9	198
1955	3.6	7.9	219
1956	3.3	7.5	227
1957	3.9	8.0	205
1958	6.1	12.6	207
1959	4.9	10.7	218
1960	5.0	10.2	204
1961	6.0	12.5	208
1962	4.9	11.0	224
1963	5.1	10.9	214

The evidence of recent deterioration in the Negro employment situation compared with whites is even more graphic when the parallel trends of unemployment and declining participation in the labor force are combined. While unemployment rose between 1948 and 1963 from 39 to 78 per 1,000 nonwhite men in the central working ages of 25 to 54, the proportion not in the labor force rose from 42 to 62 per 1,000. Among white men at the same ages, unemployment moved up from 21 to 33 per 1,000, while the proportion not in the labor force was actually reduced from 33 to 28 per 1,000. The net result of these combined effects of unemployment and departure from the labor force was an increase in those not employed from 81 per 1,000 nonwhite males (aged 25 to 54) in 1948 to 140 per 1,000 in 1963. During the same period the equivalent figures for the white population rose from 54 to 61 per 1,000.

Both the rise in unemployment and the falloff in participation between 1948 and 1963 were much sharper among older nonwhite men than among either the younger nonwhite groups or the white group of the same ages. The availability of social security benefits and private pensions cannot be the entire explanation for the decline in participation among older nonwhites. The fact that white men at the same ages showed neither the same sharp increase in unemployment (for 55- to 64-year-olds up from 27 to 53 per 1,000 for whites and from 33 to 105 per 1,000 for nonwhites), nor the same increase in withdrawal from the labor force (up from 104 to 122 per 1,000 for whites and 114 to 184 per 1,000 for nonwhites) prompts the conclusion that at least some of the Negroes' withdrawal from the labor force was directly connected with conditions of limited job opportunities.

The major increase in this squeeze-out from the labor force among nonwhites seems to have occurred after 1958, a year of recession from which there has been only imperfect recovery in many respects. Unemployment among nonwhites had in fact risen sharply during each of the postwar recessions, and since 1954 had failed to recover to the same extent as white unemployment rates during each subsequent business pickup. The familiar pattern of "first to be fired, last to be rehired" appears to have become "first to be fired, and possibly never rehired."

The same aggravated effects of disadvantage plague other groups of workers. The poorly educated of any race, like the Negroes, are affected in multiple ways: by higher rates of unemployment, by unemployment of longer duration, and by more frequent spells of unemployment—resulting to a disquieting extent in an ultimate discouragement that extinguishes the will of many to continue their search for work.

Negro Population in 1960 for the 25 Largest Cities in the United States,
Ranked by Total Population in 1960

CITY	POPULATION (IN THOUSANDS)			NEGRO AS PER CENT OF TOTAL
	TOTAL[1]	WHITE	NEGRO	
Total, 25 largest cities	30,187	23,892	5,965	19.8
Total, 10 largest cities	21,505	16,703	4,618	21.5
New York, N.Y.	7,674	6,549	1,072	14.0
Chicago, Ill.	3,513	2,685	803	22.9
Los Angeles, Calif.	2,463	2,049	333	13.5
Philadelphia, Pa.	1,967	1,439	523	26.7
Detroit, Mich.	1,656	1,174	478	28.9
Baltimore, Md.	932	606	323	34.7
Houston, Tex.	935	718	215	23.0
Cleveland, Ohio	871	619	250	28.7
Washington, D.C.	749	334	408	54.5
St. Louis, Mo.	745	530	213	28.6
San Francisco, Calif.	730	596	74	10.1
Milwaukee, Wis.	733	668	62	8.5
Boston, Mass.	682	615	62	9.1
Dallas, Tex.	674	544	129	19.1
New Orleans, La.	622	389	231	37.1
Pittsburgh, Pa.	596	496	99	16.6
San Antonio, Tex.	587	544	42	7.2
San Diego, Calif.	521	481	32	6.1
Seattle, Wash.	549	504	26	4.7
Buffalo, N.Y.	533	459	71	13.3
Cincinnati, Ohio	502	393	108	21.5
Memphis, Tenn.	496	312	184	37.1
Denver, Colo.	492	457	30	6.1
Minneapolis, Minn.	483	434	12	2.5
Atlanta, Ga.	482	297	185	38.4

[1] Includes nonwhites other than Negroes (not shown separately).

Unemployment Rates of Experienced Workers,[1] by Color and Occupation, 1963

MAJOR OCCUPATION GROUP	WHITE	NONWHITE
All occupation groups[2]	4.4	9.3
Clerical and sales workers	3.9	7.4
Craftsmen and foremen	4.6	8.2
Operatives	6.9	11.1
Private household workers	3.1	7.7
Other service workers	5.3	10.0
Farm laborers and foremen	5.0	7.1
Laborers, except farm and mine	11.0	15.2

[1] The base for the unemployment rate includes the employed, classified according to their current jobs, and the unemployed, classified according to their latest civilian job, if any; excluding unemployed persons who never had a full-time civilian job.

[2] Includes the following groups not shown separately: Professional and technical workers; managers, officials, and proprietors; and farmers and farm managers.

Employed Persons in Nonagricultural Industries, by Full- or Part-Time Status and Color, 1963

FULL- OR PART-TIME STATUS	WHITE	NONWHITE
All employed persons:		
Number (in thousands)	54,402	6,135
Per cent	100.0	100.0
At work:		
On full-time schedules[1]	85.7	78.7
On part time for economic reasons[2]	3.1	9.6
Usually work full time	1.6	2.9
Usually work part time	1.5	6.7
On part time for other reasons; usually work part time	11.2	11.7

[1] Includes persons who actually worked 35 hours or more during the survey week and those who usually work full time but worked part time because of noneconomic reasons (bad weather, illness, holidays, etc.).

[2] Includes persons who worked less than 35 hours a week because of slack work, job turnover, material shortages, inability to find full-time work, etc.

Education

Time Magazine
THE FACTS OF DE FACTO

In 1960 most of the 77,000 citizens of New Rochelle, N.Y., viewed school segregation as a disease confined to the distant likes of Little Rock, Ark. The town's ethnic mix—14 per cent Negro, 30 per cent Jewish, 45 per cent Irish and Italian Catholic—was so faithfully reflected in the high school that the Voice of America once touted it as a shining example of integrated education. Only a year later, New Rochelle became the "Little Rock of the North," convicted in a federal court of gerrymandering to promote segregation. Case in point: Lincoln Elementary School, 94 per cent Negro.

More in hurt than anger, New Rochelle defended Lincoln as a typical "neighborhood school" that, like Topsy, just grew that way. The trial told a different story. Back in 1930, the school board redrew lines to make the Lincoln district match the Negro area. It also allowed whites to transfer out—and they did. By 1949 the school was 100 per cent Negro.

The board tried to bring resident whites back to the school by revoking transfers. Instead, whites switched to private and parochial schools or moved away, making the district more Negro than ever. By 1960 Lincoln's pupils in general were academically behind every other elementary school in town. The board, nobly it thought, got a citywide vote to build a fine new Lincoln on the same spot. Negro parents countered with a federal suit on then-novel grounds: it is just as

Reprinted from "The Facts of *De Facto*," *Time, The Weekly Newsmagazine*, August 2, 1963, by permission of Time, Inc.

unconstitutional to compel Negroes to attend a *de facto* segregated school in the North as a *de jure* segregated school in the South.

Federal Judge Irving R. Kaufman did not decide that question (nor has any other federal court so far). He ruled only that gerrymandering had violated equal protection under the 14th Amendment. The outcome jogged white minds all over the North. Given free access to other schools, Lincoln's pupils on the whole did better, except for some who landed in a white school that overwhelmed them. Because two-fifths of Lincoln's pupils chose to remain, New Rochelle is now closing the 65-year-old building, assigning the children to balanced schools, and launching an extensive bus service to help keep the entire city desegregated.

ON THE ATTACK

The experience of New Rochelle is a case history in a development that is spreading across the Northern U.S.: a movement against *de facto* segregation of schools. Victory in New Rochelle spurred the N.A.A.C.P. to a successful attack on *de facto* school segregation last year (1962) in a dozen Northern communities, from Coatesville, Pa., to Eloy, Ariz. This summer (1963) it is "mobilizing direct action" in 70 cities throughout 18 Northern and Western states. School boards are responding, and many a change will have been made by September. All kinds of tools are being tried. Samples:

Open Enrollment. The most widely used method so far, it modifies the neighborhood-school concept enough to let students of mostly Negro schools transfer to mostly white schools that have sufficient room. Open enrollment was pioneered in New York City, is used or will be starting in some form next September (1963) in Baltimore, Detroit, Pittsburgh, Buffalo, San Francisco and many smaller cities. Usually only a fraction of the eligible Negro students take advantage of it.

Rezoning—which is often the same as ungerrymandering. In San Francisco, mostly white Grant School lies near mostly Negro Emerson School in a rectangular area cut by a horizontal attendance line; made vertical, the line would integrate both schools. New York City's school zoning boss, Assistant Superintendent Francis A. Turner, a Negro, is such a skilled mixmaster that balanced schools are rapidly increasing.

The Princeton Plan, so called for the New Jersey town that devised it. Formerly segregated schools are rematched, so that one school accommodates all children of perhaps three grades, a second school the next three, and so on. This works well in small communities, might do in big cities by clustering each grade group in several nearby schools to avoid long bus trips.

Recombination. An example: A Negro elementary school can be turned into a junior high school serving a wider area, or into a school for gifted or retarded children, while the original pupils are sent to other schools.

School Spotting. New schools are built only in areas of integrated housing. For fast-changing big cities, the latest idea is "educational parks," putting all new schools in one or several central clusters. Last week a New York City board of education member suggested a perfect site: the World's Fair grounds, where after 1965 an education center could accommodate 15 public schools and a teachers' college, enrolling a total of 31,000 students.

FEARS AND ILLUSIONS

All these changes stir deep fears and emotions. Negroes, demanding more than token integration, have lately attacked *de facto* segregation by street-marching protests in Los Angeles and Philadelphia, "study-in's" at the white schools of Englewood, N.J., sit-in's at the boards of education of New York and Chicago. Whites envision their neighborhood schools being flooded with poorly prepared Negro pupils or their own children being forced to integrate Negro slum schools. A feeling of "discrimination against the majority" has sparked reactions like that of white parents in Montclair, N.J., who filed a federal suit under the 14th Amendment, claiming that Negro children were allowed free transfers while theirs were not. The long-honored concept of the neighborhood school—a homey place that children can walk to, a living symbol of local pride and progress—seems in danger.

Yet behind the stresses and strains is a consensus, by many school authorities, some courts and most Negroes, that *de facto* segregation must go. The problem is to break the low-income Negro's vicious circle of slum birth to slum school to bad education to low-paid job and parenthood of more slum children. The widely accepted premise is that the circle can and must be broken at the school stage. Equally important is that segregated neighborhood schools refute the original aim of Horace Mann's "common school," strengthening democracy by serving all races, creeds and classes. Integrationists believe that schools can help to heal U.S. race relations by returning to Mann's ideal.

SEGREGATED EQUALS BAD

Nothing in theory prevents the hundreds of predominantly Negro schools in the North from excelling, but in practice a school that becomes 30 per cent to 50 per cent Negro is in for trouble. Whites pull out and it "tips" toward 100 per cent. Gone are the "motivated" bright white children who might have been models for slum kids to copy and compete with. Good teachers become hard to get (although the "spirit of the Peace Corps" is diminishing this problem, according to Cleveland's School Superintendent William B. Levenson). "Once we become concentrated, we become ignored," says a Boston Negro leader. Most of Los Angeles' 53 Negro schools are on double sessions. Chicago's Urban League calculates that in operating expenses Negro schools get only two-thirds as much per pupil as white schools.

The result is unsurprising. In Boston, where special high schools require entrance exams, one Negro boy typically complains: "I never saw that kind of math before I went for the exam." In his recent (1963) civil-rights speech, President Kennedy said: "The Negro baby born in America today has about one-half as much chance of completing a high school as a white baby, born in the same place, on the same day; one-third as much chance of completing college; one-third as much chance of becoming a professional man; twice as much chance of becoming unemployed."

BIG-CITY PROBLEMS

While small Northern cities may attack the situation in the manner of New Rochelle, big cities, with miles of Negro ghettoes, have problems that range up to hopeless. Washington, where even the most civil-righteous New Frontiersmen are prone to send their children to private schools, can hardly give classes a desegregated look when 85 per cent of public school students are Negro. Chicago, Boston and Philadelphia are marking time. A measure of New York's quandary is that some integration crusaders have proposed mass transfer of whites into Harlem schools, although few officials see it as a workable solution.

Nonetheless, the nation's biggest city school system is also the most enterprising. New York is trying to make slum schools so good that Negroes can rise more easily into an integrated society. It devised the famed Higher Horizons program, heavy on culture and counseling, which now involves 64,000 students in 76 schools. At state level, New York's Commissioner of Education James E. Allen, Jr. recently requested school boards to report by September (1963) on what steps they intend to take to balance schools with more than 50 per cent Negro enrollment.

"In the minds of Negro pupils and parents," says New Jersey's State Commissioner of Education Frederick M. Raubinger, "a stigma is attached to attending a school whose enrollment is completely or exclusively Negro, and this sense of sting and resulting feeling of inferiority has an undesirable effect on attitudes related to successful training." Raubinger has issued orders to end *de facto* segregation in three New Jersey communities. In the same vein, a former foe of "social engineering via bussing," Dr. John Fischer, president of Columbia's Teachers College, warns that schools must "take positive action to bring Negro children into the mainstream of American cultural activity." And in California, the state supreme court in June came close to outlawing *de facto* segregation. Where it exists, ruled the court, "it is not enough for a school board to refrain from affirmative discriminatory conduct." No exact racial ratio is required, but schools must take "corrective measures."

The ideal integration situation, says Psychiatrist Robert Coles, after studying Southern schools, is apparently a middle-class school with diverse ethnic groups and high teaching standards. In a forthcoming report, sponsored by the Southern Regional Council and the Anti-Defamation League of B'nai B'rith, Coles adds that young children mix naturally, ignoring adult tensions. Teen-agers take longer, but in the course of a year begin to see "them" as individuals to be judged on personal merit. As for standards, both races generally work as hard as ever. Says Coles: "We have yet to hear a Southern teacher complain of any drop in intellectual or moral climate in a desegregated room or school."

While the pressures for integration bring a troublesome measure of controversy, reaction and disillusionment, it is a fact that every sensible effort to desegregate schools—alarmists to the contrary—is likely to improve the general level of U.S. education.

Charles E. Silberman
THE NEGRO AND THE SCHOOL

It is impossible to talk about problems of Negro education without some discussion of segregation and integration . . . A great many argue that Negro children cannot receive an equal education in an all-Negro environment—that a segregated school, is inherently unequal *whatever* the reasons underlying the segregation. A number of white educators and civic leaders have expressed agreement. For example, Dr. James E. Allen, Jr., New York State Commissioner of Education,

From *Crisis in Black and White*, by Charles E. Silberman, pp. 285, 297–307. © Copyright 1964 by Random House, Inc. Reprinted by permission. Mr. Silberman is a member of the Board of Editors of *Fortune Magazine*.

announced in June of 1963 his department's conviction "that the racial imbalance existing in a school in which the enrollment is wholly or predominantly Negro interferes with the achievement of equality of educational opportunity and must therefore be eliminated from the schools of New York State." (This statement underlay the order redressing racial imbalance in Malverne which was overruled by the State Supreme Court.) Dr. Allen's statement of guiding principles went on to argue that "modern psychological and sociological knowledge seems to indicate that in schools in which the enrollment is largely from a minority group of homogeneous ethnic origin, the personality of these minority group children may be damaged. There is a decrease in motivation and thus an impairment of ability to learn. Public education in such a situation is socially unrealistic. . . ." And the Commissioner's Advisory Committee on Human Relations and Community Tensions stated a number of principles which it felt should guide local school boards, among them the conviction that "The presence in a single school of children from varied racial, cultural, socio-economic and religious backgrounds is an important element in the preparation of young people for active participation in the social and political affairs of our democracy." The Committee therefore proposed that "In establishing school attendance areas one of the objectives should be to create in each school a student body that will represent as nearly as possible a cross-section of the population of the entire school district . . ."

There is very little evidence, however, that putting lower-class Negro and middle-class white children together in the same classroom is anything more than an act of democratic faith. To take a child who comes from a poverty-stricken and intellectually-deprived background, who has received an inferior and inadequate education, and who therefore is performing several years below grade level, and to thrust him into a class with whites performing above grade level without first removing or compensating for his disabilities, may be much more damaging to his ego than keeping him in a segregated classroom. In New Rochelle, for example, where the first and most important de facto school segregation case was tried and won, the initial results seem to have been unfortunate. Negro children from the Lincoln School, in a poverty-stricken neighborhood, were transferred to the Roosevelt School, in an upper-class white neighborhood, where the average annual income was $25,000 and where in most homes both parents were college graduates. The disparity in ability was more than either the white or the Negro students could cope with. "Some of the transferees," Professor John Kaplan of Northwestern University Law School wrote in a staff report for the United States Commission on Civil Rights, "instead of being stimulated by the educational aspirations of the Roosevelt children, seemed to give up trying at all." (In a number of classes, no white child's performance was as poor as the best of the Negro children.)

Nor does contact with Negroes necessarily produce empathy on the part of white school children. On the contrary, the contact may have the reverse effect when the difference in color is accompanied by a wide difference in class, and therefore in academic performance and behavior. "The most unfortunate aspect" of the transfer of Negro students to the upper-class white school in New Rochelle, in Professor Kaplan's opinion, "has been its creation of racial stereotypes in the minds of the Roosevelt children . . . White children from a liberal background who had had no contact with Negroes before but whose home and school life taught ideals of brotherhood and the equality of man were thrown together with children of a far lower socio-economic and cultural level who happened to be Negroes." One teacher said, "Some of the Roosevelt children actually understand that this is a cultural and not a racial difference, but all they see is that the Negro children are not as bright, clean, honest, or well behaved as they."

As a result of this and similar experiences, a good many Negro community leaders are having second thoughts about the wisdom of current techniques of ending de facto segregation. "It would be unhealthy to take our children out of our own community to attend school in another," the Reverend Dr. William M. James of Harlem's Metropolitan Community Methodist Church has said. "We, in the so-called underprivileged communities, cannot look to those outside of our communities for total cure of our ills. This will not work." A good many ministers are dubious about the "open enrollment" plans which, until fairly recently, were regarded as the best solution. "Open enrollment" has a number of defects, not the least of them being the fact that painfully few Negroes take advantage of the plan. Those who do tend to be the most upwardly-mobile families in the area; the result, all too often, is that removing the brighter, more highly motivated youngsters from an all-Negro school leaves that school still all-Negro, but in worse condition than it was in before. At the same time, the youngsters who have transferred to a "white" school discover that the new school lacks a good many of the special services—reading teachers, speech teachers, guidance counselors, etc.—that they were used to or depended upon in the all-Negro school. There are real questions, too, as to whether the loss of contact with children from their own neighborhood outweighs the advantages of integration.

Large-scale transfers of Negro children to schools in white neighborhoods also raise questions whose answers are by no means obvious. Should the Negro children be put in heterogeneous classes in the new school, in which case they tend to perform at the bottom of the class if the school draws from middle-class and upper-class families? Or should they be put in homogeneous classes, i.e., classes grouped according to academic ability—in which case they are again segregated in the new school? The latter seems pointless: nothing is gained by transporting youngsters several miles in order to keep them segregated. Yet dumping youngsters who are reading several years below grade level into a class with children reading several years above grade level, as the New Rochelle experience suggests, is not likely to enhance the former group's ego nor lead to meaningful encounters between the two races.

Large-scale transfers of white students to schools in Negro neighborhoods, which a number of militant integrationists now advocate, is equally unrealistic, as Dr. Kenneth B. Clark of City College has pointed out. Such suggestions in Dr. Clark's view, "are unrealistic, irrelevant, emotional and diversionary." If the city were to try to send middle-class children into Harlem schools, he argues, it would be done "only under conditions of intense and prolonged protest" that would "clearly lead to a disruption of the educational process, and [would] not affect positively the education of any child." Some rabid integrationists are clearly prepared to pay the price; as already mentioned, Rev. Milton Galamison, chairman of the committee coordinating the integration demands of New York Negro groups, has stated bluntly that he would rather see the city school system destroyed than continue on a de facto segregated basis. It is hard to imagine any position more irresponsible to the real needs and interests of Negro children, who need the public schools even more than white middle-class children. Nor can Reverend Galamison's statement be dismissed as mere harmless rhetoric. The fact is that the public school system is in real danger. The great development of the public schools in the first half of this century, as Professor Cremin demonstrated in *The Transformation of the School,* was due to a remarkable coalition of trade unions, businessmen, and ethnic groups, each of which saw public education as the solution to its particular problem. That coalition has been breaking down in recent years, and it has not been replaced by any other; there are today relatively few powerful interest groups committed to the public schools. If Negroes join the attack on public education, the result could be its disintegration and replacement by a system of subsidies for private schools.

Some integration leaders, to be sure, see the demand for integration merely as a device to force "the white power structure" to improve the education offered Negro children. "Having a white child sit next to my Negro child is no guarantee that mine will learn," Isaiah

Robinson, chairman of the Harlem Parents Committee has said, "but it is a guarantee that he will be taught." Some activists, moreover, do not even care whether white children sit next to Negro children; they see the demand for integration simply as a lever to pry more money and services out of the school board. (The only way to get the whites to lay out the funds needed to reconstruct the schools of Harlem, in this view, is to frighten them with demands that white children be transported into Harlem's schools.) All too many Negro leaders, however—and all too many white liberals—have become prisoners of their own rhetoric, denouncing as inadequate any measure that falls short of full desegregation and attacking any proposals for compensatory education as a reversion to the old doctrine of "separate but equal."

However sincere such proponents of integration may be, there is an element of irresponsibility in their rigidity. It cannot be denied that school systems could do more than they are doing to speed desegregation, although many measures proposed might be self-defeating by leading to further reductions in the number of white students.[1] But neither can it be denied that only a small minority of Negro students would be affected even if the large cities were to take every conceivable measure to desegregate their schools; the majority of Negro youngsters would continue to attend segregated schools.

If this be so, then the thesis that Negro students cannot receive an adequate education in an all-Negro school needs to be carefully examined. It has not been; on the contrary, the thesis has been advanced without any real substantiation. To the extent that there is any evidence —and there is amazingly little—it suggests the reverse. The pioneering research by Kenneth and Mamie Clark, for example, suggested that Negro children attending Northern integrated schools had more self-hatred (or fewer positive images of themselves) than children attending segregated Southern schools.[2] The lesson of black nationalism (and of The Woodlawn Organization) suggests that Negroes must first learn pride in self and in their heritage before they can learn to relate easily to

[1] Some integrationists respond by saying, in anger, "Let the whites leave; then we'll take over the city." Their anger is understandable—but it raises a serious question as to whether their objective is integration, as they claim, or power for its own sake.

[2] See Kenneth B. Clark and Mamie Phipps Clark, "The Emergence of Racial Identification and Preference in Negro Children," reprinted in E. E. Maccoby, T. M. Newcomb, & E. L. Hartley, *Readings in Social Psychology,* Third Edition, New York: Henry Holt & Co., 1958. The Clarks showed Negro children white dolls and colored dolls, and asked them, among other questions, which doll they preferred to play with. A majority of the children in both the Southern and the Northern schools preferred to play with the white dolls—but a larger proportion of the Northern children expressed the preference, which the Clarks used as an indication of self-hatred.

people of a different color. Indeed, the fervor with which some integrationists insist that equal education is impossible in an all-Negro school sounds suspiciously like self-hatred on their part. Their arguments, moreover, carry a serious danger of becoming self-fulfilling prophecies: if you shout loudly enough and long enough that Negro youngsters cannot learn in an all-Negro school, the children almost certainly will not learn.

Let there be no misunderstanding, however: none of this discussion is intended to derogate in any way the importance of school integration. Integration is vitally important not so much for Negroes as for whites, who must learn to live in a world in which they are indeed the minority. Education, moreover, should do more than develop the powers of the intellect; it should, in addition infuse youngsters with a commitment to the brotherhood of man, with a vision of the beauty and nobility of which man is capable—and a realization of the depths of depravity to which he can sink. We have seen, in our own generation, how that greatest of all educational institutions, the German university, became the instrument of utter depravity because it had no commitment except to the intellect. Its lack of commitment was itself a commitment to amorality. There is no educational system which does not have a value system implicit within it; the value system is expressed in the way in which the system is organized and structured, even more than in the subject matter taught. There is no point in teaching about the brotherhood of man, therefore, unless the school system is organized to treat all men as brothers; a segregated school system is not likely to impart any strong convictions about racial equality.

Thus, integration is a moral imperative—the greatest moral imperative of our time. But integration should not be confused with the mere mixing of Negroes and whites in the same classroom, or in the same school, or in the same neighborhood. To throw white and black youngsters into a classroom in the name of integration, without regard to what one may reasonably expect to happen, is to violate the Commandment which prohibits the worship of false gods; it is to sacrifice the children for the sake of an abstract principle. Given the realities of population change in the large cities—more important, given the harsh and painful truth of what three hundred fifty years of exclusion have done to the personality and mentality of Negro youngsters—the public schools need techniques for meaningful integration every bit as much as they need purpose.

How, then, are we to achieve meaningful integration—integration which leads to genuine contact, to real communication with and understanding by each group of the other? The only honest answer is that genuine integration will not be possible until the schools in Negro neighborhoods—and the schools in white slum areas as well—are brought up to the level of the very best schools in each city; until the schools do their job so well that children's educational performance no longer reflects their income or their social status or their ethnic group or their color. To say this is not to suggest indefinite postponement, but to demand that the public schools stop dithering with projects and demonstrations and turn immediately to their most pressing task; neither the large cities nor the nation as a whole can afford a public school system which fails to educate between 50 and 80 per cent of its Negro students.

To say this, of course, is to contradict the current dogma, which condemns any program of compensatory education, no matter how massive, as a return to "separate but equal," hence as an expression of prejudice. Because of this tendency to label, and the accompanying competition for militancy, a good many Nego leaders who really share this view are afraid to express it, for fear of having the "Uncle Tom" or "handkerchief head" label pinned on them. They may very well be exaggerating the danger of speaking the truth, however. There is very little evidence that the mass of Negroes care very much about sending their children to school with whites, or about having whites sent to school with their children. But there is a great mass of evidence (from opinion surveys, sociological studies, and the like) suggesting that Negro parents *are* deeply concerned about the inadequate education their children are receiving, and that they desperately want better education.[3]

One group of Negro leaders, headed by Kenneth Clark and Rev. Eugene Callender, has already had the courage to face up to the realities of the education problem in central Harlem. Their views are expressed in a report issued by Harlem Youth Opportunities Unlimited, Inc. (HARYOU), a group set up with funds from the President's Committee on Juvenile Delinquency and Youth Crime. (Professor Clark serves as Chief Project Consultant; Dr. Callender, who is minister of the Church of the Master in Harlem, Moderator of the Presbytery of New York, and chairman of the board of directors of the Harlem Neighborhoods Association, serves on the HARYOU board.) The HARYOU Report (Youth in the Ghetto: A Study of Powerlessness) is quite uneven, but its chapters on education rank as perhaps the best analysis yet published of Harlem's educational problem and of the measures needed to solve it.

[3] See, for example, *Youth in the Ghetto: A Study of the Consequences of Powerlessness,* a report published by Harlem Youth Opportunities Unlimited, Inc. (HARYOU). See also, Inge Lederer Gibel, "How *Not* to Integrate the Schools," *Harper's,* November 1963; and various news reports in the *New York Times* summarizing the researches of Joseph Lyford for the Fund for the Republic.

The authors mince no words about their belief in public school integration and their distrust of many of the measures taken so far to achieve it. But they also make it clear that the children of Harlem must not be sacrificed either to the dogmas or the personal ambitions of civil rights leaders.

HARYOU's main proposition is "that this vicious cycle of educational inefficiency and social pathology can be broken only by instituting an educational program of excellence in the schools of deprived communities," and their most important recommendation is a proposal to establish compensatory nursery programs for all Harlem children. In the long run, they argue, excellence requires an end to segregation. But in the short run—"during that period required to obtain more adaptive, democratic, nonsegregated schools for all children"— compensatory education is necessary, for 50 per cent of the elementary school and 80 per cent of the junior high school students need massive remedial work if they are to be brought up to grade level. "A program for the attainment of educational excellence for the children in Harlem's schools," they argue, "cannot be delayed or obscured by ideological controversies such as 'separate but equal.'" These are important and difficult issues, but they cannot be given precedence over the fact that the present generation of Negro children have only one life within which they can be prepared to take their places in the mainstream of American society . . .

> These children cannot be sacrificed on the altar of ideological and semantic rigidities. The struggle of the civil rights groups for a better life for these children is made more difficult, if not impossible, if the methods of the struggle become dominated by inflexible emotional postures. Heroics and dramatic words and gestures, over-simplified either-or thinking, and devil hunting might provide a platform for temporary crowd pleasing, ego satisfactions or would-be "leaders," but they cannot solve the fundamental problems of obtaining high quality education in our public schools and the related problem of realistic and serious desegregation in these schools. *Meaningful desegregation of the public schools in New York City can occur only if all of the schools in the system are raised to the highest standards, and when the quality of education in these schools is uniformly high —and does not vary according to income or the social status of the neighborhood. The up-grading of quality of education in predominantly Negro and Puerto Rican schools to a level of educational excellence is an unavoidable first step in any realistic program for the desegregation of these schools.* [Emphasis added.]

Or as Abraham Lincoln put it in his first Inaugural Address, "The dogmas of the quiet past are inadequate to the stormy present . . . Let us disenthrall ourselves."

Benjamin Bloom

THE SIGNIFICANCE OF EARLY
ENVIRONMENT

There is little doubt that intelligence development is in part a function of the environment in which the individual lives. The evidence from studies of identical twins reared separately and reared together as well as from longitudinal studies in which the characteristics of the environments are studied in relation to changes in intelligence test scores indicate that the level of measured general intelligence is partially determined by the nature of the environment. The evidence so far available suggests that extreme environments may be described as *abundant* or *deprived* for the development of intelligence in terms of the opportunities for learning verbal and language behavior, opportunities for direct as well as vicarious experience with a complex world, encouragement of problem solving and independent thinking, and the types of expectations and motivations for intellectual growth.

The effects of the environments, especially of the extreme environments, appear to be greatest in the early (and more rapid) periods of intelligence development and least in the later (and less rapid) periods of development. Although there is relatively little evidence of the effects of changing the environment on the changes in intelligence, the evidence so far available suggests that marked changes in the environment in the early years can produce greater changes in intelligence than will equally marked changes in the environment at later periods of development.

Much more research is needed to develop precise descriptions and quantitative measurements of environments as they relate to the development of intelligence. More research is also needed, especially of a longitudinal nature, on the amount of change in intelligence which can

Reprinted from *Stability and Change in Human Characteristics* by Benjamin Bloom (New York: John Wiley & Sons, Inc., 1964) by permission. Pp. 88–91, 214–16, 218, 229–231.

Mr. Bloom is Professor of Education, University of Chicago, and a former president of the American Education Research Association. He is also author of *The Taxonomy of Educational Objectives.*

be produced by shifting a person from one environment to another. However, a conservative estimate of the effect of extreme environments on intelligence is about 20 I.Q. points. This could mean the difference between a life in an institution for the feeble-minded or a productive life in society. It could mean the difference between a professional career and an occupation which is at the semiskilled or unskilled level. A society which places great emphasis on verbal learning and rational problem solving and which greatly needs highly skilled and well-trained individuals to carry on political-social-economic functions in an increasingly complex world cannot ignore the enormous consequences of deprivation as it affects the development of general intelligence. Increased research is needed to determine the precise consequences of the environment for general intelligence. However, even with the relatively crude data already available, the implications for public education and social policy are fairly clear. Where significantly lower intelligence can be clearly attributed to the effects of environmental deprivations, steps must be taken to ameliorate these conditions as early in the individual's development as education and other social forces can be utilized. . . .

Our attempts to describe the development of intelligence [are] really attempts to describe stability and change in measurements of intelligence. Such measurements are based on particular tests and test problems, and these measurements are undoubtedly affected by the experiences individuals have had both in school and out of school. It seems likely that performance on these tests is responsive to the experiences individuals have had and that change in the general picture of stability and change could be produced by new developments in education and by different child-rearing practices. All this is merely an attempt to alert the reader to the view that our picture of stability and change in measured intelligence is one based on things as they now are, and this includes the particular tests to measure intelligence, the child-rearing practices of families in Western cultures, and educational practices in the schools. It is conceivable that changes in any or all of these could produce a very different picture than the one we have been able to draw. It is to be hoped that we can find ways of prolonging the growth of general intelligence throughout life. It is to be hoped that we can drastically reduce the incidence of low levels of intelligence and increase the proportion of individuals reaching high levels of measured intelligence. There is some evidence that the secular trend in the increase of height over the past 40 years is paralleled by a similar trend in the increase of general intelligence over several decades (Terman and Merrill, 1937). It will be useful for behavioral scientists to understand just why such a trend develops and how it has been influenced by various conditions in the society. Our present picture should serve as a point of departure rather than as a picture of the "natural conditions" or "actual limitations" which determine stability and change in general intelligence. . . .

The prolongation of the period of dependency for youth in the Western cultures has undoubtedly been a factor in desensitizing parents, school workers, and behavioral scientists to the full importance of the very early environmental and experimental influences. Youth are usually required to attend school until at least 16 years of age and the majority live at home and attend school until about age 18.

Another factor which has contributed to our lack of full awareness of the enormous influence of the early environment is the limited evidence on the effects of the early environment. And, even when such evidence is available from longitudinal studies of intelligence and personality, it has most frequently been interpreted as indicating little predictive significance for early measures of these characteristics. There appears to be an implicit assumption running through the culture that change in behavior and personality can take place at any age or stage in development and that the developments at one age or stage are no more significant than those which take place at another.

A central finding in this work is that for selected characteristics there is a negatively accelerated curve of development which reaches its midpoint before age 5. We have reasoned that the environment would have its greatest effect on a characteristic during the period of its most rapid development.

These findings and reasoning are supported by the results of selected studies: Lee (1951) and Kirk (1958) on intelligence . . . Sears et al. (1957) and Baldwin et al. (1949) on selected personality characteristics. Alexander (1961) and Bernstein (1960) further support the importance of the home environment on the language achievement of students in the early years of school. Additional support for the importance of the environment on early as well as later development may be found in the studies of siblings, fraternal, and identical twins reared together and reared apart (Newman, Freeman, and Holzinger, 1937; Burt, 1958). Finally, the animal research of Scott and Marston (1950) and Hebb (1949) gives support to the importance of the early environment in influencing the development of selected characteristics. The evidence . . . makes it very clear that the environment, and especially the early environment, has a significant effect on the development of selected characteristics.

We believe that the early environment is of crucial importance for three reasons. The first is based on the very rapid growth of selected characteristics in the early years and conceives of the variations in the early environment as so important because they shape these characteristics in their most rapid periods of formation. . . .

However, another way of viewing the importance of the early environment has to do with the sequential nature of much of human development. Each characteristic is built on a base of that same characteristic at an earlier time or on the base of other characteristics which precede it in development. Hebb (1949) has pointed out the differences in activity and exploratory behavior of animals reared in very stimulating environments in contrast to those reared under very confining conditions. Such differences in initial behavior are of significance in determining the animal's activity and intelligence at later stages in its development. Erickson (1950) has described stages in the development of human beings and the ways in which the resolution of a developmental conflict at one stage will in turn affect the resolutions of subsequent developmental conflicts. The entire psychoanalytic theory and practice is based on a series of developmental stages (Freud, 1933; Freud, 1937; Horney, 1936; Sullivan, 1953) with the most crucial ones usually taking place before about age 6. The resolution of each stage has consequences for subsequent stages. Similarly, other more eclectic descriptions of development (Havighurst, 1953; Piaget, 1932; Murray, 1938; Gesell, 1945) emphasize the early years as the base for later development. All these theoretical as well as empirical descriptions of development point up the way in which the developments at one period are in part determined by the earlier developments and in turn influence and determine the nature of later developments. For each of these viewpoints, the developments that take place in the early years are crucial for all that follows.

A third reason for the crucial importance of the early environment and early experiences stems from learning theory. It is much easier to learn something new than it is to stamp out one set of learned behaviors and replace them by a new set. The effect of earlier learning on later learning is considered in most learning theories under such terms as habit, inhibition, and restructuring. Although each learning theory may explain the phenomena in different ways, most would agree that the first learning takes place more easily than a later one that is interfered with by an earlier learning. Observation of the difficulties one experiences in learning a new language after the adolescent period and the characteristic mispronunciations which tend to remain throughout life are illustrations of the same phenomena.

Several explanations for the difficulties in altering early learning and for the very powerful effects of the early learning have been advanced. Schachtel (1949) and McClelland (1951) believe that the learning which takes place before language development is so powerful because it is not accessible to conscious memory. Others, such as Dollard and Miller (1950), Mowrer (1950), and Guthrie (1935), would attribute the power of early learning to the repeated reinforcement and overlearning over time such that the early learning becomes highly stabilized. More recently, the experimental work on imprinting in animals by Hess (1959) demonstrates the tremendous power of a short learning episode at critical moments in the early history of the organism. Hess has demonstrated that ducklings at ages of 9 to 20 hours may be imprinted to react to a wooden decoy duck as a mother duck in a ten minute learning experience and that the duckling will thereafter respond to the decoy duck in preference to real mother ducks.

Although it is possible that each type of explanation is sound, especially as it applies to different learning phenomena, all three tend to confirm the tremendous power of early learning and its resistance to later alteration or extinction.

The power of early learning must still, for humans, remain largely an inference drawn from theory, from descriptive developmental studies, and from quantitative longitudinal studies. In many respects, the attempts to describe the learning process as it takes place in the first few years of life are still far from satisfactory. We know more about the early learning of experimental animals than we do about human infants. In this writer's opinion, the most vital research problems in the behavioral sciences are those centered around the effects of early learning and early environments on humans. . . .

One basic finding in this work is that less and less change is likely in a group or in an individual as the curve of development of a characteristic reaches a virtual plateau. Can educational and therapeutic techniques overcome this increasing limit to change? We are, at present, somewhat pessimistic about the possibility for significant change in a characteristic once a plateau has been reached in the curve of development of that characteristic. It is possible that very powerful environmental and/or therapeutic forces may overcome and alter the most stable of characteristics—this is yet to be demonstrated.

What is quite likely is that remedial and therapeutic techniques may enable the individual to *accept* his characteristics and to have less tension, anxiety, and emotion about them. It is also likely that an individual may be helped to express his characteristics in more socially acceptable or even in socially approved ways. For example, although *aggressiveness* may become a stable characteristic of an individual, he (or she) may learn how to express it in less violent and more socially acceptable ways. Furthermore, some individuals may learn how to channel this aggressiveness so as to become very productive in scientific, scholarly, or professional pursuits. The aggressive characteristics of a juvenile delinquent may become the acceptable behavior of a soldier in combat, a policeman on dangerous duty, or a scientific worker attacking a difficult problem.

Similarly, an individual may learn to use his level of general intelligence so effectively that he can accomplish much more intellectually than do others with much higher levels of general intelligence.

Thus, although we are pessimistic about producing major changes in a characteristic after it has reached a high level of stability, we are optimistic about the possibilities of the individual being helped to learn ways of utilizing his characteristics in more effective ways, both for his own welfare and for more productive contributions to society. . . .

A central thesis of this work is that change in many human characteristics becomes more and more difficult as the characteristics become more fully developed. Although there may be some change in a particular characteristic at almost any point in the individual's history, the amount of change possible is a declining function as the characteristic becomes increasingly stabilized.

Furthermore, to produce a given amount of change (an elusive concept) requires more and more powerful environments and increased amounts of effort and attention as the characteristic becomes stabilized. In addition, the individual not only becomes more resistant to change as the characteristic becomes stabilized but change, if it can be produced, must be made at greater emotional cost to the individual. All this is to merely repeat once again a point made throughout this work: it is less difficult for the individual and for the society to bring about a particular type of development early in the history of an individual than it is at a later point in his history. There is an increasing level of determinism in the individual's characteristics with increasing age and this is reflected both in the increased predictability of the characteristic and in the decreased amount of change in measurements of the characteristic from one point in time to another.

What are some of the consequences of this increasing determinism and our ability to predict the development of a characteristic from a relatively early age?

The research summarized in this work reveals that human characteristics are, in part, determined by environmental forces which can be measured. The availability of longitudinal measurements reveals the level of prediction which can be made from one age to another. Thus Payne (1963) has demonstrated that arithmetic achievement at grade 6 can be predicted from preschool data (before age 6) with a correlation of +.68. By the end of the first grade, it can be predicted with correlations of +.85 or higher. Similarly, Alexander (1961) has shown that reading comprehension at grade 8 can be predicted with a correlation of +.73 at grade 2 and a correlation of +.88 at grade 4. Results of this type have been demonstrated on different samples. Thus these characteristics can be predicted with relatively high levels of accuracy four to six years in advance. With increased precision in the measurements of both the individual and the environment and with increased sophistication in the data-processing procedures, the length of the time interval and the level of predictive accuracy should be increased significantly.

As the characteristics develop to the criterion age or point, it becomes more highly predictive and less amenable to change. As the time interval increases the criterion becomes more difficult to predict, but the characteristic is more amenable to change.

In a static agrarian society it is possible that the development of a particular characteristic would be regarded as the responsibility of the individual and/or his family. It is quite likely that the relative isolation of the individual and his family would mean that others would be unaware of the way in which the individual is developing and perhaps few would be concerned about the effects of this development.

The rapidly changing character of urban life, the increasing interdependence of people, and the increasing complexity of the society make it especially difficult for individuals who have marked problems in adaptation and learning. The declining opportunities for unskilled workers and the increasing need for a highly educated population have raised new educational requirements for our youth. School dropouts and lack of interest in higher education become problems of concern to both the individual and the society.

All these matters point up the need for increased social responsibility. If school dropouts, delinquent behavior, and frustration with the educational requirements of a society can be predicted long in advance, can we sit idly by and watch the prophecies come true? If remedial actions and therapy are less effective at later stages in the individual's development, can we satisfy a social conscience by indulging in such activities when it is far too late? When the school environment is at variance with the home and peer group environment, can we find ways of reconciling these different environments?

REFERENCES

1. ALEXANDER, M., 1961. The relation of environment to intelligence and achievement: A longitudinal study. Unpublished Master's Thesis, Univ. Chicago.

2. BALDWIN, A. L., KALHORN, J., and BREESE, F. H., 1949. The appraisal of parent behavior. *Psychol. Monogr.*, 63, No. 4, Whole No. 299.

3. BERNSTEIN, B., 1960. Aspects of language and learning in the genesis of the social process. *J. child Psychol. Psychiat.* (Great Britain), 1, 313–324.

4. BURT, C., 1958. The inheritance of mental ability. *Amer. Psychologist,* 13, 1–15.

5. DOLLARD, J., and MILLER, N. E., 1950. *Personality and Psychotherapy.* New York: McGraw-Hill.

6. ERICKSON, E. H., 1950. *Childhood and society.* New York: Norton.

7. FREUD, A., 1937. *The ego and mechanisms of defense.* London: Hogarth Press.

8. FREUD, S., 1933. *New introductory lectures on psychoanalysis.* New York: Garden City.

9. GESELL, A., 1945. *The embryology of behavior.* New York: Harper.

10. GUTHRIE, E. R., 1935. *The psychology of learning.* New York: Harper.

11. HAVIGHURST, R. J., 1953. *Human development and education.* New York: Longmans, Green.

12. HEBB, D. O., 1949. *The organization of behavior.* New York: Wiley.

13. HESS, E., 1959. Imprinting. *Science,* 130, 133–141.

14. HORNEY, K., 1936. *The neurotic personality of our time.* New York: Norton.

15. KIRK, S. A., 1958. *Early education of the mentally retarded.* Urbana: Univ. of Illinois.

16. LEE, E. S., 1951. Negro intelligence and selective migration: A Philadelphia test of the Klineberg hypothesis. *Am. sociol. Rev.,* 16, 227–233.

17. McCLELLAND, D. C., et al., 1951. *Personality.* New York: William Sloane Associates.

18. MOWRER, O. H., 1950. *Learning theory and personality dynamics.* New York: Ronald Press.

19. MURRAY, H., 1938. *Explorations in personality.* New York: Oxford Univ. Press.

20. NEWMAN, H. H., FREEMAN, F. N., and HOLZINGER, K. J., 1937. *Twins: A study of heredity and environment.* Chicago: Univ. of Chicago Press.

21. PAYNE, ARLENE, 1963. The selection and treatment of data for certain curriculum decision problems: A methodological study. Unpublished Ph.D. Dissertation, Univ. of Chicago.

22. PIAGET, J., 1932. *The moral judgment of the child.* New York: Harcourt, Brace.

23. SCHACHTEL, E. G., 1949. "On memory and childhood amnesia," in Mullahy, P. (Ed.), *A study of interpersonal relations.* New York: Hermitage Press.

24. SCOTT, J. P., and MARSTON, M., 1950. Critical periods affecting the development of normal and maladjustive behavior of puppies. *J. genet. Psychol.,* 77, 26–60.

25. SEARS, R. R., MACCOBY, E. E., and LEVIN, H., 1957. *Patterns of child rearing.* Evanston: Row, Peterson.

26. SULLIVAN, H. S., 1953. *The interpersonal theory of psychiatry.* New Haven: Norton.

27. TERMAN, L. M., and MERRILL, M. A., 1937. *Measuring intelligence.* New York: Houghton Mifflin.

Kurt Lang
Gladys Engel Lang

RESISTANCE TO SCHOOL DESEGREGATION: A CASE STUDY OF BACKLASH AMONG JEWS[1]

Every social movement towards major social reform is bound to generate some opposition, some counterreaction, from those who see their position adversely affected by the changes sought. No one was surprised, therefore, when whites in the South resisted the desegregation of public schools and public facilities. Nor was it entirely unexpected that some Northern white groups would seriously seek to obstruct Negro progress toward the attainment of full civil rights. What did occasion some surprise—and, in some circles, bewilderment—was the unexpectedly strong resistance among groups of whites who, by virtue of their

Reprinted from *Sociological Inquiry,* 35 (Winter 1965) by permission, 94–106. Copyright © 1965.

Mr. Lang is Chairman, Department of Sociology, State University of New York. His wife teaches at Queens College. The couple also authored *Collective Dynamics.*

[1] The authors gratefully acknowledge financial assistance from the American Jewish Congress, whose officers recognized early the significance of the opposition by Jews to school desegration and the need for research as well as for community action. Without this aid, the survey data could not have been collected. Queens College helped us to hire Richard Ofshe as a research assistant. We are also deeply indebted to Donald Gelfand, Michael Goldstein, and others who volunteered coding help and to other students, too numerous for listing, who undertook some of the rather difficult interviewing assignments.

past minority group status, were expected to be active in the struggle against intolerance and discrimination or who, at the very least, were counted upon not to oppose and resist legitimate Negro demands. It is among these groups, previously judged liberal and tolerant, that one must seek evidence of any counter-movement to the political and moral crusade for equal civil rights, a phenomenon popularly dubbed "backlash."

The resistance of population groups traditionally hostile to the Negro does not constitute, in the literal sense, a "backlash" phenomenon. That term applies rather to a broadening of the base of opposition among whites as a direct reaction to the gains and demands of the civil rights movement. Conflict has sharpened as an increasing number of whites, hitherto shielded by social status and residential location from direct involvement, have suddenly found themselves directly affected by desegregation measures. The stand people have to take in this situation goes beyond generalized expressions of sympathy with the victims of Birmingham bombers and of Mississippi lynchers; they have to stand up and be counted. Nowhere has this confrontation been more direct than where the public schools are concerned. In the large metropolitan cities of the North with their sizeable Negro (and Puerto Rican) slums, measures designed to relieve overcrowding in ghetto schools and to ameliorate racial imbalance in individual schools here and there have frequently touched off violent opposition. The number of such incidents, plus the call by some Negro leaders for nothing less than citywide school desegregation, have contributed to the coalescence of scattered and sporadic resistance into a countermovement of some significance.

The particular school desegregation controversy discussed here grew out of a proposal to pair two elementary schools, located some five city blocks or .24 miles apart, so that together they could serve their school populations as a single area. As in Princeton, which lent its name to such pairing plans, this one applied to two schools close to one another but serving two quite different neighborhoods. In 1963, according to official estimates,[2] about 87 per cent of the children in one school (P.S. 149Q) were white, while about 99.5 per cent in the other (P.S. 92Q) were Negro and Puerto Rican, mostly Negro. Junction Boulevard, a moderately busy thoroughfare, separates predominantly white Jackson Heights from predominantly Negro Corona, and until the late fifties— when an adjustment explicitly aimed at sending more Negro children from Corona to the "white" school was made in school zone boundaries— it also marked off one school population from the other.

[2] New York State Commissioner, Advisory Committee on Human Relations and Community Tensions, *Desegregating the Public Schools of New York City*, New York: New York Board of Education, May 12, 1964.

The initial proposal for the pairing came from a group of white parents with children in the local public school. Their suggestion followed the summer, 1963 issuance by Dr. James E. Allen, State Commissioner of Education, of a general policy directive to local school boards that they reduce "racial imbalance." It anticipated by nearly six months the New York City Board of Education's announcement of its own intentions for the school year 1964–5. Because the proposal helped pave the way for similar suggestions elsewhere, the area of Jackson Heights became one of the first testing grounds in the city which measured the strength of forces for and against steps in the direction of better "balance." Several leaders on both sides of the local controversy quickly rose to citywide leadership in the struggle as it spread throughout the City of New York.

The two authors of this paper, former residents in the area, have been engaged in systematic participant observation since September 1963, that is, from the time the existence of a local pairing proposal first became public knowledge. In November, 1963 we undertook to supplement these observations through intensive interviews with a systematic sample of the population nearest the "white" school, specifically in a four-block apartment cooperative where the "battle" mostly raged.[3] At that time, there had been no official commitment to any plan; yet almost all the residents in the area, whether or not they had children likely to be affected, felt strongly enough to take a definite stand on the proposal to pair the schools. In this paper we have limited ourselves to an analysis of this early resistance to the plan, based mainly on the interview data supplemented by such other observations as seem pertinent. Though the study concerns one single locality, an examination of the social characteristics and general attitudes that discriminate between protagonists and opponents should help to identify the social base on which much of the Northern resistance to school desegregation proposals rests.[4]

[3] Interviews averaging 40 minutes were obtained from respondents in 188 households, selected on a random systematic basis, from a list of all households in a four-block cooperative where roughly half the school population of the high-concentration white school resided, with a deliberate oversampling of large apartments to increase the proportion of respondents with children. Respondents were predesignated, and substitutions permitted in only very special circumstances. Callbacks, sometimes as many as six, produced a 70 per cent coverage. For many reasons—such as the character of the neighborhood and the circumstances of the controversy—we experienced unusual difficulty in obtaining completed interviews. Though a quota sample would evidently have produced a larger number of interviews, we are certain that it would have resulted also in a serious misestimate of the degree of support for the plan, and of the educational level of the population.

[4] The dynamics of attitude change in response to the controversy, the hardening of positions taken early in the controversy, and their possible erosion in the face of new experience, shall be taken up on the basis of data, to be collected, following the implementation of the pairing proposal.

THE PLAN AND ITS SETTING

The plan for pairing the schools was actually approved and put into effect with only minor modifications in September, 1964, just about a year after its proposal set off the neighborhood controversy. As finally worked out, all first and second graders in the high concentration white school were transferred to the "Negro" school, while third through sixth graders attending the "Negro" school were sent to the "white" school. Thus, one school building now serves all children in grades one and two, the other, all children in the third through sixth grades. Kindergarteners, as before, continue to attend the school nearer their home. A minimum of bussing has been required; only some two to three dozen children in the combined school zone as redrawn lived beyond the legally prescribed walking distance.

While this paper makes no attempt to evaluate the plan and its effects, it is nevertheless important to note that the proposal was not simply a plan to end racial imbalance in what was *de facto* a Negro school. Included in the package were provisions for upgrading the educational facilities in *both* schools. The "Negro" school, housed in an older building, was completely renovated before the plan went into effect. It had for some time been designated a "special service school" and as such received certain extra resources and personnel for which the "white" school had heretofore not qualified. For instance, classes of near 40 children (and sometimes more) had not been atypical of the "white" school. As a result of the pairing, average class size was reduced to 27 students, and the school obtained a number of very much needed teaching specialists.

Jackson Heights, where the previously white school was located, can be considered a middle class apartment house area, even though in 1960 one third of its population still lived in one and two-family dwellings. The population grew steadily from 1940 to 1960, many of the apartment houses having been built after World War II. Where not long ago lots stood vacant in the area surrounding the "white" school, modern six-story apartment houses now directly face Corona across Junction Boulevard with its smaller and mostly much older buildings. There Negroes have been steadily replacing whites, mostly of Italian and Eastern European stock, so that Corona, together with East Elmhurst to the North, now is the second largest enclave of Negroes in the Borough of Queens.

Yet, when indicators of social status other than race are considered, the discrepancies between the two populations in the immediately adjacent areas—where the controversy centered—are not as great as some might believe. Certainly Corona ranks lower on income, education, proportion employed in the so-called middle class occupations, etc., than does Jackson Heights. But it is hardly a lower class Negro area. Despite some very obvious contrasts in the physical characteristics of the two communities and disparities to the disadvantage of Negroes, the whites in the recently settled blocks nearest the Negro district are more nearly similar to their nonwhite neighbors than are the whites living in that part of Jackson Heights farther away. There is a fairly continuous decline in a variety of socio-economic indicators, based on census tracts, as one moves from the center of Jackson Heights toward the Negro area. For example, median years of schooling completed in the census tract containing the "white" school is 11.2; in the tract with the "Negro" school, it is 10.1. Given the imperfect overlap of tracts with school zones, inferences with regard to school populations are open to challenge. Still we mean to convey the idea that this is no "Gold Coast and the Slum" situation with the two adjacent communities worlds apart.[5]

Though a few nonwhite families have moved into Jackson Heights, there is little chance in the near future of a massive invasion by lower class Negroes. Occupancy, as measured by persons per room, is at present just about as dense in the white tracts as in the Negro tracts, where buildings are older and rents consequently lower. The four-block cooperative apartment development that borders on Junction Boulevard and surrounds the "white" school, together with other cooperatives in the area, constitutes a special barrier. Carrying charges in these apartments, completed in 1958 and 1959, are modest by New York City standards, but a cash purchase of stocks at a price beyond the reach of most Negroes is an additional requirement for occupancy. While the directing boards of the cooperatives directly control occupancy on the basis of the financial solvency of applicants and limit the number of persons occupying a given apartment, this power, as far as is known, has not been used deliberately to exclude nonwhites. A few Negroes (Negro-white married couples), Orientals, and Puerto Ricans live in the cooperative.

The white residents living near the school are a "minority group" population.[6] Nearly three quarters of the respondents in the survey identified themselves as Jewish, another fifth as Catholic. Though locally dominant, more Jews than not still considered themselves members of a minority group.

Most of the people in the area studied are part of the continuing

[5] That "equal status" contacts are a condition favorable to the reduction of intergroup tensions has been amply confirmed by empirical research.

[6] Strictly speaking, the generalizations based on the sample survey apply only to the population of the cooperative development. Still, half the white school population resided there, and it was the hub of the controversy.

"middle income" exodus from the center of the city outwards. Many (40 per cent) had moved in from deteriorating areas of Brooklyn and the Bronx; only ten per cent were prior residents of the surrounding neighborhood and just six per cent had come from outside New York City limits. The move into the cooperative development was generally an "upward" move in one or more of several senses—as a first "home" after marriage, as an investment to secure sufficient living space for a growing family, or as a refuge from "overrun" neighborhoods with their multiple problems.

These residents in the aggregate are best characterized as middle mass, not middle class, insofar as many are hardly secure in status nor solidly established economically, even though the income and ambition of most differentiate them clearly from the real lower classes. Of all adults in our sample[7] only two out of five said they had continued their schooling beyond high school. A fourth were college graduates, and it was primarily the latter who expressed openly their desire to be on their way up and out of the neighborhood into a more solidly middle class milieu. The fact that only 17 per cent of the heads of household were in the professional, technical, and managerial category (including five per cent, who were teachers) must be viewed in the light of the city's unusual occupational structure. Business and white-collar supervisory occupations, not in any sense managerial, together with semi-professional jobs, not protected by licensing, account for an additional 16 per cent. All of the 15 per cent who were self-employed in "business" owned small family-run establishments. The rest, excluding a few retired, were in sales, delivery, and a variety of skilled and semi-skilled blue-collar jobs, which, as 45 per cent of the total, made up the largest group. Finally, despite the high proportion with children, 40 per cent of all women held jobs, two thirds of these full time.

MINORITY GROUP IDENTIFICATION

Discussions of conflict and controversy over racial imbalance in the public schools of New York City cannot gloss over the fact that in many areas, such as this one, the white public school population is made up to a large degree of Jewish children. Catholics, in greater proportions than 20 or 30 years ago, are receiving their primary education in parochial schools, and white Protestants cluster in the suburbs and in the independent schools of the better residential areas. For some years now, the city's public schools have been officially closed on Jewish as well as

[7] The reader is reminded that the deliberate oversampling of large apartments inflated both occupational status and education, as well as the degree of support for the plan.

the traditional Christian holidays. To what extent, then, can one rely on what is essentially a confrontation between Negroes and Jews (with an assist from Catholics) on the presumedly liberal attitudes of Jews on ethnic and racial issues?

In this particular neighborhood, Jews expressed no greater readiness to accept the pairing proposal than did their Christian neighbors. Actually the proportion of Catholics favoring the plan (33 per cent) was slightly larger than among Jews (28 per cent). It is true that fewer of the Catholics interviewed had children going to the public school or had pre-school children whom they expected to enroll someday. But whether or not one's children were involved had no statistical relationship to the side of the issue which any person was likely to favor. This *did* make a difference, however, as to whether or not the person had done something specific to support or oppose the plan, such as joining an organization, giving money, or attending a meeting. In keeping with this, the 74 per cent of the sample that was Jewish made up 88 per cent of all the "activists" on both sides. Jews were more vocal *pro* and *con*.

Racial and ethnic attitudes were gauged by a series of questions, essentially a social distance scale, where each respondent was asked whether he "would mind" being in certain types of situations involving either members of another religion or Negroes. The items, adapted from the battery employed by Louis Harris on a national sample of whites,[8] were: (1) giving preferential treatment in job opportunities to Negroes; (2) having your own teenager date a Negro; (3) having a close friend or relative marry a Negro; (4) living in a neighborhood where *a good many* of your neighbors are Negroes; (5) sitting in a restaurant where *the majority* are Negroes; (6) having your child go to a school where *about half* are Negroes. Items one, two, four and six were duplicated to apply to contact between Jews and non-Jews, with slight variations in the wording to take account of whether the respondent was Jewish or not.

An index indicating group acceptance of "outsiders" was constructed from responses to these hypothetical situations. The possible range is from 0 to 1, with 0 designating a condition where nobody "minds" contact in any of the situations and 1 a condition where all in the group "mind" every one of the situations cited.[9] Though it is quite probable that these responses underestimate the actual degree of avoidance between groups, the index seems useful for group comparisons (see Table 1).

[8] William Brink and Louis Harris, *The Negro Revolution in America*, New York: Simon and Schuster, 1964.

[9] The formula for the index is a simple one: $\frac{\Sigma \text{Rpos}}{\text{I} \times \text{N}}$ where Rpos = a response to the effect that the person "minded;" I = number of items (6 concerning Negroes, 4 concerning Jews or non-Jews), and N = number of respondents.

Judged by this index, Jews indeed turn out to "mind" contact with Negroes less than do non-Jews. But a difference of .023 is not at all meaningful, especially when compared to the difference of .233 that separates proponents and opponents of the plan. Despite their many public protestations that the plan was being rejected solely because it was educationally unsound, opposition seems to have been based on, or at least related to, underlying attitudes concerning contact with out-groups. Measured by these stated attitudes, Jews turned out to be rather less tolerant of their Christian neighbors than the latter were of Jews. Yet, one must assume that non-Jews in this predominantly Jewish apartment

TABLE 1. *"Social Distance" Index Towards Members of Other Races and Religions*

RESPONDENT	OTHER RACES INDEX VALUE	OTHER RELIGIONS INDEX VALUE
Pro-Pairing	.296	.162
Anti-Pairing	.529	.268
Jews	.459	.295
Non-Jews	.482	.106

house development were self-selected with regard to their sentiments about close contact with Jews. Indeed, this self-proclaimed tolerance among a predominantly Catholic population extended even to "not minding" close friends and relatives intermarrying.

What seems most telling is that the responses signifying a rejection by Jews of non-Jews, like their rejection of Negroes, are significantly associated with being against the pairing plan. The inference to be drawn is that the opposition by Jews represents a form of ethnocentrism, directed not solely against Negroes but reflecting, in part, a pro-ghetto outlook. The Jewish ingroupishness is dramatically expressed by the woman who phoned the local city councilman, after he had publicly endorsed the pairing, to scold him: "How could you, Mr. Councilman, do this to us, a nice Jewish boy like you?"

Minority groups living in a hostile environment find some measure of protection by sticking to "their own kind." It stands to reason that even where an individual lacks the ghetto experience there may have been ample opportunity for attitudes generated in the ghetto to have been communicated down to him by his elders. Hostility and distrust between Negroes and Jews is far from novel; one is not surprised to find opposition to the pairing proposal greatest among those who moved into the neighborhood from the now overrun Jewish sections of the Bronx and Brooklyn. Among those *against* the plan, the proportion coming from these two boroughs was nearly twice as great as among those *for* the plan. Clearly the nearness of the Negro community in Corona and the dilution of racial homogeneity in the local school was to many a potential threat.

SOCIOECONOMIC STATUS

Socioeconomic status had a considerably greater influence on individual attitudes towards the pairing proposal than did ethnic identification. Larger proportions of managerial, professional, semi-professionals, and small business owners were found among those who favored the proposal than among those opposed. Yet an even more sensitive indicator of attitude is educational level (Table 2). Most likely

TABLE 2. *Attitude on Pairing by Education*

	COLLEGE GRAD. %	SOME COLLEGE %	H. S. GRAD. %	LESS THAN H. S. GRAD. %	TOTAL %
All Respondents					
Pro-Pairing	51	32	26	20	32
Anti-Pairing	49	68	74	80	68
N = 171	100	100	100	100	100
Female Respondents and Wives of Male Respondents					
Pro-Pairing	57	35	28	13	32
Anti-Pairing	43	65	72	87	68
N = 168	100	100	100	100	100
Activists					
Pro-Pairing	61	35	29	0	38
Anti-Pairing	39	65	71	100	62
N = 74	100	100	100	100	100

to oppose the plan were those who failed to complete high school and most likely to support it were the college graduates. Note, however, that only the barest majority of college graduates endorsed the proposal.[10]

[10] The relationship between education and increase in tolerance has been documented in such studies as: Melvin Tumin, *Desegregation; Resistance and Readiness*, Princeton, New Jersey: Princeton University Press, 1958; Herbert H. Hyman and Paul B. Sheatsley, "Attitudes Towards Desegregation," *Scientific American*, 195 (December, 1956), pp. 35–39. Some doubt has been thrown on the clarity of this association by Herbert Stember, *Education and Attitude Change*, New York: Institute of Human Relations Press, 1961.

Since the issue concerns the welfare of children, it is not altogether unexpected to find that the educational achievement of wives in the households (even where males were respondents) was even more closely associated with the stand taken. Finally, the contrast between the educational level of the two groups was most marked where the active participants in the controversy are concerned. Half the activists on the "pro" side were college graduates. This alone made them somewhat unrepresentative of the residents in the area. In this respect, the activists on the "anti" side were much closer to being a cross section of the community. It is characteristic that two thirds of the women working actively against the proposal had no schooling beyond high school.

Respondents who favored the plan revealed in a variety of ways greater sensitivity to the *quality* of education their children were receiving. A larger number had been active in the local Parents Association of the school and a larger number were themselves enrolled in courses and continuing their own education. The two groups exhibit differences in their current style of life and in the ambitions most of the parents harbor for their children. Parents on both sides were interested in "advancement" and "education," but whereas the interest of most pairing supporters was sustained and continuous, that of the opposed was more likely to focus on problems and specific dissatisfactions or difficulties their children were encountering in the school, with teachers, or with other children. The difference in orientation can perhaps be illustrated by the typical educational aspirations of parents in the two opposing factions. Most respondents said they intended to send their children to college. Asked where they would send them, most of those opposed to the plan indicated their children would go to a city college (if eligible) because they were "free" and they could live at home. Those in favor were more likely to name specific colleges where they "hoped" their children might be accepted or, if they named one of the city colleges, said their children could get a good education there.

These orientations are generally linked to the occupational status of parents and to the education they themself had received. In this respect socioeconomic status seems to operate as a critical determinant of the stand taken on the pairing proposal. The image of the white liberal—Jewish or not—torn between liberal "instincts" and an overriding concern for the educational welfare of his own child, who ultimately comes to oppose the drive toward school desegregation when the issue becomes salient, simply does not fit this situation. The "backlash," for the most part, does not represent a selfish resolution of a moral dilemma. The more "liberal," the more sensitive to the ingredients that enter into a good educational milieu, the more likely was the respondent to favor this particular proposal.

The above data suggest a simple conclusion: class was more important than ethnicity in determining the likelihood that a person was on one side or the other of this school desegregation controversy. They lend no support to the proposition that Jews, just because they are Jews, will necessarily behave differently from other whites. On the contrary, Jews frequently divide along class lines, very much as other groups do.

CLASS AND MINORITY GROUP STATUS

The attitudes of a minority formed in response to past experiences are always mediated through the perspectives of current social position and often profoundly modified as a result. Hence, ingroup solidarity assumes a new and different meaning when it is turned against an outgroup clearly lower in prestige and inferior in economic standing. Whether or not and in what way a person carried the traditional attitude to the present was, to a large degree, a function of his orientation to the neighborhood, which was influenced in turn by the characteristic pattern of residential and social mobility associated with occupational status and education.

For many of the Jews against the plan, the neighborhood was in certain respects an upgraded version of the familiarly comfortable but shabby and rundown ghetto from which they had escaped. Many respondents stressed the fact that they (and others) had worked hard to get here; it was a good neighborhood and they wanted nothing to spoil it. Though surrounded by a mass of brick buildings with playgrounds completely paved and only the smallest patches of greenery in sitting areas, respondents frequently spoke about the neighborhood as if it were a part of suburbia. The low carrying charges, the modest down payment, and the soundness of the investment were almost unanimously given by the "antis" as the reason for moving into and liking the cooperative. But primary ties also exerted an attraction. Many more of those opposed to the plan than those for it had either friends or relatives (or both) living within the immediate vicinity *before* they moved in, and at the time of the interviewing more said their "three closest friends" all resided within the four-block area of the cooperative. They were more involved in informal visiting with their neighbors and they had participated more frequently in a variety of social affairs under the formal sponsorship of the cooperative. They were, in short, neighborhood-oriented localities.

Thus, insisting that they were not "prejudiced," opponents repeatedly proclaimed their welcome of any Negro who enrolled "naturally" as a *bona fide* resident within the school zone as redrawn before the pairing. "If they want to go to *our* school, let them move into our neighborhood" came to be a familiar cat call at turbulent meetings as soon as any speaker rose to support the plan. But the queries of our interviewers revealed that the number who "minded living in a neighborhood where *a good many* of your neighbors" were Negroes was actually more than twice as great as those who "minded having their child go to a school where *about half* the children were Negroes" (52 per cent compared with 24 per cent). Negroes in small numbers could evidently be assimilated; in large numbers they are a threat to the character of the neighborhood.

Finally, there is the issue of the "neighborhood school," a matter of very real concern. Any investment in housing within a given locality is, for those with children, in large part, however indirectly, an investment in the schools that serve the area. The public school in socially homogeneous neighborhoods is in a very real sense a substitute for private schooling. More than ever before, the aspirations and hopes of urban masses—just as those in suburban areas—rest on the adequacy of the schooling they receive. Far from being indifferent, the residents in this area are very concerned about the progress their children make through the grades, about possibilities for acceleration, about admission to special programs and to college, as partial insurance against future insecurity. Among this highly urbanized population, schooling is viewed as a "free" social service that is valued, not so much for its content as for its marketability. Education is a necessity if children are to retain the same relative position as their parents, but some of the magic appeal education once had for ghetto children seems to be lost as a consequence.

Supporters of the pairing, being better educated, were on the whole more socially mobile. Asked directly and early in the interview (before its main purpose had become apparent) about their plans for moving out of the neighborhood, more supporters than opponents said that for a variety of reasons (none of which had anything to do with the pairing of the schools) they intended to move out into a larger home, a better neighborhood, and so forth. They felt much less tied to the particular neighborhood and expressed much less satisfaction with their cooperative living arrangements. Despite their lower participation in the formally sponsored cooperative activities, this group, paradoxically, more frequently cited "living in a cooperative" as one of the reasons for moving into the development in the first place. Their primary group contacts were more apt to extend beyond the immediate neighborhood and they appeared much more selective with regard to the neighbors with whom they chose to be friendly. In fact, general disappointment with the people in the area is a topic they frequently discuss among themselves; their awareness of social differences with their neighbors has been sharpened by the controversy and operates as a stimulus of the desire to move out. Though any residential exodus on their part is likely to be cited as proof of hypocrisy, there is no question that being socially more mobile they were psychologically on their way up and out of the neighborhood some time before the proposal to pair the schools was initiated.

The greater cosmopolitanism of the supporters expressed itself in still another way, namely on the matter of minority group identification. As far as the "practice" of Judaism is concerned, a larger proportion of those against the plan, according to their own claim, "belong to or regularly attended" a synagogue. In spite of this, it is the "pros," though less likely to be practicing Jews, who, on being asked whether they considered themselves members of a minority group, were more likely to say "yes." Again, their response is not in terms of the immediate neighborhood, where Jews are dominant, but in terms of the society at large, where they make their way as individuals, and thus continue to be aware of the incapacities of minority group status.

The position of the masses of Jews has certainly undergone a drastic change over the past forty years: Jewish opposition to this (or any other) desegregation proposal might be attributed simply to their rise in the status system of ethnic groups. How, then, can we account for the fact that the individuals enjoying the higher socioeconomic status were less opposed to the pairing plan? The point here is the distinction between *structural mobility*, the result of general prosperity and techno-logical advance that upgrades whole groups, and *individual social mobility*, which requires that an individual free himself from his former group affiliations and leave them behind. The two types of mobility differ in their socialpsychological import. Structural mobility is compatible with parochialism, but individual social mobility provides a strong impetus toward cosmopolitanism. This mentality facilitates a loosening of particular ethnic identifications and tends to transform them into a more universalistic concern with minority group status as such. Even where Jewish affiliations are retained, as is frequently the case, their content is reinterpreted and broadened as a result.

A last point to be brought out is the difference between the attitudes of the groups toward education. Until voted out of office over the issue of school pairing, the pro-group had dominated the Parents Association and provided the school with most of its community support. When they spoke of the "quality" of education, they were much less inclined than their opponents to refer to grade achievement, promotions, and getting into special progress programs or college. Rather, the definition of quality centered on the skills and values their children were acquiring.[11] They felt some confidence that they knew what type of

---

[11] The distinction here is in some way akin to that made by Bernard C. Rosen between achievement-motivation and achievement-oriented values. (Cf. "The Achievement Syndrome: A Psycho-Cultural Dimension of Social Stratification," *American Sociological Review*, 22 [February 1957], pp. 67–73, for a discussion of their relationship to social mobility).

education their children should have, and were loath, as a result, to entrust this entirely to school officials and teachers. To a much greater degree, they felt that education had not only an instrumental value for the achievement of material advantage but also a terminal value that assured entry into the world of intellect and culture. Still, the high valuation placed on learning by these second generation Jewish parents is essentially that of the middle class; education is not the magic key to the kingdom sought by the children of immigrant parents before them.

Housing

Loren Miller
THE PROTEST AGAINST
HOUSING SEGREGATION

The Negro take-over of the centers of our great cities, and many of our smaller ones, was not foreseen by those who devised the patterns of urban residential segregation that are commonplace in the North and in the South. Their purpose was to isolate the Negro and quarantine him in the least desirable sections of those cities. That purpose failed for two reasons. The Negro population grew too rapidly for containment, and the legal props on which the containment policy depended were invalidated through ingenious use of constitutional safeguards against racial discrimination. American cities now present the spectacle of Black Belts slashing across their hearts surrounded by lily-white, or nearly lily-white, suburban developments. Comparative census statistics tell the story.

The 1960 census lists the total population of the nation's ten largest cities as 21,751,334 and their combined Negro population as 4,665,505, some 27.4 per cent of the total. Washington, D.C. is 52 per cent

Reprinted from *The Annals of the American Academy of Political and Social Science* (January, 1965) by permission.

Mr. Miller, a California judge, has been an NAACP official and is author of *The Petitioners: The Story of the Supreme Court of the United States and the Negro*.

Negro-populated; Los Angeles, 16 per cent, for example. Standard metropolitan areas lying outside those ten largest cities had a combined population of 18,271,039, of which only 809,134 were Negroes, a substantial number of whom lived in Negro sections of satellite cities and towns. The total population growth for those cities from 1930 to 1960 was 3,480,295; the Negro increase was 3,222,347. Central city growth was Negro growth. The standard metropolitan areas for those same cities had a total gain of 4,174,537 from 1930 to 1960 and a Negro increase of 146,540. Whites outgained Negroes in those suburban areas by some thirty to one.[1]

The popular version is that the existence and growth of the Negro ghetto are the results of exercise of racial prejudices of individuals, and that Black Belts can be disestablished only if we can induce a change in the hearts and minds of men. There is more to it than that—much more. Residential segregation as we know it today is the end-product of more than half a century of intensive, and aggressive, governmental sanction and support of private segregatory devices.[2] Southern and Border cities first tried to segregate Negro residents by zoning ordinances, but the United States Supreme Court invalidated such ordinances in 1917.[3] The decision came after a decade of enforcement, and was followed by informal, but effectual and unconstitutional enforcement for many years. Birmingham, for example, enforced its ordinance until about 1950.[4]

Meanwhile, housing developers and individuals had turned to the racial restrictive covenant, an agreement imposed by the subdivider or by neighborhood subscription interdicting Negro ownership or occupancy in a defined community. Courts of equity would then issue injunctions ousting the Negro who bought or rented real property in violation of the agreements.[5] Such enforcement began in 1915, and by 1948 the courts of last resort in nineteen states and the District of Columbia had directly approved the racial restrictive covenant as a constitutional method of enforcing residential segregation.[6] The Supreme Court gave them its left-handed approval in 1926,[7] but had a change of heart in 1948 and determined that judicial enforcement of covenants was

---

[1] Boundaries of standard metropolitan areas are changed from time to time. I have not weighted figures for any changes, but where boundaries have remained constant from 1930 to 1960, there is no significant variance in the figures.

[2] John Denton (ed.), *Race and Property* (Berkeley, Calif.: Diablo Press, 1964), pp. 58 ff.

[3] *Buchanan* v. *Worley*, 245 U.S. 60 (1917).

[4] *Birmingham* v. *Monk*, 185 Fed. 2d 859 (1951).

[5] McGovney, *Racial Residential Segregation by State Enforcement*, 33 Cal. Law Review 5 (1947).

[6] *Ibid.*, Note 5.

[7] *Corrigan* v. *Buckley*, 271 U.S. 323 (1926).

prohibited by the Fourteenth Amendment.[8] Three decades of *unconstitutional* enforcement after and during World Wars I and II when Negro in-migration was at its height laid the foundation for today's thriving Black Belts. The 1948 decision meant that these Black Belts could expand in the centers of the cities. They did so with great rapidity.

The federal government got into housing in the early 1930's and promptly lined up on the side of racial segregation. The first low-rent public housing was allocated on a separate-but-equal basis with "Negro" projects built in Negro communities. Later, the Public Housing Agency decided to let local housing authorities follow their own desires, which meant segregation in all but a few cities. Today, 80 per cent of public housing is still segregated. The Federal Housing Administration, the popular FHA, went further after its birth in 1934: it required insertion of racial restrictive covenants as a condition of mortgage insurance and furnished builders a model agreement. It followed that policy until 1947. Veterans Administration (VA) trailed along with FHA policies which had changed slightly when it entered the housing picture.[9]

In 1949 FHA and VA announced that they would not insure or guarantee loans for housing construction on land upon which racial restrictive covenants were imposed after February 15, 1950. The change was more apparent than real because both FHA and VA continued to insure loans when they knew that the subdivider or builder would exclude Negroes from home purchases or rentals, a policy that was followed until the fall of 1962. The all-white suburbs, some of them great cities in themselves, that ring our cities are eloquent witnesses to the efficacy of governmental sanction and support of exclusionary policies. In its initial stages, urban redevelopment was used as a device to clear out Negro slums and replace them with housing developments restricted to white occupancy. Slum clearance, ran a wry Negro joke, was Negro clearance.

Federal policies did not undergo a fundamental change—to be commented upon later—until 1962. Between 1930 and 1960, more than three million Negroes had poured into our ten largest cities, and hundreds of thousands into lesser cities, and had been segregated by court decrees until 1948, and by the working of federal housing policies and practices during the entire period.

Everybody concedes that urban residential segregation, and its rapid growth, has bred problems for Negroes. The ghetto has become what the social workers and sociologists, with their love of labels, call a trap-ghetto. One of the most persistent bits of folklore is that a particular section of a city *belongs* to the ethnic or national group that inhabits it.

[8] *Shelly* v. *Kraemer*, 334 U.S. 1 (1948).
[9] Davis McEntire, *Residence and Race* (Berkeley, Calif.: University of California Press, 1960), pp. 292–293.

That set of folk beliefs has a language of its own, bristling with military terminology. Negroes are said to "invade" or "infiltrate" a "Polish" community or another "white" community when one of their number finds residence there. Whites are stereotyped as standing heroic guard to repulse black invaders "busting blocks" and trampling on property values. The "Would-You-Want-One-To-Move-Next-Door-To-You?" inquiry is the Northern equivalent of the Southern "Would-You-Want-Your-Sister-To-Marry-One?" squelch. The usual answer is the same: a profane negative.

The trapped Negro home-buyer or tenant, who can purchase cigarettes, Cadillacs, or pornographic literature in open competition, must buy shelter in a protected seller's market and, of course, must pay a premium price for shoddy merchandise. Schools, parks, playgrounds, Boy Scout troops, political clubs, Parent-Teacher Associations, or churches, to furnish an abbreviated list, take on the color, or lack of it, of the communities in which they function. Separate institutionalism thrives in defiance of laws, Supreme Court decrees, or good will.

For obvious reasons, the Negro spends a great deal of time and protest beating against the Berlin walls that hem him in. Fair housing laws and executive decrees that interdict racial discrimination in the sale and rental of real property muster almost unanimous support from Negroes.

On the other hand, the average white urban dweller is either disinterested in or hostile to the Negro's efforts to break down the pattern of residential segregation. More often than not, the white American regards himself as having a stake in keeping the Negro in his place. "Why don't *they* stay in their own section of the city?" or "Why do *they* want to move into *our* neighborhood?" is the puzzled question. The white person who is committed to opposition to residential segregation and to support of fair housing laws or executive decrees is looked upon as a modern-day Abolitionist, a do-gooder to be tolerated but never taken too seriously. There is little appreciation for the fact that the Negro trap-ghetto and the white suburb have also trapped the American city. Toledo, Ohio, Tacoma, Washington and Berkeley, California have all repealed fair housing ordinances by popular vote. California not only invalidated its fair housing law but forbade all future fair housing legislation by the state and by its cities by a two-to-one vote.

As Negro population grows, the Black Belt nibbles or gulps its way through the heart of the city, in response to the slowdown or rapid increase of Negroes. Through a law of its own, the Black Belt never expands as rapidly as the demand for housing for Negroes grows; it is constantly overcrowded and just as constantly expanding. Overcrowding means overuse of available dwellings and a constant decay attendant on that overuse. In many instances, municipal authorities try to cope with the problem through construction of publicly owned, low-rent housing in the areas of Negro occupancy, but such a solution only compounds the essential problem. It concentrates more Negroes in the heart of the city and anchors the ghetto. Meanwhile, those displaced during construction find shelter at the edge of, and expand, the Black Belt. Some of them will ultimately flow back into the newly constructed public housing, but newcomers will take over the dwellings they vacate.

Years of overcrowding and overuse have created a crying need for urban renewal and urban redevelopment in almost every Black Belt in the nation. As close-in residential areas, Negro ghettos are not only in need of rehabilitation, but their locations have become desirable as living space for those who have tired of suburban living and who now want to return to closer proximity to their places of employment. But urban renewal and urban redevelopment call for wholesale displacement during the construction period. All too often, the city cannot cope with the displacement problem because of the racially exclusionary policies and practices of suburban communities. The Negro community is hostile to urban redevelopment out of the sad experience that it simply means a shifting of Negroes from one slum to another. City fathers, caught between the upper millstone of white suburban hostility to the residence of displaced Negroes and the nether millstone of Negro resistance, can do nothing while the heart of the city decays at an accelerated pace. Police, crime, health, and juvenile delinquency problems are compounded. Property values decline. The tax base contracts. Land cannot be put to its highest and best use. The white persons who are the fiercest proponents of residential segregation have an unperceived but very real stake in the elimination of residential segregation.

Just as the Black Belt clogs plans for urban renewal and redevelopment and hastens decay in the heart of the city, it also often prevents construction of high-speed highways or land use for civic projects such as convention halls and the like. The reason is the same: there is no place to locate the Negro population that must be displaced for such projects. Again, white supporters of residential segregation pay through the nose for the luxury of their prejudices.

Ironically, but understandably enough, the Negro is blamed for standing in the way of his city's progress. The white urban dweller sees readily enough that if the Negro were not anchored in the heart of the city, urban renewal, urban redevelopment, highway construction, and plans for the city beautiful could proceed in a much more rapid and orderly fashion. He can also see that areas of Negro residence have become desirable for close-in living. These perceptions do not move him to support fair housing laws and executive decrees or to plump for a dispersal of the Negro population. They only exacerbate his prejudices.

The Black Belt creates distrust and ill-will on the part of white city dwellers on still another plane. The Negro knows, if nobody else does, that the separate schools which his children must attend under the neighborhood plan are as unequal as statutory separate schools. They are often overcrowded. But when he looks around for a solution through drawing of new boundary lines or transporting Negro children out of the Black Belt to underused schools, a storm of opposition blows up, sometimes from the very liberals who are quite willing to support fair employment or equal accommodation legislation. The Negro is blamed because his children are backward—partially because of forced attendance at unequal schools; his insistence that they attend better schools meets condemnation. And when Negro rebellion against police maltreatment, disproportionate unemployment, and other ghetto ills finally breaks out in unfortunate, but understandable, riots and consequent looting in the Black Belt, the white urban resident is more apt than not to congratulate himself, and his neighbors, for having quarantined Negroes in the ghetto. He thanks God that they are not dispersed throughout the city where their depredations might strike him and his family.

Negro protest against residential segregation must reckon with these know-nothing attitudes. Out of long experience, Negroes have learned that voluntary efforts to change housing patterns are ineffective, after half a century of governmental sanction and support of residential segregation. They have turned to law, just as opponents of child labor, proponents of wage and hour legislation for women, and labor unions had to turn to legislation for redress of their grievances. One legal instrument is the fair housing law which forbids discrimination in the sale and rental of real property. Such laws are in effect in a score of states. Half of them interdict discrimination in all housing while the others reach housing constructed under various state and federal programs, including housing built under FHA or VA mortgage loan insurance or guarantees.

Housing discrimination became an issue in the 1960 presidential campaign, and John F. Kennedy promised to end it in all federal agencies with a stroke of the pen. He did not stroke the pen until November 20, 1962, and then he stroked it with a light touch.[10] His executive order forbade discrimination in the sale or rental of housing—and related facilities—owned or operated by the federal government or "provided in whole or in part with the aid of loans, advances, grants or contributions" made after that date. The major defect of the Order is that it falls so far short of federal possibilities. The nation's banks and savings and loan associations, commanding assets of some $400 billion, are subject to control and regulation as members of the federal banking system. They represent the major source of home financing, but the only

[10] Executive Order 11603, 27 Fed. Register 11527.

restraint put on their lending policies proscribes discrimination when they engage in FHA or VA transactions. They remain free to discriminate in conventional loans or to finance discriminatory builders. The result is that only about 25 per cent of the new housing market is covered by the Order.

The presidential Order is premised on the belief that governmental abstention from direct participation in discriminatory practices of the housing market, combined with an active campaign to encourage builders and developers to abandon those practices, meets today's needs. Negroes think much more is required. Ghettos were created by governmental action in catering to popular prejudice through a compound of judicial action, direct sanction, and approval and use of credit devices to pamper and stimulate a demand for, and enforce racial restrictions on the use of, urban land during that critical half-century when Negro in-migration was at floodtide. The Black Belts are here now; they cannot be disestablished through means that would have prevented their establishment and growth.

State fair housing laws are very important, but the South is not going to enact them, and there is a rising tide of resistance in the North. Voluntary fair housing councils have sprung up in and around every large city and do effective jobs in agitating for and implementing nondiscriminatory laws and decrees, but are impotent in the absence of legal safeguards. As the Negro sees it, the federal government must take the lead if anything effective is to be done in respect to halting the growth of Black Belts. He believes, correctly, that governmental involvement in housing will increase and that, as it increases, what government does will become increasingly crucial in determining occupancy patterns. Therefore, he reasons, the federal government must do more than abstain from aiding discrimination. It must devise affirmative methods of integration. He hopes government will become as vigilant and decisive on his side as it was in assisting residential segregation for almost thirty years.

An affirmative policy would comprehend a quick expansion of the presidential Order to cover *all* housing constructed through loans by banks and lending institutions subject to federal control and supervision. Urban renewal and urban redevelopment plans would be approved only when they contain built-in assurances that they will not compound residential segregation and, where possible, will further integration. The Housing and Home Finance Agency would require builders and developers to seek out and attract Negroes by posting proper notices of nondiscrimination as a condition of a loan from an affected lending institution, just as employers with government contracts are required to post notices that they are "equal opportunity" employers. The Agency itself would use its facilities to keep the public constantly advised that all housing constructed under loans from the affected lending institutions is open to purchase and rental without discrimination. Plans would be devised by the Agency to encourage and utilize voluntary fair housing groups and councils. In sum, the federal housing agencies would shift emphasis from their present role as mere policing agencies to undertaking leadership for nondiscrimination in housing and related industry. This is a tall order which will arouse opposition, but the need is great. The problem at hand cannot be dealt with effectively by official timidity or pious good wishes.

Last summer's outbreaks in Harlem and other ghettos are warning signals. Housing reforms, no matter how drastic, will not still all Negro discontent, nor will they lead to a quick halt of the expansion of our central city Black Belts. But a beginning must be made, and a beginning of the kind described will help dispel the mood of frustration and despair that lies back of the discontent now boiling over into riots and disturbances. Our central cities are becoming Negro cities spawning segregation in public facilities and turning political campaigns into racial contests. They are pregnant with the promise of ever-increasing and ever more bitter conflict. Government must, of course, quell disorder and conflict as is so often and so insistently urged. It is even more important to isolate and remove the causes of disorder and conflict. Residential segregation in the American city is one of the prime causes. Government which did its shameful, and successful, best to stimulate and effectuate that segregation must find ways of undoing that monumental wrong.

Nathan Glazer
Daniel Patrick Moynihan

HOUSING AND NEIGHBORHOOD: PROBLEMS IN INTEGRATION

The greatest gap by far between the conditions of life of New York's population in general and the specific part of it that is Negro is to

Reprinted from *Beyond the Melting Pot* by Nathan Glazer and Daniel Patrick Moynihan (Cambridge, Mass.: The M.I.T. Press, 1963) by permission. Copyright © 1963 by The Massachusetts Institute of Technology and the President and Fellows of Harvard College.

Mr. Glazer is Professor of Sociology, University of California, Berkeley. Mr. Moynihan, former Assistant Secretary of Labor, has been a fellow at Wesleyan University's Center for Advanced Studies.

be found in housing. Here is the greatest and most important remaining area of discrimination—important in its extent, its real consequences, and its social and psychological impact.

The Negro ghetto in New York City has not dissolved, either in Manhattan nor in the other boroughs, for the poor or the well-to-do.[1] The ghetto is not surrounded by a sharp line, and there is less sense of boundaries in New York than there is in many other cities. But in each of the four main boroughs there is a single concentrated area of Negro settlement, shading off at the edges to mixed areas, which tend with the increase in Negro population to become as concentratedly Negro as the centers. If one looks at a map of New York City on which the places of residence of the Negro population have been spotted, one will find many areas with small percentages of Negroes, and it may look as if the Negro population is spreading evenly through the city, is being "integrated." But a closer examination will reveal that these small outlying areas of Negro population are generally areas with public housing projects, and the Negro population is there because the housing projects are there. The projects in the outlying boroughs are partly Negro islands in a white sea.

There are laws forbidding discrimination in renting and selling housing, just as there is a law forbidding discrimination in employment. The city and state laws have steadily increased their coverage to the point where all housing but rooms or apartments in one's own home, and units in two-family homes in which one is occupied by the owner, must be made available without discrimination on account of race, religion, or national origin. Ninety-five per cent of city housing is now covered by the law. But the law forbidding discrimination in housing is much less effective than the law forbidding discrimination in employment. It is weaker, and provides no specific penalties, though if a landlord remains adamant, the city can bring him into court.

But the main reason the law against discrimination in housing can do less to change this situation than the law against discrimination in employment is that apartments are not controlled by big bureaucratic organizations. The big projects can be prevented from discriminating by law. But most apartments are in existing houses owned by small landlords. Long before the complaint can possibly be acted on, the apartment is gone. There is also little danger in a landlord practicing evasive action. It is fair to say that this is a law to which the run-of-the-mill landlords have responded with massive evasion. It takes elaborate measures really to get an apartment the way the law is now written. One needs a respectable-looking white friend to find out first that the apartment is available; a Negro who really wants it and is ready to take it then asks for it and is told it is not available; a second white is then required in order that he may be told that the apartment is still available, so as to get a sure-fire case; then direct confrontation plus rapid action in reporting all the details to the City Commission on Human Rights* is required. At this point, the landlord will often succumb. The Committee on Racial Equality (CORE) as well as Reform Democratic clubs and other organizations have supplied the whites for this sandwiching technique, and the elaborate advance planning and chance for immediate gratification have supplied perhaps a more satisfying activity to CORE than picketing local branches of Woolworth's. (The white pickets were generally in the majority, and were unhappy at the Negroes going past them.)

Perhaps even more significant in reducing the effectiveness of the law than landlord resistance is the perpetual housing shortage in New York City. This "temporary" situation is now as permanent as anything in life ever is. Someone beginning school in New York City during the Second World War may now be married and having children in a housing market that has the same "temporary" shortage that it had at the end of the war. Even in the absence of discrimination, the low-income tenant would find it very hard to find cheap housing when it is being demolished faster than it is being built. The housing shortage means that we deal with a situation of "discrimination for" as well as "discrimination against." Just as good jobs are reserved for friends, relatives, and insiders, so are good apartments. Indeed, the better apartments in New York descend through a chain of relatives and friends, year after year, decade after decade. The most valuable of these valuable commodities are of course the rent-controlled apartments. Rent-controlled apartments mean, as a matter of fact, discrimination against everyone who has come into the city since 1943. Even *without* any discrimination on the ground of color, Negroes (and in larger measure Puerto Ricans) would be getting a poor share of the housing market, and paying more for it, because they are in larger measure latecomers.

But the law is not only interested in improving the housing available to Negroes, it is also interested in breaking down the pattern of segregation in housing. And here it is hard for the law to be very effective, whether in conditions of housing shortage or housing plenty. It is again instructive to compare housing with jobs. The breakthrough into an area of employment *does* mean a racially mixed working force; the breakthrough into an area of white housing has up to now generally meant a period of transition ending with the extension of the all-Negro and mostly Negro neighborhood. It has not meant, the objective that so many feel is desirable and that seems so unattainable, a stable, racially mixed area.

* Formerly the Commission of Intergroup Relations. The name was changed in 1962.

This pattern of white withdrawal or flight before incoming
Negroes is found everywhere in the nation. It is perhaps mildest in New
York City, for in Manhattan, if not in the other boroughs, people act as
they do nowhere in the nation. Manhattan is unique because the struggle
for space is so intense, and so many people want to live there, that the
flight of some white elements means their immediate replacement by
other white elements. In Manhattan, therefore, one does find mixed areas
of whites, Puerto Ricans, and Negroes, and it is likely the island will
become even more mixed in the future. But one of the reasons that
people live so closely together there is because they can have so little to
do with each other. Manhattan has few communities to protect, for here a
variety of "communities" as well as many people who are connected to
none share the very same ground. One element goes to a church, a second
to a synagogue, a third to neither. One patronizes one kind of store,
another a store with a somewhat different line of similar goods, or a
different price range, located right next door to the first. One group sends
its children to public school, another to parochial school, another to
private school, and a fourth, surprisingly large, has no children at all—
which, again, is one of the reasons they are willing to live so close to
Negroes and Puerto Ricans. If the groups do not share the same
apartment houses, they do share the same blocks, parks, shopping streets.
But they are willing to share as much as this, and be as close as this,
because they really share so little. These are important considerations,
and the reason why it is unrealistic to compare Manhattan with the other
boroughs, or the rest of the metropolitan area. These areas outside
Manhattan are, to a much larger extent than Manhattan, communities,
and when a community feels threatened by what it feels is an alien
element, there is a strong tendency for those in it to move away and
reconstitute something like it, or to find something like it.

In other cities, less tolerant than New York, the community,
instead of fading away, may put up a hard shell and fight. Here,
sentiment, the governmental authorities, and the law give little support to
any violent effort to prevent Negroes from moving into white areas. The
resistance comes only from landlords, operating out of prejudice or
calculations of rational advantage, not from tenants or homeowners.
There are two other reasons New York has had little violent resistance to
the expansion of Negro neighborhoods: many are renters who will not
fight for their houses; many are Jews who would not resist a Negro move
with violence.

Around the edges of Harlem, of Bedford-Stuyvesant, and of the
other major centers of population, then, there is "integration," if one
thinks in terms of people living near one another. In the middle-class
suburban areas around New York, there are a few integrated communi-

ties, but they tend, more or less rapidly, to become more and more Negro, or less and less white, unless the houses are quite expensive—a fact that automatically limits the Negro market. The Negro population of the city and the metropolitan area is rising, and the Negro population of high and steady income is also rising; it is understandable that the Negro proportion in a desirable and pleasant area, where Negroes can buy homes, will also rise. This would be so in any case; it is also true that the transition is often speeded up by real estate men, Negro and white, encouraging people to move out. In southern Queens, in the Springfield Gardens, Laurelton, Rosedale area, a Tri-Community Council exists, and the real estate men are countered by a community organization that encourages white homeowners to stay. The same kind of effort to freeze the changeover from white to Negro occupancy is to be found in Teaneck, New Jersey, in Lakeview, Long Island, and other suburban areas. Such organizations, which tend to bring together the new and old elements in a changing community, and to teach people the great truth that people are very much alike, are desirable. They slow down the transition. Certainly they make life pleasanter while the transition goes on, and have important educational effects. But if we look at the over-all picture, we cannot but conclude that in most cases the tendencies for an area to become mostly Negro are irreversible.

Often prejudice has nothing to do with it at all, or hardly anything, and indeed the movement into the area may have begun because it showed the *least* prejudice, the *least* resistance. But the older group may still desire to live in a community of "their kind." Rising incomes and rising land prices and house prices make mobility easy. Often there are differences aside from color between the old community and the newcomers. And often the older settlers, living in older homes, and now without young children, needed only a little push to do what they were already thinking of, to move out into a smaller and more convenient house, or into a suburban apartment. Prejudice is extensive but is rarely unmixed or pure. Economic advantage in selling out, higher income permitting better housing, changing needs and wants, social interests, and other factors may play a role in the moving out of the whites.

The effect of these patterns of growth and movement has been to spread the Negro population through the city and metropolitan area, but its spread has been around a single main concentration in each borough. Harlem in Manhattan (the term has grown with the Negro community, and it is now almost synonymous with the main area of Negro occupancy) has already reached its peak as a center of Negro population. Manhattan had still in 1960 more Negroes than any other borough (397,000), but its rate of increase in 1950–1960 was by far the smallest.

Meanwhile, the centers of Negro population in the other boroughs have grown rapidly. The Bronx, which had only 25,000 in 1940, had 164,000 in 1960. Queens, which also had about 25,000 in 1940 had 146,000 in 1960. Brooklyn has grown from 110,000 in 1940 to 371,000. Harlem, which had two-thirds of the city's Negro population in 1940, has only a little more than a third today.[2]

Beyond the borders of the city, in other cities such as Newark and in suburban areas, there has been a great increase in the Negro population. Westchester has risen from 32,000 Negroes in 1940 to 56,000 in 1960. Nassau and Suffolk in this time more than doubled their Negro population. In these counties, older Negro settlements that very often consisted of servants and handymen have expanded and been joined by very different, prosperous, middle-class communities.[3]

While discrimination is the main channelizer of this population movement, we tend perhaps to minimize other factors at work in this process of Negro community formation. Even with much less prejudice directed against them, Jews have formed dense and concentrated suburban settlements. Great Neck did not become Jewish because Jews could not move anywhere else, but because it was an attractive community, and once there were enough Jews to organize synagogues and temples, to support social circles and associations, bakeries and delicatessens, it became even more attractive. There may be less in the way of specialized tastes in food and certainly less in the way of nostalgic cultural attachments to differentiate the Negro middle class from the great American average. But there is a distinctive and important religious and organizational life, and in time, and indeed perhaps the time is now, we shall have to recognize that a community that is Negro is not necessarily the outcome of discrimination, just as a Jewish community is not necessarily the product of discrimination. In the absence of discrimination these clusters would continue to exist. But there is no question that today, in a Negro community, compulsion and limitation are felt more strongly than the free decision to come together.

No one has thought very seriously about what truly integrated communities would be like. What would be the basis for common action, for social activities bringing together people of different groups? The communities of New York have always been in large measure ethnically and religiously delimited, and the social and organizational life of suburbia is lived within the distinctions created by religous affilation. If Jews set up clubs and recreational activities and social activities largely on the basis of affiliation to synagogues and Jewish community centers and other Jewish organizations—as, outside of Manhattan, they increasingly do—then what areas are left for the mingling of Negroes and Jews? They only rarely meet at work, and that does not generally affect the communities to which the workers return to live. If Catholics do the same, there is again little room for social intercourse with Negroes. There remains local politics, and one of its chief virtues is that it does remind people of the variety of our communities, and does require them all to come together.

It is the white Protestants on whom the moral injunction to form a community together with Negroes falls most heavily, at least from a theoretical point of view. For in America religion is a legitimate basis on which to erect partially distinct communities, and neither Jews nor Catholics need feel that they act in discriminatory fashion when they base their social life on a religious affiliation which does not include Negroes.* But the basis for the separation of white and Negro Protestants is much less clear. The white Protestants were generally the first settlers in the older suburban communities into which Negroes are moving. But by now, white Protestant dominance in many of these has passed in the face of a heavy Catholic and Jewish movement. Many of the white Protestants of these communities left long before the Negroes got there, two migrations back, so often there are not many white Protestants left to wonder about the basis of the division of Negro from white Methodists, Negro from white Episcopalians and Congregationalists, Negro from white Baptists. Many Protestant ministers are aware of their responsibility and their failure, and there is a good deal of discussion and soul-searching as to what can be done. Community with the Negro will become more and more a Protestant problem as religion comes more and more to serve as the major legitimate basis for separate communities within the larger community.[5]

In the center of the city, among the poor, the problem of integration is a very different one. Indeed, the search for a decent place to live is so intense that for most the additional social goal of a mixed community seems a utopian and irrelevant consideration. But ironically enough, it is here, in the center and among the poor, that the goal of integration is most earnestly sought and most widely found, for a great public agency plays an important role today in the housing of the poor in New York. The New York City Housing Authority now controls a major part of the shelter of the poor in the city of New York, and its decisions affect the way they live. In mid-1962, more than 450,000 people lived in the 116,000 apartments of the New York City Housing Authority.

---

* Negro Jews are actually only one of the many city sects that have grown up among Negroes in imitation of exotic religions. They are for the most part not really Jews, just as most Negro Muslims are not really Muslims, for they have not gone through the prescribed process of conversion. There is a sizable body of Negro Catholics, but the issue of the "integration" of Negro and white Catholics in the North does not as yet seem to have greatly concerned whites or Negroes.[4]

Nineteen thousand more apartments were under construction and being occupied, with an estimated population of 72,000, and 17,000 more apartments were being planned. Within a few years, the public housing pool will contain more than 150,000 apartments, and 600,000 people! About 40 per cent of public housing is occupied by Negroes, which means that about one out of every five or six Negroes in the city is living in a project. The project is now beginning to rival the slum as the environment for poor Negroes, and it consequently becomes more and more important to consider what kind of life is lived there, and what kind of communities are created in them.

The projects are of course integrated. There are none without some Negroes and only a few that are entirely Negro. The Housing Authority is concerned over the fact that in many projects there is a strong tendency for the white population to decline. A few years ago, it attempted to keep many projects integrated by favoring the applications of white prospective tenants in some, and of Negro and Puerto Rican tenants in others.[6] Challenged by complaints to SCAD, and by articles in the Negro press, the Authority has limited its integration efforts in recent years to the attempt to recruit a balanced tenant population for new projects. But since the over-all tendency is for the white population to fall, it is largely white tenants that are favored, within of course the over-all maximum income limitations, and the complex system of priorities that the Authority must observe. This is part of the Authority's over-all policy, within recent years, of attempting to make each project a community. Thus the Authority has also tried in many projects to reduce the numbers on relief (for some projects once contained a very large proportion of families on relief), just as it tried to get a mixture of different ethnic groups.

But the creation of a good community is a difficult thing, and the existence of a housing project that is divided between Negroes, Puerto Ricans, and whites may mean (and often does mean) only the physical proximity of groups that have very little to do with each other. In a middle-class community as we have seen, the two races separate, among other reasons, because there are too few elements of community to bind them, and their active social life goes on within racial and religious groups. In the housing project, the situation is generally worse, for the absence of ties across group lines is generally accompanied by the absence of ties even *within* the group. A powerful bureaucracy manages the project, and, whatever its intentions, its mere existence and its large functions inhibit the development of a community. There are few churches or any other kind of organization within the projects. Social isolation of tenant from tenant is common, because after all people have been bureaucratically assigned to projects and apartments, within a limited choice, rather than having located to be near friends, family, or institutions. Suspicion is also common, in part because there is fear of having transgressed one of the many rules of the Authority, and many tenants take the point of view that the less the neighbors know of them the better. The weakness of the bonds of community within the projects is true whether they are all Negro or partly Negro.

The problem of creating a community is an enormous task, and it may seem unfair to demand of a landlord that he undertake this task. But the landlord of 100,000 families is more than a landlord, and the Authority accepts, as the integration policy shows, its responsibility for helping to create community within the projects. And yet one wonders whether the mixing of the races in proper proportions will play much role in creating good communities. The improvement of the projects as communities probably depends on a host of measures that are even more difficult than affecting their racial composition: involving the people of the projects in their management and maintenance, encouraging and strengthening forms of organization among them (even when the main purpose of these organizations seems to be to attack the management), encouraging forms of self-help in them, varying their population occupationally as well as racially by greater tolerance in admissions, reducing the stark difference of the projects from their surroundings by changing their appearance, considering more seriously the impact of their design on the social life that they enfold, all this and more have been suggested. Some of the projects are integrated without any efforts by the Authority. These are the projects that for various reasons do overcome the many drawbacks and become so attractive that whites as well as Negroes want to live in them.

Integration in the projects is probably best achieved not by policies to directly affect the mixture but by policies to create good communities, making them attractive to more families. But in any case, there is not much the Authority can do to affect proportions, for the number of Negroes in public housing will depend on their future economic fate in New York. If most of the poor in New York are Negro, then most of the housing project population will have to be Negro, and the Authority will be helpless to affect the situation, short of radical changes in the entire idea of public housing.

The projects are important not only for themselves; they are also important for their impact on the rest of the city. And perhaps their most important effect has been in upsetting the balance of the slums. Large numbers of normal families living in slums (the chief candidates for the projects) have been withdrawn from them, leaving the remaining slums to become the homes of the old, the criminal, the mentally unbalanced, the most depressed and miserable and deprived. The slums now contain the very large families that are not eligible for public housing because they would overcrowd it; the families that have been ejected from the projects (or were never admitted) for being antisocial; those who have either recently arrived in the city and hardly adapted to urban life, or those who may have been here a long time but never adapted; as well as the dope peddlers and users, the sex perverts and criminals, the pimps and prostitutes whom the managers reject or eject to protect the project population. All these are now concentrated in the slums that ring the projects, and areas that were perhaps barely tolerable before the impact of the projects are now quite intolerable. As we tear down the slums, those that remain inevitably become worse. And what after all are we to do with the large numbers of people emerging in modern society who are irresponsible and depraved? The worthy poor create no serious problem—nothing that money cannot solve. But the unworthy poor? No one has come up with the answers.

The structure of the Negro neighborhood and the Negro community means that the Negro middle class, in the city at any rate, rarely escapes from the near presence of the Negro poor, as well as of the depraved and the criminal. The middle-class neighborhoods border on the lower-class neighborhoods, and suffer from robberies and attacks, and the psychic assaults of a hundred awful sights. There are the additional frustrations of the difficulty of getting a taxi to take one home, the saturation of the area by police (whose numbers make it harder to escape a summons for a minor traffic violation). Within the city, it is not easy to escape, for few neighborhoods are pure. In the small suburban towns, with their high-cost houses, strict zoning regulations, informal controls for identification and ejection of the unwanted and the troublesome, the situation is different. There, if the colored middle-class family is successful in entering, it, like the white middle class, is protected from the pressure of the social problems thrown up by modern society, and most heavily concentrated among the colored. There it can enter into the community activities that encompass both races without being burdened by the problems, actual and psychological, of the Negro poor. Its success in integration is there aided by the fact that it is successfully segregated from the Negro poor.

But in the city, no one can protect himself, for the city is free and open, and cannot fence itself off. There is thus scarcely a middle-class Negro area that does not know that close to it, on its borders and in measure in its midst, are all the problems that are so heavily concentrated in the Negro community.

This is the over-all picture, and yet, despite the housing shortage, the segregated new housing, the community problems, New York will very likely in the end be an integrated city—or rather something even better, a city where people find homes and neighborhoods according to income and taste, and where an area predominantly of one group represents its positive wishes rather than restricting prejudice.

We see the signs everywhere. In Manhattan, the western edges of the Harlem ghetto show not only the hardly integrated pattern of Negroes, mainland whites, and Puerto Ricans of different economic levels and different family patterns, close together but not mixing. There is also a large Negro element that is on the same level, economically and socially, as most of the old and new non-Puerto Rican white population. This group has older established people (as in the Morningside Gardens co-ops) and young couples and single young people, scattered through the brownstones and apartment houses. Here Negroes and whites do begin to form an interracial community that is rapidly being taken for granted, and one in which a mixed couple (the West Side is the area where they are most numerous) no longer leads to the turning of heads.

In the higher-income public projects of the City Housing Authority, the so-called middle-income housing, in co-ops like Morningside Gardens, in Title I projects like Park West Village, we find families living together, not in the indifference of forced association but in what are in large measure real communities, and where common tastes and backgrounds make interracial groups that are more than a self-conscious demonstration.

Up to now, there has been little Negro interest in co-ops, except for Morningside Gardens. But this is changing. Co-op housing is increasingly becoming the most popular answer to the problems of middle-income housing in the city. It will also draw less and less on the special type of person who is interested in the cooperative idea from an ideological point of view (that pool is becoming exhausted) and become attractive to large numbers. There is also now the model of Morningside Gardens as a successful co-op community. For all these reasons, the new co-ops have somewhat larger Negro contingents. The Negro often buys a house because he cannot get a good apartment. In the discrimination-free co-op housing, Negroes who prefer the city can find a way to stay that is not more expensive than suburban housing.

Even in Brooklyn, the Bronx, and Queens, we find, in addition to the dense all-Negro stretches, lower-income and middle-income, many individual families scattered through the most middle-class neighborhoods. Teachers, social workers, and other white-collar and professional workers may be found living on pleasant tree-lined streets with friendly neighbors.

In Greenwich Village, where few of the young bohemians who crowd the streets and coffee houses can afford to live, established Negro writers and artists live, again without meeting discrimination; and the younger and less successful find relatively easy access to the cold-water flats of the Lower East Side.

Even in suburbia, the stronghold of middle-class values, exclusiveness, and discriminatory behavior, we find the matter-of-course mixing of colored and white in many towns. In 1961 on Long Island and in Westchester and New Jersey, groups sprang up in a number of suburban communities—Great Neck was perhaps the leader—which attempted to break down their all-white character, to get sellers and real estate agents to show houses to Negroes, and to get Negroes to move in. Frances Levinson, of the New York State Committee Against Discrimination in Housing, was active in trying to coordinate the work of these varied groups. In places like Great Neck and Scarsdale, though this is only the beginning, it was apparently easier to get houses that the owners were willing to sell to Negroes than to find Negroes who could afford such houses and who wanted to move to such communities. It is perfectly understandable that if one can afford a big house in suburbia, Mount Vernon and New Rochelle and some other towns that already have large middle-class Negro communities have more to offer. For some people and in some places, we are approaching the point where we may discover that discrimination is only the first crude barrier to integration, and that people are more complicated than either racists or those who deny the reality of race believe.

It is still an effort for a Negro individual or family to live in a non-Negro neighborhood, but it is an effort that it is no longer exceptional; we can scarcely guess at the numbers who live in all the situations we have described. These situations in which white and colored live together without tension and without problems, and perhaps even comfortably enough with each other to begin finally to appreciate their real differences, mark the course of the future in New York. The only question is, how fast, and against how much resistance.

REFERENCES

1. See the valuable material on growth of New York Negro sections, and degree of segregation, in Davis McEntire, *Residence and Race*, Berkeley, Calif.: University of California Press, 1960. See, too, on the general patterns affecting the housing of Negroes, other books in this series: Nathan Glazer and Davis McEntire, Eds., *Studies in Housing and Minority Groups;* Eunice and George Grier, *Privately Developed Interracial Housing;* Chester Rapkin and William G. Grigsby, *The Demand for Housing in Racially Mixed Areas* (same place, publisher, year).

2. "Negroes in the City of New York," Commission on Intergroup Relations, City of New York, 1961.

3. *Populations of New York State: 1960,* Report No. 1, New York State Comission Against Discrimination, 1961.

4. HOWARD BROTZ, "The Black Jews of Harlem," unpublished Master's thesis, University of Chicago, 1949.

5. I accept here the argument of Will Herberg in *Protestant, Catholic, Jew,* New York: Doubleday, 1955. The discussion of the Negro problem in Protestant churches is often carried on under the general heading of the inner-city church, the urban church. See Frank S. Loescher, *The Protestant Church and the Negro,* New York: Association Press, 1948. There is need for a more up-to-date survey of this problem.

6. See Bernard Roscho, "The Integration Problem and Public Housing," *The New Leader,* July 4–11, 1960, pp. 10–13; and statements on this question by the New York City Housing Authority.

Crime and Violence

Thomas F. Pettigrew

NEGRO AMERICAN CRIME

Crime *is* prevalent among Negro Americans. Once again, white supremacists maintain this indicates the Negro is innately more prone to criminal acts than Caucasians. Asserts one such writer authoritatively: "Students are of the opinion that, with the possible exception of the Aztec, the earth has never known a bloodier race than the African Negro." (1, p. 44)

Alternatively, high Negro crime rates may be—like communicable disease and low I.Q. scores—another handmaiden of oppression. Indeed, the evidence points strongly to the explanation that racial discrimination and social class factors do in fact account for the group differential in crime.

APPARENT RACIAL CRIME RATES IN THE UNITED STATES

There is no pure index of crime. Measurement must be limited to those criminals apprehended—undoubtedly not a representative sample

Reprinted by permission from Pettigrew's *A Profile of the Negro American*, pp. 136–156. Copyright 1964, D. Van Nostrand Company, Inc., Princeton, N.J.

Mr. Pettigrew is Associate Professor, Department of Social Relations, Harvard University.

of all criminals. Even measurement of apprehended criminals is crude and approximate at best because of the lack of uniformity in laws and in crime-reporting over the United States. (2, 3, 4) Furthermore, any index of Negro crime runs the risk of being inflated by discriminatory practices of the police, the courts, and penal systems. To begin with, the laws themselves may be discriminatory; segregation legislation makes many acts a "crime" for Negroes but not for whites.[1] For these reasons, the indices which have to be used are best thought of as measures of apparent crime, not crime *per se*.

One such index relies on reported arrest data, provided annually by the Federal Bureau of Investigation in its *Uniform Crime Reports*. In 1960–61, for example, Negroes were arrested two-and-a-half to three times more frequently than other Americans, proportionate to their percentage of the population. (5) For some crimes, like forgery and counterfeiting, embezzlement and fraud, and driving while intoxicated, Negro arrest rates were approximately the same as white rates. But for other crimes, like murder and non-negligent manslaughter, aggravated assault, and gambling, Negro arrest rates were roughly five to seven times those of whites.

Arrests provide tenuous data, however. The police frequently pick up numerous suspects in connection with a single crime; and, in communities where Negroes lack political influence, the police are often more prone to arrest Negroes than whites. Sociologist Guy Johnson contends:

> The Negro is more exposed to the misuse of police power than any other group. The police custom of arresting Negroes on slight suspicion or of staging mass "roundups" of Negroes is definitely related to the Negro's lack of security and his inability to exert pressure against such abuses. . . . In some places in the South, law officers and magistrates are engaged in a sort of "racket" which involves the rounding up of Negroes on trivial charges for the sake of earning fees. (6, p. 97)

In short, arrests do not offer an accurate estimate of Negro crime. Prison commitment data furnish another index. Again, over the past few decades, Negro prison rates are high for many types of crime. Von Hentig, analyzing male felony commitments to state and federal prisons from 1930 through 1936, found Negro rates roughly three times the white rates. (7) Imprisonment for criminal homicide and aggravated

---

[1] For example, thousands of Negro Southerners have been arrested during the 1960's for seeking service at "white" lunch-counters; yet white Southerners can typically seek service if they wish at "Negro" lunch-counters with legal immunity.

assault was especially high among Negroes. And these same differences have continued. In 1950 and 1960, Negro felony commitment rates for both state and federal prisons were still about three times the white rates. (8, 9) The federal Negro commitment rate tends to remain slightly lower than the state rate, but it is particularly high among drug law felons. From 1950 to 1960, Negro drug violators constituted half of all such offenders sent to federal prisons and a fifth of all Negro commitments. (9)

But even with convictions and commitments, the exposed position of the Negro is likely to increase his rates. When compared with white defendants, the accused Negro typically has less access to bail, astute legal counsel, cash fines rather than imprisonment, appeals, and other legal protections. He is more likely to be poorly educated and unaware of his full rights. And, in many communities, he must face "a white man's court"—white judge, white clerk, white guards, white jurors. Such conditions set the stage for impaired justice, even when honest efforts are made by officials to prevent bald racial discrimination. The "legal lynching" dramatized by Harper Lee in *To Kill a Mockingbird* can still occur in some Southern courts. (10) Little wonder that accused Negroes are more often found guilty than accused whites, especially when the alleged crime is perpetrated against a white victim. (6, 11, 12, 13)

This racial difference in conviction percentage occurs not because of, but in spite of, the types of crime most frequently committed by each group. That is, fewer people accused of murder and assault—offenses with especially high Negro rates—are generally convicted than those accused of forgery, counterfeiting, and drunken driving—offenses with especially high white rates. (5, Table 10)

Negro youth likewise suffer discrimination before the law. Mary Diggs studied the disposal of juvenile cases in Philadelphia during 1948. (14) She discovered that a comparatively smaller proportion of the Negro offenders was dismissed or discharged, while a larger proportion of the Negroes was institutionalized or referred to criminal courts. Moreover, the Negro child was more likely to be referred to public rather than private agencies for treatment. Axelrad conducted a similar study of 300 of New York City's institutionalized male delinquents. (15) He noted that Negro youth, when compared to white youth, were committed younger, for less serious offenses, and with fewer previous court appearances. Not all such differences, however, can be attributed purely to racial prejudice. These practices are also consistent with a long-established juvenile court philosophy of intervening earlier in cases from socially disorganized areas. (16)

Discrimination is also evident in the sentencing and paroling of convicted Negroes. During the middle 1930's, Von Hentig noted that among males over 17 years of age Negroes were eleven times more likely to be executed and five-and-a-half times more likely to be given life sentences than whites, probabilities in excess of the arrest and commitment rates of Negroes. (7) For the 32-year period, 1930–1961, 53.9 per cent of the prisoners executed under civil authority were Negro. (17, Table 4) Statistics for armed robbery, burglary, and rape are the most revealing. Indeed, death sentences for these crimes are largely exacted in the South for Negroes convicted of crimes against whites. Of the 34 robbers and burglars put to death during this period, 29 (85 per cent) were Negro and all but one were executed in a Southern or border state; of the 442 rapists put to death, 397 (90 per cent) were Negro and all but two were executed in a Southern or border state. (17, Table 4) The rape data are all the more striking when it is remembered that over half of all convicted rapists are white. Together with anti-miscegenation laws, this record of executions for rape dramatizes the special role of sexual fears on the Southern racial scene.

Even when execution is avoided, convicted Negro felons are likely to remain in prison longer and be paroled less often than whites. Among the felons released from state prisons from 1951 through 1953, the typical Negro had served two years compared to the typical white's 21 months. (18, 19) Again the greatest difference involves rape; the median Negro rapist released during this period had served eight more months than the median white rapist.

Available evidence suggests that Negro felons adjust to prison somewhat better than whites. At Central Prison in Raleigh, North Carolina, for example, Negro felons incur fewer rule infractions than white prisoners. (20) Furthermore, throughout the country, they less often attempt to escape than white felons. (9, 1954, p. 38) Nevertheless, Negro prisoners have less chance of parole. Von Hentig discovered that 58.2 per cent of the white prisoners discharged from 1933 through 1936 were paroled compared to only 38.1 per cent of the discharged Negroes. (7) Thus, the racial composition of prison populations is the poorest index of Negro crime. The longer sentences and fewer paroles for Negro inmates cause them to increase the percentage of Negro prisoners after whites convicted of similar crimes have been released.

Negro rates of apparent crime, then, are high; though just how high in comparison with white apparent crime is difficult to determine by possible racial discrimination at every stage—arrest, conviction, sentencing, and parole. A detailed look at criminal homicide is indicated, since it has particularly high Negro rates and better data are available for analysis.

CRIMINAL HOMICIDE AMONG NEGROES

Negroes comprised 54 per cent of the reported arrests during 1961 for murder and non-negligent manslaughter. (5, Tables 23 and 29) While constituting less than 5 per cent of the area's population, Negroes made up over half of the inmates incarcerated in Pennsylvania's Western State Penitentiary for murder from 1906 through 1935. (21) Even among those admitted to Pennsylvania state prisons in 1941–1942 who were over forty-nine years of age, Negroes were more frequently charged with criminal homicide and aggressive assault than were whites. (22) For the nation as a whole in 1950, slightly over half of the male felons committed to prison for murder were Negro, though Negroes were but a tenth of the population. (8, p. 65) And from 1930 through 1961, 49 per cent of those executed for murder were Negro. (17, Table 4)

But, as just noted, these arrest, commitment, and execution data are inflated by racially discriminatory legal processes. In fact, several investigations reveal a dual code of convicting and sentencing in cases of criminal homicide. Analyzing 1931 data, Thorsten Sellin discovered that Southern states tended to give shorter sentences for homicide to Negroes, while other states tended to give shorter minimum but longer maximum homicide sentences to Negroes. (23) Johnson and Garfinkel later demonstrated that Southern courts usually give lenient sentences to Negroes who have killed other Negroes, but almost invariably give their most severe sentences to Negroes who have killed whites. (6, 12) Furthermore, Negroes accused of killing whites have the highest probability of being convicted.

To illustrate Southern judicial discrimination, Johnson provides data for Richmond, Virginia, for 1930 through 1939. Seventy-three per cent of the Negroes indicted for killing Negroes were convicted and only 6 per cent of these received life sentences; 75 per cent of the whites indicted for killing whites were convicted and only 27 per cent of these received life imprisonment or were executed; the only white indicted for killing a Negro was convicted but sentenced to less than two years; yet the five Negroes indicted for killing whites were *all* convicted and *all* given life sentences. (6) Garfinkel presents similar data for ten North Carolina counties. He shows that for each type of indictment—first degree murder, second degree murder, and manslaughter—Negroes accused of killing whites were the most likely to be convicted and given severe punishment. (12) Recent years have brought improvements in many Southern areas, but this general pattern still exists.

Equally dramatic racial differences were found by Wolfgang in his examination of criminal homicide in Philadelphia from 1948 through

1952. (13, pp. 299–307) Of those receiving a court trial, 81 per cent of the Negroes were found guilty as opposed to 62 per cent of the whites. And for each level of charge, Negroes received more severe sentences in spite of the fact that they had been more often provoked by their victims and were less likely to possess a previous police record. These data strongly suggest that racial discrimination exists in both the South and North in the convicting and sentencing of those accused of criminal homicide.

One index of homicide less subject to discriminatory practices is the cause-of-death data provided by the National Office of Vital Statistics. Instead of counting the perpetrators of the crime, it counts the victims. This procedure avoids the many pitfalls of crime statistics but involves an important assumption: namely, that whites kill whites and Negroes kill Negroes. Since this assumption is verified by recent research (13, 24), cause-of-death data provide a reasonably reliable estimate of racial differences in homicide. Since 1940, these data have shown the relative number of non-white deaths by homicide each year to be roughly ten times the white figure. (25, pp. 934, 937) Thus, 27.3 non-whites were killed per 100,000 non-whites annually from 1949 through 1951 compared to 2.6 whites. Negro homicide rates, then, remain extremely high regardless of the index chosen.

WHY IS NEGRO CRIME SO PREVALENT?

The racist argument of innate criminality rests solely on the sheer magnitude of Negro crime. A number of both logical and empirical considerations, however, conflict with this view. To begin with, the "reasoning" is circular: Negro Americans supposedly have high crime rates because they are innately criminal, and are presumed innately criminal because of their high rates. Moreover, crime must be socially, not biologically, defined. By its very nature it cannot have direct racial or genetic causation.

Even if the racist's invalid assumptions concerning the existence of relatively pure white and Negro "races" in America were correct, three different lines of evidence cast serious doubts upon his position. First, discrepancies in crime rates far larger than racial crime-rate differences in the United States are not uncommon between groups of the same race and nationality. Bonger gives an illustration from German conviction data during the years 1894–1896. (26, pp. 47–48) Compared with German domestics, German workers in manufacturing had rates 50 times higher for rape and 40 times higher for felonious assault. Modern French data provide a further example. (27) Children of domestic servants have 22 times the delinquency rate of the children of farm owners. Large group differences in apparent crime rates are not in themselves proof of a racial factor; social factors can and do cause vast differences within the same race.

Second, Negro American crime rates are by no means uniformly high. Brinton noted that the crime rate in Durham, North Carolina may vary between Negro neighborhoods as much as 500 per cent. (28) Further data are provided by the Negro communities relatively free from white control that seem to have sharply reduced rates. During the 1920's all-Negro Mound Bayor, Mississippi, was said not to have had a single murder in twenty years (29), and in 1943 all-Negro Boley, Oklahoma, was reported to have the lowest crime rate in the state. (30) St. Helena Island, near Beaufort, South Carolina, has traditionally had very little violence and crime. (31) Significantly, the island is composed largely of Negro farm owners and has been blessed with a unique history of interracial harmony.

Consider, too, the low homicide rates of East African peoples. Seventy-one per cent of the 41 tribal groups studied by Bohannan and his associates had lower homicide rates than the whites of either South Carolina or Texas in 1949–1951. (32) In fact, the median Southern state's white homicide rate for this period, 4.4 per 100,000, ranges from four to six times higher than the rates of such tribes as the Wanga and the Bukayo. Bohannan concludes: "If it needed stressing, here is overwhelming evidence that it is cultural and not biological factors which make for a high homicide rate among Negro Americans." (32, p. 237)

If there is no racial predisposition to crime, what, then, lies behind Negro American crime? The same class and discrimination considerations so vital to an understanding of health and intelligence variations again provide an explanation which can be supported by data. Negroes, when compared with other Americans, are more often lower class and poor, slum residents of the largest cities, victims of family disorganization, Southern in origin, young and unemployed, and objects of extensive discrimination—each an important social correlate of crime apart from race.

Think of the class factor. Though "white collar" crime is prevalent in the United States (33), the great bulk of recorded crime is concentrated in the lower socio-economic segments of all groups. (34) In the Nashville area, for instance, white delinquents from the lower stratum commit more serious crimes and are more often oriented toward a life of crime than white delinquents from higher strata. (35) And in Philadelphia, over 90 per cent of the homicides are perpetrated by either the unemployed or those holding the least skilled occupations. (13)

This close association between economics and recorded crime involves race insomuch as the lower socio-economic class encompasses a segment of the Negro population roughly two to three times larger than that of the white population. Thus, almost half of all non-white families, but only one-sixth of white families, had annual incomes under $2500 in 1956. (36, pp. 656–657) Yet research suggests that white-black crime differentials are not totally eliminated if socio-economic factors are held approximately constant. (37, 13, pp. 36–39) One reason for this is simply that the floor of Negro privation frequently goes below the most indigent of whites. Thus, Earl Moses attempted to examine the crime rates of Negroes and whites in four socio-economically equated areas in Baltimore; but he could not find two white districts actually as destitute as the two Negro districts. (38) He finally settled for two white areas with a greater rate of home ownership, thus vitiating his finding of greater crime rates in the Negro areas.

The special role of extreme penury in Negro crime was demonstrated during the Depression. Compared to previous decades, Spirer found that white commitments to Pennsylvania's Western State Penitentiary increased sharply during this period, but Negro commitments actually decreased. (21) These diverse trends were particularly marked for predatory crimes—robbery, burglary, larceny. Governmental aid during these lean years was apparently a significant contributor to this situation. Even with relief, bad times found many whites living below the economic levels to which they were accustomed; while relief schedules lifted impecunious Negroes above their pre-Depression income levels. Two other investigators more recently have demonstrated this phenomenon in Louisiana. (39)

Criminologists offer a number of reasons for lower-class crime. Living in the world's richest nation, surrounded by mass consumption of luxury items, and bombarded by advertisements directed primarily at the middle and upper classes, is it any wonder many lower-class persons are tempted to enter crime? Indeed, delinquent sub-cultures create a situation where law-breaking is expected behavior. (40, 41, 42, 43) In addition, the lower class, both Negro and white, has more direct association with criminal patterns. (44, 45) "Not all Negroes, working-class persons, etc., become criminals because some are presented with an excess of anti-criminal behavior patterns," explains Cressey, "but the *chances* of being presented with an excess of criminal behavior patterns are better if one is a Negro, a member of the working class, a young male, an urban dweller, and a native American than they are if one is white, middle-class, old, a rural resident or an immigrant." (46, p. 59)

This "differential association" factor assumes special importance for the poor who reside in the bleakest slums of the nation's largest urban centers, areas where criminal patterns are most conspicuous. And Negroes are disproportionately overrepresented in such big-city slums. The past two generations of constant migration have led to a significantly larger percentage of Negroes than whites residing in cities of more than a million people. The black ghettos of these metropolises are generally deep within the central city, marked by both physical and social deterioration, and witness to the most severe forms of vice and corruption.

High crime districts are characterized by a loss of any sense of community. One survey compared the opinions and actions of residents of two urban areas of similar economic standing but contrasting rates of delinquency. Figure 1 presents the results. Respondents in the high

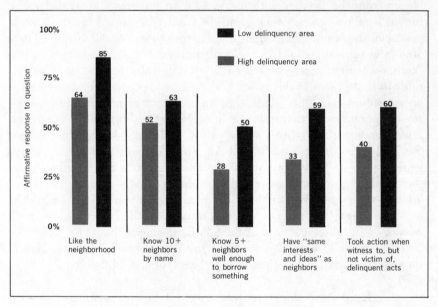

FIGURE 1—*Delinquency and Sense of Community*

(Data from: Eleanor Maccoby, J. P. Johnson, and R. M. Church, "Community integration and the social control of juvenile delinquency," *Journal of Social Issues*, 1958, 14, 38–51.)

delinquency area liked their neighbors less, and felt they had fewer "interests and ideas" in common with them. Also, persons in the high crime area less often reported taking corrective measures when they saw delinquent acts in which they were not involved. (47)

Family disorganization is similarly characteristic of such districts. There may be a direct personality relationship between violent crime and the absence of the father. In any event, there is little question that broken families are one of the agents of crime in general. Mary Diggs found that three-fourths, twice the expected ratio, of Philadelphia's Negro delinquents who came before the law during 1948 did not have both of their natural parents living at home. (14) The armed robber seems to spring most often from a background of severely impaired family life. Research on Negro offenders at the District of Columbia reformatory reveals that 84 per cent of the armed robbers came from "demoralized families," 78 per cent were reared in more than one home, and 84 per cent had histories as boys of running away from home—all percentages roughly twice those of other Negro offenders. (48)

The murderer raises additional considerations. Homicide is an intrinsic part of the South's "violent tradition." This tradition is a direct legacy from the frontier with its reliance on firearms and its distrust of formal legal processes; poverty and the Civil War caused the tradition to persist in the South even longer than in the West. (49, 50, 51, 52) There are many expressions of this regional tradition: lynching, esteem for the "hell-of-a-fellow" as a violent personality-type (50), the highest homicide rates for both races in the nation (53, 54), and a special fondness for the armed forces and guns. Thus, despite a system of nationwide congressional appointments to the service academies, Southerners are overrepresented among chief officers of the Army and Navy—though not among the leaders of the less traditional Air Force. Almost half of the Army's generals and the Navy's admirals, in 1950, were born and/or educated in the South.[2] (55) Consider, too, the results of a 1959 opinion poll which asked a representative sample of the nation: "Do you think it should be legal or illegal for private citizens to have loaded weapons in their homes?" Fifty-three per cent of the Southern sample thought it should be "legal," compared with 42 per cent of the Western sample, 35 per cent of the Northeastern sample, and 33 per cent of the Midwestern sample. (56)

Negro Americans are primarily a Southern people, and their homicide is another manifestation of this violent tradition. Consequently, Negro homicide rates vary tremendously by state; during the period 1949–1951, Texas and Florida had relatively four times the Negro homicide rate of Massachusetts and two-and-a-half times that of Connecticut and New Jersey. (57) These differences correlate highly with the state variations in the number of homicides committed by whites. Southern states, particularly those undergoing the most rapid social change, tend to have the highest rates of Negro homicide, followed by

---

[2] Southern esteem for armed service careers is also revealed by a 1947 national opinion poll. Thirty-four per cent of the Southern sample rated a regular Army captain as having an "excellent general standing" in society, compared with 25 to 27 per cent of the other regional samples. (Private communication from Professor Albert J. Reiss, Jr., of the University of Michigan.) Though the sampling errors in such a survey are large for regional differences, these data combined with other consistent evidence suggest that the "violent tradition" still lingers in the South.

the Northern states which have received large numbers of Negro migrants from the South. (57) The greater proclivity to commit homicide among Negroes, then, is partly because most Negroes are Southerners or the children of Southerners.[3]

The relevance of migration to crime is not clear. Much as with the migration and mental illness relationship, Southern-born Negroes in the North had far higher crime rates, particularly for homicide, than Northern-born Negroes prior to World War II. (58, 59) Recent work, however, casts doubt on this relationship (60), suggesting again that post-World War II Negro migrants out of the South are better prepared and qualitatively different from those of earlier years.

The widespread unemployment of ghetto youth also contributes to Negro crime rates. The greatest recent increases in American crime have occurred among the sixteen- to eighteen-year-old group. (61) This age range includes the teenagers who drop out of school and fail to find jobs. They lack money, skills, and societal acceptance; they have time on their hands and a local gang with which to affiliate. Delinquency is the natural result. James B. Conant calls this "the most dangerous social condition in America," latent with "social dynamite." (62, p. 26)

This factor assumes added importance for Negro crime rates, because Negro youth are more likely than white youth to be in this situation.[4] U.S. Department of Labor statistics show that since 1954 there has been a wide discrepancy in the racial unemployment rates of fourteen-to-nineteen-year-old teenagers. In 1962, for example, when only one in eight (12 per cent) young white males out of school were unemployed, the ratio for young non-white males was over one in five (21 per cent). In specific ghettos, the figures are much larger. In the early 1960's, in a Detroit slum with one hundred twenty-five thousand inhabitants, mostly Negro, 70 per cent of its youths between the ages of sixteen and twenty-one were out of school and out of work; in a similar Chicago slum, the figure for young Negro males was 60 per cent. (64, pp. 2–3) Even among those young men who complete high school, the racial difference remains. A 1962 survey of the 1960 graduates of a virtually all-Negro high school in Louisville, Kentucky, revealed an unemployment rate two and a half times that of predominantly white high schools, over 25 per cent to 10 per cent. (65, p. 31)

[3] Roughly two-thirds of all Negroes residing in the North in 1963 were born and reared in the South. (63)

[4] There is also an age difference between the races. A younger group on the average, Negro Americans constitute a larger percentage of youngsters and adults in the heaviest crime-committing years of 15 through 39 than they do of the total population. Though not a critical factor, this age variable can, in certain situations, explain a considerable amount of the Negro-white crime differential. (21)

Mention of unemployment introduces racial discrimination as a factor in Negro crime. Discrimination *per se* need not always lead to high crime rates; witness the relatively low crime rates of Japanese Americans. (45, p. 142) But the unique type of discrimination long practiced against Negro Americans, from slavery to enforced segregation, has been different in kind as well as degree from that practiced against other minorities, and of a type especially likely to produce crime. (6, p. 94) Job discrimination offers a case in point. In Louisville, for instance, "only a handful of Negroes" are admitted among a thousand young men enrolled in the area's apprenticeship programs. (65, p. 31) It is no accident, then, that the city's Negro high school graduates are disproportionately represented among the unemployed. The strong need to move away from such racial barriers results in unusually high Negro rates of escape crimes: gambling, drug addiction, and drunkenness. These in turn, especially drugs and alcohol, lead to other crimes, either to secure money to support the habit or to act out the less inhibited impulses released by these agents.

The loss of inhibition resulting from the use of drugs and alcohol contributes to another characteristic of Negro crime—personal violence.[5] This tendency, too, is a direct result of the Negro's oppressed status. (66, 67) Deeply frustrated by his ego-deflating role and unable to express his hostility toward the white man, the lower-status Negro often vents his aggressions in violence directed against other Negroes, especially after drinking during leisure hours. Support for this interpretation comes from Philadelphia data that indicate Negro and white homicide are quite different phenomena in several respects. (13) Thus, alcohol was involved in over two-thirds of Negro killings, but in less than half of the white killings. Negro homicides were more likely than white homicides to occur in the evening and on the week-end. They were also more likely than white killings to have been provoked by the victim and to have involved stabbing rather than a beating. Finally, the motivational and situational patterns tended to be different. Homicides triggered by jealousy or altercations over money were more common among Negroes, as were homicides involving husband and wife. Moreover, a smaller proportion of

[5] While alcohol releases inhibitions, it does not determine whether any expression of aggression will be directed outwardly or inwardly. Negroes are much more likely to direct aggression outward, as in homicide, rather than inward, as in suicide. Part of the explanation for this lies in the "violent tradition" of the South. And a clue to a further explanation is provided by a nationwide study of fourteen-to-sixteen-year-old American school children. Negro children, particularly boys, reported receiving physical punishment from their parents so much more often than white children that socio-economic differences between the groups alone cannot account for the disparity. Such physical punishment, as opposed to verbal and self-blame forms, is believed to be an important socialization determinant of outward aggression. (68)

Negro killings, compared to white homicides, took place outside the home or between strangers. In short, the Negro homicide tends to be a sudden, unpremeditated, alcohol-induced outburst between intimates in familiar surroundings, a pattern consistent with both the racial-frustration and Southern-origin explanations.

Not all Negro frustration expressed in criminal form is directed at other Negroes. Armed robbery of whites may often be motivated as much by hostility toward whites as other needs. For example, a young English scholar was accosted by several Negro youths while visiting the University of Chicago. (69, p. 598) They demanded his wallet and, when he objected, a knife was brandished. After they again insisted he yield his wallet, he argued, "Look here, I don't want to give up my wallet to you. Besides, I've just arrived from England, and I don't think this is the way to treat someone who's a visitor here." The boys looked at one another, and then one replied, "Oh. We thought you were one of those white guys," and they fled. "White guys," for these youngsters, apparently included only those whites who discriminated against them, not a white guest to their country.

Negro violence may also be encouraged by police discrimination. Johnson details the process:

> In the interplay of behavior between the police and Negro suspects, there is a reciprocal expectation of violence. The police too quickly use gun or club, and Negroes—especially those with reputations as "bad niggers"—are keyed to a desperate shoot-first-or-you'll-get-shot psychology. Thus, what starts out to be merely a questioning or an arrest for a misdemeanor may suddenly turn into violence and a charge of murder against the Negro. (6, p. 97)

The too-quick use of firearms by the police was illustrated in the 1943 Detroit race riot. In fact, Negro distrust of the city's all-white police force gave a major impetus to the spread of the riot. (70) And this distrust was justified. Fifteen Negroes but no whites were shot to death by the police in the riot, though only three of the victims had fired on the police. (70, p. 85)

Further insight into this problem is provided by Kephart's extensive research on the Philadelphia police. (71) More than half of the city's district patrolmen found it "necessary" to be more strict with Negro than white offenders. Figure 2 shows that these men harbored the most unfavorable attitudes toward Negro policemen; they more often objected to riding with a Negro patrolman, resented taking orders from a "well qualified" Negro sergeant or captain, thought there were too many Negroes on the force, and preferred that Negro police not be assigned to their districts. These findings imply that stern handling of Negroes by such white policemen may be as much or more a function of their own bigotry as it is anything unique about Negro suspects.

In a broader, societal context, Merton and other social theorists suggest how racial discrimination feeds Negro crime. They view this as simply another instance of our society's formally encouraging high aspirations and upward mobility, but at the same time effectively blocking the goals of such striving. The non-criminal "rules of the game" may be quite familiar to Negro offenders, but the supports for obeying the law are outweighed by the emphasis placed by American culture on attaining success. As Merton phrases it:

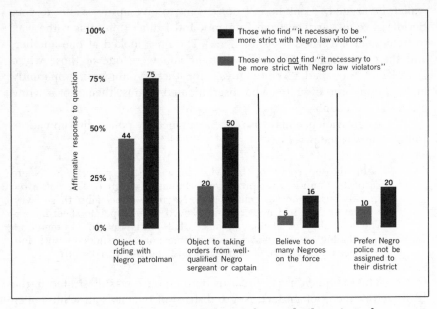

FIGURE 2—*Strictness of White Police and Their Attitudes Toward Negro Police*

(Data from: W. M. Kephart, *Racial Factors and Urban Law Enforcement.* Philadelphia: University of Pennsylvania Press, 1957; Tables 23, 25, 27, and 29.)

. . . when a system of cultural values extols, virtually above all else, certain *common* success-goals for the population at large while the social structure rigorously restricts or completely closes access to approved modes of reaching these goals *for a considerable part of the population,* deviant behavior ensues on a large scale. (72, p. 180)

Thus, crime, too, is a symptom of relative deprivation. And Negro rates need not decline just because the absolute living standards of Negroes improve. Indeed, as with other expressions of relative deprivation,

Negro crime will continue to occur at a greater rate than that of white crime as long as the group's aspirations remain far in advance of the modest attainments allowed by token desegregation.

There is nothing in this situation peculiar to Negroes. Daniel Bell highlights the fact that, repeatedly in American history, many members of ethnic groups, imbued with the success ethic but restrained from legitimate means of attainment by various types of barriers, have entered into illicit activity. (3, Chapter 7) Immigrant groups such as the Irish, Jews from Eastern Europe, and Italians have produced their "Shotgun" Kelleys, Arnold Rothsteins, and "Big Al" Capones, just as earlier Protestant groups produced their Jessie Jameses and their "robber barons." In this sense, crime is an institutionalized means for upward mobility in America, and Negroes are presently following the ascent of other groups up the ladder.

If Negroes had not become such an integral part of American society, if they had remained an isolated group refusing to share in the dominant values and aspirations of the general culture, racial discrimination would not be such a potent factor in Negro crime. Economically disadvantaged and persecuted minority groups can maintain low crime rates as long as they remain socially and culturally integrated within their own groups. (73) But as they depart from their sheltered status and begin to enter the mainstream of American life, their crime rates rise rapidly.

A RECAPITULATION

Apparent Negro American crime rates, as measured by a variety of available indices, are high. They are particularly elevated for crimes involving aggression, such as aggravated assault and homicide, and for escapist crimes, such as gambling, drug addiction, and drunkenness. And although racial discrimination still exists throughout much of the United States at each stage of the judicial process, this discrimination alone cannot account for all of the discrepancy. White supremacists are quick to interpret these data as further evidence for their theories of the genetic inferiority of Negroes as a "race." There is, however, no scientific evidence to support such claims. But there are considerable data which indicate that a multiplicity of social factors produce these criminal patterns among Negroes.

One broad set of factors is socio-economic in character. When compared with white Americans, Negroes are concentrated in those social sectors which exhibit high crime rates regardless of race. Thus, Negroes are more often lower class and poor, slum residents of the nation's largest metropolitan areas, victims of severe family disorganization, Southern in origin, young, and unemployed. Note that each of these characteristics is an important social correlate of crime apart from race—and especially for those violations with the highest Negro rates.

The other, closely related set of factors involves the special type of discrimination inflicted upon Negroes. As with other minority groups who find discriminatory barriers blocking their path toward the mainstream of success-oriented America, many Negroes turn to crime. Crime may thus be utilized as a means of escape, ego-enhancement, expression of aggression, or upward mobility. The salient feature of Negro Americans is that they have accepted and internalized American culture, but are generally denied the chief rewards and privileges of that culture. High crime rates are but one consequence of this situation.

REFERENCES

1. C. PUTNAM, *Race and Reason: A Yankee View.* Washington, D.C.: Public Affairs Press, 1961.

2. R. H. BEATTIE, "Criminal Statistics in the United States," *Journal of Criminal Law, Criminology, and Police Science,* 1960, *51,* 49–65.

3. D. BELL, *The End of Ideology.* Glencoe, Ill.: Free Press, 1959.

4. T. SELLIN, "Crime and Delinquency in the United States: An Over-all View," *Annals of the American Academy of Political and Social Science,* 1962, *339,* 11–23.

5. Federal Bureau of Investigation, *Uniform Crime Reports, 1960–61.* Washington, D.C.: U.S. Government Printing Office, 1961–62.

6. G. B. JOHNSON, "The Negro and Crime," *Annals of the American Academy of Political and Social Science,* 1941, *217,* 93–104.

7. H. VON HENTIG, "Criminality of the Negro," *Journal of Criminal Law and Criminology,* 1940, *30,* 662–680.

8. Federal Bureau of Prisons, *National Prisoner Statistics: Prisoners in State and Federal Institutions, 1950.* Leavenworth, Kansas, 1954.

9. Federal Bureau of Prisons, *Federal Prisons, 1951–1960.* No date listed.

10. HARPER LEE, *To Kill a Mockingbird.* New York: Popular Library, 1962.

11. H. C. BREARLEY, *Homicide in the United States.* Chapel Hill: University of North Carolina Press, 1932.

12. H. GARFINKEL, "Research Note on Inter- and Intra-Racial Homicides," *Social Forces,* 1949, *27,* 369–381.

13. M. E. WOLFGANG, *Patterns in Criminal Homicide.* Philadelphia: University of Pennsylvania Press, 1958.

14. MARY H. DIGGS, "Some Problems and Needs of Negro Children as Revealed by Comparative Delinquency and Crime Statistics," *Journal of Negro Education,* 1950, *19,* 290–297.

15. S. Axelrad, "Negro and White Male Institutionalized Delinquents," *American Journal of Sociology*, 1952, 57, 569–574.

16. A. K. Cohen and J. F. Short, Jr., "Juvenile Delinquency." In R. K. Merton and R. A. Nisbet (eds.), *Contemporary Social Problems*. New York: Harcourt, Brace and World, 1961.

17. Federal Bureau of Prisons, "Executions, 1961," *National Prisoner Statistics*, April 1962, 28.

18. Federal Bureau of Prisons, *National Prisoner Statistics: Prisoners Released from State and Federal Institutions, 1951*. Atlanta, Ga.: United States Penitentiary, 1955.

19. Federal Bureau of Prisons, *National Prisoner Statistics: Prisoners Released from State and Federal Institutions, 1952 and 1953*. Atlanta, Ga.: United States Penitentiary, 1957.

20. T. F. Pettigrew and G. S. Tracy, "Correlates of Prison Adjustment," Unpublished paper.

21. J. Spirer, "Negro Crime," *Comparative Psychological Monographs*, 1940, 16, no. 81, 1–81.

22. O. Pollack, "A Statistical Investigation of the Criminality of Old Age," *Journal of Clinical Psychopathology*, 1944, 5, 745–767.

23. T. Sellin, "Race Prejudice in the Administration of Justice," *American Journal of Sociology*, 1935, 41, 212–217.

24. R. C. Bensing and O. Schroeder, Jr., *Homicide in an Urban Community*. Springfield, Ill.: Thomas, 1960.

25. National Office of Vital Statistics, *Death Rates for Selected Causes by Age, Color, and Sex: United States and Each State, 1949–1951*. Washington, D.C.: U.S. Government Printing Office, 1959.

26. W. A. Bonger, *Race and Crime*. Translated by Margaret M. Hordyk. New York: Columbia University Press, 1943.

27. J. Chateau, "Le Milieu Professionnel du Père et l'Équilibre Caractériel des Enfants," *Enfance*, 1961, no. 1, 1–8.

28. H. P. Brinton, "Negroes Who Run Afoul of the Law," *Social Forces*, 1932, 11, 96–101.

29. H. C. Brearley, "The Negro and Homicide," *Social Forces*, 1930, 9, 247–253.

30. M. C. Hill and T. D. Ackiss, "Social Classes: A Frame of Reference for the Study of Negro Society," *Social Forces*, 1943, 22, 92–98.

31. T. J. Woofter, Jr., *Black Yeomanry: Life on St. Helena Island*. New York: Holt, 1930.

32. P. Bohannan (ed.), *African Homicide and Suicide*. Princeton, N.J.: Princeton University Press, 1960.

33. E. H. Sutherland, *White Collar Crime*. New York: Dryden, 1949.

34. N. J. London and J. K. Myers, "Young Offenders: Psychopathology and Social Factors," *Archives of General Psychiatry*, 1961, 4, 274–282.

35. A. J. Reiss, Jr. and A. L. Rhodes, "The Distribution of Juvenile

Delinquency in the Social Class Structure," *American Sociological Review*, 1961, *26*, 720–732.

36. D. J. BOGUE, *The Population of the United States*. Glencoe, Ill.: Free Press, 1959.

37. J. T. BLUE, "The Relationship of Juvenile Delinquency, Race, and Economic Status," *Journal of Negro Education*, 1948, *17*, 469–477.

38. E. R. MOSES, "Differentials in Crime Rates between Negroes and Whites, Based on Comparisons of Four Socio-Economically Equated Areas," *American Sociological Review*, 1947, *12*, 411–420.

39. D. A. DOBBINS and B. M. BASS, "Effects of Unemployment on White and Negro Prison Admissions in Louisiana," *Journal of Criminal Law, Criminology, and Police Science*, 1958, *48*, 522–525.

40. A. K. COHEN, *Delinquent Boys: The Culture of the Gang*. Glencoe, Ill.: Free Press, 1955.

41. A. K. COHAN and J. F. SHORT, JR., "Research in Delinquent Subcultures," *Journal of Social Issues*, 1958, *14* (3), 20–37.

42. W. B. MILLER, "Lower Class Culture as a Generating Milieu of Gang Delinquency," *Journal of Social Issues*, 1958, *14* (3), 5–19.

43. W. F. WHYTE, *Street Corner Society*. Second edition. Chicago: University of Chicago Press, 1956.

44. D. R. CRESSEY, "Epidemiology and Individual Conduct: A Case from Criminology," *Pacific Sociological Review*, 1960, *3*, 47–58.

45. E. H. SUTHERLAND and D. R. CRESSEY, *Principles of Criminology*. Sixth edition, Philadelphia: Lippincott, 1960.

46. D. R. CRESSEY, "Crime." In R. K. Merton and R. A. Nisbet (eds.), *Contemporary Social Problems*. New York: Harcourt, Brace and World, 1961.

47. ELEANOR E. MACCOBY, J. P. JOHNSON, and R. M. CHURCH, "Community Integration and the Social Control of Juvenile Delinquency," *Journal of Social Issues*, 1958, *14* (3), 38–51.

48. J. B. ROEBUCK and M. L. CADWALLADER, "The Negro Armed Robber as a Criminal Type: The Construction and Application of a Typology," *Pacific Sociological Review*, 1961, *4*, 21–26.

49. H. C. BREARLEY, "The Pattern of Violence," In W. T. Couch (ed.), *Culture in the South*. Chapel Hill: University of North Carolina Press, 1934.

50. W. J. CASH, *The Mind of the South*. New York: Knopf, 1941.

51. MABEL ELLIOTT, "Crime and the Frontier Mores," *American Sociological Review*, 1944, *9*, 185–192.

52. J. H. FRANKLIN, *The Militant South: 1800–1861*. Cambridge, Mass.: Harvard University Press, 1956.

53. A. L. PORTERFIELD and R. H. TALBERT, "A Decade of Differentials and Trends in Serious Crimes in 86 American Cities by Southern and Non-Southern Pairs," *Social Forces*, 1952, *31*, 60–68.

54. L. W. SHANNON, "The Spatial Distribution of Criminal Offenses by

States," *Journal of Criminal Law, Criminology, and Police Science,* 1954, *45,* 264–271.

55. M. JANOWITZ, *The Professional Soldier.* New York: Free Press, 1960.

56. American Institute of Public Opinion Press Release, July 21, 1959.

57. T. F. PETTIGREW and ROSALIND B. SPIER, "The Ecological Structure of Negro Homicide," *American Journal of Sociology,* 1962, *67,* 621–629.

58. S. H. TULCHIN, *Intelligence and Crime.* Chicago: University of Chicago Press, 1939.

59. L. SAVITZ, *Delinquency and Migration.* Philadelphia: Commission on Human Relations, 1960.

60. MABEL ELLIOTT, "Perspective on the American Crime Problem," *Social Problems,* 1957–58, *5,* 184–193.

61. National Committee for Children and Youth, *Social Dynamite.* Washington, D.C.: National Committee for Children and Youth, 1961.

62. *Newsweek* editors, "The Negro in America," *Newsweek,* July 29, 1963, *62,* 15–34.

63. S. A. LEVITAN, *Youth Employment Act.* Kalamazoo, Mich.: Upjohn Institute for Employment Research, 1963.

64. United States Commission on Civil Rights, *Civil Rights U.S.A. Public Schools, Southern States 1962.* Washington, D.C.: U.S. Government Printing Office, 1962.

65. J. DOLLARD, *Caste and Class in a Southern Town.* New Haven, Conn.: Yale University Press, 1937.

66. A. F. HENRY and J. F. SHORT, JR., *Suicide and Homicide.* Glencoe, Ill.: Free Press, 1954.

67. M. GOLD, "Suicide, Homicide, and the Socialization of Aggression," *American Journal of Sociology,* 1958, *63,* 651–661.

68. J. S. COLEMAN, "Community Disorganization." In R. K. Merton and R. A. Nisbet (eds.), *Contemporary Social Problems.* New York: Harcourt, Brace and World, 1961.

69. A. M. LEE and N. D. HUMPHREY, *Race Riot.* New York: Dryden, 1943.

70. W. M. KEPHART, *Racial Factors and Urban Law Enforcement.* Philadelphia: University of Pennsylvania Press, 1957.

71. R. K. MERTON, *Social Theory and Social Structure.* Revised edition. Glencoe, Ill.: Free Press, 1957.

72. A. L. WOOD, "Minority Group Criminality and Cultural Integration," *Journal of Criminal Law and Criminology,* 1947, *37,* 498–510.

Allen D. Grimshaw

URBAN RACIAL VIOLENCE IN
THE UNITED STATES: CHANGING
ECOLOGICAL CONSIDERATIONS[1]

Urban racial social violence has occurred in every geographic region of the United States.[2] It has not occurred in every city in every area. Certain similarities in its background and social context are found in the cities which have had major race riots.[3] East St. Louis, Washington, Chicago, Tulsa, and Detroit all had sharp increases in Negro population in the years immediately prior to major interracial disturbances, and there were accompanying strains in the accommodative structure, generated in part by the Negroes' assaults on it and in part by the sheer pressure of population on facilities.

Accounts of urban race riots which are in sharp disagreement on other details consistently converge in descriptions of their ecology.[4]

Reprinted from *American Journal of Sociology*, Vol. LXVI, No. 2 (September 1960), pp. 109–119, by permission of The University of Chicago Press. Copyright 1960 by The University of Chicago.

Mr. Grimshaw is Assistant Professor of Sociology, Indiana University.

[1] Based in part on my unpublished Ph.D. dissertation. "A Study in Social Violence: Urban Race Riots in the United States" (University of Pennsylvania, 1959). Indebtedness to the George L. Harrison Foundation, the Samuel S. Fels Fund, and the Albert M. Greenfield Center for Human Relations for financial assistance is gratefully acknowledged.

[2] Social violence is defined as assault upon individuals or their property solely, or primarily, because of their membership in a social (in this case, racial) category.

[3] The question of why some cities have had riots and others not cannot be fully answered until data have been collected on four types of urban areas: those characterized by combinations of high or low social tensions with weak or strong external forces of constraint. It will then be possible to isolate peculiarities of cities that have had riots. There has been no agreement as to what is decisive in causing outbreaks of violence.

[4] Other consistent patterns in major urban racial disturbances can be isolated. In view of the acknowledged defects in the materials and their frequently partisan nature, however, considerable caution is necessary in drawing conclusions about "patterns" (cf., e.g., the conclusions on the Detroit riot [1943] of the "Dowling Report" [H. J. Rushton, W. E. Dowling, Oscar Olander, and J. H. Witherspoon, *Committee To Investigate the Riot Occurring in Detroit on June 21, 1943: Factual Report* (Detroit, n.d.)] and of various "action" agencies, such as the Urban League and the National Association for the Advancement of Colored People).

Ecological patterns are found in reports of individual incidents which did not lead to riots.

Without doing too great an injustice to the data, it is possible to specify roughly four patterns of urban racial violence:

1. Spontaneous brawls over an immediate disturbance, among bystanders.

2. The "mass, unco-ordinated battle" occurring when groups of one race attack usually isolated members of the other. Mobs of one race seldom engage mobs of the other race in open battle.

3. The "urban pogrom," which is the full-scale assault of one group, almost always white, upon Negroes and which has occurred particularly where whites have assumed the tacit approval of government. These "pogroms" have resulted in the flight of large numbers of the minority community.

4. Stray assaults and stabbings on the part of individuals or small groups of one race upon individuals of the other.[5]

Three varieties of expression of social violence may be distinguished: physical assault, including lynching and other homicide; arson, bombing, and like forms of attack upon property; and looting. These occur with differential frequency and intensity in the four patterns of urban racial violence noted above and in the following types of ecological areas: (a) Negro residential areas with no, or a minimal number of, business establishments (usually the upper or middle strata of the Negro population); (b) white middle-class residential areas; (c) Negro residential areas of high density, serviced largely by white businesses; (d) "stable" mixed neighborhoods; (e) neighborhoods previously dominated by whites, now undergoing a transition in occupancy;[6] (f) white-dominated areas not contested by Negroes; and (g) white-dominated central business districts.[7]

The importance of other sites within a city, such as recreational areas and, more recently, lunch counters or schools, is determined partly by their location relative to the seven types of ecological areas and partly

[5] These four categories are a paraphrase and condensation of a typology of social violence developed by Richard D. Lambert in his study "Hindu-Muslim Riots" (unpublished Ph.D. dissertation, University of Pennsylvania, 1951), pp. 217–21. Marked parallels and some significant differences emerge from comparison of Hindu-Muslim and Negro-white violence.

[6] Called "contested areas" in Chicago Commission on Race Relations, *The Negro in Chicago* (Chicago, 1919).

[7] Obviously these ecological areas do not *cause* variant manifestations of social violence. It would be more precise to say that patterns of social organization or disorganization which are local characteristics are more likely to be associated with some outbreaks of violence than with others. For heuristic purposes, however, it is convenient to bypass the well-documented social characteristics of the areas and speak of the areas themselves as experiencing the varying manifestations.

by the local potential for violence.[8] In major riots occurring before and up to the end of World War II, two other types of locations were of particular importance in the ecology of major disturbances: public transportation facilities, particularly transfer points, and government buildings. Finally, either natural or man-made boundaries (e.g., bodies of water or large parks and large industrial complexes or railroad yards) have confined or determined the path of violence.

Three questions receive attention in this paper. First, are the patterns of urban racial violence (brawls, etc.) and particular expressions (physical assaults, etc.) differently manifested in different types of ecological areas? Attention will be directed here primarily to major urban race riots up to and including the Detroit riot of 1943. Second, have changes in urban racial violence occurred since 1943? Focus here will be on the changing role of the police and of the nature of disputes. Finally, is it possible to forecast the future of racial social violence?

ECOLOGICAL CONSISTENCIES IN RACIAL VIOLENCE DURING WORLD WAR II

During the first forty-five years of the twentieth century the United States experienced a large number of major interracial outbreaks and, particularly in the years following World War I, a host of lesser disturbances.[9] Excepting certain differences between "northern" and "southern" styles of race riots,[10] they show a remarkable degree of ecological consistency.

Negro Residential Areas with No, or a Minimal Number of, Business Establishments

Where they have existed, these Negro residential areas contain populations which, in income, in years of education completed, and in occupational status, are above the norms for the larger Negro population. These neighborhoods had few incidents. The absence of non-residential property meant an absence of opportunity for looting. Lower population density and less likelihood of large gatherings made rioting on a large

[8] While two of the bloodiest riots of this century, Chicago's in 1919 and Detroit's in 1943, started in recreational facilities, combat quickly moved away from the site of the original incident and thereafter conformed to the ecological patterns described below.

[9] Details of many of these disorders can be found in Grimshaw, op. cit. A typology of periods of racial violence in the United States is suggested in my article, "Lawlessness and Violence in America and Their Special Manifestations in Changing Negro-White Relationships," Journal of Negro History, XLIV, No. 1 (January 1959), 52–72.

[10] Grimshaw, "Lawlessness and Violence . . . ," op. cit., p. 65; "A Study in Social Violence . . . ." op. cit., pp. 36–37, 178.

scale unlikely. It is also possible, although no evidence can be found to support the claim, that the higher social and economic status of the residents enabled them to enjoy better police protection than was provided in other Negro areas.

Two varieties of racial violence might be expected to occur in these neighborhoods: arson and bombing and related forms of assault on property, and attacks on persons. In Chicago, where bombings and arson were used to intimidate real-estate dealers of both races from selling properties in "exclusive" areas, trouble might have been anticipated where middle-class Negroes were concentrated; however, there is no evidence that these neighborhoods were singled out or that they suffered from "raids" directed randomly by white hoodlums either during the major riot or in times of relative peace. It can only be concluded that insufficient evidence documents the local violence; there may have been incidents, but too few to attract the attention of authorities, or the characteristics of the neighborhoods and residents may have reduced the likelihood of incidents. In the absence of adequate documentation it seems reasonable to accept the second interpretation.

White Higher-Class Residential Neighborhoods

The experience of white residential neighborhoods, particularly those more distant from central business districts with residents of relatively high socioeconomic characteristics, was similar to that of Negro residential neighborhoods. The more isolated they were from centers in which violence occurred, the more likely they were to escape trouble, except during major outbursts of race rioting.

The single pattern of racial violence reported for such neighborhoods reflected the higher social and economic status of their white residents, many of whom employed Negro domestics.[11] During the course of several major riots such domestics were attacked by white gangs, frequently while waiting for buses or streetcars. Large mobs seldom gathered in such neighborhoods, removed as they were from the areas where rioting was concentrated, but youths frequently prowled in automobiles in search of stray Negroes,[12] and many frightened white employers kept their domestics at home until violence came to an end.

[11] With recent changes in the American social and economic structure, there have been fewer domestics. During the waves of riots during the two world wars, however, domestic service accounted for a large proportion of all Negroes who worked, particularly of Negro women.

[12] It would be interesting to see how the wider distribution of automobile ownership has spread racial disturbances to areas more remote from city centers. With television carrying news of incipient disturbances (see, e.g., William Gremley, "Social Control in Cicero," *British Journal of Sociology*, III [952] 322–38) and cars available

Negro Slums

Violence in time of major race riots has been concentrated in Negro slums, which in many cities were served largely by white businesses. Casualties and fatalities occurred most often in slums or along their fringes,[13] and destruction of property, particularly looting, was greatest there. Three subvarieties of social racial violence have occurred in Negro slums.

In a number of race riots of the "southern" style, attaining the intensity of urban "pogroms" or of mass racial war, Negro slums were completely or partially destroyed. In the Springfield, Illinois, riot of 1908, forty Negro homes were destroyed and an estimated two thousand Negroes were driven from the town by rioting whites. In the riot in East St. Louis in 1917, the Negro section was invaded, Negro residences and businesses were set on fire, and Negroes were shot down in large numbers as they attempted to flee from the burning buildings. In these, and in equally bitter disorders in Tulsa in 1921, violence was confined to Negro areas and their boundaries; however, in each case, fighting began in the central business district. Negroes then retreated to their own sections, and attacks were launched against them there by large white mobs. In Springfield there was little fighting back; in Tulsa, on the other hand, the white attackers were resisted in strength and, for a time, repulsed. In these cases, and in similar "southern" riots, all three varieties of violence occurred, although looting was minimal and was often only in the form of breaking into pawnshops and hardware stores in search of weapons and ammunition. Casualties were heavy and fatalities high, Negro victims accounting for the largest share. Arson was endemic; in Tulsa and East St. Louis the Negro sections were almost totally destroyed.

No northern city experienced racial strife in which "all-out" attacks such as these were made on Negro sections.[14] The two Harlem disturbances of 1935 and 1943 were completely limited to the Negro slum; on other occasions riots in Negro sections occurred in conjunction with more widespread violence.

The Harlem disturbances differed from other riots because of the

------

to carry people to the scene (as in the case of a Negro "move-in" in Levittown, Pennsylvania), the time may be ripe for an examination of "modern technology and the diffusion of racial disturbances." While it is too early to tell, it seems likely that the spread of the current "lunch-counter" strikes is related to the wide coverage of news by television.

[13] The Chicago riot of 1919 was an exception.

[14] Alfred McClung Lee and Norman Daymond Humphrey assert that one was narrowly averted in Detroit in 1943 (*Race Riot* [New York: Dryden Press, 1943], pp. 39–40).

sheer size of the local Negro population. A major invasion was inconceivable without a fairly well-equipped army, and only police forces
were equipped in a manner in any way adequate to cope with the 1943
disorders. On the other hand, whites in the area were relatively few and,
when outbreaks occurred, were either able to flee or to find Negroes
willing to give them shelter. There were few occasions for Negro-white
contacts, and physical clashes were usually between the resident population and the police. Most of the violence was in the form of looting of
stores and general destruction of property. While some evidence suggests
white property was singled out for attack, enough Negro establishments
were attacked to leave open the question whether the violence was racial.

In other northern urban race riots Negroes have suffered physical
violence as well as being the victims of property damage and looting.
Physical assault may be by Negroes on whites passing through their
neighborhoods in automobiles, on public vehicles, or on foot, or on
whites who found themselves in the area when major rioting began; or
there may be conflict between Negroes and the police, the Negroes
frequently being armed and, according to the police, initiating violence
by assault or by resisting arrest; or, finally, there may be conflict
following the invasion of Negro neighborhoods by bands of armed
whites, most frequently making forays by automobile. In both the
Chicago riot of 1919 and the Detroit riot of 1943, the Negro slum or the
immediately contiguous areas experienced the greatest number of casualties. Over half the fatalities in the Detroit riot occurred in Paradise
Valley. According to the reports filed by the police department, seven-
teen of thirty-four deaths in the riot were caused by justifiable shooting
by the police.[15]

With two exceptions, physical violence in these areas was usually
visited by mobs of one race upon isolated members of the other. One
exception involves large numbers of police engaged in battle with mobs
of Negroes: in both the Chicago and the Detroit riots they waged pitched
battles. The other exception has occurred when large numbers of
Negroes have caught and engaged raiding parties of whites invading
Negro sections. A more frequent occurrence than either of these, however,
was that in which white motorists passing through Negro areas, in some
cases unaware of the rioting, were stoned by Negroes or in which whites
were pulled from buses and beaten or otherwise assaulted.

Assaults on property have taken three forms. In the Chicago riot,
arson was fairly common in the Negro section, allegedly committed by
members of white gangs and "athletic clubs." Arson and bombings were
not frequent in other major northern riots; more frequent was the looting

[15] H. J. Rushton *et al.*, *op. cit.*, Exhibits 18, 19. Considerable caution is
needed in interpreting the findings of this report.

of places of business by Negroes who engaged in general destruction of property of whites. Destruction of automobiles was incidental to assaults on white motorists.

"Stable" Mixed Neighborhoods

The term "stable mixed neighborhood" has, conveniently, no precise meaning. In discussions of race riots the term has come to mean, residually, neighborhoods in which no social violence occurred. The implied meaning, however, seems to be that neighborhoods so labeled are characterized by unchanging patterns of occupancy, whatever the proportion of whites to Negroes. If this is the case, there is indirect confirmation that violence is less likely there. Studies like that of Kramer have demonstrated that more favorable interracial attitudes are to be found in such neighborhoods.[16]

Direct evidence is more problematical. Lee and Humphrey state that students reported that there was no violence in mixed neighborhoods during the Detroit riot.[17] The characteristics of these neighborhoods were not specified, either in their volume or in other writings on the Detroit riot where similar statements were made. On the other hand, in the Chicago riot of 1919 violence directed against Negroes occurred even in areas of long-established Negro occupancy, while other "adjusted" areas remained quiet.[18] If there were any residential areas in northern cities where Negroes and whites had lived amicably for long periods, they were probably few and far between, and any assertions about a lack of violence there should be looked upon with caution.[19] Areas where patterns of occupancy remained relatively unchanged over long periods of time, where friendly or, at the least, cordial relations prevailed between the two races, probably had the same experience during race riots as did the Negro residential and white middle-class neighborhoods: violence, such as it was, resulted from invasions from outside, not from the explosion of local social tensions. As in the case of Negro and white middle-class residential areas, however, there is insufficient data to state positively that "stable" neighborhoods were characterized by particular patterns of violence, during periods either of actual rioting or of relative peace.

[16] Bernard M. Kramer, "Residential Contact as a Determinant of Attitudes toward Negroes" (unpublished Ph.D. dissertation, Harvard University, 1950).

[17] *Op. cit.*, p. 17. They claimed that violence did not occur in mixed neighborhoods, among mixed groups of students, or among whites and Negroes who worked together in war plants.

[18] E.g., the North Side (see Chicago Commission on Race Relations, *op. cit.*, pp. 108–13, 119).

[19] There were "non-adjusted" neighborhoods which experienced no violence (*ibid.*, pp. 114–15).

"Contested Areas"

The term "contested area" was used by the Chicago Commission on Race Relations to describe areas previously dominated by whites but undergoing transition and those which, although not yet penetrated, are in the line of movement of the Negro population and anticipating invasion. The latter differs from the next ecological type in that the areas discussed in the next section, although close to centers of Negro population, are not contested by Negroes.

Opposition to Negro in-movement has been expressed in both an organized and a non-organized fashion. Much of the inter-racial conflict in periods of relative harmony occurred there, and much of it was, and is, organized in the form of "neighborhood improvement" or "property-owners" associations. These usually disavowed, at least verbally, violence of any variety, although the claim has been made that their publicity was often inflammatory. Whatever their official views toward violence may have been, it was in contested areas, where Negroes had already moved in, that incidents of violence most frequently occurred in periods when there were no actual riots. The incidents largely involved property, either destruction of Negro-occupied property or harassment of the owners by minor damage. Long and Johnson have noted that both the Chicago and Detroit riots were preceded by violence over the entrance of Negroes into white neighborhoods.[20] Such areas, in a pattern that continues today, also provided the scene for physical assaults.

In view of the concentration of violence in these contested areas in periods when other parts of the city were enjoying relative peace, it might be anticipated that in times of actual race rioting they would have been the focal point of violence. This is not the case; the Negro slum suffered more casualties and, in at least one major riot, that in Chicago in 1919, the highest number of casualties reported was in an area with no Negro residents. Some violence did occur in these areas, particularly along their borders and at transfer points in public transportation. In 1940, Woodward Avenue in Detroit served as a boundary line between the major concentration of Negroes in that city and an area of low-class white residence which included a large number of rooming houses. Lee and Humphrey, in their volume on the Detroit riot of 1943, include a "battle map" of major points of overt conflict. Two were located at Woodward Avenue and main cross-streets in the Mack-Davenport area and at Vernor Highway where the sharpest fighting, involving large mobs of whites, took place. Whites stoned automobiles with Negro passengers,

[20] Herman H. Long and Charles S. Johnson, *People vs. Property* (Nashville, Tenn.: Fisk University Press, 1947).

dragged Negroes from buses, and beat them. At other points up and down Woodward Avenue, Negroes occasionally took the initiative and attacked whites. However, there was no major invasion across this line, and, although some Negro penetration had occurred in areas west of Woodward Avenue, there was no major violence there. However, violence also occurred around a smaller concentration of lower-income Negroes along Michigan Avenue. Here again, the violence occurred on the peripheries rather than in surrounding contested areas.

The reason for the lack of major violence in contested areas during major race riots is not clear. A possible answer may lie in the implicit observation made by the Chicago Commission on Race Relations that the neighbors of Negro in-movers were infrequently involved in attacks upon the new tenants. It is possible that most of the violence visited upon new Negro residents is the work of individuals not themselves local residents. In its investigation of bombings the commission heard testimony of one victim that the police believed that the bombings were being done by a gang of young white "roughnecks" who were under police surveillance.[21] If this was true, and if similar acts of violence directed against property have been committed not by neighbors but by "outside fanatics,"[22] it becomes easier to understand why these sectors saw less violence during actual rioting. The perpetrating individuals or groups were, during major riots, more likely to be found where there was more action. Violence in these areas during major rioting was probably more likely to occur as a result of chance encounters or of a concentration of people, not specifically gathered for the purpose, for instance, at bus transfer points.

Except in the peak periods of major race riots, contested areas were the centers of most racial violence in northern cities through World War II. In cities which experienced no major race riots, almost all violence occurred there or in areas, such as recreation centers, with unusually high potential for trouble.

White-Dominated Areas Not Contested by Negroes

In their discussion of Negro residence areas in Chicago, the 1919 Commission on Race Relations described adjusted and non-adjusted

[21] *Op. cit.,* p. 128. Observers in Levittown, Pennsylvania, noted that most of the opposition to the Meyers family moving in was by persons not resident in the immediate neighborhood.

[22] A recent study in a Kansas City residential area found that whites were, at the least, resigned to an in-movement of Negro residents (Community Studies, Inc., *An Attitude Survey of Negro Infiltration into a White Residential Area* [Kansas City, Mo., n.d.], undertaken at the request of the Kansas City, Missouri, Commission on Human Relations). When a bomb was exploded in the neighborhood, it was interpreted as the work of a fanatic, not a resident (personal communication from William H. Gremley, executive secretary, Kansas City, Missouri, Commission on Human Relations).

areas. The second category consisted of areas of organized opposition and of unorganized opposition. The report presented materials on areas of organized opposition; of one variety of unorganized opposition, the commission said:

> There are residence districts of Chicago adjacent to those occupied by Negroes in which hostility to Negroes is so marked that the latter not only find it impossible to live there, but expose themselves to danger even by passing through. There are no hostile organizations in these neighborhoods, and active antagonism is usually confined to gang lawlessness. . . . In the section immediately west of Wentworth Avenue and thus adjoining the densest Negro residence area in the city, practically no Negroes live. . . . Wentworth Avenue has long been regarded as a strict boundary line separating white and Negro residence areas. The district has many "athletic clubs." The contact of Negroes and whites comes when Negroes must pass to and from their work at the Stock Yards and at other industries located in the district. It was in this district that the largest number of riot clashes occurred. Several Negroes have been murdered here, and numbers have been beaten by gangs of young men and boys.[23]

Of those reported injured in the Chicago riot, 34 per cent received their wounds in the "Black Belt" itself, and 41 per cent in the stockyards district of the Southwest Side.

It is difficult to find neighborhoods which have been as vehement in hostility to Negroes as the stockyards area of Chicago. Even today, the district west of Wentworth in Chicago has remained one of minimal Negro residence.[24] In 1910, Wentworth Avenue was the east-west dividing line between the Negro and white populations. Between 1910 and 1950 the Negro population increased from slightly under fifty thousand to a little over five hundred and eighty-six thousand.[25] Squeezed between Wentworth Avenue and the lake front, they spread throughout the South Side and into enclaves in western sections. The stockyards district has remained essentially white in the face of tremendous pressures of the Negro population.

Under ordinary circumstances, Chicago Negroes in 1919 would have avoided the stockyards district. They passed through it on their way to and from their work in the yards and packing houses and other industries but did not linger; as noted above, prior to the riot several

---

[23] *Op. cit.*, p. 155.

[24] Between the Chicago River and Fifty-fifth Street. This neighborhood, like Cicero and Trumbull Park, scenes of more recent disorders, has a Polish, Bohemian, and Slavic population. The residents are too poor and too foreign to go elsewhere. They are neither geographically nor socially mobile.

[25] The best ecological and demographic study of the Negro population of Chicago or, for that matter, of any northern city, is Otis D. Duncan and Beverly Duncan, *The Negro Population of Chicago* (Chicago: University of Chicago Press, 1957).

Negroes had been murdered there by gangs of young men and boys. If the situation had been normal, no Negroes would have been found there during the riot, with the possible exception of small "raiding" parties. However, the riot coincided with a major strike of Chicago's transportation lines. Negroes found themselves stranded at work; some stayed, others attempted to go home. Whether it was to protect their families or to engage themselves in rioting, or whether they did not know about the riot, is unimportant: what matters is that they got caught in the very locality most notorious for hostility to them. Many were beaten, and several slain.

No other major urban race riot has taken place where a white neighborhood characterized by such intense prejudice immediately abutted on the central concentration of Negroes. If, in Chicago, it had not been for the transportation strike, it is doubtful whether so much of the violence would have occurred where it did. More probably, battles would have been concentrated, as elsewhere, along the boundary lines. However, tension was high in the areas of Detroit immediately west of Woodward Avenue, which, however, was a contested area even in 1940: and, as has been observed, violence was largely concentrated along the dividing line itself.

White-Dominated Central Business Districts

With the exception of the Harlem disturbances, highly distinctive in many of their characteristics, in every important interracial disturbance in both northern and southern cities, Negroes were the victims of mobs in the white-dominated central business districts. In those cases where few Negroes were so assaulted, it was because the Negro population, forewarned, had not ventured downtown. Violence in central business districts took the form of physical assault and usually involved large mobs of whites and individual Negroes or small groups of them. In the Chicago riot it was reported that the white gangs of soldiers and sailors who raided the Loop, the central shopping district, in search of Negroes, "in the course of their activities . . . wantonly destroyed property of white business men."[26] This, as in other cases, was largely incidental to the main purpose of catching and assaulting Negroes. No major outbreaks of looting directed at white property were reported resulting from white mob activity.

The largest mobs of whites have usually been those which gather in the central business district. Lee and Humphrey report a mob of "10,000 people jammed around the Woodward and Davenport-Mack intersections on the northern edge of the downtown district. Cadillac

[26] Chicago Commission on Race Relations, *op. cit.*, p. 7.

Square—between City Hall and the County Building—was packed with milling murderous thousands, especially at the City Hall end."[27] The mobs engaged in a variety of types of assault, from the stoning of Negro automobiles and their occupants, to the invasion of theaters in search of Negroes. Army officers saw, from windows of the Federal Building in downtown Detroit, a mob estimated at five hundred pursuing a lone Negro on Fort Street from Woodward. Similar events occurred in every major riot.

SPECIAL ECOLOGICAL FACTORS

Two types of ecological locations warrant special mention. Violence in northern urban race riots occurred frequently at transfer points of public transportation lines, particularly where members of one race had to pass through the territory of the other. A comparison of maps noting transportation contacts between Negroes and whites with spot maps of injuries and deaths in the Chicago riot of 1919 is instructive.[28] A general strike on surface and elevated lines after the second day of the rioting magnified the importance of transportation, for, with the stopping of the street cars, a new source of danger arose to those who attempted to walk to their places of employment. Even on the first day of the riot, however, "attacks on street cars provided outstanding cases, five persons being killed and many injured."[29]

In the Detroit riot, both whites and Negroes were pulled from street cars and beaten or otherwise assaulted. The same thing occurred in the East St. Louis and Washington riots, Negroes being the major victims. Incidents in Harlem have been recorded in which white employees of the transportation systems were assaulted by Negro passengers, although this was important in neither of the major disturbances in Harlem.

Public transportation provides an opportunity to catch isolated individuals and attack them without fear of immediate reprisal. Another scene of violence is government buildings, attacks on which have occurred when it is believed that Negroes have sought shelter there or because Negroes are known to work there. Negro municipal employees were evacuated from the City Hall in Detroit when the building was threatened by white mobs. Other locations of interracial violence in major northern urban race riots have been highly specific. The rioting in

[27] Op. cit., p. 36.
[28] See the numerous maps accompanying the report of the Chicago Commission on Race Relations. Note also the special exhibits on incidents on the Detroit Street Railway (H. J. Rushton, et al., op. cit.).
[29] Chicago Commission on Race Relations, op. cit., p. 17.

Detroit began on the Belle Isle Bridge and became general apparently only after a much publicized announcement at a Negro night club. That location (Belle Isle) was on the very periphery of the Negro concentration in Detroit and fits none of the ecological classifications of areas suggested above. Once the riot was under way, activity in the original area became minimal.

RACIAL CONFLICT SINCE WORLD WAR II

In February, 1960, racial conflict appeared in a previously unexperienced form. Starting in Greensboro, North Carolina, demonstrations by Negro youth, college students, and occasional high-school students were directed against segregation at lunch counters and in restaurants.[30] At the time of this writing, only minor violence has been reported (in Chattanooga and Nashville, Tennessee, and in Portsmouth, Virginia) but large numbers of both whites and Negroes have been arrested, and the movement has expanded through seven southern states and into border cities, such as Indianapolis.

These demonstrations have differed from previous Negro-white conflicts in several significant ways. In the first place, although there is evidence of some co-ordination and the national offices of several protest organizations have "sanctioned" the demonstrations, the participants have generally claimed that the movement is spontaneous and autonomous. The spokesmen of the movements have been college students and, on occasion, high-school students. Local leadership has been drawn into the movement, largely in an advisory capacity, as instructors in techniques of "non-violent protest." The second characteristic which distinguishes these from previous interracial disturbances has been the youth and student status of the demonstrators. While other Negroes have been drawn into the situation as events have unfolded, neither the white nor the Negro leadership of affected communities has thought to characterize the initiators as "hoodlums." A third change is the restraint with which Negro participants have acted, even when subjected to considerable physical abuse by whites (also frequently youth, although occasionally not students). This refusal to respond to acts which can only be interpreted as invitations to violence (e.g., the dropping of lighted cigarettes down the backs of Negro students seated at lunch counters in a silent request for service), the quiet acceptance, even courting, of arrest, and the clearly conscious nature of the assault upon the accommodative structure, would alone differentiate these demonstrations from any previous behavior. In view of the historical patterning of race relations in

[30] *Southern School News*, VI, No. 9 (March, 1960). For detailed information on these and subsequent events, see the special report of the Southern Regional Council, *The Student Protest Movement, Winter 1960* (Report SRC-13 [rev.], April 1, 1960), and later, supplementary, reports.

the South, however, another difference in the current events is almost equally impressive: the restraint and the apparent impartiality with which local municipal officials and police forces have acted. In some instances, when stores have requested arrests of Negroes on charges of "trespassing," arrests have been entirely one-sided. In every case where opposing groups have appeared, however, arrests apparently have been relatively impartial, and almost equal numbers of each group have been taken into custody.[31]

It will be some months before the real nature of these demonstrations is known. The events seem, at least, as clearly linked to ecological factors as were earlier, more extended, race riots. Events have occurred where they did, not because of the social characteristics of residents or because of the social organization of the particular area affected, but rather because of their location in central business districts.

One other post-World War II pattern of racial violence has been directly related to an ecological circumstance: the pattern of violence and near-violence which has grown out of attempts to desegregate white southern schools in response to the Supreme Court decisions.[32] Schools have been bombed. Demonstrations, including the throwing of stones as well as epithets, have occurred on school grounds or on nearby streets. Inside the schools new Negro students have been pushed and threatened. In events related to the school problem the homes of whites and Negroes alike have been bombed, and in one case white school board members were assaulted, allegedly because of their pro-integration actions.[33]

Except for the collateral bombings and related events, disorders over school desegregation have been highly local and, with few exceptions, have involved relatively large numbers of whites and small numbers of Negroes. In almost every case the presence of legal force has prevented major assault by whites.

PROBLEMS IN FORECASTING RACIAL VIOLENCE

Considerable courage would be required to forecast major racial violence as a result of current events in the South or of continuing tension

---

[31] *Southern School News, op. cit.* However, later action has shown increasing intervention by the state and even greater proportions of Negroes arrested (see Southern Regional Council, *op. cit.*).

[32] See *Southern School News*, Vol. I, September, 1954. A dramatic presentation of some events surrounding attempted desegregation can be found in Dorothy Sterling (with Donald Gross), *Tender Warriors* (New York: Hill & Wang, Inc., 1958). A more general, if journalistic, account is that of John Bartlow Martin in *The Deep South Says Never* (New York: Ballantine Books, 1957). Among others, one specific treatment is Virgil T. Blossom, *It Has Happened Here* (New York: Harper & Bros., 1959), an account of events in Little Rock, Arkansas, by its discharged superintendent of schools.

[33] *Southern School News*, V. No. 3 (September 1958), 15.

in northern cities. Nonetheless, it is possible to note some changes in general patterning of race relations in the United States, both north and south, which may affect the probabilities.

The forecasting of racial violence requires knowledge of the history and current status of three factors:

1. *The mode and pattern of the assault upon the accommodative structure; its direct or indirect nature, the militancy with which it is pressed, and the areas in which it occurs.* In a historical review of racial violence in the United States, the writer has expressed the view that such violence has resulted from reactions of the dominant white community to real or perceived attacks on the accommodative structure and not from a conscious policy of repression and that violence in the South would be contingent on the militancy with which Negroes carried on their struggle against subordinate status.[34] That this struggle would evolve into the current campaign of non-violent action was not anticipated.

2. *The attitude and actions of agencies of external control.* There is no direct relationship between the level of tension and the eruption of social violence. While assaults on the accommodative structure doubtless lead to an increase in tensions, violence is constrained by the strength and mode of application of external agencies of control, particularly the police.[35] Changes in the latter's attitudes and in the legal use of force have had an undeniable influence in reducing the possibility of violence in the current "sit-down" campaign, particularly in large southern cities (with one marked exception: Birmingham, Alabama).

3. *The nature of the accommodative structure itself.* Negro participation in areas previously forbidden is now accepted, if with some lack of grace. At the same time Negro activities occur in areas previously considered secure and areas in which participation had been acceptable in the past are redefined. In the current disturbances the reaction of the larger national, and world, communities has consequences in redefining, frequently through increasing rigidity, local systems of accommodation. The changing structure of the accommodative system must be considered in attempting to assess interpretations of new demands by Negroes as these interpretations determine the level of tension in the white community. Concurrently, as changes in the accommodative structure occur and some demands are met, the level of aspiration of the Negro community rises, and new rebuffs generate greater tensions there.

During the period in which major urban racial disturbances occurred, the social characteristics of ecological areas within the metropolis greatly influenced the kind and intensity of local racial violence. In

[34] See n. 9.
[35] For documentation of this in another case of violence, see Lambert, *op. cit.*

recent years, and more particularly in the current events in the South, ecological factors have had a continuing but different influence on manifestations of conflict. While in the past it has been characteristic of people, now the specific ecological locale and its characteristics are of importance. Disturbances now occur where Negroes have moved into residential areas, have attempted to go to school in accordance with judicial decisions, and, most recently, have insisted on their right to eat where they buy. The whites and Negroes involved in the disturbances of the last decade have not been the populations residing in the affected locales. Indeed, particularly in the case of the current "sit-down" disturbances, there are no major concentrations in the affected areas. All involved have been transients on the sites of conflict. It is perhaps true that many of the whites who have been most active in resisting the new Negro movement have been from locales in the city characterized by more militant anti-Negro prejudices. It is certainly true that the Negroes involved have been unlike the victims and the offenders in past racial disturbances, including major riots, in the urban North.

United States Commission on Civil Rights
UNLAWFUL POLICE VIOLENCE

The Commission's study of the administration of justice concentrates on police brutality—the use of unlawful violence—against Negroes. Complaints and litigation suggest four subdivisions of the problem. The first involves the use of racially motivated brutality to enforce subordination or segregation. The second, a not altogether separate category, entails violence as a punishment. The third relates to coerced confessions. The last and largest entails the almost casual, or spontaneous, use of force in arrests. Only the first category necessarily involves racial discrimination. In the others it may, or may not, be present, but Negroes are the victims with disproportionate frequency.

In the text of this chapter the Commission briefly describes the alleged facts in 11 typical cases of police brutality. They are presented in the belief that they contribute to an understanding of the problem. The

A report by the United States Commission on Civil Rights, *Justice,* Report No. 5, 1961. (Washington, D.C.: U.S. Government Printing Office, 1961).

allegations of misconduct are supported in several cases by criminal convictions[1] or findings by impartial agencies; in others, by sworn testimony, affidavits from eye witnesses, or by staff field investigations. In no case has the Commission determined conclusively whether the complainants or the officers were correct in their statements. This is the function of a court. The Commission is of the opinion, however, that the allegations appeared substantial enough to justify discussion in this study.

Most citizens do not look upon policemen with fear. Indeed, the law officer's badge has become a symbol worthy of much respect. There is good reason for this. Many citizens call upon policemen for aid in any emergency. And it is the policeman who must enforce the criminal law. The extent of the burden on this country's approximately 200,000 policemen[2] is demonstrated by the 1,861,300 serious offenses reported in 1960.[3] In carrying out their vital mission policemen sometimes face extreme danger. The Federal Bureau of Investigation recently reported:[4]

> During 1959, 49 police employees were killed in line of duty, . . . pointing up the hazardous nature of the occupation and devotion to duty of these dedicated men. In 1960, 48 police lost their lives.

Moreover, in 1960 a total of 9,621 assaults on American policemen were reported to the FBI. This amounts to a rate of 6.3 assaults for every 100 police officers in the country.[5] The Commission's study of denials of rights to citizens by some policemen should be viewed in the context of the difficult and dangerous job that policemen are required to perform.

PATTERNS OF POLICE BRUTALITY

Enforcement of Segregation or Subordinate Status

THE KILLING OF A NEGRO IN GEORGIA: 1943.   In the early morning of January 30, 1943, Manley Poteat responded to a call for an ambulance

---

[1] In two of the incidents described in the text the officers were convicted in a Federal civil rights prosecution—the *Screws* case *infra,* at 6 and the *Clark* case *infra,* at 14. Since the Civil Rights Section of the Department of Justice became a Division in December 1957, it has obtained police brutality convictions from juries in four cases, while in two cases the defendant officers entered pleas of *nolo contendere.* See ch. 4 at 66 *infra.* In none of these cases were the victims known to be minority group members, except in the *Clark* case wherein the victim was a Canadian born Indian.

[2] Federal Bureau of Investigation, *Uniform Crime Reports—1960 at 105* (1961). The total for 3,779 cities with a total population of 103,493,753 is 195,109, which figure includes civilian employees.

[3] *Id.* at 1.

[4] *Id.* at 19 and 104.

[5] *Id.* at 106.

at the jail in Newton, Baker County, Georgia. He explained in sworn testimony later that he found an "unconscious" man crawling around in a pool of blood on the floor of a cell.[6] The man was a young Negro, Bobby Hall, a skilled mechanic who was married and had one child. He was taken to a hospital in Albany, 22 miles away, where he died approximately 1 hour after his arrival. When Walter Poteat, Manley's father, embalmed the body, he observed that it had been brutally beaten.[7]

The authorities in Albany, which is not in Baker County, were notified and saw the body; photographs were made; and the matter soon came to public attention. Sheriff Claude M. Screws—and the other officers—who beat and killed Hall were later prosecuted by the Federal Government for violation of an 1866 statute that makes it a Federal crime for an officer of the law to interfere with the constitutional rights of any person.[8] In beating and killing young Hall without justification, a Federal grand jury in Macon charged, the sheriff had deprived the victim of a number of constitutional rights including the right not to be subjected to punishment except after a fair trial and the right to equal protection of the laws. Screws was convicted, and eventually appealed to the Supreme Court, challenging the constitutionality of the statute. In the landmark decision of *Screws* v. *United States*,[9] the Supreme Court in 1945 upheld the statute, construed it strictly, and overturned the conviction because it had not been established that in killing Bobby Hall, Screws had intended to deprive him of a constitutional right.[10] Screws was later tried again under the standard set forth by the Supreme Court and acquitted.[11]

While this example of police brutality took place almost two decades ago it is still a classic case. Recent complaints coming to the attention of this Commission contain allegations that bear a striking similarity to it. For this reason the case will be described in detail.

Sheriff Screws testified at his first trial that the trouble began late that January evening in 1943 when he asked night patrolman Frank E. Jones and Deputy Sheriff Jim Bob Kelley to serve a warrant of arrest on Bobby Hall for theft of a tire. The two men brought the Negro back to Newton in the Sheriff's car. Screws continued:[12]

> I opened the door and I said, "All right, Bobby, get out" and I noticed he wasn't in any hurry to get out but when he, when I did see him come out, I saw something coming out ahead of him like that

[6] Record, p. 109, *Screws* v. *United States,* 325 U.S. 91 (1945).
[7] *Id.* at 114.
[8] 14 Stat. 27 (1866), 18 U.S.C. sec. 242 (1958).
[9] *Screws* v. *United States, supra,* note 6.
[10] A full discussion of the statute, the *Screws* case, and other aspects of the enforcement of the Civil Rights Acts are found in ch. 4 *infra.*
[11] *United States* v. *Screws,* Crim. No. 1300, M.D. Ga., Nov. 1, 1945.
[12] Record, *supra,* note 6, at 171.

(indicating) and I discovered it was a gun; and he said, "You damn white sons"—and that is all I remember what he said. By that time I knocked the gun up like that and the gun fired off right over my head; and when it did he was on the ground by then and me and Kelley and Jones ran in to him and we all were scuffling and I was beating him about the face and head with my fist. I knew Jones had a blackjack and I told him to hit him and he hit him a lick or two and he didn't seem to weaken and I said, "Hit him again!" When he fell to the ground, we didn't hit him on the ground.

At no time when I saw the deceased or Bobby Hall did he have any handcuffs on him.

The only colored prosecution witness who observed a crucial part of this event was Mrs. Annie Pearl Hall, the wife of the victim. She contradicted, in part, one vital item in the defendant's case: Mrs. Hall stated after the victim left their home under arrest, "they were handcuffing him when I went to the door."[13] All three of the officers said that he had never been handcuffed and was, therefore, able to grab the shotgun from the front seat of the car and attack them with it.

While there are many similarities between this case and others in Commission files, there is one major difference. A number of white people observed the beating of Bobby Hall and events connected with it— and appeared at the trial as witnesses. Their stories supported one another and directly contradicted that of Screws. The testimony of these witnesses may be summarized as follows: Screws and his companions had threatened to get a "nigger" that night; they took Hall to an open area in the center of town near the public pump; the three men beat him to the ground and continued for 15 to 30 minutes to pound him with a heavy object—which was later found to be a 2-pound metal blackjack; the victim was handcuffed during all of these proceedings; after the beating the shotgun was fired once—not by the unconscious victim but apparently by one of the officers for some unknown reason.[14]

One of the white eyewitnesses who appeared at the trial and swore to these facts was Mrs. Ollie Jernigan. Her husband, J. H. Jernigan, did not see the incident, but he testified that he was walking through town one day and Sheriff Screws called him over to his car where the following conversation took place:[15]

"Herschell, you know those FBI men are down here investigating that case?" He said, "Well, I understand that your wife saw it." I told him

---

[13] *Id.* at 60.
[14] This description is based primarily on the testimony of these white eyewitnesses: Mr. A. B. Edwards (*id.* at 79–82), Mrs. A. B. Ledbetter (*id.* at 83–85), Mr. A. B. Ledbetter (*id.* at 85–89), Mrs. Mabel Burke (*id.* at 105–106), and Mrs. Ollie Jernigan (*id.* at 89–92).
[15] *Id.* at 93.

"Yes." He says, "Well, you know we have always been friends and I want us to continue to be friends." I told him, "Well, I hoped we could."

The dynamics of combined prejudice and violence in this case are suggested in the testimony of James P. Willingham, a white man, who said that shortly after the killing he had a talk with his friend, Officer Frank Jones:[16]

> [He] told me that the Negro had a mighty good pistol and they had taken it away from him and the Negro acted so damn smart and went before the Court in some way trying to make them give it back to him . . . and that they went out there that night with a warrant and arrested him and handcuffed him and brought him to town and the Negro put up some kind of talk about wanting to give bond or something to that effect and they beat hell out of him; then, that when they got him up to the well they whipped him some more and he died shortly afterwards. He said the Negro attempted to shoot them at the well; said the Negro attempted to shoot them at the well with a shotgun and said he hit him with a blackjack pretty hard and I asked him about how in the world did the Negro try to shoot you and you had him handcuffed and he said well we finished him off and that is all.

Bobby Hall apparently was considered a somewhat "uppity" Negro. Evidence produced at the trial indicated that the tire theft charge was a sham for, as suggested in the Willingham testimony, Hall's major "crime" was to challenge the power of the sheriff to confiscate his pistol. Bobby Hall was not accused of any crime in connection with the weapon. He needed it, he claimed, for protection. In attempting to exercise not his civil rights but his property rights, Hall contacted a lawyer and even went before a local grand jury. But he did not recover his pistol.[17] And, while he never challenged the system of segregation, he was something of a leader among Negroes.[18]

No State or local action was taken against the alleged offenders. Prosecution by the State—which has the power to impose the supreme penalty—may be blocked in cases of this type by the fact that the potential defendant is the person who must start up the machinery of the criminal law. While the district solicitor general in the *Screws* case had formal power to prosecute, he reportedly felt "helpless in the matter" because he had "to rely upon the sheriff and policemen of the various

---

[16] *Id.* at 120.
[17] *Id.* at 67–68.
[18] Special Agent Marcus B. Calhoun of the FBI office testified at the trial that, "Mr. Screws . . . told me that he had had trouble with Bobby Hall, that he seemed to be a leader or denominated himself as such and that when a Negro got in trouble with the law that he, Bobby Hall, would advise him as to what action he should take." Record, *supra*, note 6, at 78.

counties of his circuit for investigation."[19] In the absence of an investigation and a complaint from Sheriff Screws, or by another police officer implicating Screws, no prosecution was commenced. In police brutality cases where the potential defendant is not the *chief* law enforcement officer of the county, there is a greater possibility of criminal or disciplinary action by local authorities. But even in such situations, local action against officers of the law is not common.[20]

Neither Screws nor any of his associates was ever punished. They experienced the difficulty and expense of months of litigation but a second Federal jury acquitted them. The episode did not seriously tarnish the reputation of Claude M. Screws. In 1958 he ran for the State Senate and was elected.

THE KILLING OF A NEGRO IN GEORGIA: 1958. The town of Dawson in Terrell County, Ga. is approximately 30 miles south of Newton. There on April 20, 1958, James Brazier, a Negro in his thirties, suffered a beating at the hands of officers of the law (from which he later died)—in circumstances similar to those in the *Screws* case.[21]

According to the police account, the incident started in the early evening of Sunday, April 20, 1958, when Dawson Police Officer "X" arrested James Brazier's father on a charge of driving under the influence of alcohol. When the elder Brazier resisted, he was subdued by a blackjack. James Brazier protested and, according to the policemen, threatened the officer who later returned with Officer "Y" and arrested the younger Brazier, allegedly with a warrant, for interfering with an arrest. He resisted violently and was subdued with a blackjack. Shortly thereafter he was taken to jail and examined by a local physician who found no serious injury.[22]

Brazier died 5 days later at a hospital in Columbus, Ga., from brain damage and a fractured skull. He had four to six bruised spots on his scalp from a blunt instrument which apparently also caused the skull

[19] Information from the Department of Justice, as quoted in Carr, *Federal Protection of Civil Rights* 107 (1947).
[20] See ch. 6 at 79 *infra*.
[21] The description of the Brazier case is largely based on evidence gathered in an investigation by Commission representatives in late August, 1960 and incorporated into a Commission document entitled *Report on Field Investigation in Terrell County, Georgia.* Four Negro eyewitnesses to various parts of the Brazier incident were interviewed and statements taken from them. In addition, statements were received from other Negro eyewitnesses who were not then available to be interviewed. Four white people were interviewed regarding the case.
In addition to the Brazier incident other cases in Terrell County involving alleged police brutality to Negroes were investigated on this field trip. The evidence supporting complaints in these cases was not as strong as that in the Brazier case.
[22] *Id.* at 10–12.

fracture.[23] The police claimed that Brazier was hit only once or twice at the time of the arrest.

In a sworn statement to Commission representatives Mrs. Hattie Bell Brazier, the widow of the victim, claimed that this affair had actually started months earlier. Mrs. Brazier explained that she and her husband had purchased a new Chevrolet in 1956—and another in 1958.[24] In November of 1957 James Brazier had been arrested on a speeding charge. According to Mrs. Brazier, her husband told her that Dawson Officer "Y" took him to jail, and that:[25]

> When I first entered the door of the jail, ["Y"] hit me on the back of the head and knocked me down and said, "You smart son-of-a-bitch, I been wanting to get my hands on you for a long time." I said, "Why you want me for?" ["Y"] said, "You is a nigger who is buying new cars and we can't hardly live. I'll get you yet."

Officer "Y" then allegedly hit Brazier several more times, put his foot on the small of the prostrate Negro's back (Mrs. Brazier said she saw the footprints there later), and warned him, "You'd better not say a damn thing about it or I'll stomp your damn brains out." After his release from jail, Brazier was bleeding from his ear and vomiting blood. From this time in the fall of 1957 until the second incident in April of 1958, James Brazier was under the care of a local white doctor because of these injuries. Officer "X," the policeman who accompanied "Y" during the arrest in April 1958, also allegedly made a remark about the new car at some time previous to the fatal incident.[26] It appears that James Brazier of Terrell County, like Bobby Hall of Baker County, was considered an "uppity" Negro.

[23] This information comes from the Certificate of Death of James Brazier and from an interview with a doctor who attended the victim at the Columbus Medical Center, *Report on Field Investigation in Terrell County, Georgia, supra,* note 21, at 18.

[24] Affidavit of Mrs. Hattie Bell Brazier, and *Report on Field Investigation in Terrell County, Georgia, supra,* note 21, at 14. Although their hourly wages were not high, Mrs. Brazier explained, she had three jobs and her late husband, two. They sometimes worked at menial tasks from early morning until late night. This allowed them to purchase the automobiles. Interview with Mrs. Hattie Bell Brazier, Albany, Ga., August 23, 1960.

[25] Affidavit of Mrs. Hattie Bell Brazier, and *Report on Field Investigation in Terrell County, Georgia, supra,* note 21, at 12–13.

[26] Earlier in the Spring of 1958 Mrs. Brazier alleged that Officer "X" saw the Brazier's new car and asked them how they managed to purchase it. James Brazier replied flippantly, "I works for what I gets." And "X" countered in a threatening tone, "You'll never remember paying for it." Mrs. Brazier said that this took place in her presence, and it is set out in her affidavit and in *Report on Field Investigation in Terrell County, Georgia, supra,* note 21, at 15.

The story of the fatal incident in 1958 as told by Mrs. Brazier and several other colored witnesses contradicts the account given by the officers. In her affidavit Mrs. Brazier stated that her husband had been beaten brutally by the arresting officers in full view of numerous colored people, including herself and her four children. No warrant was presented by the officers, nor was any paper observed in their hands. The officers, she said, simply ran out of their car and roughly grabbed her husband. While pulling him toward the police car, "Y" beat him repeatedly with a blackjack. Mrs. Brazier's affidavit continued:[27]

> ["Y"] then said, "You smart son-of-a-bitch, I told you I would get you." James said, "What do you want to hurt me for? I ain't done nothing. I got a heap of little chillun. [sic]." ["Y"] said, "I don't give a goddamn how many children you got, you're going away from here" . . . ["Y"] pulled out his pistol and stuck it against James' stomach and said, "I oughta blow your goddamn brains out."

Then these events allegedly occurred: James Brazier's 10-year-old son pleaded with the officers to stop beating his father and was knocked to the ground by "Y";[28] the victim was thrown onto the floor of the police car with his legs dangling outside; "Y" kicked him twice in the groin; slammed the car door on his legs; threw a hat full of sand into his bloody face, and drove off.[29]

When Brazier reached the jail, he was bloody but conscious and apparently not seriously injured by the beating he had received. Yet, when he was taken to court the next morning, he was virtually unconscious. The question that arises is whether Brazier was beaten during the interval between his arrival in jail at approximately 7 P.M. and his appearance in court at approximately 9 A.M. the next day. There is evidence that he was. It comes from several witnesses, one of whom has since died[30] and may be identified—Marvin Goshay, a Negro who was 23 years of age when he signed an affidavit on August 24, 1960 during an interview with Commission representatives in Albany, Ga. Goshay was in jail on a charge of assault and battery when Brazier was incarcerated.

[27] Affidavit of Mrs. Hattie Bell Brazier and *Report on Field Investigation in Terrell County, Georgia, supra,* note 21, at 15.

[28] Affidavit of Mrs. Hattie Bell Brazier, Affidavit of James Brazier, Jr. (aged 10), and *Report on Field Investigation in Terrell County, Georgia, supra,* note 21, at 16. Mrs. Brazier explained in a subsequent interview that the shock of this incident brought on a nervous condition in James, Jr., and forced her to send the boy to live with his grandmother in the North. Interview with Mrs. Hattie Bell Brazier, Albany, Ga., August 23, 1960.

[29] In addition to the affidavit of Mrs. Brazier this story is supported by several colored eyewitnesses interviewed by Commission representatives in Georgia. *Report on Field Investigation in Terrell County, Georgia, supra,* note 21, at 16.

[30] See note 35, *infra.*

The story, as Goshay saw it, is as follows: When James Brazier was brought into the jail he was fully dressed in suit, shirt, tie, and shoes. He talked coherently to Goshay (describing his arrest consistently with Mrs. Brazier's later testimony). Several hours later—probably around midnight—he was ordered out of the cell by Officers "X" and "Y": "They took Brazier out again," Goshay stated in his affidavit. "He asked them to wait because he wanted to put on his shoes. The police said, 'You won't need no shoes.'" This was the last time that Goshay saw him that night. Goshay next saw Brazier on the following morning. His affidavit continued:

> He had on pants, a torn undershirt, no coat, no tie, no white shirt. The last time I saw him, he had on a blue suit, white shirt, and tie. He looked worse on his head than when I saw him also . . . it was beaten worse than when I first saw him. On his back were about four long marks about a foot long. They looked reddish and bruised. His head was bleeding. We had to carry [him] to the car because he couldn't walk. He was slobbering at the mouth. When we got to the car, James, who was dazed but not completely out, didn't know enough to get in the car. Mr. ["Z"—a Dawson police officer] said if he didn't get in, he'd beat him with his blackjack.

More than a year after Brazier's death Sheriff Z. T. Mathews of Terrell County allegedly made the following statement to Mrs. Brazier:[31]

> I oughta slap your damn brains out. A nigger like you I feel like slapping them out. You niggers set around here and look at television and go up North and come back and do to white folks here like the niggers up North do, but you ain't gonna do it. I'm gonna carry the South's orders out like it oughta be done.

Also, Sheriff Mathews told reporter Robert E. Lee Baker, "You know, Cap, . . . there's nothing like fear to keep niggers in line. I'm talking about 'outlaw' niggers."[32]

No local disciplinary or criminal action was taken against any of the officers involved. The attitude of local authorities toward police was protective in this and several other cases of alleged brutality that occurred within a brief period in Dawson. Indeed, there was indignation when Negroes claimed they were "living in an atmosphere of fear."[33] As

---

[31] Affidavit of Mrs. Hattie Bell Brazier, and *Report on Field Investigation in Terrell County, Georgia, supra,* note 21, at 20. Mayor James Griggs Raines of Dawson reported in an interview with two Commission representatives that he felt that Sheriff Mathews was a bad influence on Dawson policemen. "In my opinion the Sheriff, Mathews, is unfit and has violated the Civil Rights Acts. I've seen him beat a pregnant Negro woman. He's unfit to hold office. You can quote me," the Mayor stated. *Id.* at 40.

[32] Washington Post, June 8, 1958, p. A–12.

[33] Atlanta Constitution, June 9, 1958, pp. 1–5; June 10, 1958, pp. 1, 8.

in the *Screws* case the Department of Justice was sufficiently impressed with the results of an FBI investigation to authorize Civil Rights Acts prosecutions. From August 4 to 8, 1958, the local United States Attorney presented witnesses to a Federal grand jury in Macon and requested indictments in five cases of alleged police brutality against policemen "X," "Y," and another Dawson officer.[34] The grand jury returned no indictments.[35]

In the 15 years between the death of Bobby Hall and the death of James Brazier the world had changed in many ways. But in Terrell and Baker, as in some other rural southern counties,[36] the economy, the social system, and racial attitudes remained virtually what they had been. James Griggs Raines who owns many of the buildings in Dawson and has been its Mayor, explained in a 1960 interview that, "This is a feudalistic system. But I don't know if, or how, it will be changed."[37] Few Negroes vote in these counties and in most ways they are deprived and subordinate. Officers of the law sometimes enforce this status by illegal or violent methods.[38]

Not long after Brazier died, police officer "Y" was promoted to Chief of the Dawson Police Department. Z. T. Mathews at this writing is still sheriff of Terrell County.

The Hall and Brazier cases are more dramatic than most, partly because they resulted in death. But the Commission has reviewed

[34] The Government contended that the officers had violated 18 U.S.C. sec. 242 because by these acts of brutality they had "under color of law" interfered with the constitutional rights of the victims.

[35] Although Marvin Goshay was subpoenaed by the Federal Government to testify before the grand jury sitting in Macon, he did not appear. In his sworn statement to a Commission representative Goshay explained that shortly after he received the subpoena, Officer "Y" found him walking on the street in Dawson and ordered him to jail. When the Negro asked why he was being incarcerated, "Y" replied, "You just need to be in jail." The young man was kept prisoner for 1 week, during which time the Federal grand jury met and refused indictments. One week later, "Officer ["Y"] came in and told me I could go on home," Goshay explained. "I never was brought to . . . court during this time. I just stayed in jail. I can only guess, although no one ever told me, that the only reason I was locked up was because they didn't want me to go to Macon." Goshay was slated to be a witness in a pending Federal civil suit for $177,000 brought by Mrs. Brazier against Officer "Y" and others. On March 14, 1961, Marvin Goshay was found dead—apparently of asphyxiation—in a Dawson undertaking parlor. An FBI investigation failed to uncover evidence of foul play.

[36] Those rural, southern counties which have a high percentage of nonwhites in their population are the subject of a separate and detailed analysis in this report. See part III, *supra.*

[37] *Report on Field Investigation in Terrell County, Georgia, supra,* note 21, at 5.

[38] In addition to the Brazier case, there are recent cases containing similar allegations in the files of the Commission. Some of these have been referred to the Department of Justice for possible prosecutive action.

complaints and reports of similar incidents. Reports of some of the most heinous of these have come to the Commission from the Mississippi State Advisory Committee which says that it has received "many and at times almost unbelievable reports of atrocities and brutalities" perpetrated by law enforcement officials.[39] As with many other current complaints, these

[39] Report of the Mississippi Advisory Committee to the Commission on Civil Rights, *The 50 States Report* 315, 317 (1961). The following two cases, which came to the attention of the Commission from sources other than the Mississippi Advisory Committee, are illustrative of reports from that State.

On August 9, 1958, about midday, Theodore R. Nash was stopped by a deputy sheriff 5 miles north of Winona, Miss., on a charge of reckless driving. In the car with Nash were his wife, Geraldine, his daughter, Pearlie Mae Boatman, and four small children under 6 years of age—all Negroes. Nash was a native of Mississippi but had lived in Milwaukee, Wis., since 1950. When this incident occurred, he and his family were on a vacation trip. The Nashes reported to the Commission that the following events took place: The deputy sheriff roughly ordered Nash to the nearby office of a justice of the peace. While outside the office, an altercation developed. The officer allegedly kicked Mrs. Nash, because she protested that they had not been speeding; and the justice of the peace is alleged to have struck her on the side of the head with his fist and to have dragged her along by her arms and hair because Mrs. Nash replied "No"—without adding a "Sir"—to a question from the justice. At one point the officer cocked his pistol and threatened Mr. Nash: "I just wish you would make any kind of an attempt, I would blow your damn brains out here in the street, and I wouldn't have anything to do except to write out a statement that you are tempting the law, and there won't be nothing done about it."

When the babies in the car started to cry, the officer told Nash's daughter, "If you don't quiet them, I'll take this pistol handle and beat their damn brains out into the seats and there won't be enough of them left to try to bury." Mrs. Nash was placed in jail but was soon released after fines of $19 (for resisting arrest) and $34 (for reckless driving) were paid on the spot. The officers then told the family to "Get out of here—and don't be caught in here any more" on pain of death. "They told us that they were going to stop us northern niggers from coming down there. They said these niggers get up here in the northern state[s] around these damn rich Jews, saying 'Yes' and 'No' and think that they can come down there in Mississippi doing the same thing, but before they would take that they would kill every nigger that comes down here and kill them and nothing would be done whether they were in the right or wrong. They said they make the laws and they break them as they see fit to do."

This information comes from (1) an affidavit executed by Theodore Nash on October 4, 1958, and (2) a statement given to a Commission representative on January 27, 1961, by Mr. Nash, Mrs. Nash, and Pearlie Mae Boatman, their daughter. This case was investigated by the Department of Justice. No prosecution was authorized because no corroboration beyond the story told by the Nash family regarding the violence was available. The officers alleged that Mrs. Nash attacked them and had to be subdued. Interview with Civil Rights Division attorney.

In early April 1961, a wire service photograph appeared in newspapers and magazines across the county. Life, April 7, 1961, p. 30. It showed policemen in Jackson, Miss., armed with clubs moving into a crowd of retreating, well-dressed Negroes. A German Shepherd dog on a leash had leaped upon a Negro and seemed about to bite his arm. The man was later identified to the Commission as Reverend S. Leon Whitney, the Pastor of the Farish Street Baptist Church and one of the most prominent Negro clergymen in Jackson. He suffered a severe laceration of his arm from the dog's attack. Other Negroes in the crowd also suffered injuries including an elderly man, W. R. Wren, whose arm was broken. The incident started when a group

are now under investigation by the Department of Justice and for that reason will not be considered here.

Some of the worst complaints of police brutality have included allegations that the officers involved expressed some racial motive for their conduct. The extensive violence found in the Hall and Brazier cases, for example, is rarely seen in incidents where there is no element of racial hate.

Punishment

> A student said the Batista police were so sadistic, once the policemen put you in a scout car, you had your judge and jury, trial and punishment before you get out.
>
> My most embarrassing moment came when a student asked me did the police in Detroit beat people. What could I say?[40]

The primary motivation for police brutality in the cases discussed above and in similar ones seem to have been a desire to "keep the Negro in his place." Cases of similar misconduct often occur—in many parts of the Nation—that appear to have been motivated by a desire to *punish* for reasons other than violation of local segregation customs.[41] A few examples are described in this section.

---

of Negroes applauded nine Negro students who were going into court to be tried in connection with Mississippi's first sit-in demonstration which had occurred in a public library. The applauding Negroes did not commit or threaten violence. After driving them away with clubs and dogs, the officers returned and *asked* a nearby crowd of approximately 70 white persons to disperse. United Press International dispatch as reported in the N.Y. Times, March 30, 1961, p. 19.

[40] *Detroit Hearings* 433 (attributed to a Negro columnist in the Statement of Judge Victor J. Baum).

[41] In five of the six successful police brutality prosecutions under section 242 by the Civil Rights Division, Department of Justice since January 1, 1958, the officers apparently were primarily motivated by a desire to punish for other than racial reasons. In only one of these five cases—the *Clark* case, described at 14, *infra*—was the victim known to be a minority group member; and in that case this did not appear to be a major factor. The facts in the other four "punishment" cases are as follows: (This information comes from interviews with Civil Rights Division attorneys and from the indicated annual Reports of the Attorney General.)

In *United States* v. *Koch*, Crim. No. 18,850, E.D. Ill., June 17, 1958, complaints were made to the Department of Justice alleging that prisoners of the St. Clair County Jail in East St. Louis, Ill., had been subjected to sadistic punishment for such offenses as violation of jail rules. Three deputy sheriffs were indicted and on June 17, 1958, pled guilty. See *Annual Report of the Attorney General of the United States for the Fiscal Year Ended June 30, 1958* at 177–78, and ch. 4, note 194, *infra*.

In *United States* v. *Saxon*, Crim. No. Cp. 2091, M.D. Ala., June 11, 1958, the sheriff of Coosa County, Ala., was charged with having beaten two men with his fists and a blackjack at a filling station in Goodwater, Ala. The sheriff, H. Pierce Saxon, was reportedly annoyed at a remark one of the men made concerning Saxon's bright headlights. A Federal grand jury indicted Saxon on September 11, 1957, but trial in November 1957 resulted in a hung jury. On July 11, 1958, Sheriff Saxon entered a plea of *nolo contendere* (no contest). See *Annual Report of the Attorney*

Policemen and comparable officials have absolutely no authority to punish anyone. Police may use whatever force is necessary to defend themselves and perform their public duties—beyond that they act illegally.[42] As the Wickersham Commission wrote three decades ago, "their fight against lawless men, if waged by forbidden means, is degraded almost to the level of a struggle between two law-breaking gangs."[43]

"GENTLEMEN COPS DON'T SOLVE CRIMES": DETROIT, 1959. A fight between eight Negro boys and several policemen took place in Detroit on the evening of September 10, 1959. There was a direct conflict in the stories of the policemen and the youths as to the cause of this eruption, but it is undisputed that four of the policemen were injured and sent to a hospital for treatment.

When Thaddeus Steel, one of the boys involved, arrived at the police station, a white reporter from the Detroit Free Press observed his reception and reported as follows:[44]

> A 16-year-old boy, arrested for hitting a policeman with a chair, was beaten and kicked by at least four patrolmen Thursday night after he was a prisoner in the Vernor Station garage. . . .

> Steel was brought into the police garage in a scout car, closely followed by three other cars filled with police.

General of the United States for the Fiscal Year Ended June 30, 1958 at 177, and ch. 4, note 194, *infra.*

In *Unites States v. Barber,* Crim. No. 1428, M.D. Ga., Mar. 18, 1959, a police officer of Nashville, Ga., was convicted on evidence that he had beaten John Lester Teal, the manager of a Valdosta jewelry store. Barber, while off duty and in plain clothes, had beaten Teal because he had insulted Barber's daughter in the course of an attempted repossession of a ring. As the beating was taking place, another officer, Hancock, arrived but did nothing to stop it. At the station house later Hancock allegedly held Teal while Barber beat him again. Hancock was tried but acquitted. Barber was convicted on March 18, 1959. See *Report of the Attorney General of the United States for the Fiscal Year Ended June 30, 1959* at 187, and ch. 4, note 193, *infra.*

In *United States v. Payne,* Crim. No. 55,788, N.D. Ga., Mar. 25, 1959, the evidence indicates that Herbert C. Payne, a police officer of the town of Lyerly, Ga., incited a mob to beat the victim on two separate occasions. The victim was known as the town drunk, a ne'er-do-well, and had a reputation for beating his children. The announced purpose of the attacks was to force him to leave town. Payne and a nonofficial member of the mob were indicted under section 242 and under 18 U.S.C. sec. 371 for conspiracy to violate section 242. Payne was convicted on March 25, 1959, under the conspiracy charge. See *Annual Report of the Attorney General of the United States for the Fiscal Year Ended June 30, 1959* at 188, and ch. 4, note 193, *infra.*

[42] See discussion of "Force Permissible" in Orfield, *Criminal Procedure From Arrest to Appeal* 26–27 (1947).

[43] National Commission on Law Observance and Enforcement, *Report on Lawlessness in Law Enforcement* 190 (1931).

[44] Detroit Free Press, Sept. 10, 1959, pp. 1, 3.

He sat in the back seat of the car. His face showed pain. There was a patrolman sitting next to him.

As the car halted, the patrolman left the car and yanked Steel from it by the neck. Another patrolman raced up.

"Is this him?" he shouted.

Then he threw a fist into Steel's face.

A second patrolman pushed that assailant aside and sank his fist into Steel's stomach.

Steel fell to the garage floor, moaning. . . .

The newsmen stood outside the open door of the garage.

One of the policemen saw them and shouted:

"Lower that door!"

But all were too busy slugging Steel, now prone on the floor.

They dragged him to the side and the onlookers could see only patrolmen kicking and slugging at him.

"Lower that door!" shouted one again.

Two detectives had entered the other side of the garage and strode grimly across to the newsmen. Their expressions softened as they reached them.

"Gentlemen cops don't solve crimes," one of the detectives said.

The patrolmen picked Steel up and rushed him into the station. The detectives turned and walked away. . . .

Inspector Leslie Caldwell, commander of the station, is on furlough.

Lt. Raymond Glinski, acting inspector at Vernor, said, "We can't use kid gloves on gang fighters."

"When policemen are sent to the hospital, we don't want to tap the hoodlums who hurt them on the shoulder and send them home," he said.

"After all, four policemen were hit seriously enough by juveniles to be admitted and the juvenile was released from Receiving Hospital without treatment."

Glinski said he did not want to condone beating of prisoners.

"But, after all, when it's a question of a policeman going to the hospital or a hood, I think both should go," he said.

After an investigation, Detroit Police Commissioner Herbert W. Hart decided to take no action against the police officers and announced that "no evidence to substantiate charges of police brutality" had been found.[45] "As far as I am concerned, it is a closed issue," he added.[46] When asked by the Detroit Free Press for amplification regarding the eyewitness story of its reporter, Commissioner Hart said that he did "not disbelieve" it.[47] The newspaper editorialized, "The facts stated in our

[45] Detroit Free Press, Sept. 13, 1959, p. A–1. The testimony of Commissioner Hart of this incident is found in Detroit Hearings 392–93.

[46] Detroit Free Press, supra, note 45.

[47] Ibid.

story were accurate."[48] But the editor admitted that the reporter could identify only one detective who was present at the beating.

Wayne County Prosecutor Samuel H. Olsen also ordered an investigation but did not prosecute because the alleged assailants could not be identified.[49] The Federal Government did not prosecute under the Civil Rights Acts. Several of the older Negroes were prosecuted by the State and convicted of conspiracy to commit assault and battery. Thaddeus Steel and the other juveniles were released after a hearing on similar charges by the juvenile court. . . .

POLICE BRUTALITY AND THE CONSTITUTION

In whatever category they may fall most instances of unlawful police violence involve the deprivation of rights guaranteed by the Federal Constitution. Police brutality is ordinarily treated as a violation of due process.[50] Like other matters involving constitutional rights, however, such misconduct may involve not only denials of due process but of equal protection as well. It is upon the latter, of course, that the Commission's jurisdiction depends.[51] The extent to which the two constitutional provisions overlap depends in part upon the way the equal protection clause is interpreted. In a narrow view, the latter prohibits only deliberate discrimination against a person on the basis of his membership in a racial or other minority group.[52] Thus, for instance, it would apply only to brutality directed against a Negro because he is a Negro. A broader interpretation would apply the equal protection provision in any case where a person is deliberately denied the enjoyment of a right (such as the right to be protected from physical harm while in the custody of the police)[53] that is commonly afforded others in like circumstances.[54] This view would make it applicable to instances of police brutality where there was in fact improper treatment, whether or not it was deliberately directed against the victim on account of his minority status. Thus as a practical matter, under this view, every act of police brutality would appear to constitute a denial of equal protection, since the police do not in fact brutalize all persons whom they

[48] *Ibid.*

[49] Prosecutor Olsen's description of his investigation of this incident is found in *Detroit Hearings* 502–503.

[50] See, e.g., *Screws* v. *United States,* 325 U.S. 91 (1945).

[51] See ch. 1 at 2, *supra.*

[52] This view was set forth as *dictum* in the *Slaughterhouse Cases,* 83 U.S. (16 Wall.) 36 at 81 (1873). Later cases (see notes 106 and 107 *infra*) definitely give a far broader meaning to the equal protection clause.

[53] *Catlette* v. *United States,* 132 F. 2d 902, 906–907 (4th Cir. 1943).

[54] *Lynch* v. *United States,* 189 F. 2d 476, 479 (5th Cir. 1951), *cert. denied,* 342 U.S. 831 (1951).

arrest or hold in custody. As a matter of policy the Commission's studies are confined to cases involving members of minority groups—so that they fall far short of the outer limits of the broader interpretation.

EXTENT AND EFFECTS

The Commission's studies indicate that police brutality in the United States today is a serious[55] and continuing problem in many parts of the country. Whether in the country as a whole it is increasing or decreasing is not clear. There seems to have been no marked overall abatement in recent years, although improvements have been reported in particular areas—such as Atlanta and Chicago.[56]

TABLE 1. *Allegations of Police Brutality by Race of Victim*
(Matters received by the Department of Justice,
January 1, 1958, to June 30, 1960)

	TOTAL	NEGRO AND OTHER MINORITY*	WHITE	UNKNOWN
National totals	1,328 (100%)	461 (35%)	506 (38%)	361 (27%)
Northern and Western States	433 (100%)	117 (27%)	193 (44.6%)	123 (28.4%)
Southern States	895 (100%)	344 (38.4%)	313 (35%)	238 (26.6%)

* Includes 24 cases of other minority group victims: Indian, 12; Mexican, 10; Mixed, 1; and other, 1.

[55] The seriousness of the problem of police brutality in quantitative terms is documented by the cases described in this Report; by many similar reports in Commission files not included in this Report; by the many complaints received by the Department of Justice, see app. VII, tables 2 and 3; and by the opinion of Department of Justice officials that many acts of brutality are not reported to officials due to apathy, fear, or ignorance, see ch. 4 at 58, *infra*. In qualitative terms the problem must be considered serious because any act of unlawful violence, especially by an official, is harmful to our society. The effect of such acts on the Negro community is described in Willis Ward's testimony, p. 27, *infra*. The seriousness of this situation is also suggested by this excerpt from a recent study by Bullock entitled *The Houston Murder Problem* 80–81 (1961): "Negroes also have a 'Bully' image of Houston's policemen. Whenever one hears about the police descending upon a group of Negroes, there is always raised this question: 'How many heads were whupped?' The reasons for this attitude grow out of the spread of reports concerning instances of police brutality."

Gradually and insidiously, these reports seep into the minds of Negroes and reinforce ugly images about all of Houston's policemen. Therefore, when Negroes are asked what they think of policing in Houston, their response is a series of negative attitudes that are heavily laden with disrespect. We asked this question of more than five hundred (500) people, and we got attitudinal patterns that were generally negative.

[56] See ch. 6 at 82 and 87, *infra*.

The most comprehensive statistics available on police brutality were compiled by Commission staff members from complaints that have come to the attention of the Department of Justice. These statistics, presented in the accompanying table, do not include all cases of alleged police brutality that occurred during the period in question, for as indicated below,[57] not all incidents come to the attention of the Department. The Department, nonetheless, receives notice of more such incidents than any other agency. Of course, not all the complaints that are received are valid by any means.[58] Yet they do provide at least a rough measure of the outlines of the problem.

The statistics suggest that Negroes feel the brunt of official brutality proportionately more than any other group in American society. As Table 1 shows, among the complaints of police brutality received by the Department in the two and one half year period ending June 30, 1960, the alleged victims were Negroes (who constitute approximately 10 per cent of the total population) in 35 per cent of the cases and whites in 38 per cent of the cases; in 27 per cent of the cases the race of the victim was unknown.

In terms of regions, approximately two out of every three complaints over the last few years (as seen in Table 1), and probably over the last 20 years,[59] originated in the 17 Southern States and the District of Columbia. This may indicate that police brutality is more prevalent in the South than in other regions of the country. But this is by no means certain, for these statistics may be evidence merely of a greater tendency of non-southern victims to complain to local rather than to Federal authorities.

A review of the cases and complaints from all sources suggests

[57] See ch. 4 at 57–58, *infra*.

[58] Harold R. Tyler, Jr., former Assistant Attorney General in charge of the Civil Rights Division, wrote the Commission on October 18, 1961, in this connection: "As most lawyers are aware, there has been an increasing tendency over the years for defendants and their counsel in criminal cases, particularly those of the common law variety, to raise by way of defensive matter the issue of coercion or improper treatment at the hands of the police. I feel that this phenomenon has some impact upon the nature, number, and type of complaints received by the Department of Justice. Further, Department attorneys must keep this in mind when evaluating complaints. The Department cannot be expected to prosecute complaints which are motivated by a desire on the part of the complainants to 'use' the Government to raise defensive matters collaterally, even in those situations where the facts *prima facie* might support a Section 242 prosecution. Then, too, the Government should not be expected to litigate, at least in most instances, those complaints of criminal defendants which necessarily will be aired before the courts in the complainants' own cases. Other ramifications of this point are too detailed for profitable discussion here, but the point remains that this tendency on the part of criminal case defendants, though not susceptible to statistical evaluation, is often a real problem in evaluating and acting upon complaints."

[59] See app. VII, table 3.

that brutality is largely confined to State and local police or prison forces. Several Department of Justice officials stated that while complaints do come in against Federal civilian police officers or prison guards, they are quite rare. The Wickersham Commission in 1931 also found that police brutality is almost exclusively confined to State and local agencies.[60]

Illegal violence by officers of the law casts a cloud of suspicion over the entire system of American justice. It violates highly valued constitutional rights, and may produce a pervading fear regarding the security of the person. Brutality against a few Negroes may cause many of them to distrust all police officers. This is unfortunate not only for Negroes but also for the police and the entire community. Criminal investigations rely to a great extent on information supplied by private persons. The job of crime control becomes vastly more difficult when a whole segment of the community is wary of any contact with the police. Mr. Willis Ward, a former assistant county prosecutor, testified regarding the relationship between Negro distrust of the police and the problems of crime solution at the Commission's Detroit Hearing:[61]

> It is said that there are four crimes currently in the papers today, heinous crimes, involving murder and robbery, and from what we read in the paper it would appear that the suspects are colored citizens. It would appear that perhaps in this city the people most apt to know who did it might be colored people, but the thing that shudders me is: As much as the good colored people as well as the white people want criminals apprehended and brought to justice, that if a person knows or has reason to believe it would help us to locate these culprits the chances are, 99 chances out of a hundred, if he complains he will be treated more as a suspect than as a citizen attempting to reduce crime in the city of Detroit.

SUMMARY

Police brutality—the unnecessary use of violence to enforce the mores of segregation, to punish, and to coerce confessions—is a serious problem in the United States. Much of it occurs when an ill-trained or prejudiced policeman first comes in contact with a suspect. Yet, many policemen have demonstrated that it is possible to perform their duty effectively without resorting to unlawful violence which creates suspicions about the fairness of the American system of criminal justice.

[60] Referring to brutality connected with the third degree, the Wickersham Commission wrote that there was "little evidence of the practice among Federal officials." National Commission on Law Observance and Enforcement, *op. cit. supra,* note 43 at 4.

[61] *Detroit Hearings* 381.

Raymond J. Murphy

POSTSCRIPT
ON THE LOS ANGELES RIOTS

As this book was receiving its final preparation, the most extensive and costly riot of contemporary American experience was in progress. Broad television and radio coverage made it also the most publicly witnessed spectacle of mass destruction we have known. It is too early, however, to answer with certainty or scientific accuracy many of the most important questions concerning why and how the riot in the Watts-Willowbrook Negro ghetto of the "City of Angels" started or to assess with confidence the consequences or implications for the movement for equality and civil rights. Certain impressions and observations seem, however, to be worthy of comment at this time.

The riot appears to illustrate that despite widespread legislative reforms, initiated by Congress, in the areas of social relationships and voting rights, the problems and perceptions of urban Negroes are singularly unaffected. Such legal accomplishments have fundamentally important implications of a long-range nature for the society, but their most immediate impact is in the South, where segregation and denial of voting privileges have been supported by local tradition and statute. In the urban North and West, problems of segregation and discrimination are of a much more subtle *de facto* nature, basically unaffected by the recent Congressional action. The Johnson Administration's War on Poverty does attempt to deal directly with the problems of urban unemployment and blight. However, in Los Angeles as in a number of other large cities, the effectiveness of such melioristic planning has suffered because of political bickering and delays. It is quite plausible that many of the poor, both white and Negro, have cynical responses to the promises of politicians and community leaders.

In another sense, the accomplishments and promises of "the Good Society" may be related to the riots in Los Angeles and other cities in the past two years. It has often been noted by students of revolutionary movements that the period of greatest violence occurs not when people are most deprived and repressed, but rather when things seem to be improving. This has been explained as a consequence of the frustrations experienced by persons whose expectations have been raised by material improvements in their life situations and who impatiently come to expect further gains which are not immediately obtainable. In a psychological sense, such persons compare themselves with those enjoying more of the rewards of society rather than with those less fortunate or with their own previous deprivations. Accordingly, modest gains exaggerate feelings of frustration and despair rather than diminish them. In the present case, it has been remarked by many public officials that Los Angeles, with its palm-lined streets of single-family dwelling units, its absence of rat-infested alleys, and its relatively better labor market, should not be experiencing violent racial troubles. The above theory would suggest that such improvements in living conditions trigger higher expectations among the inhabitants and a heightened sense of "relative deprivation." This could well apply to persons who have migrated into the community from the rural South as well as from urban ghettos where conditions of crowding and poverty are more acute.

All available evidence indicates that the Los Angeles riot was not planned or organized by outside agitators or by groups within the Negro community. Although the rhetoric of the Muslims was in evidence ("Get whitey!" "The blue-eyed devil's day has come!"), there is little to indicate that the violence was directed or controlled by members of this militant group. Instead, it appears to have been a collective emotional explosion of persons responding not to ideological pronouncements but to an accumulation of irritation and despair and to the excitement of the moment. It should be noted, however, that the widespread evidence of race hatred and the expressed demand that whites get out of the community, may well imply "nationalistic" sentiments among ghetto persons far more extensive than membership in such organizations as the Muslims has implied. If so, those who support integration as a solution to the Negro problem may have suffered a serious setback.

The most common explanations for the riot coming from participants have been "police brutality" and the practices of white merchants and loan sharks operating within the community. It is of some interest that most of the urban racial disturbances in recent years have been regarded by participants as a response to police brutality. This term means more than physical assault by the police. It seems probable that many Negroes include under this label such police practices as frequent questioning of innocent persons, the use of prejudicial terms ("nigger"), rude manners in relations with Negroes, and the relatively infrequent use of Negro police in ghetto areas. At this time we cannot dispassionately assess the validity of the charge of brutality. It is obvious, however, that the *perception* of denigrating and cruel treatment by the police is widespread among Negroes in the ghetto and that the police became a focal point of riot activity in Los Angeles. The selective nature of the burning and looting of business establishments made it clear that white businessmen were another major target of aggression. In one sense, both the police and the businessmen can be seen as the representatives of white authority and exploitation. The rioters' actions are thus interpretable as attacks on the symbols of white domination and white contact. The implication to be drawn here is that the narrower allegations against police and merchants may be far less significant than the broad distrust of white persons and the lack of meaningful communication between the white and Negro communities.

In the past, the most extensive communication and representation of the Negro community's needs to the white society have been through the efforts of white welfare-agency personnel and politicians working in conjunction with middle-class Negro business, professional, and religious leaders. To representatives of the white community, such contacts with the Negro middle class are both inevitable and desirable. Middle-class Negroes share many of the same goals and concerns as their white counterparts; their similarity in educational attainment invites consensual understanding of major issues, and the successful Negro business or professional man receives the attention and respect of the majority of whites who might be offended by or contemptuous of the style and rhetoric of lower-class Negro spokesmen.

Within the Negro ghettos of American cities, class structures have developed representing not only different life styles but differing goals and aspirations as well. (A number of articles in this book illustrate this.) Lower-class people have complained that Negro middle-class leaders do not lead the masses. The integrationist aspirations of the Negro middle class may not square with the immediate concrete needs of the uneducated and unemployed. The lower-class members of the ghetto, for example, may prefer to have better and newer segregated schools in the community than the promise of eventual integrated schools or such awkward temporary solutions as "bussing." The apparent inability of middle-class Negro leaders to control or influence the rioters in Los Angeles demonstrates and highlights the lack of communication within the Negro community.

There is also evidence to suggest that the rift between the classes has been heightened by the riot. It seems entirely possible at this time that the vacuum created by the apparent rejection of middle-class leadership may be filled by persons representing a more militant nationalistic emphasis to the solution of Negro problems or by political opportunists who see possibilities for developing a "safe" and reliable base for realizing career aspirations. Either of these developments could have important implications for the course and development of the Negro movement. Negro middle-class leaders face estrangement both from the white community, because of their apparent inability to lead, and from the Negro, because of their apparent lack of concern for the problems of the masses. In such a situation, the response may be to express a more militant position on civil rights in the hopes of winning support among the lower class. Such a strategy, however, might lead to further alienation from established white support.

Finally, we feel it of some importance to mention that the forces most active in civil rights demonstrations (CORE, SNCC, etc.) have been strangely silent to date in the Los Angeles situation. This may represent an effort to disassociate themselves from violent attempts to solve racial problems, or it might indicate an inability to speak with, or for, those who triggered an orgy of fire and bloodshed in the warm August summer of 1965.

Assimilation and Identity

Milton M. Gordon

ASSIMILATION IN AMERICA:
THEORY AND REALITY*

Three ideologies or conceptual models have competed for attention on the American scene as explanations of the way in which a nation, in the beginning largely white, Anglo-Saxon, and Protestant, has absorbed over 41 million immigrants and their descendants from variegated sources and welded them into the contemporary American people. These ideologies are Anglo-conformity, the melting pot, and cultural pluralism. They have served at various times, and often simultaneously, as explanations of what has happened—descriptive models—and of what should happen—goal models. Not infrequently they have been used in such a fashion that it is difficult to tell which of these two usages the writer has had in mind. In fact, one of the more remarkable omissions in

Reprinted from the Spring 1961 issue of *Daedalus* by permission of *Daedalus*, published by the American Academy of Arts and Sciences, Brookline, Massachusetts. Vol. 90, No. 2, *Ethnic Groups in American Life*.

Mr. Gordon, Professor of Sociology, University of Massachusetts, is author of *Assimilation in American Life* (Oxford University Press, 1964).

* The materials of this article are based on a larger study of the meaning and implications of minority group assimilation in the United States, which I have carried out for the Russell Sage Foundation and which is scheduled to be published as a book by the Foundation.

the history of American intellectual thought is the relative lack of close analytical attention given to the theory of immigrant adjustment in the United States by its social scientists.

The result has been that this field of discussion—an overridingly important one since it has significant implications for the more familiar problems of prejudice, discrimination, and majority-minority group relations generally—has been largely preempted by laymen, representatives of belles lettres, philosophers, and apologists of various persuasions. Even from these sources the amount of attention devoted to ideologies of assimilation is hardly extensive. Consequently, the work of improving intergroup relations in America is carried out by dedicated professional agencies and individuals who deal as best they can with day-to-day problems of discriminatory behavior, but who for the most part are unable to relate their efforts to an adequate conceptual apparatus. Such an apparatus would, at one and the same time, accurately describe the present structure of American society with respect to its ethnic groups (I shall use the term "ethnic group" to refer to any racial, religious, or national-origins collectivity), and allow for a considered formulation of its assimilation or integration goals for the foreseeable future. One is reminded of Alice's distraught question in her travels in Wonderland: "Would you tell me, please, which way I ought to go from here?" "That depends a good deal," replied the Cat with irrefutable logic, "on where you want to get to."

The story of America's immigration can be quickly told for our present purposes. The white American population at the time of the Revolution was largely English and Protestant in origin, but had already absorbed substantial groups of Germans and Scotch-Irish and smaller contingents of Frenchmen, Dutchmen, Swedes, Swiss, South Irish, Poles, and a handful of migrants from other European nations. Catholics were represented in modest numbers, particularly in the middle colonies, and a small number of Jews were residents of the incipient nation. With the exception of the Quakers and a few missionaries, the colonists had generally treated the Indians and their cultures with contempt and hostility, driving them from the coastal plains and making the western frontier a bloody battleground where eternal vigilance was the price of survival.

Although the Negro at that time made up nearly one-fifth of the total population, his predominantly slave status, together with racial and cultural prejudice, barred him from serious consideration as an assimilable element of the society. And while many groups of European origin started out as determined ethnic enclaves, eventually, most historians believe, considerable ethnic intermixture within the white population took place. "People of different blood" [sic]—write two American historians about the colonial period, "English, Irish, German, Huguenot, Dutch, Swedish—mingled and intermarried with little thought of any difference."[1] In such a society, its people predominantly English, its white immigrants of other ethnic origins either English-speaking or derived largely from countries of northern and western Europe whose cultural divergences from the English were not great, and its dominant white population excluding by fiat the claims and considerations of welfare of the non-Caucasian minorities, the problem of assimilation understandably did not loom unduly large or complex.

The unfolding events of the next century and a half with increasing momentum dispelled the complacency which rested upon the relative simplicity of colonial and immediate post-Revolutionary conditions. The large-scale immigration to America of the famine-fleeing Irish, the Germans, and later the Scandinavians (along with additional Englishmen and other peoples of northern and western Europe) in the middle of the nineteenth century (the so-called "old immigration"), the emancipation of the Negro slaves and the problems created by post-Civil War reconstruction, the placing of the conquered Indian with his broken culture on government reservations, the arrival of the Oriental, first attracted by the discovery of gold and other opportunities in the West, and finally, beginning in the last quarter of the nineteenth century and continuing to the early 1920's, the swelling to proportions hitherto unimagined of the tide of immigration from the peasantries and "pales" of southern and eastern Europe—the Italians, Jews, and Slavs of the so-called "new immigration," fleeing the persecutions and industrial dislocations of the day—all these events constitute the background against which we may consider the rise of the theories of assimilation mentioned above. After a necessarily foreshortened description of each of these theories and their historical emergence, we shall suggest analytical distinctions designed to aid in clarifying the nature of the assimilation process, and then conclude by focusing on the American scene.

ANGLO-CONFORMITY

"Anglo-conformity"[2] is a broad term used to cover a variety of viewpoints about assimilation and immigration; they all assume the desirability of maintaining English institutions (as modified by the American Revolution), the English language, and English-oriented cultural patterns as dominant and standard in American life. However, bound up with this assumption are related attitudes. These may range from discredited notions about race and "Nordic" and "Aryan" racial superiority, together with the nativist political programs and exclusionist immigration policies which such notions entail, through an intermediate position of favoring immigration from northern and western Europe on amorphous, unreflective grounds ("They are more like us"), to a lack of opposition to any source of immigration, as long as these immigrants and their descendants duly adopt the standard Anglo-Saxon cultural patterns. There is by no means any necessary equation between Anglo-conformity and racist attitudes.

It is quite likely that "Anglo-conformity" in its more moderate aspects, however explicit its formulation, has been the most prevalent ideology of assimilation goals in America throughout the nation's history. As far back as colonial times, Benjamin Franklin recorded concern about the clannishness of the Germans in Pennsylvania, their slowness in learning English, and the establishment of their own native-language press.[3] Others of the founding fathers had similar reservations about large-scale immigration from Europe. In the context of their times they were unable to foresee the role such immigration was to play in creating the later greatness of the nation. They were not all men of unthinking prejudices. The disestablishment of religion and the separation of church and state (so that no religious group—whether New England Congregationalists, Virginian Anglicans, or even all Protestants combined—could call upon the federal government for special favors or support, and so that man's religious conscience should be free) were cardinal points of the new national policy they fostered. "The Government of the United States," George Washington had written to the Jewish congregation of Newport during his first term as president, "gives to bigotry no sanction, to persecution no assistance."

Political differences with ancestral England had just been written in blood; but there is no reason to suppose that these men looked upon their fledgling country as an impartial melting pot for the merging of the various cultures of Europe, or as a new "nation of nations," or as anything but a society in which, with important political modifications, Anglo-Saxon speech and institutional forms would be standard. Indeed, their newly won victory for democracy and republicanism made them especially anxious that these still precarious fruits of revolution should not be threatened by a large influx of European peoples whose life experiences had accustomed them to the bonds of despotic monarchy. Thus, although they explicitly conceived of the new United States of America as a haven for those unfortunates of Europe who were persecuted and oppressed, they had characteristic reservations about the effects of too free a policy. "My opinion, with respect to immigration," Washington wrote to John Adams in 1794, "is that except of useful mechanics and some particular descriptions of men or professions, there is no need of encouragement, while the policy or advantage of its taking place in a body (I mean the settling of them in a body) may be much questioned; for, by so doing, they retain the language, habits and principles (good or bad) which they bring with them."[4] Thomas Jefferson, whose views on race and attitudes towards slavery were notably liberal and advanced for his time, had similar doubts concerning the effects of mass immigration on American institutions, while conceding that immigrants, "if they come of themselves . . . are entitled to all the rights of citizenship."[5]

The attitudes of Americans toward foreign immigration in the first three-quarters of the nineteenth century may correctly be described as ambiguous. On the one hand, immigrants were much desired, so as to swell the population and importance of states and territories, to man the farms of expanding prairie settlement, to work the mines, build the railroads and canals, and take their place in expanding industry. This was a period in which no federal legislation of any consequence prevented the entry of aliens, and such state legislation as existed attempted to bar on an individual basis only those who were likely to become a burden on the community, such as convicts and paupers. On the other hand, the arrival in an overwhelmingly Protestant society of large numbers of poverty-stricken Irish Catholics, who settled in groups in the slums of Eastern cities, roused dormant fears of "Popery" and Rome. Another source of anxiety was the substantial influx of Germans, who made their way to the cities and farms of the mid-West and whose different language, separate communal life, and freer ideas on temperance and sabbath observance brought them into conflict with the Anglo-Saxon bearers of the Puritan and Evangelical traditions. Fear of foreign "radicals" and suspicion of the economic demands of the occasionally aroused workingmen added fuel to the nativist fires. In their extreme form these fears resulted in the Native-American movement of the 1830's and 1840's and the "American" or "Know-Nothing" party of the 1850's, with their anti-Catholic campaigns and their demands for restrictive laws on naturalization procedures and for keeping the foreign-born out of political office. While these movements scored local political successes and their turbulences so rent the national social fabric that the patches are not yet entirely invisible, they failed to influence national legislative policy on immigration and immigrants; and their fulminations inevitably provoked the expected reactions from thoughtful observers.

The flood of newcomers to the westward expanding nation grew larger, reaching over one and two-thirds million between 1841 and 1850 and over two and one-half million in the decade before the Civil War. Throughout the entire period, quite apart from the excesses of the Know-Nothings, the predominant (though not exclusive) conception of what the ideal immigrant adjustment should be was probably summed up in a letter written in 1818 by John Quincy Adams, then Secretary of State, in answer to the inquiries of the Baron von Fürstenwaerther. If not the earliest, it is certainly the most elegant version of the sentiment, "If they don't like it here, they can go back where they came from." Adams declared:[6]

> They [immigrants to America] come to a life of independence, but to a life of labor—and, if they cannot accommodate themselves to the character, moral, political and physical, of this country with all its compensating balances of good and evil, the Atlantic is always open to them to return to the land of their nativity and their fathers. To one thing they must make up their minds, or they will be disappointed in every expectation of happiness as Americans. They must cast off the European skin, never to resume it. They must look forward to their posterity rather than backward to their ancestors; they must be sure that whatever their own feelings may be, those of their children will cling to the prejudices of this country.

The events that followed the Civil War created their own ambiguities in attitude toward the immigrant. A nation undergoing wholesale industrial expansion and not yet finished with the march of westward settlement could make good use of the never faltering waves of newcomers. But sporadic bursts of labor unrest, attributed to foreign radicals, the growth of Catholic institutions and the rise of Catholics to municipal political power, and the continuing association of immigrant settlement with urban slums revived familiar fears. The first federal selective law restricting immigration was passed in 1882, and Chinese immigration was cut off in the same year. The most significant development of all, barely recognized at first, was the change in the source of European migrants. Beginning in the 1880's, the countries of southern and eastern Europe began to be represented in substantial numbers for the first time, and in the next decade immigrants from these sources became numerically dominant. Now the notes of a new, or at least hitherto unemphasized, chord from the nativist lyre began to sound—the ugly chord, or discord, of racism. Previously vague and romantic notions of Anglo-Saxon peoplehood, combined with general ethnocentrism, rudimentary wisps of genetics, selected tidbits of evolutionary theory, and naive assumptions from an early and crude imported anthropology produced the doctrine that the English, Germans, and others of the "old immigration" constituted a superior race of tall, blonde, blue-eyed "Nordics" or "Aryans," whereas the peoples of eastern and southern Europe made up the darker Alpines or Mediterraneans—both "inferior" breeds whose presence in America threatened, either by intermixture or supplementation, the traditional American stock and culture. The obvious corollary to this doctrine was to exclude the allegedly inferior breeds; but if the new type of immigrant could not be excluded, then everything must be done to instill Anglo-Saxon virtues in these benighted creatures. Thus, one educator writing in 1909 could state:[7]

> These southern and eastern Europeans are of a very different type from the northern Europeans who preceded them. Illiterate, docile, lacking in self-reliance and initiative, and not possessing the Anglo-Teutonic conceptions of law, order, and government, their coming has served to dilute tremendously our national stock, and to corrupt our civic life. . . . Everywhere these people tend to settle in groups or settlements, and to set up here their national manners, customs, and observances. Our task is to break up these groups or settlements, to assimilate and amalgamate these people as a part of our American race, and to implant in their children, so far as can be done, the Anglo-Saxon conception of righteousness, law and order, and popular government, and to awaken in them a reverence for our democratic institutions and for those things in our national life which we as a people hold to be of abiding worth.

Anglo-conformity received its fullest expression in the so-called Americanization movement which gripped the nation during World War I. While "Americanization" in its various stages had more than one emphasis, it was essentially a consciously articulated movement to strip the immigrant of his native culture and attachments and make him over into an American along Anglo-Saxon lines—all this to be accomplished with great rapidity. To use an image of a later day, it was an attempt at "pressure-cooking assimilation." It had prewar antecedents, but it was during the height of the world conflict that federal agencies, state governments, municipalities, and a host of private organizations joined in the effort to persuade the immigrant to learn English, take out naturalization papers, buy war bonds, forget his former origins and culture, and give himself over to patriotic hysteria.

After the war and the "Red scare" which followed, the excesses of the Americanization movement subsided. In its place, however, came the restriction of immigration through federal law. Foiled at first by presidential vetoes, and later by the failure of the 1917 literacy test to halt the immigrant tide, the proponents of restriction finally put through in the early 1920's a series of acts culminating in the well-known national-origins formula for immigrant quotas which went into effect in 1929. Whatever the merits of a quantitative limit on the number of immigrants to be admitted to the United States, the provisions of the formula, which discriminated sharply against the countries of southern and eastern Europe, in effect institutionalized the assumptions of the rightful dominance of Anglo-Saxon patterns in the land. Reaffirmed with only slight modifications in the McCarran-Walter Act of 1952, these laws, then, stand as a legal monument to the creed of Anglo-conformity and a telling reminder that this ideological system still has numerous and powerful adherents on the American scene.

THE MELTING POT

While Anglo-conformity in various guises has probably been the most prevalent ideology of assimilation in the American historical experience, a competing viewpoint with more generous and idealistic overtones has had its adherents and exponents from the eighteenth century onward. Conditions in the virgin continent, it was clear, were modifying the institutions which the English colonists brought with them from the mother country. Arrivals from non-English homelands such as Germany, Sweden, and France were similarly exposed to this fresh environment. Was it not possible, then, to think of the evolving American society not as a slightly modified England but rather as a totally new blend, culturally and biologically, in which the stocks and folkways of Europe, figuratively speaking, were indiscriminately mixed in the political pot of the emerging nation and fused by the fires of American influence and interaction into a distinctly new type?

Such, at any rate, was the conception of the new society which motivated that eighteenth-century French-born writer and agriculturalist, J. Hector St. John Crèvecoeur, who, after many years of American residence, published his reflections and observations in *Letters from an American Farmer*.[8] Who, he asks, is the American?

> He is either an European, or the descendant of an European, hence that strange mixture of blood, which you will find in no other country. I could point out to you a family whose grandfather was an Englishman, whose wife was Dutch, whose son married a French woman, and whose present four sons have now four wives of different nations. *He* is an American, who leaving behind him all his ancient prejudices and manners, receives new ones from the new mode of life he has embraced, the new government he obeys, and the new rank he holds. He becomes an American by being received in the broad lap of our great *Alma Mater*. Here individuals of all nations are melted into a new race of men, whose labours and posterity will one day cause great changes in the world.

Some observers have interpreted the open-door policy on immigration of the first three-quarters of the nineteenth century as reflecting an underlying faith in the effectiveness of the American melting pot, in the belief "that all could be absorbed and that all could contribute to an emerging national character."[9] No doubt many who observed with dismay the nativist agitation of the times felt as did Ralph Waldo Emerson that such conformity-demanding and immigrant-hating forces represented a perversion of the best American ideals. In 1845, Emerson wrote in his Journal:[10]

> I hate the narrowness of the Native American Party. It is the dog in the manger. It is precisely opposite to all the dictates of love and magnanimity; and therefore, of course, opposite to true wisdom. . . . Man is the most composite of all creatures. . . . Well, as in the old burning of the Temple at Corinth, by the melting and intermixture of silver and gold and other metals a new compound more precious than any, called Corinthian brass, was formed; so in this continent,—asylum of all nations,—the energy of Irish, Germans, Swedes, Poles, and Cossacks, and all the European tribes,—of the Africans, and of the Polynesians,—will construct a new race, a new religion, a new state, a new literature, which will be as vigorous as the new Europe which came out of the smelting-pot of the Dark Ages, or that which earlier emerged from the Pelasgic and Etruscan barbarism. *La Nature aime les croisements.*

Eventually, the melting-pot hypothesis found its way into historical scholarship and interpretation. While many American historians of the late nineteenth century, some fresh from graduate study at German universities, tended to adopt the view that American institutions derived in essence from Anglo-Saxon (and ultimately Teutonic) sources, others were not so sure.[11] One of these was Frederick Jackson Turner, a young historian from Wisconsin, not long emerged from his graduate training at Johns Hopkins. Turner presented a paper to the American Historical Association, meeting in Chicago in 1893. Called "The Significance of the Frontier in American History," this paper proved to be one of the most influential essays in the history of American scholarship, and its point of view, supported by Turner's subsequent writings and his teaching, pervaded the field of American historical interpretation for at least a generation. Turner's thesis was that the dominant influence in the shaping of American institutions and American democracy was not this nation's European heritage in any of its forms, nor the forces emanating from the eastern seaboard cities, but rather the experiences created by a moving and variegated western frontier. Among the many effects attributed to the frontier environment and the challenges it presented was that it acted as a solvent for the national heritages and the separatist tendencies of the many nationality groups which had joined the trek westward, including the Germans and Scotch-Irish of the eighteenth century and the Scandinavians and Germans of the nineteenth. "The frontier," asserted Turner, "promoted the formation of a composite nationality for the American people. . . . In the crucible of the frontier the immigrants were Americanized, liberated, and fused into a mixed race, English in neither nationality nor characteristics. The process has gone on from the early days to our own." And later, in an essay on the role of the Mississippi Valley, he refers to "the tide of foreign immigration which has risen so steadily that it has made a composite American people whose amalgamation is destined to produce a new national stock."[12]

Thus far, the proponents of the melting pot idea had dealt largely with the diversity produced by the sizeable immigration from the countries of northern and western Europe alone—the "old immigration," consisting of peoples with cultures and physical appearance not greatly different from those of the Anglo-Saxon stock. Emerson, it is true, had impartially included Africans, Polynesians, and Cossacks in his conception of the mixture; but it was only in the last two decades of the nineteenth century that a large-scale influx of peoples from the countries of southern and eastern Europe imperatively posed the question of whether these uprooted newcomers who were crowding into the large cities of the nation and the industrial sector of the economy could also be successfully "melted." Would the "urban melting pot" work as well as the "frontier melting pot" of an essentially rural society was alleged to have done?

It remained for an English-Jewish writer with strong social convictions, moved by his observation of the role of the United States as a haven for the poor and oppressed of Europe, to give utterance to the broader view of the American melting pot in a way which attracted public attention. In 1908, Israel Zangwill's drama, *The Melting Pot*, was produced in this country and became a popular success. It is a play dominated by the dream of its protagonist, a young Russian-Jewish immigrant to America, a composer, whose goal is the completion of a vast "American" symphony which will express his deeply felt conception of his adopted country as a divinely appointed crucible in which all the ethnic divisions of mankind will divest themselves of their ancient animosities and differences and become fused into one group, signifying the brotherhood of man. In the process he falls in love with a beautiful and cultured Gentile girl. The play ends with the performance of the symphony and, after numerous vicissitudes and traditional family opposition from both sides, with the approaching marriage of David Quixano and his beloved. During the course of these developments, David, in the rhetoric of the time, delivers himself of such sentiments as these:[13]

> America is God's crucible, the great Melting Pot where all the races of Europe are melting and re-forming! Here you stand, good folk, think I, when I see them at Ellis Island, here you stand in your fifty groups, with your fifty languages and histories, and your fifty blood hatreds and rivalries. But you won't be long like that, brothers, for these are the fires of God you've come to—these are the fires of

God. A fig for your fueds and vendettas! Germans and Frenchmen, Irishmen and Englishmen, Jews and Russians—into the Crucible with you all! God is making the American.

Here we have a conception of a melting pot which admits of no exceptions or qualifications with regard to the ethnic stocks which will fuse in the great crucible. Englishmen, Germans, Frenchmen, Slavs, Greeks, Syrians, Jews, Gentiles, even the black and yellow races, were specifically mentioned in Zangwill's rhapsodic enumeration. And this pot patently was to boil in the great cities of America.

Thus around the turn of the century the melting-pot idea became embedded in the ideals of the age as one response to the immigrant receiving experience of the nation. Soon to be challenged by a new philosophy of group adjustment (to be discussed below) and always competing with the more pervasive adherence to Anglo-conformity, the melting-pot image, however, continued to draw a portion of the attention consciously directed toward this aspect of the American scene in the first half of the twentieth century. In the mid-1940's a sociologist who had carried out an investigation of intermarriage trends in New Haven, Connecticut, described a revised conception of the melting process in that city and suggested a basic modification of the theory of that process. In New Haven, Ruby Jo Reeves Kennedy[14] reported from a study of intermarriages from 1870 to 1940 that there was a distinct tendency for the British-Americans, Germans, and Scandinavians to marry among themselves—that is, within a Protestant "pool"; for the Irish, Italians, and Poles to marry among themselves—a Catholic "pool"; and for the Jews to marry other Jews. In other words, intermarriage was taking place across lines of nationality background, but there was a strong tendency for it to stay confined within one or the other of the three major religious groups, Protestants, Catholics, and Jews. Thus, declared Mrs. Kennedy, the picture in New Haven resembled a "triple melting pot" based on religious divisions, rather than a "single melting pot." Her study indicated, she stated, that "while strict endogamy is loosening, religious endogamy is persisting and the future cleavages will be along religious lines rather than along nationality lines as in the past. If this is the case, then the traditional 'single-melting-pot' idea must be abandoned, and a new conception, which we term the 'triple-melting-pot' theory of American assimilation, will take its place as the true expression of what is happening to the various nationality groups in the United States."[15] The triple melting-pot thesis was later taken up by the theologian, Will Herberg, and formed an important sociological frame of reference for his analysis of religious trends in American society, *Protestant-Catholic-Jew*.[16] But the triple melting-pot hypothesis patently takes us into the realm of a society pluralistically conceived. We turn now to the rise of an ideology which attempts to justify such a conception.

CULTURAL PLURALISM

Probably all the non-English immigrants who came to American shores in any significant numbers from colonial times onward—settling either in the forbidding wilderness, the lonely prairie, or in some accessible urban slum—created ethnic enclaves and looked forward to the preservation of at least some of their native cultural patterns. Such a development, natural as breathing, was supported by the later accretion of friends, relatives, and countrymen seeking out oases of familiarity in a strange land, by the desire of the settlers to rebuild (necessarily in miniature) a society in which they could communicate in the familiar tongue and maintain familiar institutions, and, finally, by the necessity to band together for mutual aid and mutual protection against the uncertainties of a strange and frequently hostile environment. This was as true of the "old" immigrants as of the "new." In fact, some of the liberal intellectuals who fled to America from an inhospitable political climate in Germany in the 1830's, 1840's, and 1850's looked forward to the creation of an all-German state within the union, or, even more hopefully, to the eventual formation of a separate German nation, as soon as the expected dissolution of the union under the impact of the slavery controversy should have taken place.[17] Oscar Handlin, writing of the sons of Erin in mid-nineteenth-century Boston, recent refugees from famine and economic degradation in their homeland, points out: "Unable to participate in the normal associational affairs of the community, the Irish felt obliged to erect a society within a society, to act together in their own way. In every contact therefore the group, acting apart from other sections of the community, became intensely aware of its peculiar and exclusive identity."[18] Thus cultural pluralism was a fact in American society before it became a theory—a theory with explicit relevance for the nation as a whole, and articulated and discussed in the English-speaking circles of American intellectual life.

Eventually, the cultural enclaves of the Germans (and the later-arriving Scandinavians) were to decline in scope and significance as succeeding generations of their native-born attended public schools, left the farms and villages to strike out as individuals for the Americanizing city, and generally became subject to the influences of a standardizing industrial civilization. The German-American community, too, was struck a powerful blow by the accumulated passions generated by World War I —a blow from which it never fully recovered. The Irish were to be the dominant and pervasive element in the gradual emergence of a pan-

Catholic group in America, but these developments would reveal themselves only in the twentieth century. In the meantime, in the last two decades of the nineteenth, the influx of immigrants from southern and eastern Europe had begun. These groups were all the more sociologically visible because the closing of the frontier, the occupational demands of an expanding industrial economy, and their own poverty made it inevitable that they would remain in the urban areas of the nation. In the swirling fires of controversy and the steadier flame of experience created by these new events, the ideology of cultural pluralism as a philosophy for the nation was forged.

The first manifestations of an ideological counterattack against draconic Americanization came not from the beleaguered newcomers (who were, after all, more concerned with survival than with theories of adjustment), but from those idealistic members of the middle class who, in the decade or so before the turn of the century, had followed the example of their English predecessors and "settled" in the slums to "learn to sup sorrow with the poor."[19] Immediately, these workers in the "settlement houses" were forced to come to grips with the realities of immigrant life and adjustment. Not all reacted in the same way, but on the whole the settlements developed an approach to the immigrant which was sympathetic to his native cultural heritage and to his newly created ethnic institutions.[20] For one thing, their workers, necessarily in intimate contact with the lives of these often pathetic and bewildered newcomers and their daily problems, could see how unfortunate were the effects of those forces which impelled rapid Americanization in their impact on the immigrants' children, who not infrequently became alienated from their parents and the restraining influence of family authority. Were not their parents ignorant and uneducated "Hunkes," "Sheenies," or "Dagoes," as that limited portion of the American environment in which they moved defined the matter? Ethnic "self-hatred" with its debilitating psychological consequences, family disorganization, and juvenile delinquency, were not unusual results of this state of affairs. Furthermore, the immigrants themselves were adversely affected by the incessant attacks on their culture, their language, their institutions, their very conception of themselves. How were they to maintain their self-respect when all that they knew, felt, and dreamed, beyond their sheer capacity for manual labor—in other words, all that they *were*—was despised or scoffed at in America? And—unkindest cut of all—their own children had begun to adopt the contemptuous attitude of the "Americans." Jane Addams relates in a moving chapter of her *Twenty Years at Hull House* how, after coming to have some conception of the extent and depth of these problems, she created at the settlement a "Labor Museum," in which the immigrant women of the various nationalities crowded together in the slums of Chicago could illustrate their native methods of spinning and weaving, and in which the relation of these earlier techniques to contemporary factory methods could be graphically shown. For the first time these peasant women were made to feel by some part of their American environment that they possessed valuable and interesting skills —that they too had something to offer—and for the first time, the daughters of these women who, after a long day's work at their dank "needletrade" sweatshops, came to Hull House to observe, began to appreciate the fact that their mothers, too, had a "culture," that this culture possessed its own merit, and that it was related to their own contemporary lives. How aptly Jane Addams concludes her chapter with the hope that "our American citizenship might be built without disturbing these foundations which were laid of old time."[21]

This appreciative view of the immigrant's cultural heritage and of its distinctive usefulness both to himself and his adopted country received additional sustenance from another source: those intellectual currents of the day which, however overborne by their currently more powerful opposites, emphasized liberalism, internationalism, and tolerance. From time to time, an occasional educator or publicist protested the demands of the "Americanizers," arguing that the immigrant, too, had an ancient and honorable culture, and that this culture had much to offer an America whose character and destiny were still in the process of formation, an America which must serve as an example of the harmonious cooperation of various heritages to a world inflamed by nationalism and war. In 1916 John Dewey, Norman Hapgood, and the young literary critic, Randolph Bourne, published articles or addresses elaborating various aspects of this theme.

The classic statement of the cultural pluralist position, however, had been made over a year before. Early in 1915 there appeared in the pages of *The Nation* two articles under the title "Democracy *versus* the Melting-Pot." Their author was Horace Kallen, a Harvard-educated philosopher with a concern for the application of philosophy to societal affairs, and, as an American Jew, himself derivative of an ethnic background which was subject to the contemporary pressures for dissolution implicit in the "Americanization," or Anglo-conformity, and the melting-pot theories. In these articles Kallen vigorously rejected the usefulness of these theories as models of what was actually transpiring in American life or as ideals for the future. Rather he was impressed by the way in which the various ethnic groups in America were coincident with particular areas and regions, and with the tendency for each group to preserve its own language, religion, communal institutions, and ancestral culture. All the while, he pointed out, the immigrant has been learning to speak English as the language of general communication, and has participated in the over-all economic and political life of the nation. These developments in which "the United States are in the process of becoming a federal state not merely as a union of geographical and administrative unities, but also as a cooperation of cultural diversities, as a federation or commonwealth of national cultures,"[22] the author argued, far from constituting a violation of historic American political principles, as the "Americanizers" claimed, actually represented the inevitable consequences of democratic ideals, since individuals are implicated in groups, and since democracy for the individual must by extension also mean democracy for his group.

The processes just described, however, as Kallen develops his argument, are far from having been thoroughly realized. They are menaced by "Americanization" programs, assumptions of Anglo-Saxon superiority, and misguided attempts to promote "racial" amalgamation. Thus America stands at a kind of cultural crossroads. It can attempt to impose by force an artificial, Anglo-Saxon oriented uniformity on its peoples, or it can consciously allow and encourage its ethnic groups to develop democratically, each emphasizing its particular cultural heritage. If the latter course is followed, as Kallen puts it at the close of his essay, then,[23]

> The outlines of a possible great and truly democratic common-wealth become discernible. Its form would be that of the federal republic; its substance a democracy of nationalities, cooperating voluntarily and autonomously through common institutions in the enterprise of self-realization through the perfection of men according to their kind. The common language of the commonwealth, the language of its great tradition, would be English, but each nationality would have for its emotional and involuntary life its own peculiar dialect or speech, its own individual and inevitable esthetic and intellectual forms. The political and economic life of the commonwealth is a single unit and serves as the foundation and background for the realization of the distinctive individuality of each *natio* that composes it and of the pooling of these in a harmony above them all. Thus "American civilization" may come to mean the perfection of the cooperative harmonies of "European civilization"—the waste, the squalor and the distress of Europe being eliminated—a multiplicity in a unity, an orchestration of mankind.

Within the next decade Kallen published more essays dealing with the theme of American multiple-group life, later collected in a volume.[24] In the introductory note to this book he used for the first time the term "cultural pluralism" to refer to his position. These essays reflect both his increasingly sharp rejection of the onslaughts on the immigrant and his culture which the coming of World War I and its attendant fears, the "Red scare," the projection of themes of racial superiority, the continued exploitation of the newcomers, and the rise of the Ku Klux Klan all served to increase in intensity, and also his emphasis on cultural pluralism as the democratic antidote to these ills. He has since published other essays elaborating or annotating the theme of cultural pluralism. Thus, for at least forty-five years, most of them spent teaching at the New School for Social Research, Kallen has been acknowledged as the originator and leading philosophical exponent of the idea of cultural pluralism.

In the late 1930's and early 1940's the late Louis Adamic, the Yugoslav immigrant who had become an American writer, took up the theme of America's multicultural heritage and the role of these groups in forging the country's national character. Borrowing Walt Whitman's phrase, he described America as "a nation of nations," and while his ultimate goal was closer to the melting-pot idea than to cultural pluralism, he saw the immediate task as that of making America conscious of what it owed to all its ethnic groups, not just to the Anglo-Saxons. The children and grandchildren of immigrants of non-English origins, he was convinced, must be taught to be proud of the cultural heritage of their ancestral ethnic group and of its role in building the American nation; otherwise, they would not lose their sense of ethnic inferiority and the feeling of rootlessness he claimed to find in them.

Thus in the twentieth century, particularly since World War II, "cultural pluralism" has become a concept which has worked its way into the vocabulary and imagery of specialists in intergroup relations and leaders of ethnic communal groups. In view of this new pluralistic emphasis, some writers now prefer to speak of the "integration" of immigrants rather than of their "assimilation."[25] However, with a few exceptions,[26] no close analytical attention has been given either by social scientists or practitioners of intergroup relations to the meaning of cultural pluralism, its nature and relevance for a modern industrialized society, and its implications for problems of prejudice and discrimination —a point to which we referred at the outset of this discussion.

CONCLUSIONS

In the remaining pages I can make only a few analytical comments which I shall apply in context to the American scene, historical and current. My view of the American situation will not be documented here, but may be considered as a series of hypotheses in which I shall attempt to outline the American assimilation process.

First of all, it must be realized that "assimilation" is a blanket term which in reality covers a multitude of subprocesses. The most crucial distinction is one often ignored—the distinction between what I have elsewhere called "behavioral assimilation" and "structural assimilation."[27] The first refers to the absorption of the cultural behavior patterns of the "host" society. (At the same time, there is frequently some modification of the cultural patterns of the immigrant-receiving country, as well.) There is a special term for this process of cultural modification or "behavioral assimilation"—namely, "acculturation." "Structural assimilation," on the other hand, refers to the entrance of the immigrants and their descendants into the social cliques, organizations, institutional activities, and general civic life of the receiving society. If this process takes place on a large enough scale, then a high frequency of intermarriage must result. A further distinction must be made between, on the one hand, those activities of the general civic life which involve earning a living, carrying out political responsibilities, and engaging in the instrumental affairs of the larger community, and, on the other hand, activities which create personal friendship patterns, frequent home intervisiting, communal worship, and communal recreation. The first type usually develops so-called "secondary relationships," which tend to be relatively impersonal and segmental; the latter type leads to "primary relationships," which are warm, intimate, and personal.

With these various distinctions in mind, we may then proceed.

Built on the base of the original immigrant "colony" but frequently extending into the life of successive generations, the characteristic ethnic group experience is this: within the ethnic group there develops a network of organizations and informal social relationships which permits and encourages the members of the ethnic group to remain within the confines of the group for all of their primary relationships and some of their secondary relationships throughout all the stages of the life cycle. From the cradle in the sectarian hospital to the child's play group, the social clique in high school, the fraternity and religious center in college, the dating group within which he searches for a spouse, the marriage partner, the neighborhood of his residence, the church affiliation and the church clubs, the men's and the women's social and service organizations, the adult clique of "marrieds," the vacation resort, and then, as the age cycle nears completion, the rest home for the elderly and, finally, the sectarian cemetery—in all these activities and relationships which are close to the core of personality and selfhood—the member of the ethnic group may if he wishes follow a path which never takes him across the boundaries of his ethnic structural network.

The picture is made more complex by the existence of social class divisions which cut across ethnic group lines just as they do those of the white Protestant population in America. As each ethnic group which has been here for the requisite time has developed second, third, or in some cases, succeeding generations, it has produced a college-educated group which composes an upper middle class (and sometimes upper class, as well) segment of the larger groups. Such class divisions tend to restrict primary group relations even further, for although the ethnic-group member feels a general sense of identification with all the bearers of his ethnic heritage, he feels comfortable in intimate social relations only with those who also share his own class background or attainment.

In short, my point is that, while *behavioral assimilation* or acculturation has taken place in America to a considerable degree, *structural assimilation,* with some important exceptions has not been extensive.[28] The exceptions are of two types. The first brings us back to the "triple melting pot" thesis of Ruby Jo Reeves Kennedy and Will Herberg. The "nationality" ethnic groups have tended to merge within each of the three major religious groups. This has been particularly true of the Protestant and Jewish communities. Those descendants of the "old" immigration of the nineteenth century, who were Protestant (many of the Germans and all the Scandinavians), have in considerable part gradually merged into the white Protestant "subsociety." Jews of Sephardic, German, and Eastern European origins have similarly tended to come together in their communal life. The process of absorbing the various Catholic nationalities, such as the Italians, Poles, and French Canadians, into an American Catholic community hitherto dominated by the Irish has begun, although I do not believe that it is by any means close to completion. Racial and quasi-racial groups such as the Negroes, Indians, Mexican-Americans, and Puerto Ricans still retain their separate sociological structures. The outcome of all this in contemporary American life is thus pluralism—but it is more than "triple" and it is more accurately described as *structural pluralism* than as cultural pluralism, although some of the latter also remains.

My second exception refers to the social structures which implicate intellectuals. There is no space to develop the issue here, but I would argue that there is a social world or subsociety of the intellectuals in America in which true structural intermixture among persons of various ethnic backgrounds, including the religious, has markedly taken place.

My final point deals with the reasons for these developments. If structural assimilation has been retarded in America by religious and racial lines, we must ask why. The answer lies in the attitudes of both the majority and the minority groups and in the way these attitudes have interacted. A saying of the current day is, "It takes two to tango." To apply the analogy, there is no good reason to believe that white

Protestant America has ever extended a firm and cordial invitation to its minorities to dance. Furthermore, the attitudes of the minority-group members themselves on the matter have been divided and ambiguous. Particularly for the minority religious groups, there is a certain logic in ethnic communality, since there is a commitment to the perpetuation of the religious ideology and since structural intermixture leads to intermarriage and the possible loss to the group of the intermarried family. Let us, then, examine the situation serially for various types of minorities.

With regard to the immigrant, in his characteristic numbers and socioeconomic background, structural assimilation was out of the question. He did not want it, and he had a positive need for the comfort of his own communal institutions. The native American, moreover, whatever the implications of his public pronouncements, had no intention of opening up his primary group life to entrance by these hordes of alien newcomers. The situation was a functionally complementary standoff.

The second generation found a much more complex situation. Many believed they heard the siren call of welcome to the social cliques, clubs, and institutions of white Protestant America. After all, it was simply a matter of learning American ways, was it not? Had they not grown up as Americans, and were they not culturally different from their parents, the "greenhorns?" Or perhaps an especially eager one reasoned (like the Jewish protagonist of Myron Kaufmann's novel, *Remember Me To God,* aspiring to membership in the prestigious club system of Harvard undergraduate social life) "If only I can go the last few steps in Ivy League manners and behavior, they will surely recognize that I am one of them and take me in." But, alas, Brooks Brothers suit notwithstanding, the doors of the fraternity house, the city men's club, and the country club were slammed in the face of the immigrant's offspring. That invitation was not really there in the first place; or, to the extent it was, in Joshua Fishman's phrase, it was a " 'look me over but don't touch me' invitation to the American minority group child."[29] And so the rebuffed one returned to the homelier but dependable comfort of the communal institutions of his ancestral group. There he found his fellows of the same generation who had never stirred from the home fires. Some of these had been too timid to stray; others were ethnic ideologists committed to the group's survival; still others had never really believed in the authenticity of the siren call or were simply too passive to do more than go along the familiar way. All could now join in the task that was well within the realm of the sociologically possible—the build-up of social institutions and organizations within the ethnic enclave, manned increasingly by members of the second generation and suitably separated by social class.

Those who had for a time ventured out gingerly or confidently, as the case might be, had been lured by the vision of an "American" social structure that was somehow larger than all subgroups and was ethnically neutral. Were they, too, not Americans? But they found to their dismay that at the primary group level a neutral American social structure was a mirage. What at a distance seemed to be a quasi-public edifice flying only the all-inclusive flag of American nationality turned out on closer inspection to be the clubhouse of a particular ethnic group —the white Anglo-Saxon Protestants, its operation shot through with the premises and expectations of its parental ethnicity. In these terms, the desirability of whatever invitation was grudgingly extended to those of other ethnic backgrounds could only become a considerably attenuated one.

With the racial minorities, there was not even the pretense of an invitation. Negroes, to take the most salient example, have for the most part been determinedly barred from the cliques, social clubs, and churches of white America. Consequently, with due allowance for internal class differences, they have constructed their own network of organizations and institutions, their own "social world." There are now many vested interests served by the preservation of this separate communal life, and doubtless many Negroes are psychologically comfortable in it, even though at the same time they keenly desire that discrimination in such areas as employment, education, housing, and public accommodations be eliminated. However, the ideological attachment of Negroes to their communal separation is not conspicuous. Their sense of identification with ancestral African national cultures is virtually nonexistent, although Pan-Africanism engages the interest of some intellectuals and although "black nationalist" and "black racist" fringe groups have recently made an appearance at the other end of the communal spectrum. As for their religion, they are either Protestant or Catholic (overwhelmingly the former). Thus, there are no "logical" ideological reasons for their separate communality; dual social structures are created solely by the dynamics of prejudice and discrimination, rather than being reinforced by the ideological commitments of the minority itself.

Structural assimilation, then, has turned out to be the rock on which the ships of Anglo-conformity and the melting pot have foundered. To understand that behavioral assimilation (or acculturation) without massive structural intermingling in primary relationships has been the dominant motif in the American experience of creating and developing a nation out of diverse peoples is to comprehend the most essential sociological fact of that experience. It is against the background of "structural pluralism" that strategies of strengthening intergroup harmony, reducing ethnic discrimination and prejudice, and maintaining the rights of both those who stay within and those who venture beyond their ethnic boundaries must be thoughtfully devised.

REFERENCES

1. ALLAN NEVINS and HENRY STEELE COMMANGER, *America: The Story of a Free People* (Boston: Little, Brown, 1942), p. 58.

2. The phrase is the Coles's. See Stewart G. Cole and Mildred Wiese Cole, *Minorities and the American Promise* (New York: Harper & Brothers, 1954), ch. 6.

3. MAURICE R. DAVIE, *World Immigration* (New York: Macmillan, 1936), p. 36, and (cited therein) "Letter of Benjamin Franklin to Peter Collinson, 9th May, 1753, on the condition and character of the Germans in Pennsylvania," in *The Works of Benjamin Franklin, with notes and a life of the author,* by Jared Sparks (Boston, 1828), vol. 7, pp. 71–73.

4. *The Writings of George Washington,* collected and edited by W. C. Ford (New York: G. P. Putnam's Sons, 1889), vol. 12, p. 489.

5. THOMAS JEFFERSON, "Notes on Virginia, Query 8;" in *The Writings of Thomas Jefferson,* ed. A. E. Bergh (Washington: The Thomas Jefferson Memorial Association, 1907), vol. 2, p. 121.

6. *Niles' Weekly Register,* vol. 18, 29 April 1820, pp. 157–158; also, Marcus L. Hansen, *The Atlantic Migration, 1607–1860,* pp. 96–97.

7. ELLWOOD P. CUBBERLY, *Changing Conceptions of Education* (Boston: Houghton Mifflin, 1909), pp. 15–16.

8. J. HECTOR ST. JOHN CRÈVECOEUR, *Letters from an American Farmer* (New York: Albert and Charles Boni, 1925; reprinted from the 1st edn., London, 1782), pp. 54–55.

9. OSCAR HANDLIN, ed., *Immigration as a Factor in American History* (Englewood Cliffs: Prentice-Hall, 1959), p. 146.

10. Quoted by Stuart P. Sherman in his Introduction to *Essays and Poems of Emerson* (New York: Harcourt Brace, 1921), p. xxxiv.

11. See Edward N. Saveth, *American Historians and European Immigrants, 1875–1925,* New York: Columbia University Press, 1948.

12. FREDERICK JACKSON TURNER, *The Frontier in American History* (New York: Henry Holt, 1920), pp. 22–23, 190.

13. ISRAEL ZANGWILL, *The Melting Pot* (New York: Macmillan, 1909), p. 37.

14. RUBY JO REEVES KENNEDY, "Single or Triple Melting-Pot? Intermarriage Trends in New Haven, 1870–1940," *American Journal of Sociology,* 1944, *49:* 331–339. See also her "Single or Triple Melting-Pot? Intermarriage in New Haven, 1870–1950," *ibid.,* 1952, *58:* 56–59.

15. ————, "Single or Triple Melting-Pot? . . . 1870–1940," p. 332 (author's italics omitted).

16. WILL HERBERG, *Protestant-Catholic-Jew* (Garden City: Doubleday, 1955).

17. NATHAN GLAZER, "Ethnic Groups in America: From National Culture to Ideology," in Morroe Berger, Theodore Abel, and Charles H. Page, eds., *Freedom and Control in Modern Society* (New York: D. Van Nostrand, 1954), p. 161; Marcus Lee Hansen, *The Immigrant in American History* (Cambridge: Harvard University Press, 1940), pp. 129–140; John A. Hawgood, *The Tragedy of German-America* (New York: Putnam's, 1940), *passim*.

18. OSCAR HANDLIN, *Boston's Immigrants* (Cambridge: Harvard University Press, 1959, rev. edn.), p. 176.

19. From a letter (1883) by Samuel A. Barnett; quoted in Arthur C. Holden, *The Settlement Idea* (New York: Macmillan, 1922), p. 12.

20. JANE ADDAMS, *Twenty Years at Hull House* (New York: Macmillan, 1914), pp. 231–258; Arthur C. Holden, *op. cit.*, pp. 109–131, 182–189; John Higham, *Strangers in the Land* (New Brunswick: Rutgers University Press, 1955), p. 236.

21. JANE ADDAMS, *op. cit.*, p. 258.

22. HORACE M. KALLEN, "Democracy *versus* the Melting-Pot," *The Nation*, 18 and 25 February 1915; reprinted in his *Culture and Democracy in the United States* (New York: Boni and Liveright, 1924); the quotation is on p. 116.

23. KALLEN, *Culture and Democracy* . . . , p. 124.

24. *Op. cit.*

25. See W. D. Borrie *et al.*, *The Cultural Integration of Immigrants* (a survey based on the papers and proceedings of the UNESCO Conference in Havana, April 1956), Paris, UNESCO, 1959; and William S. Bernard, "The Integration of Immigrants in the United States" (mimeographed), one of the papers for this conference.

26. See particularly Milton M. Gordon, "Social Structure and Goals in Group Relations,"; and Nathan Glazer, "Ethnic Groups in America; From National Culture to Ideology," both articles in Berger, Abel, and Page, *op. cit.*; S. N. Eisenstadt, *The Absorption of Immigrants* (London: Routledge and Kegan Paul, 1954); and W. D. Borrie *et al.*, *op. cit.*

27. MILTON M. GORDON, "Social Structure and Goals in Group Relations," p. 151.

28. See Erich Rosenthal, "Acculturation without Assimilation?" *American Journal of Sociology*, 1960, *66:* 275–288.

29. JOSHUA A. FISHMAN, "Childhood Indoctrination for Minority-Group Membership and the Quest for Minority-Group Biculturism in America," in Oscar Handlin, ed., *Group Life in America* (Cambridge: Harvard University Press, forthcoming).

Ralph Ellison
REFLECTIONS OF A WRITER

Anything and everything was to be found in the chaos of Oklahoma; thus the concept of the Renaissance Man has lurked long within the shadow of my past, and I shared it with at least a half dozen of my Negro friends. How we actually acquired it I have never learned, and since there is no true sociology of the dispersion of ideas within the American democracy, I doubt if I ever shall. Perhaps we breathed it in with the air of the Negro community of Oklahoma City, the capital of that state whose Negroes were often charged by exasperated white Texans with not knowing their "place." Perhaps we took it defiantly from one of them. Or perhaps I myself picked it up from some transplanted New Englander whose shoes I had shined of a Saturday afternoon. After all, the most meaningful tips do not always come in the form of money, nor are they intentionally extended. Most likely, however, my friends and I acquired the idea from some book or from some idealistic Negro teacher, some dreamer seeking to function responsibly in an environment which at its most normal took on some of the mixed character of nightmare and of dream.

One thing is certain, ours was a chaotic community, still characterized by frontier attitudes and by that strange mixture of the naïve and sophisticated, the benign and malignant, which makes the American past so puzzling and its present so confusing; that mixture which often affords the minds of the young who grow up in the far provinces such wide and unstructured latitude, and which encourages the individual's imagination—up to the moment "reality" closes in upon him—to range widely and, sometimes, even to soar.

We hear the effects of this in the southwestern jazz of the thirties, that joint creation of artistically free and exuberantly creative adventurers, of artists who had stumbled upon the freedom lying within the restrictions of their musical tradition as within the limitations of their

From *Shadow and Act*, by Ralph Ellison, pp. xii–xviii. © Copyright 1964 by Ralph Ellison. Reprinted by permission of Random House, Inc.

Mr. Ellison is a major American novelist whose book *Invisible Man* won the National Book Award in Fiction.

social background, and who in their own unconscious way have set an example for any Americans, Negro or white, who would find themselves in the arts. They accepted themselves and the complexity of life as they knew it, they loved their art and through it they celebrated American experience definitively in sound. Whatever others thought or felt, this was their own powerful statement, and only nonmusical assaults upon their artistic integrity—mainly economically inspired changes of fashion —were able to compromise their vision. . . .

I recall that much of so-called Kansas City jazz was actually brought to perfection in Oklahoma by Oklahomans. It is an important circumstance for me as a writer to remember, because while these musicians and their fellows were busy creating out of tradition, imagination and the sounds and emotions around them a freer, more complex and driving form of jazz, my friends and I were exploring an idea of human versatility and possibility which went against the barbs or over the palings of almost every fence which those who controlled social and political power had erected to restrict our roles in the life of the country. Looking back, one might say that the jazzmen, some of whom we idolized, were in their own way better examples for youth to follow than were most judges and ministers, legislators and governors (we were stuck with the notorious Alfalfa Bill Murray). For as we viewed these pillars of society from the confines of our segregated community we almost always saw crooks, clowns or hypocrites. Even the best were revealed by their attitudes toward us as lacking the respectable qualities to which they pretended and for which they were accepted outside by others, while despite the outlaw nature of their art, the jazzmen were less torn and damaged by the moral compromises and insincerities which have so sickened the life of our country.

Be that as it may, our youthful sense of life, like that of many Negro children (though no one bothers to note it—especially the specialists and "friends of the Negro" who view our Negro American life as essentially nonhuman) was very much like that of Huckleberry Finn, who is universally so praised and enjoyed for the clarity and courage of his moral vision. Like Huck we observed, we judged, we imitated and evaded as we could the dullness, corruption and blindness of "civilization." We were undoubtedly comic because, as the saying goes, we weren't supposed to know what it was all about. But to ourselves we were "boys," members of a wild, free outlaw tribe which transcended the category of race. Rather we were Americans born into the forty-sixth state, and thus, into the context of Negro-American post-Civil War history, "frontiersmen." And isn't one of the implicit functions of the American frontier to encourage the individual to a kind of dreamy wakefulness, a state in which he makes—in all ignorance of the accepted limitations of the possible—rash efforts, quixotic gestures, hopeful testings of the complexity of the known and the given?

Spurring us on in our controlled and benign madness, was the voracious reading of which most of us were guilty and the vicarious identification and empathic adventuring which it encouraged. This was due, in part, perhaps to the fact that some of us were fatherless—my own father had died when I was three—but most likely it was because boys are natural romantics. We were seeking examples, patterns to live by, out of a freedom which for all its being ignored by the sociologists and subtle thinkers was implicit in the Negro situation. Father and mother substitutes also have a role to play in aiding the child to help create himself. Thus we fabricated our own heroes and ideals catch-as-catch can, and with an outrageous and irreverent sense of freedom. Yes, and in complete disregard for ideas of respectability or the surreal incongruity of some of our projections. Gamblers and scholars, jazz musicians and scientists, Negro cowboys and soldiers from the Spanish-American and First World Wars, movie stars and stunt men, figures from the Italian Renaissance and literature, both classical and popular, were combined with the special virtues of some local bootlegger, the eloquence of some Negro preacher, the strength and grace of some local athlete, the ruthlessness of some businessman-physician, the elegance in dress and manners of some head-waiter or hotel doorman.

Looking back through the shadows upon this absurd activity I realize now that we were projecting archetypes, recreating folk figures, legendary heroes, monsters even, most of which violated all ideas of social hierarchy and order and all accepted conceptions of the hero handed down by cultural, religious and racist tradition. But we, remember, were under the intense spell of the early movies, the silents as well as the talkies; and in our community, life was not so tightly structured as it would have been in the traditional South—or even in deceptively "free" Harlem. And our imaginations processed reality and dream, natural man and traditional hero, literature and folklore, like maniacal editors turned loose in some frantic film-cutting room. Remember, too, that being boys, yet in the play-stage of our development, we were dream-serious in our efforts. But serious, nevertheless, for *culturally* play is a preparation, and we felt that somehow the human ideal lay in the vague and constantly shifting figures—sometimes comic but always versatile, picaresque and self-effacingly heroic—which evolved from our wildly improvisionary projections—figures neither white nor black, Christian nor Jewish, but representative of certain desirable essences, of skills and powers physical, aesthetic and moral.

The proper response to these figures was, we felt, to develop ourselves for the performance of many and diverse roles, and the fact that certain definite limitations had been imposed upon our freedom did not lessen our sense of obligation. Not only were we to prepare but we were to perform—not with mere competence but with an almost reckless verve; with, may we say (without evoking the quaint and questionable notion of *negritude*), Negro American style? Behind each artist there stands a traditional sense of style, a sense of the felt tension indicative of expressive completeness; a mode of humanizing reality and of evoking a feeling of being at home in the world. It is something which the artist shares with the group, and part of our boyish activity expressed a yearning to make any and everything of quality *Negro American;* to appropriate it, possess it, re-create it in our own group and individual images.

And we recognized and were proud of our group's own style wherever we discerned it—in jazzmen and prize fighters, ballplayers and tap dancers; in gesture, inflection, intonation, timbre and phrasing. Indeed, in all those nuances of expression and attitude which reveal a culture. We did not fully understand the cost of that style but we recognized within it an affirmation of life beyond all question of our difficulties as Negroes.

Contrary to the notion currently projected by certain specialists in the "Negro problem" which characterizes the Negro American as self-hating and defensive, we did not so regard ourselves. We felt, among ourselves at least, that we were supposed to be whoever we would and could be and do anything and everything which other boys did, and do it better. Not defensively, because we were ordered to do so; nor because it was held in the society at large that we were naturally, as Negroes, limited—but because we demanded it of ourselves. Because to measure up to our own standards was the only way of affirming our notion of manhood.

Hence it was no more incongruous, as seen from our own particular perspective in this land of incongruities, for young Negro Oklahomans to project themselves as Renaissance Men than for white Mississippians to see themselves as ancient Greeks or noblemen out of Sir Walter Scott. Surely our fantasies have caused far less damage to the nation's sense of reality, if for no other reason than that ours were expressive of a more democratic ideal. Remember, too, as William Faulkner made us so vividly aware, that the slaves often took the essence of the aristocratic ideal (as they took Christianity) with far more seriousness than their masters, and that we, thanks to the tight telescoping of American history, were but two generations from that previous condition. Renaissance Men, indeed!

I managed, by keeping quiet about it, to cling to our boyish ideal during three years in Alabama, and I brought it with me to New York, where it not only gave silent support to my explorations of what was then an unknown territory, but served to mock and caution me when I became interested in the communist ideal. And when it was suggested that I try my hand at writing, it was still with me; thus I went about writing rashly unaware that my ambitions as a composer had been fatally diverted.

THAT SAME PAIN, THAT SAME PLEASURE: AN INTERVIEW*

RICHARD G. STERN   Last night we were talking about the way in which your literary situation has been special, the way in which you as a Negro writer have vaulted the parochial limitations of most Negro fiction. Accepting this, not debating it, would you want to talk a bit about the sources of the strength by which you escaped them?

RALPH ELLISON   Well, to the extent that one cannot ever escape what is given I suppose it had less to do with writing per se than with my desire, beginning at a very early age, to be more fully a part of that larger world which surrounded the Negro world into which I was born. It was a matter of attitude. Then there were the accidents through which so much of that world beyond the Negro community became available to me. Ironically, I would have to start with some of the features of American life which it has become quite fashionable to criticize in a most unthinking way—the mass media. Like so many kids of the twenties, I played around with radio—building crystal sets and circuits consisting of a few tubes, which I found published in the radio magazines. At the time we were living in a white middle-class neighborhood, where my mother was custodian for some apartments, and it was while searching the trash for cylindrical ice-cream cartons which were used by amateurs for winding tuning coils that I met a white boy who was looking for the same thing. I gave him some of those I'd found and we became friends. Oddly enough, I don't remember his family name even though his father was pastor of the leading Episcopal church in Oklahoma City at that time, but his nickname was Hoolie and for kids of eight or nine that was enough.[1] Due to a rheumatic heart Hoolie was tutored at home and spent

---

* From pp. 3–23 of *Shadow and Act*. Reprinted by permission of *December Magazine*.

[1] Thanks to the Reverend Kenneth R. Coleman, Chaplain of the Episcopal Church at Yale University, to whom (in 1963) I related the circumstances of this old friendship, I was put in touch with the Reverend R. A. Laud Humphreys, Historiographer of the Episcopal Diocese of Oklahoma, who in turn kindly interested himself in the mystery of my childhood friend. Thus I now know not only that "Hoolie" is the son of the Reverend Franklin Davis and Mrs. Davis, but that his real name is Henry Bowman Otto Davis. He is now an electronics expert connected with the Air Force.

a great deal of time playing by himself and in taking his parents' elaborate radio apart and putting it back together again, and in building circuits of his own. For all of his delicate health, he was a very intelligent and very alive boy. It didn't take much encouragement from his mother, who was glad to have someone around to keep him company, for me to spend much of my free time helping with his experiments. By the time I left the community, he had become interested in short-wave communication and was applying for a ham license. I moved back into the Negro community and began to concentrate on music, and was never to see him again, but knowing this white boy was a very meaningful experience. It had little to do with the race question as such, but with our mutual loneliness (I had no other playmates in that community) and a great curiosity about the growing science of radio. It was important for me to know a boy who could approach the intricacies of electronics with such daring and whose mind was intellectually aggressive. Knowing him led me to expect much more of myself and of the world.

The other accident from that period lay in my mother's bringing home copies of such magazines as *Vanity Fair* and of opera recordings which had been discarded by a family for whom she worked. You might say that my environment was extended by these slender threads into the worlds of white families whom personally I knew not at all. These magazines and recordings and the discarded books my mother brought home to my brother and me spoke to me of a life which was broader and more interesting, and although it was not really a part of my own life, I never thought they were not for me simply because I happened to be a Negro. They were things which spoke of a world which I could some day make my own.

STERN Were you conscious at this time of peculiar limitations upon your freedom of action, perhaps even your freedom of feeling?

ELLISON Well, now, remember that this was in Oklahoma, which is a border state and as the forty-sixth state was one of the last of our territories to achieve statehood. Although opened to American settlers in 1889, at the time of my birth it had been a state only seven years. Thus it had no tradition of slavery, and while it was segregated, relationships between the races were more fluid and thus more human than in the old slave states. My parents, like most of the other Negroes, had come to the new state looking for a broader freedom and had never stopped pushing against the barriers. Having arrived at the same time that most of the whites had, they felt that the restriction of Negro freedom was imposed unjustly through the force of numbers and that they had the right and obligation to fight against it. This was all to the good. It made for a tradition of aggressiveness and it gave us a group social goal which was not as limited as that imposed by the old slave states. I recognized limitations, yes; but I thought these limitations were unjust and I felt no innate sense of inferiority which would keep me from getting those things I desired out of life. There were those who stood in the way but you just had to keep moving toward whatever you wanted.

As a kid I remember working it out this way: there was a world in which you wore your everyday clothes on Sunday, and there was a world in which you wore your Sunday clothes every day—I wanted the world in which you wore your Sunday clothes every day. I wanted it because it represented something better, a more exciting and civilized and human way of living; a world which came to me through certain scenes of felicity which I encountered in fiction, in the movies, and which I glimpsed sometimes through the windows of great houses on Sunday afternoons when my mother took my brother and me for walks through the wealthy white sections of the city. I know it now for a boy's vague dream of possibility. Hoolie was part of it, and shop-window displays of elegant clothing, furniture, automobiles—those Lincolns and Marmons! —and of course music and books. And for me none of this was hopelessly beyond the reach of my Negro world, really; because if you worked and you fought for your rights, and so on, you could finally achieve it. This involved our American Negro faith in education, of course, and the idea of self-cultivation—although I couldn't have put it that way back during the days when the idea first seized me. Interestingly enough, by early adolescence the idea of Renaissance Man had drifted down to about six of us, and we discussed mastering ourselves and everything in sight as though no such thing as racial discrimination existed. As you can see, quite a lot of our living was done in the imagination.

STERN   At one part of your life you became conscious that there was something precious in being a Negro in this country at this time. Can you remember when you discovered this?

ELLISON   Well, part of it came from the affirmation of those things in the Negro environment which I found warm and meaningful. For instance, I had none of the agricultural experience of my mother, who had grown up on a farm in Georgia, and although in twenty minutes you could move from Oklahoma City into deep farm country, I shared none of the agricultural experience of many of my classmates. I was of the city, you see. But during the fall cotton-picking season certain kids left school and went with their parents to work in the cotton fields. Now, most parents wished their children to have no contact with the cotton patch, it was part of an experience which they wanted to put behind them. It was part of the Old South which they had come west to forget. Just the same, those trips to the cotton patch seemed to me an enviable experience because the kids came back with such wonderful stories. And it wasn't the hard work which they stressed, but the communion, the playing, the eating, the dancing and the singing. And they brought back jokes, *our* Negro jokes—not those told about Negroes by whites—and they always returned with Negro folk stories which I'd never heard before and which couldn't be found in any books I knew about. This was something to affirm and I felt there was a richness in it. I didn't think too much about it, but what my schoolmates shared in the country and what I felt in their accounts of it—it seemed much more real than the Negro middle-class values which were taught in school.

Or again: I grew up in a school in which music was emphasized and where we were taught harmony from the ninth through the twelfth grades, and where much time was give to music appreciation and the study of the shorter classical forms but where jazz was considered disreputable. Of course, this is part of the story of jazz even today. So much of the modern experimentation in jazz springs—as far as Negro jazz modernists are concerned—from a misplaced shame over the so-called low-class origins of jazz. These are usually men of Negro middle-class background who have some formal training in music and who would like for jazz to be a "respectable" form of expression tied up with other forms of revolt. They'd like to dry up the deep, rowdy stream of jazz until it becomes a very thin trickle of respectable sound indeed. Be that as it may, despite my teachers, the preachers and other leaders of the community, I was with those who found jazz attractive, an important part of life. I hung around the old Blue Devils Orchestra out of which the famous Basie band was formed. I knew these people and admired them. I knew Jimmy Rushing, the blues singer, who then was not quite the hero of the middle-class people whom I knew, that he is today after years of popular success. But for us, even when he was a very young man, a singer who came home to the city once in a while, Jimmy represented, gave voice to, something which was very affirming of Negro life, feelings which you couldn't really put into words. Of course, beyond jazz there was all the boasting, the bragging that went on when no one but ourselves was supposed to be listening, when you weren't really being judged by the white world. At least when you *thought* you weren't being judged and didn't care if you were. For instance, there is no place like a Negro barbershop for hearing what Negroes really think. There is more unself-conscious affirmation to be found here on a Saturday than you can find in a Negro college in a month, or so it seems to me.

Getting back to your question, I suppose my attitude toward these elements of Negro life became a discipline toward affirming that which felt desirable to me over and beyond anything which we were taught in school. It was more a matter of the heart than of the mind.

STERN You found something precious, special, and associated it with jazz. Now, between finding that jazz was a vehicle for special qualities which you admired in Negroes and finding that literature was a vehicle, you yourself wanted to employ—

ELLISON I wanted to be a composer but not a jazz composer, interestingly enough. I wanted to be a symphonist.

STERN How about that then?

ELLISON Well, I had always listened to music and as far back as I can remember I had the desire to create. I can't remember when I first wanted to play jazz or to create classical music. I can't remember a time when I didn't want to make something, whether it was a small one-tube radio or a crystal set, or my own toys. This was a part of the neighborhood where I spent most of my childhood. There were a number of us who were that way.

STERN Did your desire to be a symphony composer rather than a jazz instrumentalist stand for a sort of denial of your own cultural situation as a Negro?

ELLISON No, no. You see, what is often misunderstood nowadays is that there wasn't always this division between the ambitions of jazz musicians and the standards of classical music; the idea was to master both traditions. In school the classics were pushed at us on all sides, and if you danced, if you shared any of the social life of the young people, jazz was inescapable; it was all around you. And if you were a *musician* you were challenged by its sounds and by the techniques required to produce them. In fact, we admired such jazzmen as the late bassist Walter Page and the trumpeter Icky Lawrence over all other local musicians, because although they usually played in jazz bands, they could go into any theater pit and play the scores placed before them. They played the arrangements for the silent movies at sight and we found this very impressive. Such men as Lawrence and Page—and there were several others—had conservatory training as well as a rich jazz experience and thus felt no need to draw a line between the two traditions. Following them, our ideal was to master both. It wasn't a matter of wanting to do the classics because they denied or were felt to deny jazz, and I suppose my own desire to write symphonies grew out of an attraction to the bigger forms and my awareness that they moved many people as they did me in a different way. The range of mood was much broader.

STERN Can you describe the difference in your own feelings about the two forms?

ELLISON   I can try, but since I shall be trying to recall emotions having to do with the non-verbal medium of music, and at a time when I was a very young and inarticulate boy, I can only give you vague impressions. You see, jazz was so much a part of our total way of life that it got not only into our attempts at playing classical music but into forms of activities usually not associated with it: into marching and into football games, where it has since become a familiar fixture. A lot has been written about the role of jazz in a certain type of Negro funeral marching, but in Oklahoma City it got into military drill. There were many Negro veterans from the Spanish-American War who delighted in teaching the younger boys complicated drill patterns, and on hot summer evenings we spent hours on the Bryant School grounds (now covered with oil wells) learning to execute the commands barked at us by our enthusiastic drillmasters. And as we mastered the patterns, the jazz feeling would come into it and no one was satisfied until we were swinging. These men who taught us had raised a military discipline to the level of a low art form, almost a dance, and its spirit was jazz.

On the other hand, I became a member of the school band while in the eighth grade and we played military music, the classical marches, arrangements of symphonic music, overtures, snatches of opera, and so on, and we sang classical sacred music and the Negro spirituals. So all this was a part of it, and not only did we have classes in music appreciation right through school, on May Day we filled the Western League Ball Park wrapping maypoles and dancing European folk dances. You really should see a field of little Negro kids dancing an Irish jig or a Scottish fling. There must have been something incongruous about it for the few whites who came to see us, but there we were and for us the dance was the thing. Culturally everything was mixed, you see, and beyond all question of conscious choices there was a level where you were claimed by emotion and movement and moods which you couldn't put into words. Often we wanted to share both: the classics and jazz, the Charleston and the Irish reel, spirituals and the blues, the sacred and the profane. I remember the breakfast dances, the matinée dances along with the tent meetings, and the more formal Afro-Methodist Episcopal Christmas services which took place in our church; they all had their special quality. During adolescence I remember attending sunrise services, which took place before Christmas morning. It was a very sacred service, but I remember my mother permitting me to leave after the services were over to attend a breakfast dance. She didn't attend dances herself and was quite pious by that time, but there was no necessary clash between these quite different celebrations of Christmas, and for me the two forms added quite a bit to my sense of the unity of the life I lived. Just the same, there were certain yearnings which I felt, certain emotions, certain needs for other forms of transcendence and identification which I could only associate with classical music. I heard it in Beethoven, I heard it in Schumann. I used to hear it in Wagner—he is really a young man's composer; especially a young bandsman with plenty of brass. I was always a trumpeter, so I was always listening for those composers who made the most use, the loudest use, of the brass choir. Seriously though, you got glimpses, very vague glimpses, of a far different world than that assigned by segregation laws, and I was taken very early with a passion to link together all I loved within the Negro community and all those things I felt in the world which lay beyond.

STERN So pretty early you had a sense of being part of a larger social or cultural complex?

ELLISON Put it this way: I learned very early that in the realm of the imagination all people and their ambitions and interests could meet. This was inescapable, given my reading and my daydreaming. But this notion, this vague awareness, was helped along by the people I came to know. On the level of race relations, my father had many white friends who came to the house when I was quite small, so that any feelings of distrust I was to develop toward whites later on were modified by those with whom I had warm relations. Oklahoma offered many opportunities for such friendships. I remember also an English actress named Emma Bunting—I wonder what happened to her? Anyway, when I was a child, Emma Bunting used to bring over a repertory company each summer, and when she performed in Oklahoma City, her maid, a very handsome Negro woman named Miss Clark, used to stay with us. There was no segregation in the downtown theatres during that period—although it came later—and my mother went frequently to plays and was very proud of a lace bag which Emma Bunting had given her. You see, there is always some connection. Miss Clark brought not only the theatre into our house but England as well. I guess it's breaks in the pattern of segregation which count, the accidents. When I reached high school I knew Dr. Ludwig Hebestreit, a conductor who formed the nucleus of what became the Oklahoma Symphony—a German for whom I used to cut the grass in exchange for trumpet lessons. But these lessons were about everything else. He'd talk to me about all that lay behind music, and after I'd performed my trumpet lesson and had been corrected he'd say, "You like such and such a composition, don't you?" And I'd say, "Yes," and he'd sit down at the piano with a piece of scoring paper and in a few minutes he would have written out passages of the orchestration and show me bar by bar how the sounds were blended.

"The strings are doing this," he'd say, "and the trumpets are playing this figure against the woodwinds," and so on.

Most of it was over my head, but he made it all so logical and, better still, he taught me how to attack those things I desired so that I could pierce the mystery and possess them. I came to feel, yes, that if you want these things and master the technique, you could get with it. You could make it yours. I came to understand, in other words, that all that stood between me and writing symphonies was not simply a matter of civil rights—even though the civil rights struggle was all too real. At that time my mother was being thrown into jail every other day for violating a zoning ordinance by moving into a building in a section where Governor Alfalfa Bill Murray had decided Negroes shouldn't live . . .

STERN   You went on then to Tuskegee, and you studied music seriously, and came up to New York more or less intending to . . .

ELLISON   To go back to Tuskegee. I came up during my junior year hoping to work and learn a little about sculpture. And although I did study a bit, I didn't get the job through which I hoped to earn enough money for my school expenses, so I remained in New York, where I soon realized that although I had a certain facility with three-dimensional form I wasn't really interested in sculpture. So after a while I blundered into writing.

STERN   The music you had given up by this time?

ELLISON   No, no, I was still trying to be a musician. I was doing some exercises in composition under Wallingford Riegger, and although I was much behind his advanced students I stayed there and studied with him until I had to have a tonsillectomy. It turned out to be a pretty chronic case and caused a lot of trouble, and by the time I tried to go back to my classes my mother died out in Ohio and I left New York for a good while. It was during the period in Dayton, I started trying seriously to write and that was the breaking point.

STERN   Can you remember why you started to write or how?

ELLISON   I can remember very vividly. Richard Wright had just come to New York and was editing a little magazine. I had read a poem of his which I liked, and when we were introduced by a mutual friend he suggested that I try to review a novel for his magazine. My review was accepted and published and so I was hooked.

STERN   You were launched . . .

ELLISON   Oh no, not really launched.

STERN   You were conscious that such a thing was possible. Was Wright famous at that time?

ELLISON   No, Wright hadn't written *Native Son.* He had published *Uncle Tom's Children,* which was the real beginning of his fame, and he was already working on *Native Son.* I remember the first scene that he showed me, it was the poolroom scene—it isn't the first scene but it was one of the first written and I was to read the rest of the book as it came out of the typewriter.

STERN   At that time were you dissatisfied with the sort of work Wright was doing?

ELLISON   Dissatisfied? I was too amazed with watching the process of creation. I didn't understand quite what was going on, but by this time I had talked with Wright a lot and he was very conscious of technique. He talked about it not in terms of mystification but as writing know-how. "You must read so-and-so," he'd say. "You have to go about learning to write *consciously.* People have talked about such and such a problem and have written about it. You must learn how Conrad, Joyce, Dostoievsky get their effects . . ." He guided me to Henry James and to Conrad's prefaces, that type of thing. Of course, I knew that my own feelings about the world, about life, were different, but this was not even a matter to question. Wright knew what he was about, what he wanted to do, while I hadn't even discovered myself. I knew only that what I would want to express would not be an imitation of his kind of a thing.

STERN   So what sort of thing did you feel Wright was not doing that you wanted to do?

ELLISON   Well, I don't suppose I judged. I am certain I did not judge in quite so conscious a way, but I think I felt more complexity in life, and my background made me aware of a larger area of possibility. Knowing Wright himself and something of what he was doing increased that sense of the possible. Also, I think I was less interested in an ideological interpretation of Negro experience. For all my interest in music, I had been in love with literature for years and years—if a writer may make such a confession. I read everything. I must have read fairy tales until I was thirteen, and I was always taken with the magical quality of writing, with the poetry of it. When I came to discover a little more about what I wanted to express I felt that Wright was overcommitted to ideology—even though I, too, wanted many of the same things for our people. You might say that I was much less a social determinist. But I suppose that basically it comes down to a difference in our concepts of the individual. I, for instance, found it disturbing that Bigger Thomas had none of the finer qualities of Richard Wright, none of the imagination, none of the sense of poetry, none of the gaiety. And I preferred Richard Wright to Bigger Thomas. Do you see? Which gets you in on the—directs you back to the difference between what Wright was him-self and how he conceived of the individual; back to his conception of the quality of Negro humanity.

STERN Did you think you might write stories in which Negroes did not appear?

ELLISON No, there was never a time when I thought of writing fiction in which only Negroes appeared, or in which only whites appeared. And yet, from the very beginning I wanted to write about American Negro experience and I suspected that what was important, what made the difference, lay in the perspective from which it was viewed. When I learned more and started thinking about this con-sciously, I realized that it was a source of creative strength as well as a source of wonder. It's also a relatively unexplored area of American experience simply because our knowledge of it has been distorted through the overemphasis of the sociological approach. Unfortunately many Negroes have been trying to define their own predicament in exclusively sociological terms, a situation I consider quite short-sighted. Too many of us have accepted a statistical interpretation of our lives and thus much of that which makes us a source of moral strength to America goes unappreciated and undefined. Now, when you try to trace American values as they find expression in the Negro community, where do you begin? To what books do you go? How do you account for Little Rock and the sit-ins? How do you account for the strength of those kids? You can find sociological descriptions of the conditions under which they live but few indications of their morale.

STERN You felt as you were starting to get serious about writing that you had a special subject to write about?

ELLISON Yes, I think so. Well, let's put it this way: Sometimes you get a sense of mission even before you are aware of it. An act is demanded of you but you're like a sleepwalker searching for some important object, and when you find it you wake up to discover that it is the agency through which that mission, assigned you long ago, at a time you barely understood the command, could be accomplished. Thus while there appeared to be no connection between my wanting to write fiction and my mother's insistence, from the time I was a small boy, that the hope of our group depended not upon the older Negroes but upon the young, upon me, as it were, this sense of obligation got into my work immediately. Of course, these are very complicated matters, because I have no desire to write propaganda. Instead I felt it important to explore the full range of American Negro humanity and to affirm those qualities which are of value beyond any question of segregation, economics or previous condition of servitude. The obligation was always there and there is much to affirm. In fact, all Negroes affirm certain feelings of identity, certain foods, certain types of dancing, music, religious experiences, certain tragic attitudes toward experience and toward our situation as Americans. You see, we do this all within the community, but when it is questioned from without—that's when things start going apart. Like most Americans we are not yet fully conscious of our identity either as Negroes or Americans. This affirmation of which I speak, this insistence upon achieving our social goal, has been our great strength and also our great weakness because the terms with which we have tried to define ourselves have been inadequate. We know we're not the creatures which our enemies in the white South would have us be and we know too that neither color nor our civil predicament explain us adequately. Our strength is that with the total society saying to us, "*No, No, No, No,*" we continue to move toward our goal. So when I came to write I felt moved to affirm and to explore all this—not as a social mission but as the stuff of literature and as an expression of the better part of my own sense of life.

STERN Somebody has described a literary situation as one which commemorates what a man feels is passing or threatened. Did you feel that your work might be a commemoration of values which were disappearing as you wrote about them?

ELLISON How shall I say? Yes, I do feel this. Now just how consciously I was concerned with it at the time I wrote I don't know. When I started writing *Invisible Man* I was reading Lord Raglan's *The Hero,* in which he goes into figures of history and myth to account for the features which make for the mythic hero and at the same time I got to thinking about the ambiguity of Negro leadership during that period. This was the late forties and I kept trying to account for the fact that when the chips were down, Negro leaders did not represent the Negro community.

Beyond their own special interests they represented white philanthropy, white politicians, business interests, and so on. This was an unfair way of looking at it, perhaps, but there was something missing, something which is only now being corrected. It seemed to me that they acknowledged no final responsibility to the Negro community for their acts and implicit in their roles were constant acts of betrayal. This made for a sad, chronic division between their values and the values of those they were supposed to represent. And the fairest thing to say about it is that the predicament of Negroes in the United States rendered these leaders automatically impotent, until they recognized their true source of power—which lies, as Martin Luther King perceived, in the Negro's ability to suffer even death for the attainment of our beliefs. Back in the forties only preachers had real power through which to effect their wills but most of these operated strictly within the Negro community. Only Adam Powell was using the power of the Negro church to assert the Negro's political will. So at that time a thick fog of unreality separated the Negro group from its leaders— But let me tell you a story: At Tuskegee during graduation week countless high-powered word artists, black and white, descended upon us and gathered in the gym and the chapel to tell us in high-flown words what the Negro thought, what our lives were and what our goals should be. The buildings would be packed with visitors and relatives and many guardians of race relations—Northern and Southern. Well, the Negro farm people from the surrounding countryside would also come to the campus at the same time. Graduation week was a festival time for the surrounding Negro community, and very often these people would have children and relatives taking part in the ceremonies in progress in the chapel and the gym. But do you know that while the big-shot word artists were making their most impressive speeches, the farm people would be out on the old athletic field dancing square dances, having picnics, playing baseball and visiting among themselves as though the ceremonies across the wide lawns did not exist; or at best had no connection with the lives they led. Well, I found their celebrations much more attractive than the official ceremonies and I would leave my seat in the orchestra and sneak out to watch them; and while my city background had cut me off from the lives they led and I had no desire to live the life of a sharecropper, I found their unrhetorical activities on the old football field the more meaningful.

STERN   The familiar liberal hope is that any specialized form of social life which makes for invidious distinctions should disappear. Your view seems to be that anything that counts is the result of such specialization.

ELLISON   Yes.

STERN   Now, a good many people, millions, are damaged permanently, viciously, unfairly by such distinctions. At the same time, they contribute, as you more than perhaps any writer in the world have seen, to something marvelous. Some sort of decision probably has to be made by an individual who is sensitive to this paradox—I wonder what yours is. Do you want the preservation of that which results in both the marvelous and the terrible, or do you feel that the marvelous should not endure while the terrible endures along with it?

ELLISON   I am going to say something very odd. In the first place, I think that the mixture of the marvelous and the terrible is a basic condition of human life and that the persistence of human ideals represents the marvelous pulling itself up out of the chaos of the universe. In the fairy tale, beauty must be awakened by the beast, the beastly man can only regain his humanity through love. There are other terms for this but they come to much the same thing. Here the terrible represents all that hinders, all that opposes human aspiration, and the marvelous represents the triumph of the human spirit over chaos. While the terms and the conditions are different and often change, our triumphs are few and thus must be recognized for what they are and preserved. Besides, I would be hard put to say where the terrible could be localized in our national experience, for I see in so much of American life which lies beyond the Negro community the very essence of the terrible.

STERN Yes, but the last few days we have been talking about some of the particular meannesses which are characteristic of the Negro situation . . . just the fact that there are four Negro congressmen, when adequate representation would mean that there'd be twenty . . .

ELLISON Yes.

STERN And hundreds of things of this sort, many of which result in crippling injustices and meannesses. Now, can this go on? And if it doesn't go on, will this mean the elimination of that which you have commemorated in fiction?

ELLISON Well, what I have tried to commemorate in fiction is that which I believe to be enduring and abiding in our situation, especially those human qualities which the American Negro has developed despite and in rejection of the obstacles and meannesses imposed upon us. If the writer exists for any social good, his role is that of preserving in art those human values which can endure by confronting change. Our Negro situation is changing rapidly, but so much which we've gleaned through the harsh discipline of Negro American life is simply too precious to be lost. I speak of the faith, the patience, the humor, the sense of timing, rugged sense of life and the manner of expressing it which all go to define the American Negro. These are some of the things through which we've confronted the obstacles and meannesses of which you speak and which we dare not fail to adapt to changed conditions lest we destroy ourselves. Times change but these possessions must endure forever—not simply because they define us as a group, but because they represent a further instance of man's triumph over chaos. You know, the skins of those thin-legged little girls who faced the mob in Little Rock marked them as Negro but the spirit which directed their feet is the old universal urge toward freedom. For better or worse, whatever there is of value in Negro life is an American heritage and as such it must be preserved. Besides, I am unwilling to see those values which I would celebrate in fiction as existing sheerly through terror; they are a result of a tragicomic confrontation of life.

I think that art is a celebration of life even when life extends into death and that the sociological conditions which have made for so much misery in Negro life are not necessarily the only factors which make for the values which I feel should endure and shall endure. I see a period when Negroes are going to be wandering around because, you see, we have had this thing thrown at us for so long that we haven't had a chance to discover what in our own background is really worth preserving. For the first time we are given a choice, we are making a choice. And this is where the real trouble is going to start. The South could help. If it had a sense of humor, you know, the South could say, "All right, we will set aside six months and there will be complete integration—all right, you don't have to integrate the women—but there will be complete integration as far as anything else is concerned. Negroes may go anywhere, they may see how we entertain, how we spend our leisure, how we worship, and so on," and that would be the end of the whole problem. Because most Negroes could not be nourished by the life white Southerners live. It is too hag-ridden, it is too obsessed, it is too concerned with attitudes which could change everything that Negroes have been conditioned to expect of life. No, I believe in diversity, and I think that the real death of the United States will come when everyone is just alike.

As for my writer's necessity of cashing in on the pain undergone by my people (and remember I write of the humor as well), writing is my way of confronting, often for the hundredth time, that same pain and that same pleasure. It is my way of seeing that it be not in vain.

E. U. Essien-Udom

THE APPEALS AND CHALLENGES OF THE BLACK NATIONALIST MOVEMENT

Can the majority of Negroes be assimilated into American society? Do they really want to be assimilated? What "price" will they

Reprinted from *Black Nationalism: A Search for an Identity in America*, by E. U. Essien-Udom by permission of The University of Chicago Press. Copyright © 1962 by The University of Chicago.

Mr. Essien-Udom is a Nigerian scholar who studied at the University of Chicago.

have to pay for assimilation or non-assimilation? If they want to be assimilated, what are they themselves doing to facilitate this process? If not, are there discernible attitudes among Negroes which impede this process? Were there a rational choice, can the Negro subculture successfully resist the pressure for conformity exerted upon it by the dominant culture? Can they (Negroes) revitalize and regenerate the subculture?

Negroes will argue, and often glibly, that they are not concerned with assimilation but with integration (i.e., total acceptance without discrimination) and that the prospects for the former are very remote. Hence, they dismiss the question as academic. Although the probability of assimilation is remote, the question is not psychologically insignificant for the Negroes. It is significant, in part, because one's attitude toward assimilation may or may not foster the feeling of separateness and will determine the intensity of one's effort to merge into the larger culture and society. However, the question is particularly important during this period of rapid improvement in the Negro's status and the trend toward integration. These changes, in themselves, are sources of anxiety to many Negroes.[1] Although Negroes do not express their concern publicly, the writer found that it was widely, but privately, voiced in and outside the Muslim movement. This concern and their ambivalent attitudes—be it at the level of conscious or unconscious awareness—explain, in part, why so many Negroes pay attention to black nationalism but do not actively support the Muslim movement, which is only a specific manifestation of their uncertainties. This question involves the "destiny" of the Negro people in America. We should seek to understand it; we should not explain it away. The price for assimilation is clear; the price for non-assimilation is not obvious. If, however, the sense of separateness and ethnic consciousness, now developing, were to dominate, society at large will have to pay a price for minority exclusiveness, especially for the kind now fostered by the Muslim movement.

Ideologically and culturally, however, the assimilationist strand has been stronger among Negroes. The dominance of this strand is already discernible and much stronger among the middle- and upper-class Negroes and intellectuals.[2] But this strand is somewhat weaker

[1] It is interesting to note that a report of a two-year study of Negro and white attitudes toward integration, prepared for the State Commission on Civil Rights in Connecticut by Elmo Roper, revealed that although 90 per cent of Negroes questioned hoped for integration and favored it (in most phases of activities), 37 per cent voiced some misgivings for racial mixing in purely social affairs, especially, "parties," 46 per cent whites questioned objected to racial mixing in purely social affairs. "Connecticut Ends Study of Integration" by David Anderson, *New York Times*, April 14, 1961, p. 21.

[2] Elmo Roper, the chairman of the Connecticut Civil Rights Commission report, referred to previously, explains that Negroes harboring racial prejudice against

among the lower classes because the realities of their social situation do not support their assimilationist mentality. Consequently, the sense of separateness and ethnic consciousness actually dominate their lives. This feeling has always been present but they lacked positive articulation. The intensification of these feelings is one of the most important developments in the contemporary social situation of American Negroes.

Perhaps, the black nationalists' agitation is the loudest expression of a "manifesto of identity"—the Negroes' conscious, though slow, awakening to their heritage of abuse and degradation, and, especially, to their possible destiny as human beings. It may well signal the beginning of the end of the Negroes' aimless and vain desire to hide their dark skins behind a white mask. The manifesto of identity is a subjectivity: its voice reflects the past and the present and perhaps the future as well. It requires no real objects and relationships for its expression; yet in a significant way, the manifesto brings to public attention "voices from within the veil" and subtle and imperceptible changes which are occurring among the black masses. They are voices heralding perhaps the psychological and spiritual liberation of the black masses from the shackles of a past that still haunts the present. The manifesto announces their "presence" in America and their impatience and disaffection with the limitations imposed upon their "equality in opportunity." Their impatience and disaffection cannot be disassociated from the important changes (most contributing significantly to the general improvement of the Negroes) in the United States as a whole and in the Negro community or from the rising protest of millions in the non-white world against discrimination and exploitation based solely on racial or religious distinctions.

The "voices from within the veil" and the manifesto of identity do not deny the Negro's Americanism. Indeed, they affirm what is commonly known: that the Negro is American in heart, loyalties, and in everything else. In its mild forms the manifesto of identity is best expressed in the "Negro History Week" and by such organizations as the American Society of African Culture or the Afro-American Heritage Association. Its voice is a reaffirmation of the Negroes' faith in the possibilities offered by the pluralistic character of American society for their cultural, intellectual, and spiritual development. In its extreme form, the Muslim movement is the best example; it reveals how deeply the cancer of American racism has infected all its parts, making the oppressed and the oppressor mutually depraved.

---

white people are either well-educated Negroes who have come up from the South and are resentful of their treatment there, or else are northern Negroes of poor education. *Christian Science Monitor*, April 14, 1961, p. 6.

The study of black nationalism illustrates the desperate character of the social situation of the lower-class Negroes in the large northern cities and the tensions which arise from this situation. We tried to show that their life is devoid of meaning and purpose. They are estranged from the larger society which they seek to enter, but which rejects them. Similarly, they are estranged from their own group which they despise. The result of this feeling of dual alienation is apathy, futility, and emptiness of purpose. In a psychological sense, many are lonesome within and outside their own group. They are rootless and restless. They are without an identity, i.e., a sense of belonging and membership in society. In this situation, there is neither hope nor optimism. In fact, most lower-class Negroes in these large cities see little or no "future" for themselves and posterity. This is partly because they have no faith in themselves or in their potential as black men in America and especially because important decisions which shape their lives appear entirely beyond their control. We should stress, however, that the sense of social estrangement and alienation is not limited to the Negroes. In fact, it is a problem common to urban dwellers. The consequence for a meaningful life is, in varying degrees, the same for Negroes as well as others in comparable social situations. The point, however, is that the impact of contemporary urban tensions and anxieties on an already marginal and despised group is dramatic and paralyzing. It corrupts the personality of its victims, depriving them of any sense of human worth and dignity.

Three more factors in the contemporary social situation of Negroes help to explain the growing sense of separateness and ethnic consciousness among the Negro masses: the bifurcation of the Negro caste, i.e., the emergence of a real Negro middle class and the Negro's re-definition of himself not only in terms of the whites but in relation to this "new" class; his re-definition of himself in relation to Africa; and his reactions to the traditional Negro institutions and leadership groups in terms of these new definitions.

The bifurcation of the caste, especially in the North, is an important development of which the implications are not generally recognized. Nevertheless, the emergence of a Negro middle class may have serious consequences for the Negro masses, creating an "imbalance" within the Negro community. One obvious consequence is that lower-class Negroes are beginning to re-define themselves not only in relations to the white society but also to the Negro middle- and upper-class "society." For this reason, they resent middle-class Negroes whose social situation is incomparably better than theirs. This situation is important for understanding the character of race relations in the North. First, the position of the middle-class Negroes tends to obscure the problems of the lower-class Negroes, in part because Negro "progress" (with some justification) is defined largely in middle-class terms; it is measured by the conspicuous consumption of the middle- and upper-class Negroes, who, in fact, have found their identity with the white middle-class. As individuals, they can escape the open contempt which Northern whites have for the less fortunate of their race. They, too, display haughtiness toward the lower-class Negroes. The "bonds of solidarity in chains" which previously characterized the relationship between them is no longer apparent, i.e., the fact that in the past middle- and upper-class Negroes were able to identify with the struggles and aspirations of lower class Negroes. The interests of the middle class are different and, in some measure, lower-class Negroes are estranged from them. But, like middle classes everywhere, the essentially middle-class Negro leadership takes for granted that its strivings represent unquestionably the interest of the masses. This may well be, but the estrangement between the two classes is incontestable. The important point is that precisely because lower-class Negroes are beginning to define themselves in relations to the Negro "image" portrayed by the middle-class and are attracted to it, they are also repelled by it because their actual conditions do not permit genuine indentification with the middle-class Negroes. As it is in their relations with the white society, lower-class Negroes tend to withdraw and disassociate themselves from the middle- and upper-class Negroes. This estrangement suggests the beginning of class consciousness and conflict among the Negro masses, directed not against whites, but against the Negro middle and upper classes. This development aggravates tensions in the Negro community and produces distrust of the middle-class leadership among the lower-class Negroes.

These Negroes feel powerless not only in relation to the white-power complex but also to what appears to them as the monopoly of power by Negro middle-class leadership. Black nationalism, especially the Muslim movement, reflects this sense of dual marginality and impotence in both power centers. But an important distinction should be made here: Although black nationalism is a general reaction against whites as "possessors" of vital social, economic, and political power, the nationalists do not question, except in utopian and religious terms, the legitimacy of the white power monopoly, nor have they sought to alter it. Instead, their sense of impotence produces a need for withdrawal and racial separation (a desire for a homeland) as the means by which Negroes might become masters of their destiny. However, the Muslim movement reflects the increasing class consciousness and conflict[3] among the lower-class Negroes and questions, specifically the legitimacy of the Negro middle-class leadership. In other words, the movement questions

[3] That this conflict has not found widespread organized expression is not important for our analysis.

the "monopoly" of power by the middle-class leadership in defining both the "needs" and "destiny" of the Negro people in America. It questions the trend toward integration which its leaders see as a trend toward assimilation. Furthermore, its leaders question the "balance" between the ideal of integration and the definition of lower-class Negro "needs" in practical terms. The Muslim movement, in a real sense, is an attempt to alter the power relationship within the Negro community. The concerns now voiced by the black nationalists may well determine the character and style of future Negro leadership in their communities.

Another defect in the contemporary social situation of the urban Negro masses is the impotence of traditional Negro institutions in dealing with either the psychological or practical needs of their community. For a long time, these institutions and leadership groups have been the interpreters of the social scene for the masses of Negroes. Of these, the Negro church is the most important. There is evidence that the Negro church has lost its significance for the urban proletarian who seeks to define his situation in terms of the church. However, where its influence is still felt, the Negro church is particularly culpable for its general lack of concern for the moral and social problems of the community. Rather than face the problem of the degradation of its people and take positive action for moral, cultural, and economic reconstruction, it has been accommodatory. Fostering indulgence in religious sentimentality, and riveting the attention of the masses on the bounties of a hereafter, the Negro church remains a refuge, an escape from the cruel realities of the here and now. Furthermore, evidence abounds of the misuse of the pulpit for furthering personal ambitions at the expense of the already harshly exploited masses. The grim fact is that the pulpit, with exceptions spread far and wide, has become during the present century and especially in the large cities of the North, a route to social mobility for the charlatans in the Negro community. There is some evidence, however, of growing realization of their social responsibilities among many Negro church leaders. The most important evidence is the Southern Christian Leadership Conference, led by the Rev. Dr. Martin Luther King, Jr.[4] The same concern was shown by Dr. Joseph H. Jackson, President of the five-million-member National Baptist Convention, who recently announced the purchase of 600 acres of farmland for resettlement of Negro tenant and sharecropper families dispossessed of any means of livelihood by whites in Fayette and Haywood Counties as reprisals for their attempt to exercise the right to vote.[5] In large measure, however, both the Negro

[4] See Martin Luther King, Jr., *Stride Toward Freedom: The Montgomery Story* (New York: Harper and Brothers, 1958).
[5] *The New York Courier,* March 25, 1961, Sec. 2, p. 18. The *Courier* editorially described Dr. Jackson's action as "Statesmanship in the Pulpit."

Church and other traditional leadership groups do not seem to appreciate how debased the life of the urban lower-class Negro is, nor the magnitude of effort in thought and action required for the reconstruction of the "Souls of Black Folk."

Lastly, the liberation movements and the emergence of the independent African states have had a significant impact on the Negro's total redefinition of himself, in relation to both his situation in America and to Africa. These events have not only awakened an unprecedented interest in Africa but have led, in a limited way at least, to what may be called "an African orientation." This does not mean that their effort to redefine themselves in relation to Africa is an expression of their desire to emigrate there. The practical importance of their African orientation should not be exaggerated. It should be balanced against the strong integration and assimilationist trends. We may observe, however, that recent developments in Africa have led a great many Negroes to identify with the struggles and aspirations of the African people. This, together with the domestic developments and changes, appears to create a psychological situation fostering and intensifying the sense of separateness and ethnic consciousness among the masses. This psychological situation fosters among Negroes a new self-image, pride, and an impatient and urgent desire for equality, personal dignity and self-assertion. In some measure, the consequences of their "new" psychology are evident in the confidence shown by southern Negro student "sit-in" demonstrations. Similarly, the emotional appeal, though otherwise limited, of black nationalism to the Northern urban Negro masses suggests the same psychological changes.[6] We might add, qualifiedly, that the Negro's need for an identity and his desire for equality and dignity lead him increasingly to merge his aspirations with those of millions throughout the non-white world who are protesting against discrimination and exploitation. They, too, are caught in the "revolution of rising expectations!"

Elijah Muhammad, then, emerges against this background of tensions, change, and of neglect by the traditional Negro institutions and leaders; the failure of the white society to extend "equality in opportunity" to the Negro people, the Negro's dual sense of alienation and

[6] It is interesting to note that Dr. Joseph H. Jackson announced recently that the National Baptist Convention has sent a three-man commission to Liberia with a view to arranging for purchase of 5,000 acres of land for young Negroes interested in resettling there. Although, Dr. Jackson stressed that his project was not a "back-to-Africa" movement, it is significant that this is the first commission of this nature sent to Africa since the abortive effort of Garvey in the twenties. *The Courier,* p. 18. For our analysis, what we describe as "an African Orientation" is important because for the first time in recent history, some Negroes are beginning to look to Africa as a possible alternative to the United States. Some are interested in business and cultural ties, but there are many who are interested in emigration.

marginality; and the increasing sensitivity of the masses to their lowly material fortunes and the anxieties about their "destiny" in America. Keeping this background in mind, and disregarding but not condoning the excesses of Muhammad's ideological concoctions or racial mysticism, it is clear that his is a unique effort to reconstruct the Negro soul, by providing a "world" (a *mystique*) in which one could be black and unashamed, and by regenerating the Negro's moral and social values. So far as the writer knows, no Negro has ever dared to tackle the bewildering problems of the "Negro in the mud" with equal vigor and such obdurate determination as Mr. Muhammad. Seen in this light, and in the light of the limited alternatives open to these Negroes, the Nation of Islam, with its moral and economic reforms, provides a way out for these Negroes. The ideological and racialist excesses are more symptomatic and symbolic than crucial in themselves. They reflect the harsh cruelties, discontent, and the grave social malaise which afflicts millions of Negroes in America. Stated simply, the message of the Nation of Islam is this: Despite important, though slow, changes which have occurred in the Negro's formal status as citizens, the lot of the masses of Negroes in the North has not changed in substance. Evidence of pauperization, cultural disorientation, and moral degradation persist in spite of, and perhaps because of, the façade of public progress. These, Muhammad asserts, exist in spite of the fact that inequalities between blacks and whites are not legislated in the North; that the subordination of the masses of Negroes in the North reveals a few stubborn facts of social life which no amount of declarations of good intentions or wishful optimism can obviate. The first, he says, is the unequal distribution of political and economic power between blacks and whites. The possibility of an equalization of this distribution of vital social power is too remote to warrant speculation; but for a long time, there shall exist Negro communities, and the position of Negroes is likely to remain marginal. Thus, Negro striving for advancement, Mr. Muhammad says, is fundamentally circumscribed by their awareness of this fact. Their formal freedom is concomitantly limited by the substantive limitations as well as by their perception of the limitations. Yet within these restrictions, Negroes can give meaning to their freedom.

Formal freedom, insists Muhammad, without a substantive basis is, in effect, meaningless. Substantive freedom, a people's style of life— material, cultural, moral and a sense of human dignity—cannot be bestowed upon people who do not want it, and if they do, are not prepared to help themselves and make the sacrifice necessary for its attainment; they must help create the conditions for it. Thus, if the masses of Negroes are to rise in the social scale, if they are to gain respect from others, if they are to be regarded as human beings rather than social outcasts, they must become consciously aware of their predicament, their degradation which is the bond of their common identity. They must also become conscious of their opportunities, however limited, and must take advantage of them. It is pointless to indulge in the fantasy that through some biological miracle black Americans will be transformed into white Americans or that the Negro communities will disappear in the foreseeable future.

Norman Podhoretz
MY NEGRO PROBLEM—AND OURS

> *If we—and . . . I mean the relatively conscious whites and the relatively conscious blacks, who must, like lovers, insist on, or create, the consciousness of the others—do not falter in our duty now, we may be able, handful that we are, to end the racial nightmare, and achieve our country, and change the history of the world.*
>
> James Baldwin

Two ideas puzzled me deeply as a child growing up in Brooklyn during the 1930's in what today would be called an integrated neighborhood. One of them was that all Jews were rich; the other was that all Negroes were persecuted. These ideas had appeared in print; therefore they must be true. My own experience and the evidence of my senses told me they were not true, but that only confirmed what a day-dreaming boy in the provinces—for the lower-class neighborhoods of New York belong as surely to the provinces as any rural town in North Dakota—discovers very early: *his* experience is unreal and the evidence of his senses is not to be trusted. Yet even a boy with a head full of fantasies incongruously synthesized out of Hollywood movies and English novels cannot altogether deny the reality of his own experience—especially when there is so much deprivation in that experience. Nor can he altogether gainsay the evidence of his own senses—especially such evidence of the senses as comes from being repeatedly beaten up, robbed, and in general hated, terrorized, and humiliated.

And so for a long time I was puzzled to think that Jews were

Reprinted from *Commentary* (February 1963) by permission; copyright © 1963 by The American Jewish Committee.

Mr. Podhoretz is Editor of *Commentary*. Though his main interests are literary, he frequently writes on social issues. His collected essays appear in *Doings and Undoings*.

supposed to be rich when the only Jews I knew were poor, and that Negroes were supposed to be persecuted when it was the Negroes who were doing the only persecuting I knew about—and doing it, moreover, to *me*. During the early years of the war, when my older sister joined a left-wing youth organization, I remember my astonishment at hearing her passionately denounce my father for thinking that Jews were worse off than Negroes. To me, at the age of twelve, it seemed very clear that Negroes were better off than Jews—indeed, than *all* whites. A city boy's world is contained within three or four square blocks, and in my world it was the whites, the Italians and Jews, who feared the Negroes, not the other way around. The Negroes were tougher than we were, more ruthless, and on the whole they were better athletes. What could it mean, then, to say that they were badly off and that we were more fortunate? Yet my sister's opinions, like print, were sacred, and when she told me about exploitation and economic forces I believed her. I believed her, but I was still afraid of Negroes. And I still hated them with all my heart.

It had not always been so—that much I can recall from early childhood. When did it start, this fear and this hatred? There was a kindergarten in the local public school, and given the character of the neighborhood, at least half of the children in my class must have been Negroes. Yet I have no memory of being aware of color differences at that age, and I know from observing my own children that they attribute no significance to such differences even when they begin noticing them. I think there was a day—first grade? second grade?—when my best friend Carl hit me on the way home from school and announced that he wouldn't play with me any more because I had killed Jesus. When I ran home to my mother crying for an explanation, she told me not to pay any attention to such foolishness, and then in Yiddish she cursed the *goyim* and the *schwartzes*, the *schwartzes* and the *goyim*. Carl, it turned out, was a *schwartze*, and so was added a third to the categories into which people were mysteriously divided.

Sometimes I wonder whether this is a true memory at all. It is blazingly vivid, but perhaps it never happened: can anyone really remember back to the age of six? There is no uncertainty in my mind, however, about the years that followed. Carl and I hardly ever spoke, though we met in school every day up through the eighth or ninth grade. There would be embarrassed moments of catching his eye or of his catching mine—for whatever it was that had attracted us to one another as very small children remained alive in spite of the fantastic barrier of hostility that had grown up between us, suddenly and out of nowhere. Nevertheless, friendship would have been impossible, and even if it had been possible, it would have been unthinkable. About that, there was nothing anyone could do by the time we were eight years old.

Item: The orphanage across the street is torn down, a city housing project begins to rise in its place, and on the marvelous vacant lot next to the old orphanage they are building a playground. Much excitement and anticipation as Opening Day draws near. Mayor LaGuardia himself comes to dedicate this great gesture of public benevolence. He speaks of neighborliness and borrowing cups of sugar, and of the playground he says that children of all races, colors, and creeds will learn to live together in harmony. A week later, some of us are swatting flies on the playground's inadequate little ball field. A gang of Negro kids, pretty much our own age, enter from the other side and order us out of the park. We refuse, proudly and indignantly, with superb masculine fervor. There is a fight, they win, and we retreat, half whimpering, half with bravado. My first nauseating experience of cowardice. And my first appalled realization that there are people in the world who do not seem to be afraid of anything, who act as though they have nothing to lose. Thereafter the playground becomes a battleground, sometimes quiet, sometimes the scene of athletic competition between Them and Us. But rocks are thrown as often as baseballs. Gradually we abandon the place and use the streets instead. The streets are safer, though we do not admit this to ourselves. We are not, after all, sissies—that most dreaded epithet of an American boyhood.

Item: I am standing alone in front of the building in which I live. It is late afternoon and getting dark. That day in school the teacher had asked a surly Negro boy named Quentin a question he was unable to answer. As usual I had waved my arm eagerly ("Be a good boy, get good marks, be smart, go to college, become a doctor") and, the right answer bursting from my lips, I was held up lovingly by the teacher as an example to the class. I had seen Quentin's face—a very dark, very cruel, very Oriental-looking face—harden, and there had been enough threat in his eyes to make me run all the way home for fear that he might catch me outside.

Now, standing idly in front of my own house, I see him approaching from the project accompanied by his little brother who is carrying a baseball bat and wearing a grin of malicious anticipation. As in a nightmare, I am trapped. The surroundings are secure and familiar, but terror is suddenly present and there is no one around to help. I am locked to the spot. I will not cry out or run away like a sissy, and I stand there, my heart wild, my throat clogged. He walks up, hurls the familiar epithet ("Hey, mo'f——r"), and to my surprise only pushes me. It is a violent push, but not a punch. A push is not as serious as a punch. Maybe I can still back out without entirely losing my dignity. Maybe I can still say, "Hey, c'mon Quentin, whaddya wanna do *that* for. I dint do nothin' to *you,*" and walk away, not too rapidly. Instead, before I can stop myself, I push him back—a token gesture—and I say, "Cut that out, I don't wanna fight, I ain't got nothin' to fight about." As I turn to walk back into the building, the corner of my eye catches the motion of the bat his little brother has handed him. I try to duck, but the bat crashes colored lights into my head.

The next thing I know, my mother and sister are standing over me, both of them hysterical. My sister—she who was later to join the "progressive" youth organization—is shouting for the police and screaming imprecations at those dirty little black bastards. They take me upstairs, the doctor comes, the police come. I tell them that the boy who did it was a stranger, that he had been trying to get money from me. They do not believe me, but I am too scared to give them Quentin's name. When I return to school a few days later, Quentin avoids my eyes. He knows that I have not squealed, and he is ashamed. I try to feel proud, but in my heart I know that it was fear of what his friends might do to me that had kept me silent, and not the code of the street.

Item: There is an athletic meet in which the whole of our junior high school is participating. I am in one of the seventh-grade rapid-advance classes, and "segregation" has now set in with a vengeance. In the last three or four years of the elementary school from which we have just graduated, each grade had been divided into three classes, according to "intelligence." (In the earlier grades the divisions had either been arbitrary or else unrecognized by us as having anything to do with brains.) These divisions by IQ, or however it was arranged, had resulted in a preponderance of Jews in the "1" classes and a corresponding preponderance of Negroes in the "3's," with the Italians split unevenly along the spectrum. At least a few Negroes had always made the "1's," just as there had always been a few Jewish kids among the "3's" and more among the "2's" (where Italians dominated). But the junior high's rapid-advance class of which I am now a member is overwhelmingly Jewish and entirely white—except for a shy lonely Negro girl with light skin and reddish hair.

The athletic meet takes place in a city-owned stadium far from the school. It is an important event to which a whole day is given over. The winners are to get those precious little medallions stamped with the New York City emblem that can be screwed into a belt and that prove the wearer to be a distinguished personage. I am a fast runner, and so I am assigned the position of anchor man on my class's team in the relay race. There are three other seventh-grade teams in the race, two of them all Negro, as ours is all white. One of the all-Negro teams is very tall—their anchor man waiting silently next to me on the line looks years older than I am, and I do not recognize him. He is the first to get the baton and crosses the finishing line in a walk. Our team comes in second, but a few minutes later we are declared the winners, for it has been discovered that the anchor man on the first-place team is not a member of the class. We are awarded the medallions, and the following day our home-room teacher makes a speech about how proud she is of us for being superior athletes as well as superior students. We want to believe that we deserve the praise, but we know that we could not have won even if the other class had not cheated.

That afternoon, walking home, I am waylaid and surrounded by five Negroes, among whom is the anchor man of the disqualified team. "Gimme my medal, mo'f——r," he grunts. I do not have it with me and I tell him so. "Anyway, it ain't yours," I say foolishly. He calls me a liar on both counts and pushes me up against the wall on which we sometimes play handball. "Gimme my mo'f——n' medal," he says again. I repeat that I have left it home. "Les search the li'l mo'f——r," one of them suggests, "he prolly got it *hid* in his mo'f——n' *pants*." My panic is now unmanageable. (How many times had I been surrounded like this and asked in soft tones, "Len' me a nickel, boy." How many times had I been called a liar for pleading poverty and pushed around, or searched, or beaten up, unless there happened to be someone in the marauding gang like Carl who liked me across that enormous divide of hatred and who would therefore say, "Aaah, c'mon, le's git someone else, *this* boy ain't got no money on 'im.") I scream at them through tears of rage and self-contempt, "Keep your f——n' filthy lousy black hands offa me! I swear I'll get the cops." This is all they need to hear, and the five of them set upon me. They bang me around, mostly in the stomach and on the arms and shoulders, and when several adults loitering near the candy store down the block notice what is going on and begin to shout, they run off and away.

I do not tell my parents about the incident. My team-mates, who have also been waylaid, each by a gang led by his opposite number from the disqualified team, have had their medallions taken from them, and they never squeal either. For days, I walk home in terror, expecting to be caught again, but nothing happens. The medallion is put away into a drawer, never to be worn by anyone.

Obviously experiences like these have always been a common feature of childhood life in working-class and immigrant neighborhoods, and Negroes do not necessarily figure in them. Wherever, and in whatever combination, they have lived together in the cities, kids of different groups have been at war, beating up and being beaten up: micks against kikes against wops against spicks against polacks. And even relatively homogeneous areas have not been spared the warring of the young: one block against another, one gang (called in my day, in a pathetic effort at gentility, an "S.A.C.," or social-athletic club) against another. But the Negro-white conflict had—and no doubt still has—a special intensity and was conducted with a ferocity unmatched by intramural white battling.

In my own neighborhood, a good deal of animosity existed between the Italian kids (most of whose parents were immigrants from Sicily) and the Jewish kids (who came largely from East European immigrant families). Yet everyone had friends, sometimes close friends, in the other "camp," and we often visited one another's strange-smelling houses, if not for meals, then for glasses of milk, and occasionally for some special event like a wedding or a wake. If it happened that we divided into warring factions and did battle, it would invariably be half-hearted and soon patched up. Our parents, to be sure, had nothing to do with one another and were mutually suspicious and hostile. But we, the kids, who all spoke Yiddish or Italian at home, were Americans, or New Yorkers, or Brooklyn boys: we shared a culture, the culture of the street, and at least for a while this culture proved to be more powerful than the opposing cultures of the home.

Why, *why* should it have been so different as between the Negroes and us? How was it borne in upon us so early, white and black alike, that we were enemies beyond any possibility of reconciliation? Why did we hate one another so?

I suppose if I tried, I could answer those questions more or less adequately from the perspective of what I have since learned. I could draw upon James Baldwin—what better witness is there?—to describe the sense of entrapment that poisons the soul of the Negro with hatred for the white man whom he knows to be his jailer. On the other side, if I wanted to understand how the white man comes to hate the Negro, I could call upon the psychologists who have spoken of the guilt that white Americans feel toward Negroes and that turns into hatred for lack of acknowledging itself as guilt. These are plausible answers and certainly there is truth in them. Yet when I think back upon my own experience of the Negro and his of me, I find myself troubled and puzzled, much as I was as a child when I heard that all Jews were rich and all Negroes persecuted. How could the Negroes in my neighborhood have re-garded the whites across the street and around the corner as jailers? On the whole, the whites were not so poor as the Negroes, but they were quite poor enough, and the years were years of Depression. As for white hatred of the Negro, how could guilt have had anything to do with it? What share had these Italian and Jewish immigrants in the enslavement of the Negro? What share had they—down-trodden people themselves breaking their own necks to eke out a living—in the exploitation of the Negro?

No, I cannot believe that we hated each other back there in Brooklyn because they thought of us as jailers and we felt guilty toward them. But does it matter, given the fact that we all went through an unrepresentative confrontation? I think it matters profoundly, for if we managed the job of hating each other so well without benefit of the aids to hatred that are supposedly at the root of this madness everywhere else, it must mean that the madness is not yet properly understood. I am far from pretending that I understand it, but I would insist that no view of the problem will begin to approach the truth unless it can account for a case like the one I have been trying to describe. Are the elements of any such view available to us?

At least two, I would say, are. One of them is a point we frequently come upon in the work of James Baldwin, and the other is a related point always stressed by psychologists who have studied the mechanisms of prejudice. Baldwin tells us that one of the reasons Negroes hate the white man is that the white man refuses to *look* at him: the Negro knows that in white eyes all Negroes are alike; they are faceless and therefore not altogether human. The psychologists, in their turn, tell us that the white man hates the Negro because he tends to project those wild impulses that he fears in himself onto an alien group which he then punishes with his contempt. What Baldwin does *not* tell us, however, is that the principle of facelessness is a two-way street and can operate in both directions with no difficulty at all. Thus, in my neighborhood in Brooklyn, *I* was as faceless to the Negroes as they were to me, and if they hated me because I never looked at them, I must also have hated them for never looking at *me.* To the Negroes, my white skin was enough to define me as the enemy, and in a war it is only the uniform that counts and not the person.

So with the mechanism of projection that the psychologists talk about: it too works in both directions at once. There is no question that the psychologists are right about what the Negro represents symbolically to the white man. For me as a child the life lived on the other side of the playground and down the block on Ralph Avenue seemed the very embodiment of the values of the street—free, independent, reckless, brave, masculine, erotic. I put the word "erotic" last, though it is usually stressed above all others, because in fact it came last, in consciousness as in importance. What mainly counted for me about Negro kids of my own age was that they were "bad boys." There were plenty of bad boys among the whites—this was, after all, a neighborhood with a long tradition of crime as a career open to aspiring talents—but the Negroes were *really* bad, bad in a way that beckoned to one, and made one feel inadequate. *We* all went home every day for a lunch of spinach-and-potatoes; *they* roamed around during lunch hour, munching on candy bars. In winter *we* had to wear itchy woolen hats and mittens and cumbersome galoshes; *they* were bare-headed and loose as they pleased. *We* rarely played hookey, or got into serious trouble in school, for all our street-corner bravado; *they* were defiant, forever staying out (to do what delicious things?), forever making disturbances in class and in the halls, forever being sent to the principal and returning uncowed. But most important of all, they were *tough;* beautifully, enviably tough, not giving a damn for anyone or anything. To hell with the teacher, the truant officer, the cop; to hell with the whole of the adult world that held *us* in its grip and that we never had the courage to rebel against except sporadically and in petty ways.

This is what I saw and envied and feared in the Negro: this is what finally made him faceless to me, though some of it, of course, was actually there. (The psychologists also tell us that the alien group which becomes the object of a projection will tend to respond by trying to live up to what is expected of them.) But what, on his side, did the Negro see in me that made me faceless to *him?* Did he envy me my lunches of spinach-and-potatoes and my itchy woolen caps and my prudent behavior in the face of authority, as I envied him his noon-time candy bars and his bare head in winter and his magnificent rebelliousness? Did those lunches and caps spell for him the prospect of power and riches in the future? Did they mean that there were possibilities open to me that were denied to him? Very likely they did. But if so, one also supposes that he feared the impulses within himself toward submission to authority no less powerfully than I feared the impulses in myself toward defiance. If I represented the jailer to him, it was not because I was oppressing him or keeping him down: it was because I symbolized for him the dangerous and probably pointless temptation toward greater repression, just as he symbolized for me the equally perilous tug toward greater freedom. I personally was to be rewarded for this repression with a new and better life in the future, but how many of my friends paid an even higher price and were given only gall in return.

We have it on the authority of James Baldwin that all Negroes hate whites. I am trying to suggest that on their side all whites—all American whites, that is—are sick in their feelings about Negroes. There are Negroes, no doubt, who would say that Baldwin is wrong, but I suspect them of being less honest than he is, just as I suspect whites of self-deception who tell me they have no special feeling toward Negroes. Special feelings about color are a contagion to which white Americans seem susceptible even when there is nothing in their background to account for the susceptibility. Thus everywhere we look today in the North, we find the curious phenomenon of white middle-class liberals with no previous personal experience of Negroes—people to whom

Negroes have always been faceless in virtue rather than faceless in vice—discovering that their abstract commitment to the cause of Negro rights will not stand the test of a direct confrontation. We find such people fleeing in droves to the suburbs as the Negro population in the inner city grows; and when they stay in the city we find them sending their children to private school rather than to the "integrated" public school in the neighborhood. We find them resisting the demand that gerrymandered school districts be re-zoned for the purpose of overcoming de facto segregation; we find them judiciously considering whether the Negroes (for their own good, of course) are not perhaps pushing too hard; we find them clucking their tongues over Negro militancy; we find them speculating on the question of whether there may not, after all, be something in the theory that the races are biologically different; we find them saying that it will take a very long time for Negroes to achieve full equality, no matter what anyone does; we find them deploring the rise of black nationalism and expressing the solemn hope that the leaders of the Negro community will discover ways of containing the impatience and incipient violence within the Negro ghettos.[1]

But that is by no means the whole story; there is also the phenomenon of what Kenneth Rexroth once called "crow-jimism." There are the broken-down white boys like Vivaldo Moore in Baldwin's *Another Country* who go to Harlem in search of sex or simply to brush up against something that looks like primitive vitality, and who are so often punished by the Negroes they meet for crimes that they would have been the last ever to commit and of which they themselves have been as sorry victims as any of the Negroes who take it out on them. There are the writers and intellectuals and artists who romanticize Negroes and pander to them, assuming a guilt that is not properly theirs. And there are all the white liberals who permit Negroes to blackmail them into adopting a double standard of moral judgment, and who lend themselves—again assuming the responsibility for crimes they never committed—to cunning and contemptuous exploitation by Negroes they employ or try to befriend.

And what about me? What kind of feelings do I have about Negroes today? What happened to me, from Brooklyn, who grew up fearing and envying and hating Negroes? Now that Brooklyn is behind me, do I fear them and envy them and hate them still? The answer is yes, but not in the same proportions and certainly not in the same way. I now live on the upper west side of Manhattan, where there are many Negroes and many Puerto Ricans, and there are nights when I experience the old apprehensiveness again, and there are streets that I avoid when I am

---

[1] For an account of developments like these, see "The White Liberal's Retreat" by Murray Friedman in the January 1963 *Atlantic Monthly*.

walking in the dark, as there were streets that I avoided when I was a child. I find that I am not afraid of Puerto Ricans, but I cannot restrain my nervousness whenever I pass a group of Negroes standing in front of a bar or sauntering down the street. I know now, as I did not know when I was a child, that power is on my side, that the police are working for me and not for them. And knowing this I feel ashamed and guilty, like the good liberal I have grown up to be. Yet the twinges of fear and the resentment they bring and the self-contempt they arouse are not to be gainsaid.

But envy? Why envy? And hatred? Why hatred? Here again the intensities have lessened and everything has been complicated and qualified by the guilts and the resulting over-compensations that are the heritage of the enlightened middle-class world of which I am now a member. Yet just as in childhood I envied Negroes for what seemed to me their superior masculinity, so I envy them today for what seems to me their superior physical grace and beauty. I have come to value physical grace very highly, and I am now capable of aching with all my being when I watch a Negro couple on the dance floor, or a Negro playing baseball or basketball. They are on the kind of terms with their own bodies that I should like to be on with mine, and for that precious quality they seem blessed to me.

The hatred I still feel for Negroes is the hardest of all the old feelings to face or admit, and it is the most hidden and the most overlarded by the conscious attitudes into which I have succeeded in willing myself. It no longer has, as for me it once did, any cause or justification (except, perhaps, that I am constantly being denied my right to an honest expression of the things I earned the right as a child to feel). How, then, do I know that this hatred has never entirely disappeared? I know it from the insane rage that can stir in me at the thought of Negro anti-Semitism; I know it from the disgusting prurience that can stir in me at the sight of a mixed couple; and I know it from the violence that can stir in me whenever I encounter that special brand of paranoid touchiness to which many Negroes are prone.

This, then, is where I am; it is not exactly where I think all other white liberals are, but it cannot be so very far away either. And it is because I am convinced that we white Americans are—for whatever reason, it no longer matters—so twisted and sick in our feelings about Negroes that I despair of the present push toward integration. If the pace of progress were not a factor here, there would perhaps be no cause for despair: time and the law and even the international political situation are on the side of the Negroes, and ultimately, therefore, victory—of a sort, anyway—must come. But from everything we have learned from observers who ought to know, pace has become as important to the

Negroes as substance. They want equality and they want it *now*, and the white world is yielding to their demand only as much and as fast as it is absolutely being compelled to do. The Negroes know this in the most concrete terms imaginable, and it is thus becoming increasingly difficult to buy them off with rhetoric and promises and pious assurances of support. And so within the Negro community we find more and more people declaring—as Harold R. Isaacs recently put it in these pages[2]— that they want *out:* people who say that integration will never come, or that it will take a hundred or a thousand years to come, or that it will come at too high a price in suffering and struggle for the pallid and sodden life of the American middle class that at the very best it may bring.

The most numerous, influential, and dangerous movement that has grown out of Negro despair with the goal of integration is, of course, the Black Muslims. This movement, whatever else we may say about it, must be credited with one enduring achievement: it inspired James Baldwin to write an essay[3] which deserves to be placed among the classics of our language. Everything Baldwin has ever been trying to tell us is distilled here into a statement of overwhelming persuasiveness and prophetic magnificence. Baldwin's message is and always has been simple. It is this: "Color is not a human or personal reality; it is a political reality." And Baldwin's demand is correspondingly simple: color must be forgotten, lest we all be smited with a vengeance "that does not really depend on, and cannot really be executed by, any person or organization, and that cannot be prevented by any police force or army: historical vengeance, a cosmic vengeance based on the law that we recognize when we say, 'Whatever goes up must come down.' " The Black Muslims Baldwin portrays as a sign and a warning to the intransigent white world. They come to proclaim how deep is the Negro's disaffection with the white world and all its works, and Baldwin implies that no American Negro can fail to respond somewhere in his being to their message: that the white man is the devil, that Allah has doomed him to destruction, and that the black man is about to inherit the earth. Baldwin of course knows that this nightmare inversion of the racism from which the black man has suffered can neither win nor even point to the neighborhood in which victory might be located. For in his view the neighborhood of victory lies in exactly the opposite direction: the transcendence of color through love.

Yet the tragic fact is that love is not the answer to hate—not in

[2] "Integration and the Negro Mood," *Commentary*, December 1962.
[3] Originally published last November in the *New Yorker* under the title "Letter from a Region in My Mind," it has just been reprinted (along with a new introduction) by Dial Press under the title *The Fire Next Time* (128 pp., $3.50).

the world of politics, at any rate. Color is indeed a political rather than a human or a personal reality and if politics (which is to say power) has made it into a human and a personal reality, then only politics (which is to say power) can unmake it once again. But the way of politics is slow and bitter, and as impatience on the one side is matched by a setting of the jaw on the other, we move closer and closer to an explosion and blood may yet run in the streets.

Will this madness in which we are all caught never find a resting-place? Is there never to be an end to it? In thinking about the Jews I have often wondered whether their survival as a distinct group was worth one hair on the head of a single infant. Did the Jews have to survive so that six million innocent people should one day be burned in the ovens of Auschwitz? It is a terrible question and no one, not God himself, could ever answer it to my satisfaction. And when I think about the Negroes in America and about the image of integration as a state in which the Negroes would take their rightful place as another of the protected minorities in a pluralistic society, I wonder whether they really believe in their hearts that such a state can actually be attained, and if so *why* they should wish to survive as a distinct group. I think I know why the Jews once wished to survive (though I am less certain as to why we still do): they not only believed that God had given them no choice, but they were tied to a memory of past glory and a dream of imminent redemption. What does the American Negro have that might correspond to this? His past is a stigma, his color is a stigma, and his vision of the future is the hope of erasing the stigma by making color irrelevant, by making it disappear as a fact of consciousness.

I share this hope, but I cannot see how it will ever be realized unless color does *in fact* disappear: and that means not integration, it means assimilation, it means—let the brutal word come out—miscegenation. The Black Muslims, like their racist counterparts in the white world, accuse the "so-called Negro leaders" of secretly pursuing miscegenation as a goal. The racists are wrong, but I wish they were right, for I believe that the wholesale merging of the two races is the most desirable alternative for everyone concerned. I am not claiming that this alternative can be pursued programmatically or that it is immediately feasible as a solution; obviously there are even greater barriers to its achievement than to the achievement of integration. What I am saying, however, is that in my opinion the Negro problem can be solved in this country in no other way.

I have told the story of my own twisted feelings about Negroes here, and of how they conflict with the moral convictions I have since developed, in order to assert that such feelings must be acknowledged as honestly as possible so that they can be controlled and ultimately disregarded in favor of the convictions. It is *wrong* for a man to suffer because of the color of his skin. Beside that clichéd proposition of liberal thought, what argument can stand and be respected? If the arguments are the arguments of feeling, they must be made to yield; and one's own soul is not the worst place to begin working a huge social transformation. Not so long ago, it used to be asked of white liberals, "Would you like your sister to marry one?" When I was a boy and my sister was still unmarried, I would certainly have said no to that question. But now I am a man, my sister is already married, and I have daughters. If I were to be asked today whether I would like a daughter of mine "to marry one," I would have to answer: "No, I wouldn't *like* it at all. I would rail and rave and rant and tear my hair. And then I hope I would have the courage to curse myself for raving and ranting, and to give her my blessing. How dare I withhold it at the behest of the child I once was and against the man I now have a duty to be?"

E. Franklin Frazier
"SOCIETY":
STATUS WITHOUT SUBSTANCE

There is a phase of the world of make-believe of the black bourgeoisie which requires special treatment, namely, the activities of those persons who constitute its "society." Although Negro "society" was not created by the Negro press, it is the Negro press which feeds and perpetuates the illusions of this element in the black bourgeoisie. The activities of "society" are not simply a form of social life engaged in for pleasure and friendly social intercourse. They are engaged in primarily in order to maintain status or as a part of the competition for status. The activities of "society" serve to differentiate the black bourgeoisie from the masses of poorer Negroes and at the same time compensate for the exclusion of the black bourgeoisie from the larger white community. However, the behavior and standards of consumption which are maintained by "society" generally lack the economic base which such activities presuppose. "Society" thus provides one of the main escapes from the world of reality into a world of make-believe.

Reprinted with permission of The Free Press from *Black Bourgeoisie* by E. Franklin Frazier. Copyright © 1957 by The Free Press, a Corporation. Chapter IV.
     Mr. Frazier, a former president of the American Sociological Association, also wrote *The Negro Family in the United States*.

EVOLUTION OF "SOCIETY"

"Society" among Negroes had its roots among the house servants who enjoyed a certain prestige among the other slaves on the plantation during their social gatherings. An ex-slave, who wrote his autobiography after escaping to freedom, has provided a vivid account of the status of this group on a plantation.

> It was about ten o'clock when the aristocratic slaves began to assemble, dressed in the cast-off finery of their master and mistress, swelling out and putting on airs in imitation of those they were forced to obey from day to day.
>
> House servants were, of course, "the stars" of the party; all eyes were turned to them to see how they conducted, for they, among slaves, are what a military man would call "fugle-men." The field hands, and such of them as have generally been excluded from the dwelling of their owners, look to the house servants as a pattern of politeness and gentility. And indeed, it is often the only method of obtaining any knowledge of the manners of what is called "genteel society"; hence, they are ever regarded as a privileged class; and are sometimes greatly envied, while others are bitterly hated.[1]

After Emancipation, some of the social distinctions which had grown up among the slaves continued to function. Negroes who were free before the Emancipation Proclamation or who could boast of a distinguished family background set themselves apart from the masses of freedmen and constituted a distinct upper social class. Many of them boasted of their "blood," which generally referred to their white ancestry. A mulatto witness of the history of Negroes during the years following the Civil War has left a rather satirical account of the emergence of "society" among them in the nation's capital.

> There is another element in this strange heterogeneous conglomeration, which for want of a better name has been styled society and it is this species of African humanity which is forever and ever informing the uninitiated what a narrow escape they had from being born white. They have small hands, aristocratic insteps and wear blue veins, they have auburn hair and finely chiselled features. They are uneducated as a rule (i.e.) the largest number of them, though it would hardly be discovered unless they opened their *mouths* in the presence of their superiors in intellect, which they are very careful not to do. In personal appearance, they fill the bill precisely so far as *importance* and pomposity goes—but no farther. They are opposed to manual labor, their physical organization couldn't stand it, they prefer light work such as "shuffling cards or dice" or "removing the spirits of Frumenta from the gaze of rude men" if somebody else becomes responsible for the damage. Around the festive board, they are unequalled for their verbosity and especially for their aptness in

tracing their ancestry. One will carry you away back to the times of William the Silent and bring you up to 18 so and so, to show how illustrious is his lineage and pedigree. His great, great grandfather's mother-in-law was the Marchioness So and So and his father was ex-Chief Justice Chastity of S. C. or some other southern state with a polygamous record.[2]

Washington became, in fact, the center of Negro "society" and retained this distinction until after the first World War. This was owing partly to the fact that until the mass migrations of Negroes to northern cities, Washington with around 90,000 Negroes had a larger Negro community than any city in the United States until 1920. The preeminence of Washington as the center of Negro "society" was due more especially to other factors. Because of its relatively large Negro professional class, including teachers in the segregated public school system, doctors, dentists, and lawyers, and large numbers of Negroes employed in the federal government, Negroes in the nation's capital had incomes far above those in other parts of the country. This enabled Washington's "colored society" to engage in forms of consumption and entertainment that established its pre-eminence among American Negroes. Moreover, the Negro "society" which developed in Washington was composed of the upper-class mulattoes who, in fleeing from persecution and discriminations in the South, brought to Washington the social distinctions and color snobbery that had been the basis of their ascendancy in the South.

The first World War, which initiated a period of increased social as well as physical mobility in the Negro population, set in motion social and economic forces that inaugurated a new stage in the evolution of Negro "society." First, family background and color snobbishness based upon white ancestry became less important for membership among the social elite. Although in Charleston, South Carolina, in Atlanta, Georgia, in New Orleans, and in other southern cities, Negro "society" might continue to boast of the white or mulatto ancestors, in New York, Chicago, and Detroit, those who were becoming "socially" prominent were beginning to ask, "What is his profession?" or "What is his income?" Even in Washington, where a light complexion had been so important in "society," these questions were being asked. "Blue veins" and "auburn hair and finely chiseled features" were beginning to be ridiculed as a basis of social prominence. A newspaper edited by a pure black Negro carried articles each week showing up the foibles of the mulattoes who constituted Negro "society."[3]

During a decade or so following the first World War, in both northern and southern cities education and occupation increasingly supplanted family background and a light complexion as a basis for admission to the social elite among Negroes. For example, in New York, Chicago, and Philadelphia, Negroes who had constituted Negro "society" because they were mulattoes and acted like "gentlemen" were pushed aside because they were engaged in personal services. The Negro doctors, dentists, lawyers, and businessmen, who could not boast of white ancestors or did not know their white ancestors, were becoming the leaders of Negro "society." Even if they did not act like "gentlemen," they were able to imitate white "society" in their standards of consumption and entertainment. In fact, they tended to ridicule the so-called "culture" and exclusiveness of the older Negro "society."

During this transition period in the development of Negro "society," the "socially" prominent among Negroes were developing the new social values and new orientation towards the American environment that have become characteristic of Negro "society" at the present time. Although among isolated enclaves in the Negro communities of both southern and northern cities there is an attempt to constitute a "social" elite after the manner of the older Negro "society," such Negroes are generally looked upon as curiosities. Family background has little significance in Negro "society" of the present day, although there is an unavowed color snobbishness which has ceased to have much importance. Education from the standpoint of fundamental culture has completely lost its significance. There is still a certain snobbishness in regard to one's occupation, but the most important thing about one's occupation is the amount of income which it brings. Therefore, at the present time, Negro "society" is constituted largely of professional and business men and women with large incomes that enable them to engage in conspicuous consumption. From time to time the incomes of these Negro professional men who are "socially" prominent are revealed to have been derived from traffic in narcotics and performing abortions, while it is difficult at times to determine whether "socially" prominent businessmen are engaged in legitimate or illegitimate business.[4]

THE GAUDY CARNIVAL

One may get some idea of the nature of "society" in the make-believe world of the black bourgeoisie from an article entitled "Society Rulers of 20 Cities," which was published in the May, 1949 issue of *Ebony*. The rulers of "society" included five wives of physicians, three wives of dentists, three women school teachers, two wives of morticians, a social worker, the owner of a newspaper, the wife of a lawyer, a banker's daughter, a concert pianist, and the wife of a college president. Of course, there are Negro women in these cities who would challenge the "social" ascendency of these so-called leaders, since there is much competition to be known as a ruler of "society." In northern cities, especially, there are wives of politicians and businessmen who, because of their ability to engage in conspicuous consumption, would not accept these so-called leaders. Nevertheless, the rulers of "society" reported in *Ebony* are representative, on the whole, of the leaders in "society" among the black bourgeoisie both with respect to the source of income and the style of life of this element among the black bourgeoisie.

One of the rulers of colored society, a physician's wife who works every day, is celebrated for her three big parties each year. The ruler of society in a southern city has gained fame because she entertains Negroes who have a national reputation. Another has gained notoriety because she is a friend of Lena Horne and gave a cocktail party for the famous movie actress. A former social worker is reported to have won her position in "society" because certain white writers and white "playboys" have paid attention to her. Another gave lavish debutante parties for her daughters. A southern ruler of society seemingly won eminence because her husband gave her a Cadillac automobile and a mink coat. The eminence of one school teacher in society seems to stem from the fact that she gives expensive parties and drives a Mercury automobile. A physician and his wife who had been to Europe proved their "social" eminence by giving a "continental" dinner consisting of nine courses for fifty-six guests which required four hours and thirty-five minutes to consume. In one case the reader learns that a particular ruler of "society" is noted for receptions in her home, the walls and ceilings of which, including the bathroom, are covered with mirrors. Details are supplied concerning the other rulers of "society" who own Cadillacs, have elaborate recreation rooms, and supply unlimited food and liquor to their guests.

For that section of the black bourgeoisie which devotes itself to "society," life has become a succession of carnivals. In cities all over the country, Negro "society" has inaugurated Debutante Balls or Cotillions which provide an opportunity every year for the so-called rich Negroes to indulge in lavish expenditures and create a world of fantasy to satisfy their longing for recognition. Very often these "rich" Negroes mortgage their homes in order to maintain the fiction that they are able to indulge in these vast spectacles of make-believe. In Philadelphia the Debutante Ball known as the "Pink Cotillion" is reputed to excel all others in the country. At this Debutante Ball, noted for the money spent on decorations and the expensive gowns and jewels worn by the women, an award is made each year to some distinguished Negro. This award consists of a diamond cross of Malta. During the years 1949, 1950, and 1951, the diamond cross of Malta was presented successively to Marian Anderson, Dr. Ralph Bunche, and Mrs. Mary McCleod Bethune.[5] The Debutante

Balls are written up in the Negro press, with pictures, in order to show the splendor and wealth of those who participate in this world of make-believe.[6]

The Debutante Balls are only one manifestation of the carnival spirit of Negro "society" which never slackens, especially since the black bourgeoisie has been enjoying unusual prosperity during recent years. The weekly accounts in the Negro press of the activities of Negro "society" are invariably stories of unbridled extravagance. These stories include a catalogue of the jewelry, the gowns, and mink coats worn by the women, often accompanied by an estimate of the value of the clothes and jewelry, and the cost of the parties which they attend. One constantly reads of "chauffeured" Cadillac cars in which they ride to parties and of the cost of the homes in which they live. The carnival spirit of Negro "society" with its emphasis upon conspicuous consumption has permeated the Negro colleges, where the fraternities and sororities compete with each other to excel in the amount of money spent for flowers, decorations and entertainment. It was reported in the Negro press that during the Christmas holidays in 1952, nine Greek letter societies meeting in four cities spent $2,225,000.[7] Most of the persons attending the college fraternities and sororities were not, of course, college students, but as the article stated, top "social" and intellectual leaders. For these top "social" and intellectual leaders, the fraternities and sororities represented their most serious interest in life.

PLAYING SERIOUSLY

For a large section of the black bourgeoisie, their activities as members of "society" are their most serious or often their only serious preoccupation. Their preoccupation with "society" has its roots in the traditions of the Negro community in the United States. As we have seen above, in their position of house servants during slavery, Negroes acquired from their white masters notions of what constituted "social" life or "society." After emancipation they continued in the role of personal servants, and therefore saw the white man only in his home or when he was engaged in recreation. They never saw the white man at work in the shop or factory and when he engaged in the serious matter of business. As a consequence they devoted much time and much of their meager resources in attempting to carry on a form of "social" life similar to the whites'. For many Negroes, it appears that "social" life became identified with the condition of freedom. "Social" life among the masses of Negroes was a free and spontaneous expression of their desire to escape from the restraints of work and routine. But for those who set themselves apart as Negro "society," "social" life became a more formalized activity. Among the Negro elite as well as among the masses, "social" life acquired a significance that it did not have among white Americans.

The great significance which "social" life has for Negroes has been due to their exclusion from participation in American life.[8] The numerous "social" clubs and other forms of voluntary associations which have existed among them provided a form of participation that compensated for their rejection by the white community. At the same time these various "social" clubs have been a part of the struggle of Negroes for status within their segregated communities. The elite, who have set themselves apart as Negro "society" and have attempted to maintain an exclusive "social" life, have been extremely conscious of their inferior status in American life. For them "social" life has not only provided a form of participation; it has represented an effort to achieve identification with upper-class whites by imitating as far as possible the behavior of white "society."

The exclusion of middle-class Negroes from participation in the general life of the American community has affected their entire outlook on life. It has meant that whites did not take Negroes seriously; that whites did not regard the activities of Negroes as of any real consequence in American life. It has tended to encourage a spirit of irresponsibility or an attitude of "play" or make-believe among them. Consequently, Negroes have "played" at conducting their schools, at running their businesses, and at practicing their professions.[9] The spirit of play or make-believe has tended to distort or vitiate the ends of their most serious activities. For example, in a number of cities where Negro doctors have been excluded from joining the white professional association, they have set up "reading societies," supposedly to offset such exclusion. But, on the whole, these "reading societies" have turned out to be "social" clubs for drinking and playing poker. Playing, then, has become the one activity which the Negro may take seriously.

In fact, great importance is attached to "Negro society" in the Negro press because it is a serious preoccupation among the black bourgeoisie. One can get some notion of its importance from an editorial in the September, 1953, number of *Ebony* entitled "Is Negro Society Phony?" The editorial asserts that those who say that Negro "society" is a pretense are envious of those who have been accepted by "society." It goes on to show that members of American white "society" have achieved entrance in the same manner as the members of Negro "society." Then the editorial points out that people like Dr. Bunche, Louis Armstrong, Marian Anderson, Mary McCleod Bethune and Joe Louis have won their places in Negro "society" by achievement. The article concludes with the statement that brains rather than blood should be the basis for admission to Negro "society" and that if this is made the basis of acceptance, then Negro youth will seek recognition by Negro "society." It seemingly never occurred to the writer of the editorial that Negroes with brains would prefer not to seek escape in the world of make-believe of the black bourgeoisie.

The exaggerated importance which the black bourgeoisie attaches to "society" is revealed in the emphasis placed by the Negro press upon the "social" aspects of events concerning Negroes. When it was announced recently that a Negro businessman had been named a member of the American delegation to the United Nations, it was stated in a leading Negro publication that he was invading the "glittering international UN scene—the most exclusive and powerful *social* set in the world."[10] The news item added that the nominee had "already made plans to acquire new formal wear" and that he was preparing his wardrobe for his entrance into the United Nations. In fact, generally when white middle-class people have sought the co-operation of the black bourgeoisie in some serious community project, they have found it difficult unless it could be interpreted as a "social" event. For example, such liberal middle-class white groups as the League of Women Voters and League of Women Shoppers have constantly complained that they could not interest middle-class Negro women. On the other hand, let us take the following account of an interracial group of women who raised money for the fight against infantile paralysis. There appeared in the February 25, 1954, issue of *Jet,* under the section labeled "People Are Talking About," the statement that $1,500 was raised by a group of fifteen white and colored "society" women who wore over $500,000 worth of furs and gowns.

Anyone who achieves any distinction in any field may become a "socialite" in the Negro press. It is not simply that, as a Negro journalist stated, "anybody not in the criminal class can get a 'personal' or 'social' note in the Negro paper."[11] This suggests only a small-town attitude which may be found among any people. In making a "socialite" of a Negro, the Negro press is attributing to him or to her the highest conceivable status and recognition. For example, when a Negro anthropologist, who never attended "social" functions, gave a lecture in Chicago, the account in the Negro press referred to him as a "socialite." Consequently, one learns in the Negro press that wives of gamblers, policemen, waiters, college professors, doctors, lawyers, petty civil servants, and public school teachers are all "socialites"—often when their husbands are not so designated. It should be pointed out, however, that being called a "socialite" in the Negro press is generally regarded as a high compliment by the members of the black bourgeoisie, whatever may be their occupations.

As a consequence of the prestige of "society," many Negro professional men and women take more seriously their recreation than their professions. Once the writer heard a Negro doctor who was prominent "socially" say that he would rather lose a patient than have his favorite baseball team lose a game. This was an extreme expression of the relative value of professional work and recreation among the black bourgeoisie. At the same time, it is indicative of the value which many Negro professional men and women, including college professors, place upon sports. Except when they are talking within the narrow field of their professions, their conversations are generally limited to sports— baseball and football. They follow religiously the scores of the various teams and the achievements of all the players. For hours they listen to the radio accounts of sports and watch baseball and football games [on] television. They become learned in the comments of sportswriters. Often they make long journeys in order to see their favorite teams—white or Negro—play baseball and football games. Although they may pretend to appreciate "cultural" things, this class as a whole has no real appreciation of art, literature, or music. One reads, for example, under what "People Are Talking About" in the September 2, 1954, issue of *Jet*, that a "wealthy" Negro doctor in Detroit is planning to install a "Hammond organ" on his "luxurious yacht." The decor of their homes reveals the most atrocious and childish tastes. Expensive editions of books are bought for decoration and left unread. The black bourgeoisie, especially the section which forms Negro "society," scarcely ever read books for recreation. Consequently, their conversation is trivial and exhibits a childish view of the world.

The prominent role of sports in the "serious playing" of Negro "society" stems partly from certain traditions in the Negro community. It reflects to some extent the traditions of the "gentleman" who engaged in no serious work. But in addition, preoccupation of Negro "society" with sports is related to its preoccupation with gambling, especially poker. This latter preoccupation is especially significant because it is related to the religious outlook of the black bourgeoisie, especially Negro "society."

FROM CHURCH TO CHANCE

The black bourgeoisie cannot escape completely from the religious traditions of the Negro masses, since many of those who are achieving middle-class status have come from the masses. They are often haunted by the fears and beliefs which were instilled in them during their childhood. However, they are glad to escape from the prohibitions which the Baptists and Methodists placed upon dancing, card playing, and gambling. They want to escape from the concern of the Baptists and Methodists with sin and death and salvation. The middle-class Negro is like the "suburban agnostic" with whom Mary Kingsley compared the missionary-made African, who keeps the idea of the immortality of the soul and a future heaven but discards the unpleasant idea of hell.[12] The middle-class Negro will tell you that he believes in a Supreme Being, some vague entity who runs the universe, and the immortality of the soul, but he does not believe in hell because he thinks that man has his hell on earth. As a rule, the black bourgeoisie do not give themselves to reflection on these matters. They are regarded as impractical and unpleasant questions which should be left to a few "queer" Negroes, who should spend their time more profitably in making money. An outstanding educated Negro minister, who is a sort of a mystic, was generally regarded with amusement by the black bourgeoisie, and he sought a more congenial audience in an interracial church and as a visiting preacher in white colleges.

When the middle-class Negro abandons the traditional religion of his ancestors, he seldom adopts a new philosophical orientation in regard to existence and the world about him. Since he is as isolated intellectually as he is socially in the American environment, he knows nothing of humanistic philosophy and he rejects materialism because of his prejudices based upon ignorance. Negro intellectuals have nothing to offer him, since they have never developed a social philosophy, except perhaps a crude and unsophisticated opportunism. Therefore, as a rule, the middle-class Negro is the prey of all forms of spiritualism. He avoids the fantastic extravagances of Father Divine's cult, partly because lower-class Negroes are associated with it. He concedes, however, that Father Divine "does some good" because his followers are "honest and faithful domestic servants." Nevertheless, the black bourgeoisie are interested in "psychic" phenomena because, according to them, "scientists do not know everything." Therefore, the little reading in which they indulge is often concerned with "faith healing" and popular accounts of "psychic" phenomena. In some cities it has become a fad for members of Negro "society" to make a novena though they are not Catholics, and they have reported that this religious exercise has resulted in their securing a dress or mink coat which they have always desired.

Without the traditional religion of the Negro and a philosophy to give them an orientation towards life, the black bourgeoisie, especially the element among them known as Negro "society," have often become the worshippers of the God of Chance. This new faith or dependence upon chance finds its extreme expression in their preoccupation with gambling, including the "numbers" (the illegal lotteries in American cities), betting on horses, and more especially poker. At one time the black bourgeoisie regarded the "numbers" as a lower-class form of gambling and restricted themselves to betting on horses. Likewise, playing poker was formerly regarded by them as a pastime for the sporting element among Negroes. But with the emergence of the new Negro "society," playing the "numbers" has become respectable. This is not strange, since some members of "society" derive their incomes from the "numbers." Therefore, it is not unusual for Negro professional men and their wives to play the "numbers" daily. Even the wives of Negro college professors are sometimes "writers" or collectors of "numbers" for the "numbers racket."

But poker has become the most important form of recreation for members of "society" among the black bourgeoisie. In fact, poker is more than a form of recreation; it is the one absorbing interest of Negro "society." It is the chief subject of conversation. Negro "society" women talk over the telephone for hours on the last poker game. According to an article in *Ebony*, March, 1953, the bane of many "society" editors is that "social" affairs turn into poker games, though the latter "can be exciting" when the stakes involve "homes, lots, and automobiles." Even a chance encounter of members of Negro "society" will lead to a poker game. Moreover, poker has tended to level all social barriers among Negroes. At the richly furnished homes of Negro doctors, chauffeurs, waiters, gasoline station attendants gather with college professors to play poker. So important has poker become among the black bourgeoisie that the measure of a man has become the amount of stakes which he can place at a poker game.

In many cities of the United States, the black bourgeoisie usually spend their weekends in what might be called "poker marathons" or "poker orgies" which last sometimes from Friday night until Monday morning. Some poker players who still have old-fashioned religious ideas may leave the poker table long enough to go to church, because, as they say, they believe in God. But usually most of them, being refreshed with food, remain throughout the "marathon." Some college professors boast of leaving the poker table and going directly to lecture to their classes on Monday. Likewise, Negro surgeons have been heard to boast of leaving the poker table and going directly to perform an operation. Because of their devotion to poker, some middle-class Negroes form groups and journey periodically from city to city in order to engage in these gambling orgies. News of these orgies, with details emphasizing the high stakes played are the main topic of conversation among Negro "society." The importance of poker may be measured by the fact that some middle-class Negroes assert that poker is the one thing in life that prevents them from going crazy. Therefore, the role of poker as a "religious" force in the lives of the black bourgeoisie can not be discounted. . . .

The activities of Negro "society" are an extreme expression of the world of make-believe.

REFERENCES

1. AUSTIN STEWARD, *Twenty-two Years a Slave, and Forty Years a Freeman* (Rochester. Allings and Cory, 1857), pp. 30–32.

2. Manuscript document by John E. Bruce in the Schomburg Collection, New York.

3. It is difficult to find a file of *The Washington Bee,* which published these attacks on the mulattoes.

4. See Drake and Cayton, *op. cit.,* pp. 470ff.

5. See *Jet,* December 27, 1951.

6. See, for example, pictures of Dr. Bunche being presented with the diamond cross of Malta in *The Philadelphia Tribune,* January 2, 1951.

7. See *The Pittsburgh Courier. Washington Edition,* January 10, 1953.

8. Compare Myrdal, *op. cit.,* pp. 918–19, 952–55.

9. Once I was asked to write a criticism of an article which a Negro had written in a scientific journal. The dean of a Negro college, who read the article and my criticism, objected to what I wrote on the grounds that I had treated the article in the scientific journal seriously!

10. See *Jet,* August 12, 1954, p. 6. Italics mine.

11. Cited in Myrdal, *op. cit.,* p. 919.

12. MARY H. KINGSLEY, *Travels in West Africa, Congo Français, Corisco and Cameroons.* (London: Macmillan, 1897), pp. 660–61.

Part Three
Prospects and
Strategies

We begin this section on prospects and strategies with an historical overview by Martin Oppenheimer and George Lakey. They summarize the major historical developments that preceded the present civil rights struggle, with special attention to the post-World-War-II period.

Many students of the Negro movement regard conventional political means as inadequate to the demands of the hour. They believe something should happen fast—that the enormity of the problem demands a directness of action that is difficult, if not impossible, to achieve through established legal channels of a complex democratic society. The next four articles constitute an analysis of the direct and radical approaches to the problems that have caused the Negro movement and those resulting from it.

Tom Kahn retains a strong commitment to representative democracy while advocating extensive changes in the social and economic structure of American society. Not only, he says, will self-help in the Negro community be inadequate; but also small-scale efforts by the federal government will fail. He asks us to face the possibility that comfortable notions of slow but steady progress are delusions. Kahn suggests that there can be no full justice for the Negro and no real success for the Negro movement without far-reaching, perhaps radical, changes in our political and economic system.

Arthur I. Waskow counters the misgivings many people have about the role of law violation in the civil rights movement by pointing out the historical and philosophical grounds for civil disobedience. His paper can be viewed as a reply to some of the negative attitudes towards civil disobedience expressed by Eric Hoffer in Part One.

Judgment of the effectiveness of civil rights efforts usually rests on an assessment of whether or not the expressed goals of the demonstrations are achieved. However, Frederic Solomon and his colleagues have reported an interesting study of a possible side effect—what sociologists call a "latent function"—of civil rights activity. If, as their paper indicates, civil rights activity has certain desirable effects on the Negro community apart from the achievement of expressed goals, the utility and advisability of such activities must be reassessed.

Elinson describes and analyzes the most significant of the many groups that have dissented from the programs and strategies of the mainstream of the civil rights movement while interacting with it. Most of the articles in this reader clearly assume that the goal of the Negro movement is racial equality and that the means to this end will be found within the broad confines of the existing economic and political system. The groups discussed by Elinson reject one or both of these assumptions. The black nationalists advocate black supremacy and racial separation; the leftist authoritarians, whether Communists or not, advocate violent revolution; and the new anarchists, many of whom are dedicated to a policy of nonviolence, advocate radical changes in the entire organization of society. All of these groups provide opposition and competition, in varying degrees, to the views and programs advocated by the majority of the most prominent civil rights groups and leaders.

It is the editors' view that the most significant and promising arena for the Negro Movement lies in political action. To explore the problem of successful political activity for the Negro Movement, we have included two articles that analyze the Negro's situation through the facts of his political background.

The selection from Banfield and Wilson's authoritative book, *City Politics,* discusses the role of Negroes in the political life of American cities—especially big cities in the North. The article by Samuel Lubell provides a thorough analysis and historical survey of the participation of Negro voters in politics on the national level.

The concluding piece, with which the editors strongly concur, argues forcefully for a strategy of political coalition within the confines of the democratic electoral process. Author Bayard Rustin suggests that such a coalition could include the leadership of Negroes, organized labor, liberal intellectuals, and some elements of the white working class. He sees its major goal as that of enlarging the responsibility of the federal government in the promotion of full employment, adequate housing, quality education, and equal opportunity.

Martin Oppenheimer
George Lakey

THE CIVIL RIGHTS MOVEMENT
IN AMERICAN HISTORY

Most of those now active in civil rights and other direct action movements in this country were born in the mid-1940's. They know about World War II, the depression, and the social protest of the New Deal era only through the pages of history textbooks. About the great tradition of Negro protest which led to the present movement, they know even less, for it is hardly mentioned in most high school and even college history courses.

There is no real "beginning" to the history of Negro protest; it is, of course, rooted in Africa. Slave revolts were common occurrences aboard ship, throughout the West Indies (resulting in the independence of the island of San Domingo), in the plantation South, and even in the North prior to the Civil War. Many of these revolts were integrated, involving white indentured servants and poor farmers—the famous raid on Harpers Ferry by John Brown was also interracial. The happy slave dwelling amidst the scent of magnolia blossoms and mint juleps is a myth.

After the Civil War, freed Negroes had some measure of political rights in the South, which was occupied by federal troops until 1877. They elected a number of Negro congressmen and two senators (both from Mississippi). In general, Negroes holding public office during the

Reprinted from *A Manual for Direct Action* by Martin Oppenheimer and George Lakey (Chicago: Quadrangle Books, 1965), pp. 3–14, by permission of Quadrangle Books.

Mr. Oppenheimer teaches sociology at Haverford College and has worked extensively with the Congress of Racial Equality. Mr. Lakey is Executive Secretary of the Friends' Peace Committee.

Reconstruction era performed well, again contrary to myth, especially when compared with the behavior of other public figures in a time of widespread corruption and public immorality. After the Compromise of 1876, which made Hayes President of the United States, federal troops were withdrawn from the South and Negroes began to lose many of their hard-won rights. But it was not until the break-up of the frequently integrated Populist, or People's, party, in 1896 that Jim Crow laws as we know them today began to be passed. In some states such laws were not passed until about 1910. With the passing of the Populist movement, sometimes called the "Agrarian Crusade," came the end of Negro politics and of the two-party system in the South until our own time.

The disillusionment of many Negroes with current politics at that time, resulting partly from the collapse of Populism and partly from the desertion of the Negro by Northern liberalism, led to the rise of Booker T. Washington as a popular Negro leader. Washington became a symbol of non-involvement in integrationist agitation, and his followers, informally organized into what became known as the "Tuskegee Machine" (after the college which Washington helped to found), emphasized vocational training, hard work, and keeping one's nose clean.

NEGROES MOVE TO THE BIG CITY

As Negroes moved into Northern cities around the turn of the century (in part because of the collapse of the cotton market), they came into contact with many new ideas. The philosophy of Booker T. Washington was no longer adequate for many, and the result was the formation, in 1905, of the "Niagara Movement" by W. E. B. DuBois. This was the forerunner of the National Association for the Advancement of Colored People, which was organized in its present form in 1910. The NAACP quickly became active in drives to establish laws against lynching, and pushed an integrationist viewpoint.

World War I took many Negroes to France, where they came into contact with an entirely different way of handling the "race problem"—the French treated Negroes as equals. They also met Negroes from Africa who conveyed to them many of the African ideas of independence beginning to take shape at that time. The result was that many returning "doughboys" were unwilling to accept their pre-war status as second-class citizens. A series of racial incidents in a number of cities took place in the summer of 1919, frequently involving Negro ex-soldiers, and race riots broke out. This became known as "Red Summer."

Some disillusionment with the "gradual" tactics of the NAACP resulted. This, together with a new sense of race pride brought back by the ex-soldiers, contributed to the rise of the Universal Negro Improvement Association, led by Marcus Garvey, a Jamaican. Garveyism, as it became known, was a nationalistic, "back-to-Africa" movement which recruited hundreds of thousands of Negroes to its ranks in the few years it was able to command attention. But Garvey had not trained his followers; the movement was authoritarian, and once Garvey was deported (as a result of a mail fraud conviction) his lieutenants began to squabble and the movement died. The present Nation of Islam, however, can be traced historically and ideologically to Garveyism.

All of these events in the development of the civil rights movement took place while the American Negro was moving in large numbers from the country to the city, and from the South to the North. With this movement to find jobs and a better way of life (a movement which continues today), came all of the social problems which we have come to associate with "urbanization": family break-ups, crime, delinquency, bad housing, unemployment, poor schools (not that country schools had been any better), and the evils of the urban political machine. But at least two factors served to balance this picture to some degree for the Negro: contact with new ideas, new visions of equality; and contact with and membership in trade unions. Both factors broadened the cultural and political horizon of the ex-farmer population, and some unions (as well as some churches) trained many of today's leaders of Negro protest.

The depression, which began in 1929, hit the Negro particularly hard. Several important developments paralleled the New Deal decade (1932 to 1941). First, the attempts made by the Roosevelt administration to solve the depression problem, even though inadequate, swung the Negro voter into the Democratic party column in large numbers in the North (he did not vote in large numbers in the South anyway). Second, some Negroes engaged in a brief flirtation with the Communist party, but this did not last long; the zigs and zags of party policy in these years disillusioned most Negroes. They gradually understood that "The Negro Question" was secondary to the current needs of Soviet Foreign policy. Third, the process of urbanization continued. With it came the confidence of numbers gathered in one place; the growth of a better educated and financially more independent middle and professional class to serve the large numbers; and the growth of a powerful bloc of voters who were able to obtain favors.

Success in obtaining small favors leads to demands for bigger favors. These favors lead to a better way of life, at least for some; to an education which gives a broader view, and thus to still wider demands. Morale improves, committees and lobbies are formed, and still more demands are made and achieved. All of these pressures had an effect upon the federal executive, judiciary, and legislature, and in turn these branches of government, by taking measures to improve the lot of the Negro, have provoked pressures for still further equality in citizenship.

In 1941, just prior to our entry into World War II, A. Philip Randolph, head of the Brotherhood of Sleeping Car Porters, organized the March on Washington Movement. The threat of the march—which never came off—led to the signing, by President Roosevelt, of an executive order establishing a federal Fair Employment Practices Commission. In 1949 President Harry S. Truman signed another executive order putting equality of treatment in the armed forces into effect "as rapidly as possible." Within about four years this was accomplished. Other orders, for example, an Interstate Commerce Commission ruling forbidding discrimination in interstate bus travel, followed.

In the courts, the NAACP bore the brunt of the action in a long series of educational cases which finally resulted in the famous Supreme Court decision in *Brown* v. *Board of Education* on May 17, 1954, stating that "separate educational facilities are inherently unequal." A year later the Court supplemented that decision with an order requiring school authorities to begin steps to comply "with all deliberate speed." Unfortunately, the emphasis so far has been on the deliberate, not on the speed.

In the Congress, the first civil rights bill since 1875 was passed on September 9, 1957, under President Eisenhower, and in the summer of 1960 a second bill was passed under the Eisenhower administration. A third bill was passed in 1964 . . .

NEGROES RESPOND TO WORLD WAR II

World War II, like World War I, had important repercussions in the Negro community. First, it alleviated the depression to a large degree, giving Negroes a chance at a limited number of skilled jobs. Second, it again thrust Negro soldiers, even though they were still segregated, into contact with new situations and new ideas. Third, it once more showed American Negroes the hypocrisy of a nation which claimed to be fighting against fascism and for democracy, yet failed to treat a tenth of its population as first-class citizens.

Randolph's March on Washington Movement (which, by the way, was the first American Negro protest action officially to endorse the principle of nonviolent direct action) led to a series of efforts, even during the war, to protest discrimination. On June 16, 1942, for example, during a Madison Square Garden rally in New York, lights in Harlem were turned out in response to Randolph's call. During that summer, the still intact MOWM organization organized several marches to protest the execution of a Negro, Odell Walker, in Virginia. That same year, the Congress of Racial Equality (CORE) was founded in Chicago. Organized mainly by white pacifists, it took over many of the principles laid down by Randolph for MOWM. It went immediately to work in the field of public accommodations and began to stage the first sit-ins at restaurants. CORE's experience in these early years was to come in handy later. In 1947, the Fellowship of Reconciliation, out of which CORE had developed, cooperated with CORE in recruiting twenty-three persons who carried out a project called a "Freedom Ride" in the upper South to test an early Supreme Court decision on interstate travel. In 1948, partly to offset the possible effect of Henry Wallace's Progressive party campaign, both major parties put anti-discrimination planks into their platforms.

As the Cold War iced over the American scene in the late 1940's, open protest slowed down. The prosperity of most Americans also helped to gloss over the continuing problem of "The Other America," including Negroes. Still, even the Cold War served to focus some attention on discrimination, for, as the U.S. and the U.S.S.R. competed for the favors of African, Asian, and Latin American nations (many predominantly non-white), our treatment of both Americans and visiting persons of color became a daily scandal on the front pages of the world press. As their African cousins began to overcome centuries of foreign oppression, more and more American Negroes asked themselves when their own yoke would be removed.

On December 1, 1955, Mrs. Rosa Parks, a Negro seamstress and formerly the secretary of the local NAACP, boarded a bus in downtown Montgomery, Alabama. She was tired and sat down in the first seat behind the section reserved for whites. Several white passengers boarded. The bus driver ordered her and three other Negro passengers to move back. She refused and was arrested. In protest, the vast majority of the Negro community refused to ride Montgomery buses from December 5 until November 14, 1956, and walked to work or organized car pools. They returned to the buses only after a Supreme Court decision on November 13, 1956, declared Alabama's state and local bus segregation laws unconstitutional.

This was the Montgomery Bus Boycott, the first major campaign in the nonviolent direct action movement which is still underway. The campaign catapulted onto the stage of American history a young Baptist minister, the Rev. Martin Luther King, Jr., who soon became the symbol of American Negro protest throughout the world. After Montgomery it seemed only a matter of time before a major revival of Negro protest would take place. Lobbying and court battles seemed outmoded or overly slow in achieving significant progress, and King's tactics seemed both an alternative and a way for the ordinary citizen to become involved in the struggle.

Late in the fall of 1956 a group of Northern Negroes, encouraged by whites close to a variety of pacifist organizations, and organized by A. Philip Randolph, called for a massive "Prayer Pilgrimage" to the Lincoln Memorial in Washington. This became the first of a series of revivals of the March on Washington idea, which reached its high point in the massive march of August, 1963. The 1956 effort was not particularly successful—with a Negro population in Washington of some 400,000 at that time, only 20,000 attended the ceremonies. One observer pointed out that it would take more than prayer to move the nation's white power structure.

YOUTH JOINS THE MOVEMENT

On October 25, 1958, and again on April 18, 1959, the idea of the march was repeated, but with emphasis on youth. These were the two Youth Marches for Integrated Schools, organized chiefly by Bayard Rustin, a Negro radical pacifist with many years of experience in mass movements. The two youth marches turned out, respectively, 8,000 and 25,000 young people, and contributed significantly to the continuing growth of civil rights concern on American college campuses. But a specific technique which people could use in their own communities to get things done had not yet been widely developed.

In 1957, in Oklahoma City, a fourteen-year-old Negro girl, Barbara Ann Posey, joined the NAACP's Youth Council. There she learned the story of Rev. King and the Montgomery Bus Boycott. She went to New York City to attend a youth rally and was much impressed with that city's integrated facilities. When she returned to Oklahoma City she was determined to do something about locally segregated facilities. A sit-in on August 19, 1958, was the result. This appears to have been the first formal sit-in by predominantly Negro students, and it resulted in the desegregation of all but one of the five stores selected for action. On Sunday, August 24, 1958, twenty pairs of Negro youths visited twenty white churches; they were refused at only three, making Oklahoma City the first community to have a "kneel-in," or "pray-in," though neither of these terms had been invented yet.

News of the Oklahoma City sit-ins spread to other NAACP Youth Councils. Sit-ins took place in Wichita and Kansas City, Kansas; and in Enid, Tulsa, and Stillwater, Oklahoma, that year. In Tallahassee there was a bus boycott, though with less result than in Montgomery. Other local demonstrations protested resistance to school integration, especially in Virginia. But the sit-in idea did not catch hold for another year and a half.

At 4:30 P.M. on Feb. 1, 1960, four Negro students at North

Carolina A & T College in Greensboro entered the F. W. Woolworth store in downtown Greensboro and deliberately sat down at the lunch counter. They waited for service knowing that Negroes traditionally were not served. They were not served. They sat and waited until the store closed for the day, and left. The following day they were back with other students. Girls from Bennett College soon joined in. As crowds of whites began to threaten the Negro students in the store, the four boys realized they had bitten off quite a chunk. They went to the head of the local NAACP chapter for help. He called the CORE national office in New York. CORE immediately sent a field secretary who organized workshops in nonviolence.

The Greensboro action was quickly picked up by newspapers and radio, and within a few days Durham and Winston-Salem students were staging their own "sit-ins." Within two weeks sit-ins were taking place in Virginia and South Carolina, and within two months the movement (for such it was) spread to nearly eighty cities as far removed as Xenia, Ohio, and Sarasota, Florida. Some facilities in six Southern communities were desegregated quickly, and more were to follow. But more than 1,000 students and their sympathizers were arrested, and hundreds were harassed in one way or another, including tear gas, police dogs, burning cigars on clothing, beatings, and suspension or expulsion from college.

The sit-in movement continued to spread and gained varying degrees of success in more than 130 communities in the upper and middle South. Sit-ins were succeeded by other direct action techniques—movie stand-ins, church pray-ins, beach wade-ins. But no integration was achieved in any of the deep Southern states of South Carolina, Georgia, Alabama, Mississippi, or Louisiana at that time. The "easy" victories had been achieved; now the students were up against the hard core of segregation, and the sit-ins and other actions to secure integrated public accommodations began to bog down.

The 1960 Sit-In Movement was, according to most observers of civil rights history in this country, a turning point. It marked the beginning of a new wave of Negro protest, one which is still underway today. It also put nonviolent direct action on "the agenda" of social change in a wider sense for Americans. Perhaps less important in the long run, but certainly critical for the history of this decade, the sit-ins indirectly contributed what was probably the decisive margin in the narrow victory won by the late President Kennedy in November, 1960. Many observers believe that the personal intervention of Kennedy on behalf of Rev. Martin Luther King, Jr., after King was arrested in the course of demonstrations in Atlanta that October, was crucial in swinging Negro votes to the Kennedy-Johnson ticket. Several states in which the

Negro vote was probably decisive went for the winning ticket by very small margins—notably Texas, South Carolina, and Illinois.

SNCC IS ORGANIZED

In April, 1960 the Student Nonviolent Coordinating Committee (SNCC) was organized in Raleigh, North Carolina. For more than a year, SNCC was chiefly a coordinating group. Then, as it began to grapple with the problems of segregation in the deep South, it began to develop its own staff and full-time volunteer organization, apart from its participating member groups. This was a necessary step forward as the integrationist struggle moved from the campus and from a primary interest in public accommodations into the Negro community, and into contact with the basic problems of that community.

It was the Freedom Rides of 1961, the bus rides to test interstate transportation integration, which acted as the bridge to this new emphasis. For the Freedom Rides—the first organized by CORE, and others later in the summer organized by SNCC—took students from the campus and put them in touch with the wider Negro community. This contact quickly developed into a concern with one of the chief problems of the Negro community in the South—voting and registration to vote. SNCC decided that voter registration efforts would be next on the agenda of the civil rights movement in the South.[1] This effort, which began as early as the fall of 1960 in the thinking of some SNCC people, picked up steam after the 1961 Freedom Rides and received most of its public acclaim during the summer of 1964. Hundreds of students from all over the United States went to Mississippi to help in voter registration and the associated "freedom school" projects organized by the Council of Federated Organizations (COFO), a group composed of CORE, SNCC, the NAACP, and Rev. King's Southern Christian Leadership Conference (SCLC). As we know, three of the workers in this project . . . were killed in the campaign to bring civil rights and liberties to the people of Mississippi . . . The bombing of churches and other centers of Freedom Schools and voter registration activity, the intimidation of civil rights workers and potential and actual registered voters, and shootings into the homes of leading figures in the Freedom Movement continue.

In the North, too, a shift in tactics has occurred. In the early days of the Southern sit-ins, most Northern civil rights actions took the form of picketing to support the Southern movement. Soon, however, these support groups began to act on problems in their own communities. But, partly reflecting the primarily middle class and student composition of

[1] For more information on the history of SNCC see Howard Zinn's *SNCC: The New Abolitionists*, Boston, The Beacon Press, 1964.

direct action groups in these early days, these efforts were mainly directed toward public accommodations. In the North this meant integration of facilities that required the expenditure of money: clubs, swimming pools, and above all suburban middle-income and upper-income housing. But in the effort to integrate basically middle class facilities, it became necessary to recruit larger numbers of people, especially Negroes, to gain more power. And as larger numbers of Negroes were recruited into the active movement, organizations such as CORE became more working class in composition. The new composition was quickly reflected in new demands: better slum housing, better schools in Negro neighborhoods, more jobs. Just as in the South SNCC was thrown into the Negro community in its effort to register voters, so in the urban North CORE began to establish more direct contract with the urban Negro ghettos in order to involve the larger numbers of people needed to move toward the newer goals. Community organization became part and parcel of American "race relations."

Civil rights today moves beyond mere integration *into* existing American society. By the nature of the fact that civil rights involves basic issues confronting *all* Americans (jobs, automation, education, housing, urban renewal, and, through all of these, politics), the movement now goes beyond the relations between the races and involves the relationship of men to all other men, and the relationship between all men and the basic decision-making processes of our society.

Unfortunately, the shift in focus by the nonviolent direct action civil rights organizations to the Negro community and its problems has been slow and relatively recent. Meanwhile, the civil rights movement has contributed to raising the sights of American Negroes, but without always succeeding in attaining the demands of the day. The resistance of local and even national power structures to change continues, and while civil rights groups may be able to achieve lunch counter integration, it is another thing to achieve decent schools, housing, and jobs. These demands involve many more changes in the basic rules of our society. Above all, the demand for jobs in a nation where the entire job market (even for whites) is unable to keep up with an expanding population, a market which within a few years may even be decreasing, involves fundamental issues that challenge the very foundations of our economy. Success cannot be easy, yet these are the very issues which are closest to the everyday needs of the Negro ghettos, both North and South.

Direct Action and Radicalism

Tom Kahn

PROBLEMS OF THE NEGRO MOVEMENT

The civil rights movement has entered a critical period. Without new tactics and fresh approaches, its future success is by no means assured. The struggle for freedom may be eternal, but specific movements never are: they adapt and prosper, or they falter into the graveyard of history.

If this seems too stark an introduction to an analysis of the civil rights movement, it may hopefully balance a contrary tendency. Immediacy and spontaneity are energizing attributes in both people and movements. But they must harmonize with, not undermine, long-range perspectives. Otherwise, there is a danger of sinking into a project-centered provincialism and, in the civil rights movement, a disinclination to discuss structural obstacles to Negro freedom.

Consideration of these obstacles is already viewed in some circles as alien to the pressing concerns of the movement. And to suggest that they are not surmountable by the civil rights organizations alone is viewed as an indirect way of asserting their insurmountability—hence as the latest guise of gradualism.

This last reaction springs largely from a vision of American society which, if lacking depth, has a certain validity. That vision sees the

Reprinted from *Dissent* (Winter 1964) by permission of Dissent Publishing Association.

Mr. Kahn is Executive Secretary of the League for Industrial Democracy and served as an assistant to Bayard Rustin in organizing the 1963 march on Washington.

civil rights movement as the only dynamic force for social change in this country today. It follows, then, that the broad range of problems confronting the Negro must be solved by the civil rights movement—or they will not be solved at all. Militant optimism rules out the latter possibility and therefore dictates either a continued picture of an omnipotent civil rights movement or an evasion of the knottier problems it faces.

A major reason for this dilemma is the absence of a vital democratic Left in the United States. The "sit-in" generation was not affected by a militant labor movement struggling for social transformations. Rather it saw in the AFL-CIO an apparently overbureaucratized and complacent institution, itself tainted by racism. Nor did this generation grow up in an intellectual atmosphere enlivened by radical or socialist ideas. Rather it came to consciousness in the Eisenhower-McCarthy decade, when relative prosperity and the witch-hunt combined to enthrone mediocrity and discourage nonconformist thought. (How significant that so many sit-inners, seeking intellectual ancestors, turn back to Gandhi and Thoreau!)

We are far enough into the new decade to sense that it is qualitatively different from its predecessor. The intellectual blackout has lifted; critics of the "affluent society" seem to be more numerous; increasing technological unemployment has caused some stirrings in the labor movement; the Kennedy-Johnson administrations have been more sensitive to the need for reform.

All this would seem to bode well for the civil rights movement. But the problem is that the new atmosphere of the 60s is due primarily to the dramatic impact of the civil rights movement *itself*—not to a broad social-reform movement of which Negroes are part. Until now the Negro's struggle has proceeded in relative isolation.

This is not to say that the struggle lacks sympathy among other segments of the population. Sympathy it has. What it lacks is corresponding organization and movement. Unemployment among Negroes is at least 12 per cent, but there is no mass movement of the unemployed with which the civil rights movement could forge mutually reinforcing links. The labor movement has so far failed to assume responsibility for "the other America." Similarly, the integration of schools and housing, especially in the industrial centers, is stymied by a complex of socio-economic problems for whose solution no powerful urban reform movement now exists. Fifteen per cent of the Negro labor force is still on the farms, but there is no strong organization of small farmers to cope with galloping agricultural mechanization and its miserable human consequences.

If substantially correct, the foregoing analysis would seem to justify either variety of social pessimism earlier described—a single-minded focusing upon a messianic civil rights movement, or an ostrich-like posture in regard to the structural obstacles to Negro freedom.

Actually, it poses a challenge. Most of all, it is a challenge to white Americans in the liberal, labor, and radical communities to rescue the Negro from isolation—not merely by sympathizing with his struggle, not alone by joining it, but by radically altering the context in which it takes place.

Ever since the March on Washington, civil rights activity has been in a relative lull. A causal relationship may be suggested: energy for local protest activity was diverted into and exhausted by preparations for the gigantic March.

The March did sop up a lot of energy *and* frustration—enough to prevent predicted race riots. Actually, the Washington March stimulated local marches in several areas (Long Island, New Jersey, California, etc.), and the call issued by the national March office for a Day of Mourning following the Birmingham atrocity elicited impressive results on short notice. Moreover, the seeming quiet on the Southern front cannot be attributed to March exhaustion, since Southern participation was not that great.

No; the reasons for the lull are fundamental to the difficulties now being faced by the movement, and the evidence of these difficulties will remain even if the Spring brings a fresh outburst of demonstrations.

Nineteen sixty-three was a traumatic year for the civil rights movement, as the words March, Birmingham children, Medgar Evers, construction sites, rent strike,. and Dallas suggest. This was to be "freedom year"—"Free by '63!" as the NAACP slogan had it. It was also a record year for civil rights legislation on the state level.

But measured in concrete gains, the "freedom year" was disappointing. In Birmingham a glorious movement, symbolized by hundreds of fearless children, failed in its objectives. In Cambridge, Md., whether or not the leadership's strategy was sound, there was defeat. Despite the unprecedented March on Washington (which did prompt addition of Part III and FEPC to the civil rights draft of the House Judiciary Subcommitte), Congress slumbered, the Attorney General compromised, and prospects for a strong bill dimmed. As the pace of school desegregation diminished in the South, the courage of James Meredith threatened to become a tokenistic mockery. Meanwhile, eleven freedom fighters gave their lives, while thousands were jailed and brutalized.

It may be argued that these specific disappointments are over-weighted, that they are taken out of context, that they should be balanced by a recitation of victories. Granted, the picture is distorted if only defeats or failures are listed. The fact remains, however, that *in not a single city has the civil rights movement scored a breakthrough victory.*

With regard to the South, this is due at least in part to the higher stakes for which the movement is playing. Package demands—combining integration of public accommodations with jobs and/or school integration and/or biracial commissions—have become increasingly prominent in demonstrations, eclipsing the earlier single-demand approach associated with lunch-counter sit-ins. Victories are harder to chalk up because more basic demands are being made on the local white power structures. While the broadening of demands is a step in the right direction, it does not follow that local civil rights groups can themselves, through their usual tactics, generate sufficient pressure to win these demands. It appears that the Southern movement has entered a transitional phase whose outcome depends largely on national developments.

As for the North, it is unnecessary to list defeats. The trends are unmistakable and dangerous. While the South adjusts itself to the least discommoding forms of tokenism, the metropolitan centers of the North are becoming increasingly segregated with respect to housing and schools. As the nonviolent direct-action movement has fanned out of the South, it has been frustrated by the diffused yet deeply built-in character of discrimination and segregation in the big cities. Here the white power structure is a harder target to pinpoint. Often steeped in liberal rhetoric, it proclaims its impotence in the face of the "impersonal" and "objective" historical forces that are transforming our cities into ghettoes.

There is a sense in which many urban politicians are sincere in describing these forces as "objective"—i.e., the sense that these forces are set in motion not so much by the subjective racism of specific individuals, but have to do primarily with economics. And before the alleged mystery of economics, most Americans throw up their hands.

Again, the present lull may be over before these words see print. Still, the foregoing review suggests that its causes may persist. A similar impression is conveyed by the stock-taking now proceeding among many civil rights activists.

In strategic terms the crisis confronts the movement as a rising frustration in the Negro community, on the one hand, and a burgeoning white counter-revolution, on the other. The latter is perhaps the most distinctive development in race relations this year. It has manifested itself not only in Southern retaliatory violence but in the shifting attitudes of non-Southern whites as reflected in the Harris polls.

It is my contention that by tracing rising black frustration to its roots, we simultaneously bare the roots of the white counter-revolution. And their common soil is economics.

It takes a lot of running to stand still on the treadmill of this technologically advancing society. When you know you're running hard and everyone tells you you're moving at a fast clip, and yet the scenery around you remains the same, the   most appropriate word to describe your reactions is . . . frustration.

Running fast to stand still is essentially the position in which the Negro finds himself today. This harsh fact cannot be obscured by dramatic progress in the integration of public accommodations. Lunch-counters, hotels, parks, and the like are the easiest targets of direct action and boycotts. There are enough of these establishments to accommodate everybody; in fact overcrowding them is profitable. Once the sit-in movement in a city integrates all the lunch-counters, thus securing a given establishment from segregationist competition, lunch-counters enjoy a potentially larger consumer market.

Overcrowding in employment, housing, and schools has vastly different consequences. If the segregated lunch-counter is a hollow relic of the *ancien regime*, one which would inevitably topple at an early stage in the revolution, the more fundamental, institutional forms of discrimination appear quite compatible with modern socio-economic trends. This is the inescapable conclusion that emerges from an examination of the Negro's situation in employment, housing and schools. . . .

I spoke earlier of the relative isolation of the Negro struggle. A major reason for the absence of activity among the nation's dispossessed stems from the very nature of class unemployment. It tends to induce passivity, not revolt. Its effects are attritional, not cataclysmic. In contrast with the Great Depression, when masses of workers were more or less suddenly laid off, increasing numbers of today's unemployed are simply never hired. Many of today's youth will never enter into the productive process at all. And largely because our society has never guaranteed the right to work, most of the unemployed have not yet fully perceived that they are victims of social injustice. This, by contrast, is not true of the Negro. If the spirit and dynamic of his struggle can be injected into the white "other America," then the problems of both may be solved.

The increasingly obvious confluence of class and caste factors may set the spark and ignite a new movement. But there is little chance of such a movement effecting progressive social change without a profound reorganization of American politics. Speaking before the Washington SNCC Conference, Jack Conway, Executive Director of the Industrial Union Department, AFL-CIO, asserted that

> wage earners, minority groups, middle- and low-income city people in general, older people—all of us who make up an overwhelming majority of the society—have a broad interest . . . in justice, in full employment, in social security, in a world at peace, in a community where there is no exploitation of one group by another. No party, not even the Democratic Party which elected President Kennedy, had

finally brought these people together into an effective political party . . . We have not yet created this broader based party we need so badly, and because we do not have this party, with its commitments reaching into every community of the United States, it is uncertain what way legislation and political events will go in the next year, and in the next four years, and perhaps following eight years.

The nation can ill afford such uncertainty. The deepening racial and economic crises alone—not to mention international problems—require that we make fundamental decisions about our future and that those decisions be acted upon.

Our present political alignments render such decisions well-nigh impossible. Instead of illuminating the basic issues, the two major parties adopt similar platforms. The differences within the parties are sharper than between them. Consequently, party affiliation is practically no indication of political program.

Beneath the irrational surface of party politics are coalitions rationally designed to perpetuate minority rule. Despite the preponderance of Democrats in both houses of Congress, a coalition of Dixiecrats and conservative Republicans maintains effective control of Congressional machinery. The nation limps into the age of cybernation with 14 of the 20 standing committees of the House dominated by rural representatives, with 12 of 19 important Senate committees chaired by Southerners. The seniority system is only part of this archaic rules structure of Congress.

Nor are these rules merely a matter of parliamentary mechanics; they are a matter of politics. Seniority is determined along party lines, and the parties must take responsibility for those it elevates to power. So long as Eastland is senior member of the Senate Judiciary Committee, a Democratic majority in the Senate means he is chairman of that committee.

Responsible party government is impossible so long as Humphrey and Eastland are in the same party. A realignment of the two parties into distinctly liberal and conservative entities is a prerequisite for democratic social change. The alternative is the present political stalemate.

One impetus toward political realignment is the reapportionment of legislative districts, increasing the representation of liberal urban areas. Most important perhaps is the increasing tension between the Dixiecrat and liberal wing of the Democratic party. The separation of the Dixiecrats from the Democratic party would deprive them of the political power they wield on the national scene. The voter-registration drives of Southern Negroes will help undermine racist power at its source.

These tendencies should be explicitly and vigorously encouraged by the liberal-labor-Negro coalition in 1964, traditional party loyalists notwithstanding. Roy Wilkins' announcement that the NAACP will actively seek the defeat of Congressmen opposed to civil rights legislation is a potentially significant move in this direction. The test question for Congressional candidates should be:

If elected, do you pledge to vote against any candidate for a committee chairmanship who opposes the party's platform in the area of the committee's concern?

The determination of political allegiances on the basis of answers to this question might take us a long way toward the kind of principled politics without which we are not likely to achieve civil rights, or social justice, or economic reform.

Arthur I. Waskow

"CREATIVE DISORDER" IN THE RACIAL STRUGGLE

It is now ten years since the day on the Supreme Court's calendar that some Americans call "black Monday" and some others have called "Black-and-White-Together Monday." The efforts to achieve and to resist racial equality have during this past decade been carried on in three ways: through the politics of order, in courtroom and legislature and newspaper column; through the politics of violence, in sporadic bombings and clashes of mobs, police, and detachments of the Army; and through a third kind of politics that has been neither orderly nor violent, and that has brought more real and permanent change than either of the others.

It is characteristic of our attitude toward this third kind of politics that we do not even have a separate word for it. The best we can do with the sort of politics that lies between order and violence is to call it "disorder" and "nonviolence." Such new or newly revived political techniques as the sit-in, the mass public demonstration, the economic boycott, the rent strike, and the school boycott leave our lawyers puzzled, our police upset, and our public conscience divided. The occasional

Reprinted from *The Correspondent* (Autumn 1964), No. 32, by permission.

Mr. Waskow is a fellow at the Institute for Policy Studies in Washington and is author of *The Worried Man's Guide to Peace* and *From Race Riot to Sit In: 1919 and the 1960's*.

mention or brief use of techniques that are still not violent but seem somewhat more "disorderly"—like telephone jamming or highway blocking—has been even more puzzling, upsetting, and divisive.

It is not always easy to draw distinctions between the politics of order, disorder, and violence. Efforts by the Student Nonviolent Coordinating Committee to get Negro voters registered in Albany, Georgia—seemingly a thoroughly "orderly" notion that fits into traditional election politics—have been closely connected with street marches for equal access to public accommodations and economic boycotts against discriminatory employers, which are unconventional and sometimes "disorderly" techniques. After mass public demonstrations by Negroes in Southern cities have met brutal violence from white mobs or police, some Negroes outside the official civil rights movement have responded with street violence of their own. It is not easy to disentangle the politics of disorder from the politics of violence in such a case, just as it is not easy to disentangle the politics of disorder from the politics of order in the previous case.

Yet we have a sense of some crucial differences, and perhaps they can be expressed this way: All three forms of politics, of course, are concerned with bringing about change. But they differ in the extent to which people using the different forms tend to focus on the changes to be achieved, as against worrying about the system that is to be changed or those who defend that system. In the politics of order, people divide their attention between the changes to be accomplished and the accepted rules of society concerning the legitimate ways of bringing about change. In the politics of violence, people divide their attention between the changes to be accomplished and those powerful people who get in the way of change—the enemy. In the politics of disorder, people tend to reduce greatly their interest in both the given rules and the enemy; instead they focus very strongly on the changes to be accomplished. To oversimplify a bit, we might say that in the politics of order, men follow the rules; in the politics of violence, they attack their enemies; in the politics of disorder, they pursue change. Perhaps that is why the use of "disorder" in the racial struggle has actually brought about more change.

Both because the politics of disorder has triggered more change than either of the other techniques in the conflict over racial equality and integration, and because it is a fuzzier and less conventional approach than the others, it deserves careful study. One aspect of the politics of disorder—the approach that has come to be known as "nonviolence," that traces its history to Gandhi, and that has its chief spokesman in Martin Luther King—has received a good deal of public attention. But not all the recent disorder conflict has been "nonviolent" in the pure Gandhian sense. As we are using the term, "disorder" is certainly not violent in deed. But nonviolence has come to mean specifically the Gandhian politics of love, the confrontation of conscience, and conversion through example and dignity. There has been much in the politics of racial disorder that has nothing to do with love or the confrontation of conscience—but nothing to do with outright violence, either. By Gandhi's standards, one should hate the oppressive system but love the oppressor himself as a human being; in a great deal of disorderly politics, young Negroes are expressing intense anger not only for the segregation system but for the segregationists themselves or even, in a few cases, for all whites. And yet this anger is expressed by pursuing change, not by attacking the enemy; it is pursued with no outright act of violence, though perhaps with a "violent" heart and mind. What might be called the "not-quite-violent" and the "nonviolent" approaches both go to make up the politics of disorder.

Disorder has not been a monopoly of those who favored racial integration. In parts of the South, segregationists have cut off bank credit or refused to sell tools and food to Negroes who tried to integrate some facilities; white parents have picketed school boards that tried to end *de facto* segregation in the schools, and have kept their children home in protest. When Mississippians feared that Federal marshals might try to arrest Governor Ross Barnett for contempt of court, thousands of them sat down around the Governor's Mansion to interpose their bodies—perhaps intending a "not-quite-violent" resistance—between him and the forces of law and order.

But there has been much more fertility of invention of new forms of "disorder" on the side favoring racial integration and equality, and there have been many more people to carry out these new forms of disorder. This is scarcely surprising. It is the people who are "outside" a particular system of political order who have to invent new techniques that look disorderly to people inside the system. In the same way, back in the seventeenth and eighteenth centuries, urban lawyers and merchants who could not get the old crowd of politicians to pay attention to their grievances (and who were scarcely represented in parliament) used the illegal and disorderly device of political pamphleteering against the established order. In the same way, nineteenth-century workers who could not get their employers or the elected legislators to pay attention used unionization and the strike—which at first were illegal—to call attention to their grievances. In both these cases, using the politics of disorder not only got the immediate grievances looked after but also got the new techniques accepted into the array of authorized and approved political methods. Thus the "criminal libel" of political pamphleteering is now enshrined as freedom of the press, and the "criminal conspiracy" of striking is now enshrined in our system of free labor unions. One century's disorder became the next century's liberty under ordered law.

In the United States, Negroes have been the group most thoroughly excluded from power, and they are now proving themselves the most ingenious at inventing new forms of disorder and at reinvigorating old forms. Some of these have long been just on the borderline between "order" and "disorder"; others were only recently clearly illegal and were considered totally disorderly, but have now begun to be accepted into the army of legitimate political techniques; and yet others still seem beyond the pale.

The "borderline" forms of disorder have been the public march or demonstration and the economic boycott. Presumably, picketing or parading are forms of free speech and therefore perfectly legal. In many places, however, this form of public free speech has been limited by controls over numbers, the density of the demonstrators, the routes that parades can take, and so on. In many cities, the civil rights movement challenged some of these rules, by sending such large numbers of marchers that there was considerable interference with orderly traffic and business.

Different police departments reacted in opposite ways to the "disorderly" marches. Some, particularly but not solely in the South, treated such public marches as irretrievably illegal. Indeed, some police officers took this reaction so far that they exceeded any conceivable interpretation of their constitutional powers, by treating as illegal any sort of public civil rights demonstration even if it completely avoided interfering with traffic or business. Thus Chief Laurie Pritchett of Albany, Georgia, has arrested single individuals as soon as they emerged on a public street carrying signs demanding integration.

On the other hand, in some Northern cities the winds of change in 1963 were strong enough to blow down all the normal restraints on public protest, and to get mass marches of political anger and protest treated as if they were parades of legionnaires having fun or Irishmen honoring St. Patrick. Thus when a quarter of a million people marched down Detroit's streets to demand immediate steps toward racial equality, although they were paralyzing traffic in what might easily have been considered a disorderly act of political protest, the Mayor himself marched at their head. In the Great March on Washington for Jobs and Freedom, another quarter-million people carrying a message of political protest interrupted not only the traffic but also the normal flow of governmental work, yet were similarly hailed and protected, not attacked or arrested as were Coxey's Army and the bonus marchers of earlier days. So far as "official" America is concerned, the mass public protest march, however disorderly, seems to have become accepted not only as legal, but even as harmless—at least if it deals with racial equality.

Like public demonstrations, the economic boycott has generally been treated as if it were somewhere on the borderline between "order" and "disorder." When Negroes in some Southern cities have organized boycotts against companies that discriminated in hiring or serving Negroes, some officials have tried to charge them with "illegal restraint of trade"; but most of these attacks have come to nought, and even in most parts of Mississippi, economic pressures against segregationist businesses are now treated as legal techniques. Some Negro leaders have avoided legal difficulties by transforming "boycotts" against segregationist businesses into "selective buying campaigns" in favor of integrationist business. In the North—for example in Philadelphia, where a well-organized "selective buying campaign" in favor of department stores that hired without regard to race was highly successful—selective buying has come to be regarded as fully legitimate, though of course it is not especially welcomed by the "official" business and political interests.

Much more startling has been the increasing legitimation of certain kinds of disorder that only four years ago seemed clearly illegal. The sit-in and all its cognate acts of "trespass," the school boycott and its "truancy," the rent strikes and their "erosion of property rights" have all become far more nearly tolerable forms of disorder.

The sit-in and all its permutations—kneel-ins, live-ins, wade-ins, learn-ins, read-ins—were first taken as a major challenge to what might be called the "territorial" sense of private property, the sense that along with ownership goes a defensible "boundary." As the courts began working on the problem, however, it became clear that under the force of the equal-protection clause of the Fourteenth Amendment there would be only a partial restructuring of this "territorial" notion of property. The Supreme Court of Delaware held that the police could not intervene to protect an owner's "territorial" rights if he were using them to discriminate racially, since that would involve the state in racial discrimination. This left the owner free to use "self-help"—possibly including a limited amount of force—to impose racial segregation, if he wished. It also left the sit-inner free to sit in, so far as the state was concerned. In short, it made legitimate a certain form and amount of disorder—but probably only on the racial question, and only in places affected with a public interest.

If the exclusion were not racial, at least so far as the Delaware decision went, the owner could still call the police to enforce his territorial boundaries. Democrats, for instance, could presumably still get police to exclude Republican sit-inners from a Democratic caucus. And if the place were not affected with a public interest, presumably the police could still enforce a racial exclusion. Thus, for example, Black Muslims could presumably still call police to keep white sit-inners out of the mosque.

A view different from Delaware's—in some ways more restricted, in some ways more expansive—was set forth by the Department of Justice in a brief before the United States Supreme Court, as friend of the court in five sit-in cases. The Department was more restrictive in arguing that only when racial exclusion or segregation in public places was clearly not the mere whim of an individual owner but rather the result of a long-standing public custom having practically the force of law were the police forbidden to intervene to arrest sit-inners. For then, the Department argued, the conjunction of custom and police action would have the force of unconstitutional state action. This outlook would still leave an individual shop-owner free to have a Negro sit-inner arrested if his community had no tradition or custom of racial exclusion. But on the other hand, the Justice Department in some ways went further than Delaware by arguing that the owner could not himself use violence to reject a sit-inner, since the permission to use private violence was also a grant from the state. In other words, the Justice Department brief would have required a nonviolent confrontation between sit-inner and proprietor, each trying through calm moral suasion or angry political pressure and argument to accomplish his ends.

In short, disorder without violence would be permitted. In this respect, the Justice Department—and the courts too—are far in advance of the American Bar Association, which has formally deplored demonstrations which involve trespass.

Both the original Southern argument and the farthest developed NAACP argument were quite different from this Justice Department case for the legitimacy of disorder; and they are far more like each other in their basic theory of law and politics than either is like the Justice Department brief. Originally, the South argued that states and localities have a right to create and defend the established order of segregation by law if they wish; and even when that argument collapsed, the South continued to argue that states and localities had a right to use police power to defend a *privately* established system of segregation. As for the NAACP, it is now arguing that any public business licensed by the state is an arm of the state and must forego segregation; in other words, that the state has an affirmative duty to create and uphold a new established order of racial integration. Both the South and the NAACP, then, see the task of government as securing *order* by enforcing one set of values or another. The Justice Department now sees the role of government in some aspects of the race question to be rather the prevention of outright violence, while certain kinds of *disorder* are permitted to exist because private groups are struggling over which set of values should prevail.

Obviously the Justice Department did not come easily to the position that disorder without violence was better than any order imposed by governmental enforcement. Indeed, the Justice Department is usually extremely fearful of disorder and very insistent on the value of order, as might be expected from its institutional role. The Department came to its position in this particular stubborn set of cases because, despite the official rhetorical commitment of American society to the ultimate achievement of racial integration, there is a deep conflict in day-to-day American life as to *which* "order," which set of values should be enforced by the state—integration or segregation. The conflict runs so deep that instead of acting the way a government usually would—enforcing a particular set of values by the use of police powers if necessary—the Federal government and the states restrict themselves to proclamation of particular sets of values and the prevention of outright private violence. (The Federal government, through constitutional amendments a century ago, the Supreme Court ten years ago, and the President and Congress more recently, have proclaimed their support for integration; the Southern states, through repeated statements of high officials and through such institutions as the Mississippi State Sovereignty Commission, have proclaimed their support for segregation; and "unofficial" muttered rhetoric in many a Northern city and suburb has agreed in essence with the South.) At least before passage of the civil rights bill, the Federal government has been unwilling to use its police powers to do more than prevent or stop violence. Presumably the passage of that bill would indicate that an effective new consensus had been reached on using Federal power to enforce the racial integration of certain kinds of public places. But in actuality, stubborn opposition in parts of the South will probably still leave the country without a full consensus, and in enforcing the bill, the Federal government (especially if Southern states continue to try to block it) will probably for some time yet behave more as an agency to prevent outright violence than as an agency to establish and enforce a new order.

The other major forms of previously illegal disorder—the school boycott and the rent strike—have begun to become legitimate in much the same way as the sit-in. Deliberately refusing to go to school is truancy, and urging children to stay out of school is illegal. But no one punished 9,000 Boston students last June when they invented the one-day school boycott and the substitute one-day "Freedom School"; nor did anyone punish either the 250,000 Chicago and 360,000 New York students who later adopted the boycott method, or their parents and civil-rights leaders who suggested and led it. The aim of the school boycotts was to force an end to *de facto* school segregation, accomplished in some Northern cities by gerrymandering school districts to follow racial lines and in others by failure to act affirmatively to cope with segregation based on residential discrimination. The legal status of *de facto* segregation, especially the second kind, is still under debate; but the school boycotts have done much to reduce the political viability of such patterns of official behavior. In New York, for example, the boycott stirred anguished protests from school officials and *The New York Times*, but it also forced school officials to grapple for the first time with the problem of integrating big-city schools. Of course the acceptance of such techniques is not universal. Atlanta, in January, suspended several dozen students for truancy when they cut classes to demonstrate against the school board for faster integration. But the emergence of the school boycott as a political weapon, which "official" figures in government, business, and the press have deplored but tolerated, points to the new openness of the political system to certain forms of disorder.

The third form of disorder to move toward acceptability has been the rent strike. In the late autumn of 1963, several groups in New York City began to focus on the problem of slum housing—some of them the older civil-rights groups like CORE, but especially newer organizations that looked on many Negro problems as difficulties bred more of poverty than of race, like the Community Council on Housing led by Jesse Gray. Where housing was utterly inadequate, as it was in hundreds of Harlem tenements that Negro families had to share with rats, bitter cold and driving rain, the tenants began to refuse to pay their rent. At least in New York City, this form of disorder was quickly assimilated by the law. Drawing partly on New York's rent-control law which gives tenants statutory rights to their apartments in the absence of good cause to evict them, several local courts held that landlords who provided no heat, shelter, or freedom from vermin were not really providing housing at all. Hence they were not entitled to rent, and could not claim nonpayment of rent as good cause to evict the tenants. One judge ruled that the rent should be paid into a special fund under the supervision of the courts, from which withdrawals could be made only to pay for repairs of the tenements. Another judge ruled that tenants could voluntarily set up such a "repair fund" if they wished, but had no obligation to do so or to pay their rent in any other way until the landlord had put his property back in livable shape. Thus the rent strike quickly won the support of New York law, and can hardly be viewed as "disorderly" so far as New York goes.

The idea at once began to be discussed in other cities, however; and in many places the housing laws and courts were by no means so likely to support the rent strike. For at least at first glance, the rent strike seems to invade the notion of private property as the right to a cash return for the owner, and to leave the decision as to what is a "fair" return to the tenant rather than to orderly determination by the courts and housing officials. Thus some landlords, even in New York, claimed that the rent strike amounted to the expropriation of property. In New

York, partly because of the background and tradition of rent-control law, these landlords were immediately confronted with the argument that non-payment of rent in abominably maintained apartments was no more an expropriation of property than was the condemnation and destruction of food found to be diseased and poisonous. But in some places, unlike New York, it is the landlord's view that is written into the law; and therefore police would presumably try to evict rent strikers.

The logic of creative disorder would suggest that in such places there might be nonviolent mass sit-downs to prevent the police from removing furniture or evicting tenants. Such nonviolent resistance would then be more likely to force the acceptance of the rent strike in the New York fashion, either by law or in practice. Since the problem of housing lies near the heart of the civil rights question in many Northern cities, it is conceivable that the rent strike will be developed into one of the most potent forms of disorder without violence. Bad housing furthermore affects poverty-stricken whites in much of the nation, so that the rent strike may be one of the earliest of the new forms of creative disorder to be taken over by groups not especially concerned with Negro rights or racial integration.

Finally, in addition to forms of disorder that have long been accounted legal and forms that have recently become practically legal, there is one form of disorder that has been only tentatively tried by the movement for racial equality, that has failed a number of times and succeeded only a few, and that still seems in almost all localities to be outside the pale of legitimacy. That form of disorder is the disruption of some activity that is strategically necessary to the society at large, rather than merely a single institution. Thus the original suggestion by some integration leaders that failure to pass a civil rights bill quickly might bring sit-ins to Capitol Hill and into Congressional offices brought a great outcry and a swift retreat to the much milder disorder of the March on Washington. Sit-ins in mayors' and governors' offices have been roundly condemned and, so far, generally ineffective. In Danville, Virginia, student protest groups, after suffering brutal street violence from police, tried briefly to disrupt the city government. They placed hundreds of telephone calls to City Hall, saying "Freedom!" and hanging up when their calls were answered, interrupting the normal flow of city business as conducted by telephone. But their tactic brought no immediate results, and they abandoned it.

One of the most detailed plans for general social disruption was set forth last fall, in the days of post-March frustration and post-Birmingham-bombing disillusion, in a memo by Diane Nash Bevel to the Student Nonviolent Coordinating Committee (SNCC). She proposed the creation of a large nonviolent army, 25,000 strong, uniformed and militant, that would undertake such campaigns as surrounding and paralyzing Southern state capitols where governors set their faces utterly against integration, stopping transportation by blocking airports, highways, and railroads with their bodies, etc. This proposal never came near serious consideration by SNCC, was bitterly attacked by the normally pro-integration *Washington Post,* and was hastily dismissed by other civil rights organizations. So far, it seems, the sort of disorder that would be involved in broad-scale social disruption has not become "legitimate" in most parts of the country.

That this sort of disorder may not remain forever forbidden may be seen from the little-publicized events of November, 1963, in Chester, Pennsylvania. The civil rights movement in that industrial suburb of Philadelphia began its campaign to end *de facto* segregation and to improve the quality of some abysmal schools by using the comparatively legitimate disorder of a school boycott and public picketing. After several days of merely picketing, the demonstrators (still not using violence) blocked all entrance to one of the most overcrowded and most heavily Negro schools, and forced the city to close it. Then, and over the next few days, the crowds converged on Chester's City Council in numbers so huge as to force the abandonment of Council sessions and on one occasion the flight of the Councilmen. More than 100 demonstrators were arrested. But after several days of social disruption, Chester not only permanently closed the dilapidated, 95 per cent Negro school that had been the focus of the protest—but also, and more important, freed the demonstrators who had been arrested. In other words, for Chester the technique of social disruption had become at least partially legitimate.

It does not follow that social disruption will necessarily become an acceptable technique of disorder across much of the country, in much the same way as have the sit-in, the rent strike, and the school boycott. For, of course, disruption is a much more radical technique than the others. It is not a more *violent* technique than the others, and there is no reason to assume that it will provoke violence any more than the others will. But it is certainly a considerable "escalation" of disorder without violence. For what disruption essentially does is challenge the entire society as a racially discriminatory *system.* The other forms of disorder challenge only a particular incident or institution that is segregated or discriminatory. In a sense, the sit-in, the rent strike, and the school boycott are, in the politics of disorder, equivalent to a riot in the politics of violence—that is, they are ways for two different social groups to carry on conflict against each other without violence, just as a riot is a way for two social groups to carry on conflict against each other by using violence. Disruption, however, is equivalent in the politics of disorder to insurrection in the politics of violence, and an insurrection is quite different from a riot. For insurrection is a way for one social group to carry on conflict not merely against another social group, but against the society as a whole, or against the government. Inventing a way to carry on an insurrection without violence is a major act of creativity, but it is an act likely to arouse more hostility than carrying on a "riot" without violence.

What then is the future of the politics of disorder within and outside the integration movement? Will the new political forms wither away as integrationists win more and more victories, or will the techniques outlive the particular issues? Which of the techniques are likely to prove most effective and creative? Is disorder often likely to escalate from the boycott or the sit-in to full-scale social disruption, or will the hostility to this form of attack prevent its being often used?

The answers to these questions will depend mostly upon three factors: the response of government to the use of controlled forms of disorder; the success or failure of controlled forms of disorder in attracting public attention to and bringing about a resolution of particular conflicts; and the degree of inventiveness and self-discipline in the Negro community as it tries to create new techniques to cope with whatever failures may occur in the use of controlled disorder. As to government: if the local police try to smash equivalents of a "riot" that use no violence, they are much more likely to find real riots blossoming before them. Or alternatively they are likely to find Negroes who have tried sit-ins or boycotts, and have suffered under the full weight of police power used against them, turning in desperation to more radical acts of social disruption. If boycotts and sit-ins are suppressed, the choice between violent riots and social disruption without violence may well depend in part on the amount of naked violence used by government officials in suppressing such techniques of controlled disorder. Sit-ins that are suppressed by police brutality or police permission for mobs to use brutality are quite likely to be followed by riots. Arrests and other official pressures that do not use outright violence may be more likely to bring an "escalation" of disorder without violence. Since brutality is more likely in the South and careful arrests in the North, this factor may weight the scales somewhat toward riot in the South and social disruption in the North.

The second factor, that of the success or failure of controlled disorder in bringing about change, may also suggest that social disruption is more likely in the North. For controlled, small-scale acts of disorder are less likely to catch the public eye in a great Northern metropolis than in a middle-sized Southern town, and frustrated protestants who see their efforts at controlled disorder going for naught may well continue to try such disruptive techniques as blocking New York's

Triborough Bridge. In other words, the greater scale of much Northern
society may seem to require the escalation of disorder if it is to have any
effect—and the greater complexity of Northern society is likely to make it
more vulnerable to disruption.

On the Negro and integrationist side, the question will be
whether there is in existence a leadership committed to avoiding violence
and capable of inventing new forms of disorder without violence. If so,
the chances for riot would decrease, as compared to the chances of an
escalated form of disorder. So far, Negro leadership in the North and
South have seemed about equally imaginative in inventing new ways of
carrying on conflicts without violence.

Judging from what has happened so far—the increasing acceptance in most parts of the country that many forms of controlled disorder
are legitimate—it seems likely that the suppression of disorder may occur
chiefly in the South. Elsewhere, more limited forms of disorder are likely
to win their point. This development is not yet absolutely certain; some
Bostonians have talked about arresting those who plan school boycotts,
and there have been a few arrests in the New York rent strike. But the
trend of governmental action outside the South seems to be toward more
and more acceptance of most forms of disorder other than disruption.

If this trend continues, there are two different kinds of response
that officials might make to the use of limited disorders. First, the
governments concerned, local and national, may step back and allow sit-
ins, boycotts, and rent strikes to be "fought out" just as most labor strikes
and lockouts are, so long as neither side uses violence. Or instead,
governments may respond to the pressures of disorder by changing the
law or vigorously enforcing laws that are already on the books; in other
words, they may let creative disorder become a guide to the state of
public opinion in the same way that the free press is.

There is some evidence that parts of the Federal government
have already taken the second tack. Certainly it was no accident that the
late President Kennedy waited till after the 1963 disorder in Birmingham
before presenting a comprehensive civil rights bill to Congress. And the
process by which the House Judiciary Committee strengthened the
Administration's bill owed much to the march of events out on the street.
Because of the wide range of disorderly protest after Birmingham (jobs,
restaurants, votes, schools), the Administration felt compelled to send
Congress a bill which (though shallow in each section) had many
sections, and was broad enough to cover almost every area from
employment to voting to education to the courts. Such a bill provided an
excellent starting place for section-by-section strengthening, all across its
broad front. Then, again because of militant disorder all through the
summer, the Justice Department was too busy with legal problems across

the country to pay more than lackadaisical attention to the bill-drafting process in sub-committee. By the time Justice realized its own bill was being strengthened all across the board, the process had gone too far to be reversed without a struggle. As for the congressmen themselves, it was the militant protests that kept some of them conscious of the danger of widespread violence, that brought home to others with great emotional impact (as when the Birmingham Sunday school was bombed or students were jailed in Americus, Georgia, under capital charges) the nature of the resistance to racial integration. The demonstrations worked quietly on the minds and hearts of older "unexcited" Democrats on the subcommittee like Byron Rogers of Colorado, until suddenly they were joining with young men like Robert Kastenmeier of Wisconsin in saying it was *their* responsibility, as the majority and as Congressmen, to write as good a bill as they could—not the responsibility of the Justice Department or the Republicans or anyone else. And it was the demonstrations, finally, that led Republican leader William McCulloch of Ohio to tell his men that blood might be on their hands if for partisan reasons they helped Southerners block the bill and then violence followed.

As things stand now, it looks as if many of the forms of limited disorder will be accepted as legitimate in most of the country. Indeed, they may well be accepted not only as legitimate but as reasonable methods for persuading legislators to change their minds—akin to free speech, in other words. If this is the direction of change—if the Congress and local governments really take sit-ins, marches, boycotts, and rent strikes as expressions of public desires and change their behavior accordingly—then it is rather unlikely that disorder will escalate to efforts at social disruption, except in cases of great local strain and frustration. And if the new forms of disorder do become acceptable expressions of liberty under law, what can we expect them to mean outside the realm of civil rights and racial struggle?

The new techniques are likely to be borrowed for use by groups other than their inventors. It is easy to imagine the desperate white miners of eastern Kentucky, without jobs for many years, sitting-in on Federal unemployment compensation offices in order to demand jobs or extended unemployment insurance. It is easy to imagine school boycotts by students protesting a compulsory civil-defense shelter program in their schools, or students protesting the firing of a professor, or students protesting against their schools being put in a split-shift schedule. It is easy to imagine a rent strike by the many whites who live in slum dwellings as bad as Harlem's. In other words, if the new forms of disorder become legitimate, there is no reason to expect that only Negroes will find them useful and necessary.

The new techniques are also likely to revivify the practice of that kind of democracy in which all the citizens participate directly, in which each man has an active share in the shaping of his own destiny and that of his society. For it is in the nature of the new forms of disorder that they are creative in two ways. Not only do they help to reshape society, but they help to reshape those who carry on the disorder. It takes a much deeper commitment on the part of larger numbers of people to carry on a school boycott, or a rent strike, or a march, than it does to pursue a more orderly politics. The new forms of disorder involve large numbers of people in the process of politics, and they make that process immediate, relevant, and productive for people who before were outside of politics and fearful or distrustful of it. As the disorderly pamphleteering press focused the talents of the middle class and the disorderly labor movement focused the energies of working men, so the new forms of disorder have the power to create a politically alive citizenry out of the last of the excluded, the only slave class in American history. Thus, while the goal of disorder is to create racial Freedom Tomorrow, the very process of racial disorder can create individual Freedom Now. What was disorder in 1954, on Desegregation Monday, can be liberty this year.

Fredric Solomon
Walter L. Walker
Garrett J. O'Connor
Jacob R. Fishman

CIVIL RIGHTS ACTIVITY AND REDUCTION IN CRIME AMONG NEGROES

INTRODUCTION

In this preliminary report, data are presented on a possible reduction in crime among Negroes in certain cities during periods of

Reprinted from the *Archives of General Psychiatry*, March 1965, Vol. 12, pp. 227–236. Copyright 1965 by the American Medical Association.

Dr. Solomon is a NIMH Fellow in psychiatry at the Center for Youth and Community Studies, Howard University. Mr. Walker is Senior Staff Associate at the Center. Dr. O'Connor is Psychiatry Instructor, The Henry Phipps Psychiatric Clinic, Johns Hopkins Hospital. Dr. Fishman is Assistant Professor of Psychiatry and Neurology and Director, Center for Youth and Community Studies, Howard University.

organized community action for civil rights in those cities. The existence of such a phenomenon has been remarked upon by leaders of "direct action" civil rights groups in several communities. Yet, to date there has been no documentation of this phenomenon except for newspaper accounts of the one-day "March on Washington for Jobs and Freedom" of Aug. 28, 1963.

According to the *Washington Evening Star*, there were only seven "major crimes" recorded by the District of Columbia police in the 24-hour period ending at 8:00 A.M. on Aug. 29, 1963.[1] The *Star* noted that during the same time period in the previous week, there had been 19 such crimes. Thus, reported major crime in Washington apparently dropped 63% for the day of and the night after The March.

Somewhat more surprising is an article which appeared in the *New York Times*. A reporter spent most of August 28th in Harlem and then wrote a story about the serious but happy mood that seemed to pervade Harlem on that day.[2] The story in the *Times* concluded with the following:

> Police cars patrolled Harlem's streets all day, thinking it would be a big day for robberies, with so many Negro residents away from home, for the trip to Washington.
> But in the evening, the desk sergeant of the 26th Precinct reported no robberies or other crime.

It has been our opinion that in the long run, the effects of the civil rights movement on the self-image and social behavior of the American Negro will be as important as the movement's direct effect on segregation patterns. Two of us have already written extensively about the student civil rights demonstrators themselves—their attitudes, behavior and motivations, and the psychological significance of antisegregation activities in their life histories to date.[3-5] The present paper represents the initial phase of an inquiry into possible community-wide "side effects" of the civil rights movement.

Data will be presented which, in a preliminary way, tend to document the existence of an association between well-organized direct action for civil rights and a substantial reduction in crimes of violence committed by Negroes. We shall discuss the findings, their limitations, and their implications and shall offer some thoughts about further research.

HISTORICAL NOTE

The historic Niagara Movement in 1905 was the foundation for a national organization whose declared purpose was to wage a war against racial injustice, the National Association for the Advancement of Colored People. Since its inception, the NAACP has sought the support of both Negroes and whites in an effort to mount an effective protest against lynching, unfair characterization of the Negro in the news and entertainment media, job and housing discrimination, and segregated public accommodations. Almost from the very beginning, the NAACP sought redress for racial injustice in the nation's courts. Citizen participation in NAACP efforts was invited largely in the area of fund-raising to support the enormous costs of litigation. There was very little the lower-class Negro citizen was asked to do, personally, to strike a blow for his rights.

During the World War I period, the National Urban League began its work of helping Negro immigrants from the rural South adjust to urban living. This organization typically worked on two levels. First, attempts were made to educate and train Negroes to live in an urban setting. Almost every segment of the Negro community was involved in teaching, learning, or fund-raising. Second, the Urban League undertook to negotiate with employers in an effort to open new opportunities for Negroes. Although the Urban League has been, in a sense, a "grassroots" organization it rarely has urged its constituency to mount a public protest against prevailing systems of injustice.

It has been said that the work of the NAACP and the Urban League has laid the economic, legal, and educational groundwork for the present civil rights movement. The 1954 Supreme Court decision and the successful adjustments to urban living made by many Negroes serve as testimony to the effectiveness of their efforts.

However, it is not the use of legal skill, negotiation, or education which is the focus of this paper. We are concerned here with the process of direct action which began on a large scale in the 1955 Montgomery, Ala., bus boycott, found new expression in the student "sit-in" movement; was dramatized by the "Freedom Rides"; and continues to express itself in the street demonstrations and voter registration efforts of today. What is direct action? Whom does it involve? How does it differ from other civil rights activities?

In the context of the so-called Negro Revolt, direct action is a nonviolent confrontation between the prevailing power structure of the community and an emerging center of power which demands changes in the legal, social, political, and economic fabric of the community. The main thrust of direct action has been via nonviolent public demonstrations, civil disobedience, economic boycott, and various actions designed to test the legality of local laws and customs.

Direct action involves different segments of the Negro community, depending on the particular technique being used. Economic boycotts and voter registration campaigns often directly commit a majority of the Negro community to the effort. Sit-ins and street demonstrations traditionally involve college-age Negroes, but there is mounting evidence that a wider segment of the Negro population is becoming directly involved in these especially active forms of protest.

Those members of the Negro community not directly involved in direct action are often indirectly and vicariously involved nonetheless. The violent reactions of whites, that is often the price of direct action, strikes close to home. Friends and relatives are often directly involved. The "battle plans" are drawn up in the Negro areas and are often public knowledge there. Negroes are often questioned about the movement by their white employers. There is strong community pressure to actively join in the "fight for freedom."

Contrast, then, the community involvement characteristic of a direct action movement with that of a local community's involvement in a battery of NAACP lawyers fighting a legal battle in the Supreme Court in Washington. Clearly, the average man sees himself as more immediately involved in a direct action, where willingness to be counted is the major requirement for participation, than he is in a legal battle that requires long years of professional training for participation in the front line.

METHODOLOGY

For three cities (two in the Deep South and one in a border state) data were collected from various sources, including official crime reports, medical records, newspaper accounts, and individual interviews with residents. Originally, a systematic attempt had been made to obtain relevant and reliable crime records from 16 cities, 12 of them Southern. This was largely unsuccessful because of a number of problems. For example, two cities with crucial roles in the history of the civil rights struggle had changed their crime reporting criteria and the organization of their reports from year to year within the period in which we were interested. In another city, a Negro colleague of professorial rank in a local college, was denied access to the police reports which he had seen on the shelves of the public library just the day before. A general problem in the crime statistics which we *were* able to obtain was the absence of racial breakdown in most of the data.

Two central crime information agencies were contacted for their help—The Uniform Crime Reporting Section of the Federal Bureau of Investigation and The Crime Information Center of the National Council on Crime and Delinquency. They were of limited assistance; and we have drawn some inferences from data from several cities; but we have found only one Southern city with the kind of published crime reports that would be maximally useful to us in this research, and that is "city Z." Using an alternate approach, we have obtained hospital emergency room statistics and other relevant data from a small town which we shall call "town X," and we have a fairly reliable picture of developments there. Finally, via interviews, we collected some important anecdotal material which describes direct interaction between delinquent gangs and a young civil rights leader in "city A."

In evaluating crime data our focus has been upon major crimes committed by Negroes, with special emphasis upon aggravated assaults. There are several reasons for this focus. Local police departments report major crimes to the FBI under the heading of "Part I Offenses." (Other offenses in this category aside from aggravated assault are homicide, manslaughter, rape, robbery, burglary, larceny, and auto theft. Minor offenses, such as drunkenness or gambling are much less uniformly reported by police departments and are not considered accurate indices of local crime pictures.) Of major crimes against persons, aggravated assault is by far the most frequent, so that variations in the number of assaults from year to year (or month to month) are likely to be statistically more meaningful than would be variations in homicide or rape, for example. Furthermore, aggravated assaults frequently result in some kind of medical attention to the victims; so medical personnel in hospital emergency rooms may keep records that may usefully supplement what appears (or does not appear) in police reports. Finally, as the FBI *Manual on Uniform Crime Reporting* states, assaults are a fairly sensitive "index of social disorder in a community."[6]

Of course, one must always keep in mind that, except for homicide and armed robbery, *all* crime statistics are reflecting merely the top of an iceberg of unreported crime. It has been suggested that most criminal acts never come to the attention of the police.[7]

There is another problem in doing a study of this kind. There is a paucity of written material about the chronological development of direct action for civil rights in various geographical areas. There is a great need, we feel, for someone to chronicle the contemporary history of these developments. For our part, we have relied upon the *New York Times Index* for cities Z and A, an unpublished document written by college students detailing developments in town X, and interview material for all three communities.

CITY Z

City Z is a large industrial and educational center located in the Deep South. The city has had a reputation for being "progressive," within the confines of segregation. Many of the city's Negro college students come from the North. The city has a well-established Negro middle class. Although the police force is interracial, the Negro officers customarily restrict their arrest power to Negro suspects.

The civil rights movement in city Z, according to local citizens, began in 1960 primarily as a student movement in response to the initial sit-ins in Greensboro, N.C. However, the white community's reaction to the students' increased pressure for equality soon welded the whole Negro community (and its established leaders) into a unified force in support of direct action.

Two economic boycotts of downtown stores with segregated facilities and employment practices were nearly 100% effective in terms of participation. In the Christmas season of 1960 and again at Easter of 1961, reportedly no more than a handful of Negroes could be seen shopping downtown on any given day. In response to this boycott by the whole Negro community, as well as in response to numerous public demonstrations by students, the major downtown stores finally did upgrade employment opportunities for Negroes, and all their lunch counters were desegregated by the end of 1961. There was virtually no organized civil rights protest activity in 1962, in sharp contrast to the extremely active years of 1960 and 1961. (Late in 1963, public protests resumed, focusing upon segregated eating places.)

Crime statistics included in city Z's annual police reports reflect trends which suggest that civil rights activities may be related to a reduction of crime in the Negro community. The general police and crime activity over the four-year period 1959 through 1962 is reflected in Table 1.

TABLE 1. *General Police and Crime Activity, 1959–1962*

	1959	1960*	1961*	1962
Population	487,000	Data missing	Data missing	504,000
Police-patrolmen	519	519	538	541
Total Part I Offenses (major crime)	16,809	17,290	19,414	20,431

* Years of sustained civil rights activity.

This indicates that city Z's slow increase in population was matched by a roughly proportional increase in patrolmen. Major crime has also increased in the city's general population.

Various direct action protests were common occurrences in city Z in 1960 and 1961; there were no such activities in 1959 and very few in 1962. Table 2 shows that in 1960 the number of Negro vs Negro assaults coming to the attention of the police decreased 31% from the 1959 figure. During 1961, the Negro vs. Negro assaults remained at this low 1960

TABLE 2. *Aggravated Assaults (Known Offenses, by Race)*

	1959	1960*	1961*	1962
Negro attacks Negro	531	371	373	536
White attacks white	85	79	100	101
Negro attacks white	8	9	13	19
White attacks Negro	5	5	5	9

* Years of sustained civil rights activity.

figure. However, in 1962—a year which saw civil rights activity in only one month—the annual rate for Negro vs Negro assaults returned to the 1959 figure.

Aggravated assaults within the white community did *not* vary in the same manner as did the Negro vs Negro assaults. On an annual basis, the figures for cross-race assaults are too small to be particularly noteworthy.

The known offense data concerning aggravated assault cases are reported not only annually but also on a month-by-month basis. Such figures would appear useful in making a closer inspection of the possible relationship between variations in civil rights activity and changes in Negro crime rates. These *monthly* data, however, are not broken down by race, as were the *annual* data reported in Table 2. Therefore, any inferences from these data of an association between civil rights activity and assaults by Negroes must be based on the knowledge that whites account for only a small proportion of the total reports of aggravated assault. For the period 1959–1962, only 16.5% of the reported and recorded assaults were attributed to whites; thus, in any given month, one might assume that Negroes account for about four out of five of the "known offenses" in the aggravated assault category.

It is of some interest to note, as in the top line of Table 3,

TABLE 3. *Aggravated Assaults (Known Offenses)*

	1959	1960*	1961*	1962
Monthly average (all races)	52	38	41	59
Annual assaults by Negroes	539	380	386	575
Annual assaults by whites	90	84	105	110
Annual grand total	629	464	491	711

* Years of sustained civil rights activity.

monthly averages for assaults in city Z. In the period 1959 through 1962 there were 16 months in which newsworthy civil rights protest activity occurred (15 months in 1960 and 1961, one month in 1962). The average number of assaults in these "civil rights months" was 39; the average number of assaults in "noncivil rights months" was 52, one third higher than in the "civil rights months."

Of all the 48 months from 1959 through 1962, only three had less than 30 reported assaults. These were the months of October, 1960 (27), November, 1960 (23), and January, 1961 (25). It turns out that this period (October, 1960–January, 1961) was an especially significant one in terms of the history of city Z's civil rights movement. We have already noted the successful boycott of downtown stores which occurred from about December 15, 1960 to January 15, 1961. But this was preceded by a peak of mass activity in October and November, 1960. Mass arrests of demonstrators and the confinement of the city's civil rights leaders both took place during these two months of unusually low rates of assault.

It is also interesting to note that, except for the period just mentioned it was largely in the warmer months of 1960 and 1961 that most of the civil rights activity took place. Crime, especially assault, is at its greatest during the warmer months. The months of May, June, and July in both 1960 and 1961 were all months of civil rights activity, whereas these same months in 1959 and 1962 were inactive, as far as direct action for civil rights is concerned. The average number of assaults in these civil rights months, compared with these noncivil rights months was 46 vs. 56.

Certain anecdotal material from interviews appears relevant to the process by which the direct action for civil rights might have affected a violence-prone segment of the Negro community in city Z.

In 1960 and 1961, a student civil rights leader decided to spend as much time as he could in poolrooms and bars talking with lower-class Negroes about "the issues" over which the civil rights groups were then doing battle with the "white power structure." Although his success in gaining really active recruits was limited, he discovered several surprising things. First of all, virtually everyone in the bars and poolrooms was well acquainted with all the details of the sit-ins and boycotts as they occurred. Secondly, the two issues of mistreatment by the police and segregated employment were very meaningful ones to these people, and they found common cause with the civil rights demonstrators over them. Thirdly, and most impressive, a sense of the hope and of the power of organized direct action began to creep into the lives of these ordinarily rather hopeless people. This is illustrated, somewhat humorously, in the following incident which the student observed from a distance. One afternoon during the boycott, a bartender became verbally abusive to a patron who was apparently speaking rather loudly. Some of the other patrons told the bartender, "Let him talk! Let him talk!" When the bartender persisted and became even more abusive, all the customers joined in telling him, "You better let him talk or we'll *all* leave." The bartender let him talk.

The student placed this incident in the perspective of a "definite change of attitude" in the lower-class people with whom he had chosen to acquaint himself. During the period of direct action civil rights activity, "a 'cat' would have something to live for—not just a five day week, then get it off his chest by getting drunk on Saturday night."

CITY A

Our second, designated city A, is in the Deep South not far from city Z. It has a population of 60,000, virtually no Negro middle class, and a reputation for police brutality and unequal administration of justice. Details of the crime picture are not available from its Police Department. City A is brought up here only because the young leader of the civil rights movement there has been quite successful in converting members of delinquent juvenile gangs into nonviolent workers for civil rights. The leader was interviewed several times, and his reports were corroborated by others familiar with his work.

The leader's work with the gangs grew out of necessity, not design. Soon after he had begun organizing meetings and protest marches and had come into conflict with the police, he discovered that his group's activities were receiving unasked for "protection" of a violent sort. For example, young people from delinquent gangs would "protect" a civil rights meeting in a church by standing outside throwing bricks at white policemen. Soon the civil rights leader—a former seminary student —was able to persuade the delinquents that they were needed instead as guards *against* violence, assigning them the job of "policing the area to make sure no violence occurred and to make sure nobody was waiting outside who should be inside at the meeting."

Over the next two years, about 200 members of four different gangs of out-of-school, out-of-work Negro teenagers received some training in nonviolent techniques and have become rather effective workers for voter registration, thus aiding the regular members of the local civil rights group, most of whom are in school or have jobs. Reportedly, delinquency among the gang members has diminished markedly, although sometimes the civil rights leader has had to personally "cool off" gang wars and personal rivalries to avert the bloodshed that used to be the order of the day.

TOWN X

Town X, which has a population of less than 20,000, is situated in a rural part of a border state. The Negro population is about one third of the total. The town is controlled by a small number of wealthy whites who are adamant segregationists.

At the time of the Civil War, at least half of the Negroes were enslaved, and town X was the major slave trading center for the area. Geographical factors have made the city isolated, and even today it lacks a train service. In the 1920's the city became a "Company town" in which almost the entire labor force, white and Negro, were employed by one firm. After the second World War, however, various factors caused the decline of the "Company," so that early in the 1950's its machinery finally ground to a reluctant halt.

This alteration in the economic status quo produced a meteoric rise in unemployment. A federal report in 1962 described the town as "economically distressed." Despite the founding of numerous small industries during the last ten years the unemployment rate among Negroes is still between 30% and 40%. The new factories, being obligated to the city council, apparently preferred white workers, and as more and more Negro job applications were ignored, the first stirrings of racial unrest were heard in the community. For the Negroes benevolent exploitation by a small group had been replaced by total inattention. The disintegration of the Company had removed the barriers of social structure which had, for years, kept the Negro community in a state of enforced "contentment." A Negro adult from town X summed it up recently: "At one time we coloreds here used to admire the whites and look up to them. But, then something happened—I don't know, everybody was out of work—and they didn't look so good any more."

Later in 1961, members of several interested organizations visited town X to investigate conditions there as they affected Negroes. Gradually, the local chapter of the NAACP (which had been virtually inactive for years and was composed mainly of middle-class Negroes) was superseded by the formation of a local committee for nonviolent direct action. Early in 1962 demonstrations took place which were met with resistance from the white community. Throughout the year outside help continued to arrive in the town, and further sit-ins and picketing took place. About 90% of those arrested for misdemeanors in 1962 civil rights activities were so-called Freedom Riders from outside town X. Because of some disagreements within the local movement, the winter of 1962–1963 was quiet and relatively uneventful.

The spring of 1963 heralded the arrival of Congress of Racial Equality (CORE) officials and members of student organizations. The local nonviolent action group was under new leadership, and demonstrations were in active progress by May. A mass arrest took place, which highlighted the movement in the national press. In June, the Negro community had an explosive reaction when two teenagers were sent to reform school for illegal demonstrating. Prior to this incident, some local leaders had experienced difficulty in raising crowds to demonstrate; but now, they had to beseech them to remain in their homes, lest violence should ensue from inadequately planned demonstrations. An army of police reinforcements occupied the town and the situation resembled one of martial law for much of the summer. Gradually, the mutual fear of violence eased, and negotiations were resumed. Demonstrations were suspended in August and September while a temporary compromise was being worked out.

Perhaps the most important single fact about the movement in town X is that it was conducted almost entirely by *lower-class* Negroes. After the pattern of most revolutionary movements, a few key leaders were middle class. But, in fact, most middle-class Negroes remained aloof from the action, and by their passivity incurred hostility and contempt as "Uncle Toms," with the result that their property was sporadically damaged by angry youngsters on the periphery of the movement.

Because of the longitudinal nature of the civil rights action outlined above (five months of maximal organization in 1963, some activity in 1962, none in 1961), town X was thought to be a propitious place to investigate the incidence of crime among Negroes in temporal relation to the movement. For the purpose of the study it was decided to investigate the period of May through September for the years 1961, 1962, and 1963. It is felt that this period reflects the situation in terms of a progression from virtual inactivity to explosive action. This progression seems to be reflected in data on major crime in the town. The police reports of town X for the months of May through September show that the number of Part I Offenses recorded during this five-month period in 1963 was 31, a very low figure. During this period in previous years, records show 49 reported offenses in 1962 and 73 in 1961. By way of contrast, the number of reported offenses in the four months *before* direct action began in 1963 and in the three months after it had subsided, showed approximately the same crime rate as the previous two years (see Table 4). Unfortunately, these figures do not include reports of assaults,

TABLE 4. *Town X Part I Offenses (Murder, Robbery, Burglary, Larceny)*

	1961	1962	1963
May–Sept.	73	49	31
Jan.–April	38	49	35
Oct.–Sept.	21	31	30
Total (annual)	132	129	96
Total adult arrests by the police force—all offenses	(Data missing)	386	429

and there is no racial breakdown, although it is known that Negroes *normally account for about 50%* of the arrests for "major crime" in town X.[a]

Because the relevant police records with racial breakdowns are unavailable, we thought of studying the Emergency Case records of the General Hospital in an effort to estimate the number of injuries resulting from assaults by Negroes during the time periods in question. Table 5

TABLE 5. *Town X Emergency Room Cases—Assaults by Negroes*

	May	June	July	Aug.	Sept.	Total
1961	1	7	7	2	4	21
1962	1	4	0	7	1	13
1963 All cases	0	1	4	4	1	10
1963 "Ordinary" cases	(0)	(0)	(0)	(4)	(1)	5

This table represents the number of injury cases arising from assaults by Negroes in town X, which were treated in the Emergency Room of the local public general hospital. The figures include only assaults which occurred within the city limits and do not take into consideration the assaults perpetrated by members of the migrant labor force (see text). The bracketed figures in the last row are corrected to *exclude* assaults directly connected with civil rights action—eg, injuries incurred during clashes with the police. The period represented is May through September of 1961, 1962, and 1963.

shows the incidences including those arising from racial rioting and police violence. The last line in Table 5 is corrected to exclude these cases, and represents the "routine" number of cases treated. Both tables exclude assaults perpetrated in the local labor camps, as it is felt that those were essentially nonconnected with the movement. We were told that the Negro migrant workers, who come to the area during the summer months to harvest the crops, would not associate themselves in any way with the movement, and, in fact, stayed away from the town because they were "scared." (Parenthetically, it *is* interesting to note that the incidence of assault among the migrant workers showed no appreciable change. Indeed a slight increase was apparent, whereas the "routine" cases from local Negroes diminished sharply).

While it is felt that these figures do not represent the total number of assaults, they would seem to reflect a fairly constant proportion of the incidences and thus be suitable for our purposes. The

[a] An examination of Magistrate's Court's gross records of people arraigned on a variety of crimes indicates a similar trend. In the summer of 1962, 53% fewer *local Negroes* were arraigned on the various charges than were arraigned in the summer of 1961. The summer of 1963 saw a slight rise in the total, in that a reduction of only 25% below the 1961 figure was apparent. It is fair to assume, though, that the reason 1963 showed more cases than 1962 is that a substantial number of disorderly conduct and trespass arrests took place as part of 1963's civil rights effort by local Negroes. (The 1962 civil rights arrests, it will be recalled, were largely of people from out of town, though that year's efforts were obviously watched by the local populace with avid interest.)

one Negro physician in the community quite independently supported the accuracy of the trend shown in these hospital records in stating that "during the summer of 1963 I stitched only three or four cases, when in other years I would have seen a dozen in the same period of time."

Many local leaders were interviewed in conjunction with the study, and their anecdotal impressions are of some interest. For example, the Public Health Inspector, whose duty it is to control the spread of venereal disease, particularly among crime-prone lower-class Negroes well known to him, observed: "Many of the contacts I sought, who would normally have been in jail, were living at home or could be found with their friends."

One of the principal Negro leaders estimates that there was much less crime in general: "People became interested in the movement, and were reluctant to do anything to jeopardize its progress. Most of the 1962 arrests were Freedom Riders—not locals. By 1963 there was a unification of common interest, and people who before were indigent and depressed, suddenly found that they had something to live and fight for."

Another local movement leader had anticipated trouble from the "winos" (alcoholics) and for this reason she felt that they should not be included in the protest marches. However, she was surprised to find that with special attention from the sober and more responsible members, they behaved themselves admirably and turned out to be exemplary, if somewhat passive, demonstrators. A student leader attests to this and quotes the case of a young alcoholic who had a long history of arrests. "He apparently was accustomed to being in the County Jail, but while the movement was strong and active he never was in trouble, although he continued to drink." When the student returned to the town later in the year, months after all activity had ceased, he met the man leaving the jail; he had just been released and was heading for a bar.

Many factors may influence this apparent decrease in the incidence of crimes involving personal violence. Most of the local people quoted above mentioned that a temporary ban on retail sales of alcohol and the imposition of a curfew were important inhibitors. One reliable report, however, indicates that "bootlegged" alcohol was readily available for anyone who wanted it. Group identification and interest in the Cause, strengthened by the persuasion of the leaders, were the factors most commonly selected for mention. One leader said that during the marches "We found ourselves breaking ranks to intervene in sidewalk scuffles and family squabbles, so that there may well have been more than an indirect influence."

The civil rights struggle in town X was not totally devoid of incidental violence. A student civil rights worker, who spent the summer in town X, indicts a small splinter group for the violence which did occur in the early summer of 1963. "There was a great deal of interest during early July in the movement from this group—young, violent types. As soon as the police had a permanent hold, and the movement continued to threaten to demonstrate but never did, they provided the biggest lobby to continue demonstrations, even at gun and bayonet point, and constantly threatened to act on their own if the movement itself would not. They spoke to us often about this, because we (the college student staff) also wanted to resume demonstrations. They never carried out any of their major threats, although one assumes that they were the group responsible for the various crimes related to the movement from the Negro ward," such as throwing bricks at policemen and attacking the property of whites and so-called Uncle Toms.

Nevertheless, there are certain factors in town X that make it quite surprising that *more* violence did not occur. Among the lower-class Negroes of town X, there is a great contempt for the local police force. Arrests and jail sentences do not carry any social stigma; imprisonment is merely something unpleasant which must be endured. On one occasion during the summer, a group of jeering Negroes surrounded a white policeman who had drawn his gun, and dared him to shoot. The same attitude of sullen hostility was in evidence toward the dogs which were used occasionally by the police. (The dogs were returned to their kennels, we understand, when it became clear that they had failed to have the desired effect on the demonstrators.) In other words, town X could be considered a "tough" town with a "tough" population of unemployed Negroes, many of whom became actively involved in direct action programs for civil rights. The fact that crimes of violence apparently *decreased* during this tense summer would hardly have been a predictable phenomenon.

COMMENT

The material we have presented raises many questions, certainly more questions than it has answered. We hasten to state categorically that the findings are suggestive, but by no means conclusive.

There seem to us to be four areas that warrant discussion and exploration:

1. To what extent are the data reliable?

2. Assuming the data *are* reliable and suggest a diminished incidence of crime committed by Negroes during periods of direct action for civil rights, what are the possible explanations for this relationship?

3. What implications might all this have for an understanding of violence in populations of the poverty-stricken and socially disadvantaged?

4. What further research is indicated to shed light on the effect of organized social movements on the behavior of lower-class populations?

We have already remarked that probably the majority of criminal acts go unreported and that collection of crime data by police departments is often quite unreliable. One can never be sure what factors, including chance, may be operating to influence the crime reporting process. Even when one finds a police department (such as the one in city Z) that prides itself on its crime reporting, there is still much to be desired in the uniformity of crime reporting from city to city.

Nonetheless, even taking these limitations into account, it is interesting that the statistics we have collected show the definite trend that they do, and that supplementing the police statistics with hospital Emergency Room records (as we have done in town X) reveals the same trend. It is possible to argue that this apparent trend is based on a change in contact between the police and the Negro community. Perhaps the police were so busy with civil rights demonstrators that their contact with or recording of crimes of violence within the Negro community was altered; i.e., their attention and concentration of forces were elsewhere. Or, perhaps, during economic boycotts Negroes are more careful to shield crime from the eyes of the police and white authorities. If these be so, any drop in crime rate is more illusory than real.

While these are real possibilities, there is at least anecdotal evidence to the contrary. During periods of "racial tension" in the South, the police force generally pays particularly close attention to the Negro sections of town and keeps a close vigil for potential violence of all kinds. Furthermore, where we have been able to supplement police data with medical information, as in town X, the incidence of medically recorded injuries resulting from personal violence has shown a decrease during civil rights activity.

Obviously, it would further strengthen the case for our hypothesis if we could present parallel data from comparable communities which have had no direct action civil rights programs. Unfortunately, we have not yet been able to obtain appropriately comparative data.

Assuming for the time being, then, that the reduction in the incidence of crime was *real*, not merely apparent, how might this be explained?

Perhaps when there are important events upon which the attention of any community is focused there is distraction from the forms of behavior which might otherwise lead to crime. Is the reduction of crime in these instances an epiphenomenon of the focusing of group attention on unusual public events? (There are some reports, for example, that crime in Washington, DC was reduced somewhat during the period following President Kennedy's assassination. Would the same have been true of the 1962 Cuban Crisis or of a World Series?)

Or, perhaps the explanation lies in a deterrent effect of the increased number of policemen on patrol during periods of protest, or the potentiality of such an increase. In city Z, at least, this "deterrence" could not have been a large factor in the sustained diminution of assaults during 1960 and 1961. The major form of protest during that time was an economic boycott which did not involve the local police very extensively.

There is some sociological and psychological data that might suggest a basis for the possible existence of a causal relationship between organized direct action for civil rights and reduced crime among Negroes. A long-term effect of segregation upon lower-class Negroes has been a blocking off of their social and self-assertion—economically, socially, and psychologically.[8,3,5] Open expression of their resentment against second-class status has been blocked off in both South and North. We would agree with other authors that this damming-up of resentment is one reason for the high incidence of crime among lower-class Negroes;[8,9] this is further supported by the fact that the vast majority of violent acts by Negroes are directed toward other Negroes. To put it another way, one might say that for the lower-class Negro, avenues have been closed off by the social structure, so that violent crime against members of his own race is one of the channels of least resistance open to him for the expression of aggression. When he becomes aggressive *against segregation,* the Negro's sense of personal and group identity is altered; race pride partially replaces self-hatred, and aggression need not be directed so destructively at the self or the community. The concept of "prosocial acting out" has been set forth elsewhere[3,4] to describe risky, aggressive, somewhat impulsive actions which the actor sees himself taking "for the good of society." These actions are thus distinguished from the diffuse lashing out against social institutions that characterizes "antisocial acting out"—although in some cases, the psychodynamic roots of the two types of behavior may be quite similar.

When large scale direct action civil rights activities are launched in a community, the leaders face a herculean task of community organization. The members of the community must be recruited, trained, and organized into a disciplined, nonviolent army. Networks of communication and transportation must be arranged, for large numbers of people must be united behind a single effort. It is the pooling of resources, the setting up and certifying of goals, priorities, and methods in a community effort to produce social change that draws neighbors together in an organization whose very existence would tend to discourage crime (particularly crimes of violence against each other). If the community organization process is successful, each man, through the combined strength of his and his neighbors' efforts, can have that seat at the "community bargaining table" that has traditionally been denied him. Each man learns that possibly his personal welfare and certainly the welfare of the movement requires unity in the Negro community. As a result of the need for unity, people begin to know their neighbors and their neighbors' problems. A spirit of common concern pervades the community and serves to discourage crimes of violence.

The data we have presented do not indicate any long-lasting effect of organized civil rights activity upon the crime pictures of city Z and town X—although seemingly permanent gains have been made with the juvenile gangs of city A. In looking at the crime data from city Z and town X, it is clear that after the major civil rights action had ceased, the number of reported crimes by Negroes returned fairly promptly to the frequency that was customary before the "movement" began. It is impressive, though, that a reduced crime rate for Negroes was sustained in city Z for two full years before going back up to former levels. Furthermore, when crime rates returned to frequencies comparable to earlier years, there was no "rebound phenomenon" of a net *increase* in violence which (had it occurred) might have been attributed to frustration of hopes which had been "stirred up" by the civil rights movement. Indeed, in city Z the 1962 frequency of assaults by Negroes is somewhat *below* what one would expect in view of the increase in population over 1959.

It is apparent from these data that direct or vicarious participation in the partial successes of civil rights direct action movements did not solve all the problems of violence-prone, socially disadvantaged Negroes. In recent months in town X, for example, the leaders of the civil rights movement have become less and less interested in equal access to public accommodations but increasingly adamant about obtaining federal relief of poverty and unemployment in the area. Whether civil rights leaders across the nation are feeling a continuing responsibility to plan for and press for improvements in the life conditions of the low-income Negro is a question that cannot be dealt with here, although there are several recent signs pointing in this direction.[b] This shift in emphasis by civil rights groups represents an increasingly sophisticated awareness of the multifaceted nature of the problems faced by Negroes, both North and South. In spite of successes in the South, however, the direct action civil rights groups have been largely unable to organize the socially disadvan-

[b] For example, in November, 1963, the "militant" Student Nonviolent Coordinating Committee (SNCC) held its annual leadership conference on the theme of "Food and Jobs." The meeting was held in Washington and featured conference-workshops with federal officials on the subject of existing programs that could possibly be of aid to the rural Negro in the South.

taged Negroes of the North—perhaps because they have been perceived by the residents of Northern Negro slums as being mainly interested in public accommodations and voting rights. At this point in time, the deprived Northern Negro is cynical about the value of a public accommodations law or the right to vote. He lives in areas of the country where there are few statutory or semilegal sanctions to prevent him from eating at a lunch counter, going to a movie, or voting. Yet, he is still denied equal employment opportunities, good housing, and respect from police officers. The Northern slum Negro sees himself as still not being "free," and until effective methods are found to combat his problems, he will often choose between the unfortunate alternatives of either accepting his fate or lashing out with hate and violence. In our opinion it seems unlikely that the civil rights groups will be able to effectively organize the socially deprived Negro in the urban North; it may instead be the black "hate" groups that will be successful, unless substantial efforts are made to relieve the social and economic deprivation of the Northern Negro.

This brings us to our concluding remarks. We feel it should be emphasized that if our findings are verified, there is then a very strong argument that the kind of community organization and psychological mobilization inherent in the civil rights struggle may be of prime importance in the development and implementation of various crime prevention programs and "anti-poverty" programs. It would appear that such programs—which, after all, are often aimed at lower-class Negroes —could learn a great deal from the interactional and motivational processes involved in the direct action civil rights movement. Yet, surprisingly little research has been done or is being done on just *how* the movement functions and the process of its development. The study of process requires a multidimensional approach including both that of statistical reporting and anecdotal observations. This technique requires considerable further development. It is our hope that the need for such research will have been made more apparent by this presentation.

SUMMARY

Data are presented which suggest a substantial reduction in crimes of violence by Negroes in three cities during periods of organized protests and "direct action" for civil rights in those cities. The findings are based on official crime reports, medical records, newspaper accounts, and interviews with residents of the three communities (two cities in the Deep South and one in a border state).

It is hypothesized that Negroes release long dammed-up resentment of segregation by asserting themselves (directly or vicariously) in direct action for civil rights. Such emotional expression, when it occurs in a framework of community organization may reduce the need for aggressive outbursts of a violent sort, thus reducing the incidence of such crimes.

We note that further research into the functioning of the civil rights movement may produce fruitful implications for programs to prevent crime and battle poverty.

REFERENCES

1. Crime Drops Overnight, March Plans Credited, *Washington Evening Star*, Aug 29, 1963, p. B-1.

2. TALESE, G.: A Happy Day in Harlem, *New York Times*, Aug 29, 1963, p. 19.

3. FISHMAM, J. R., and SOLOMON, F.: Youth and Social Action: I. Perspectives on Student Sit-In Movement, Amer J Orthopsychiat 33:872–882 (Oct) 1963.

4. SOLOMON, F., and FISHMAN, J. R.: Youth and Social Action: II. Action and Identity Formation in First Student Sit-In Demonstration, J Soc Issues 20: 36–45 (April) 1964.

5. SOLOMON, F., and FISHMAN, J. R.: Psychosocial Meaning of Nonviolence in Student Civil Rights Activities, Psychiatry 27:91–99 (May) 1964.

6. Federal Bureau of Investigation: 1964 Manual for Uniform Crime Reporting, Department of Justice.

7. PEARL, A.: Personal communication to the authors.

8. KARDINER, A., and OVESEY, L.: Mark of Oppression: Psychosocial Study of American Negro, New York: W. W. Norton & Company, Inc., 1951.

9. MYDRAL, G.: American Dilemma, New York: Harper & Brothers, 1944.

Howard Elinson

RADICALISM AND
THE NEGRO MOVEMENT

There are two important reasons for discussing groups with radical views on race relations in the context of an analysis of the Negro movement. First, the radicals and the mainstreamers have common roots: the desire of one for rapid integration and of the other for radical separation both stem from a deep dissatisfaction with the seemingly permanent hypocrisy of the ideals of equality coupled with the realities of racism. Second, the successes or failures of each group are of consequence to the other. Our understanding of the mainstream is inadequate if we are not sensitive to its relationship to the radicals.

For the purpose of the present article, we must make explicit the distinction between the terms "mainstream" and "radical." The use of the word "radical," like the expression "extremism" in the 1964 Presidential contest, indicates a moral and political judgment. For the purpose of this paper, we regard as radicals individuals and groups who, while supporting the cause of the Negro, dissent from any of several such traditional American values as racial equality, the restriction of social movements to legal and nonviolent means, and political change through the usual processes of representative democracy. Further, most of those we refer to as radicals see American society as so evil and corrupt that any significant improvement in the lot of the Negro would require some sort of revolutionary structural transformation rather than gradual piecemeal reforms. While dissent from these traditional values is a defining characteristic of the radical groups we are interested in, it is by no means the only way in which they diverge from common American values. We will also consider the rejection of such ideals as progress, material comfort, and conventional social organization. Three radical groupings will be discussed: the black nationalists, the authoritarian left, and the new anarchists.

BLACK NATIONALISTS

Perhaps the best known radicals in the Negro movement are the black nationalists. The national publicity given the Black Muslims and their one-time spokesman Malcolm X has made the existence of black nationalism a matter of common knowledge.[1] The basic ideological commitment of all such nationalist groups is to a separate social existence for the American Negro. Ideas on how this separate existence might be accomplished vary from group to group and from time to time. However, several formulations are common: (1) a separate territory either in the form of an all-Negro geographical region (the key element in Black Muslim doctrine); (2) the conscious development of Negro ghettos as voluntary arenas for a separate group life; (3) the development of a Negro economy that runs parallel to the white economy but excludes whites, thus protecting Negroes from dependence on the white man's mercy for economic survival; (4) the exclusion of white businesses from Negro neighborhoods; and (5) the development of all-Negro factories and agricultural communities.

Separatists generally insist on social segregation of the races founded on voluntarily segregated churches, voluntary associations, and kinship systems. Underlying these separatist notions are the ideas that whites as a *race* are morally inferior to Negroes (in some versions, evil incarnate) and that white hatred and exploitation of Negroes are so extensive, and whites so unrepenting and unyielding, that only radical separation can improve the status of the Negro. Corollary to this is the conviction that white liberal efforts on behalf of the Negro are not only insincere, but are machinations to guarantee the continued exploitation of Negroes.

Popular knowledge concerning black nationalism tends to be vague and inaccurate. The greatest misconceptions concern its size and "militancy." Although exact membership figures are impossible to come by, it can be stated that the least accurate sources of information about the size of radical groups are, most often, the groups themselves or their enemies. Both are inclined to exaggerate. Muslim spokesmen have claimed as many as 250,000 followers. The figure of 100,000 has been widely circulated by other Muslims and many journalists—perhaps in an effort to make the movement appear more menacing or to add to its news-worthiness. Even so reputable a sociologist as Arnold Rose repeats this figure in an article in a scholarly journal.[2] A count of the number of Black-Muslim mosques around the country and their approximate seating capacity, careful tabulation of attendance figures at public rallies, and the independent estimates of *Time, Newsweek,* and *The New York Times* suggest that the actual membership is between five and ten thousand.[3]

While it is true that radical movements often wield influence greatly in excess of their numerical strength, numbers do have meaning. The significance of a group with 5 or 10 thousand members can hardly be likened to that of a group with 100 or 250 thousand devotees. This is especially true of such groups as the Muslims, because they particularly lack one major advantage that can overcome low membership: members in strategic positions. The membership is drawn almost entirely from lower-class Negroes, and there are few Muslims, if any, in significant positions in business, labor, or government. The other black-nationalist groups are even smaller. E. U. Essien-Udom estimates the number of nationalists in Harlem, the center of the movement, at about 5,000—a figure that includes the large Muslim Mosque No. 7 in Harlem. Therefore, it seems safe to conclude that there are no more than 15,000 organized black nationalists in the United States at the present time— and probably considerably fewer than that.

While the *organized* influence of the Muslims and other nationalists is small, their ideologies transmitted by the mass media have an effect of unknown magnitude on the Negro masses. Certainly many Negroes who do not accept a separatist solution to their problems agree with nationalist attacks on whites. During the Summer 1965 riots in Los Angeles, some Negroes interviewed by the press would begin "I'm not a Muslim but," and then proceed to use Muslim rhetoric (e.g., "blue-eyed devils"). In most cases, the nationalists articulate and fan racial animosities rather than create them.

The second illusion about black nationalists is that they are "militant" in the sense that they are tougher, more courageous, and more dangerous to white interests than the mainstream civil rights groups. Surely this idea started with the nationalists themselves. They portray themselves as belligerent and determined anti-whites. The press convey the image to the public by quoting their words about the white man as "a walking, talking devil, the one with the guilty blue eyes, whom Allah will destroy," or by printing such pictures as that of a nationalist book store in Harlem with its large sign reading "The God Damn White Man—read this book." While the Muslims look to Allah for the white man's destruction, the secular groups advocate massive civil disobedience, some of them talking about guerrilla warfare and other forms of violent conflict with white society. Bayard Rustin, Tom Kahn, and Irving Howe have pointed out that most of the militancy of the black nationalist poses no real threat to whites.[4] Howe calls those suggestions of such things as guerrilla warfare "vicarious indulgence in violence, often merely theoretic and thereby all the more irresponsible."[5] Certainly, appeals for violence could be the prelude to organized patterns of actual violent conflict. Some radical groups attempt to enlarge and extend riots in Negro neighborhoods, because they see these riots as revolutions or rehearsals for revolutions. However, most nationalist activities are quite removed from the planning or organizing of armed rebellions. Rather, they articulate an ideology that vents anger by expressing hatred of whites, pride in being a Negro, and determination for revenge. The ideology allows Negroes to avoid the painful truths about the impossibility of a satisfactory separate existence and the difficulties of obtaining an integrated existence. By embracing utopian goals—with no clear ideas as to how these goals might be obtained—the nationalists are aligned more closely with the other-worldly Negro church than with civil rights groups that have a practical purpose.

THE AUTHORITARIAN LEFT

The attempt by leftist authoritarians to play upon the discontent of American Negroes is an old and recurring theme in the history of American radical politics.[6] From the time of the '30's when the Communist Party of the United States attempted to bring Negroes into the party to the present time, when Maoists see the Negro lower class as the true proletariat of Marxist theory, little seems to have changed.

The political radical left is characterized by a bewildering number of miniscule groups with names and programs that appear similar to the outsider.[7] It is beyond the scope of our discussion to indicate the subtle differences that cause such bitter divisions between various groups on the authoritarian left. Nevertheless, some basic distinctions are essential. By far the most important thing to note is the present role of the American Communist Party. Many persons far removed from leftist politics continue to think of the Communist Party as a vital revolutionary group having actual or potential significance in shaping the direction of the Negro's quest for greater opportunities. In truth, the Party is weak, small, and demoralized. The unpopularity of its views, the wave of disillusionment that swept the party as a result of the brutalities of Stalinism, awareness of the totalitarian nature of international Communism, and vigorous suppression and harassment by the federal government have greatly reduced its size and influence.[8] The recent "party line" on the Negro problem has been neither radical nor revolutionary. Instead, it has argued that all that can be done in the present political situation is to support the civil rights reforms proposed by liberals and, if possible, work for stronger reform measures. It is unlikely that the few regular CPUSA Communists who are in civil rights groups have intentions of subverting those groups, although their basic politicoeconomic outlook is alien to many people in the civil rights movement. Of course, the "party line" is subject to change, and what is left of party discipline could bring about a change in the attitudes and behavior of many party members. The party itself is not very active in the civil rights area, or for that matter, in any other area. The W. E. B. Du Bois Clubs have party members in leadership positions and follow a line similar to that of the party. A danger to the Negro movement is that the unsought and undesired support of the regular Communist Party or of groups such as the Du Bois Clubs will be used to discredit the movement as "Red." Accusations of Communist influence have been made by members of the radical right who favor segregation of the Negro. Occasionally these charges are picked up by more moderate politicians.

Perhaps more dangerous to the civil rights movement than the regular CPUSA are either the various small groups that are oriented towards Communist China, or the leftist authoritarians in underdeveloped areas, such as Castro or Sukarno. These groups have combined the extreme practices of the old-time Communist Party with some disturbing innovations. They have taken the rigid Marxism-Leninism of the old Communist Party, with only slight modifications. The chief element of their doctrine is the assumption that no significant changes are possible for the Negro within the existing society and that the only instrument of historical change is violent revolution. One consequence of these views is that while such groups say they are interested in the problems of the American Negro, they often actively *oppose* efforts to solve those problems by labeling such efforts as useless or inconsequential. The best examples of this are their traditional disparagement of the electoral system and their advice that Negroes throw away their franchise by not voting, by casting blank ballots, or by voting for obscure third-party candidates. Recently, for example, in New York City, the Progressive Labor Movement, a Peking-oriented Communist group, scoffed at the proposal for a civilian review board which would hear cases of alleged police brutality. The idea of a civilian review board in New York and elsewhere has long been a key demand of the Negro community, and the absence of such a board has been one of the most deeply felt grievances. The Progressive Labor Movement opposes the idea by arguing that only a revolution can solve the problems of police brutality; that piecemeal efforts such as a review board merely distract the Negro masses from the revolutionary struggle.[9]

Many of those sympathetic to the problems of the American Negro and anxious to find realistic solutions to those problems are understandably disturbed by the antics of the authoritarian left. The efforts of these groups to divert Negroes from practical efforts to improve their conditions may be morally indefensible; however, evil intentions and potential for evil are not the same thing. It should be kept in mind that the groups on the authoritarian left are exceedingly small and have little direct influence. Some are nothing more than a handful of people with a ditto machine and a post office box. Most Americans, white and black, are either in sufficient accord with American values or sufficiently apathetic that they are totally uninterested in the possibility of a Communist revolution in this country. Even at the depths of the Great Depression, surprisingly few whites or Negroes were attracted to movements of the totalitarian left.

THE NEW ANARCHISTS

The most recent group of radicals to arrive on the American scene seems potentially the most important. It has been variously labeled the new radicals, new left, and spontaneous left.[10] It consists of a very loose connection of groups and individuals. The expression which seems to us to capture their most important characteristics is "new anarchists." There are no civil rights organizations in which all the members are new anarchists. However, there are several in which the new anarchists are sufficiently prominent to be a dominating force. The Student Nonviolent Coordinating Committee, the Congress of Racial Equality in some areas —particularly Berkeley and New York City—and a new organization, Students for a Democratic Society, are presently the organizations in which the new anarchists hold sway. Many of the new anarchists use the issues raised by the Negro movement to secure civil rights as their springboard for broad and radical protest against various aspects of society. These broader interests have found expression in the student protests at Berkeley and in student opposition to recent American foreign policy.

Few observers have correctly judged the nature and the mood of the new anarchists. Roland Evans and Robert Novak of the *Washington Post* have sensed the sharp differences between the new anarchists and the "mainstreamers" in the civil rights movement.[11] They have been inclined to see Communist infiltration as a major element in understanding SNCC's radicalism. However, the radicalism of SNCC is very different from the radicalism of the Communist Party. In fact, the Communist Party's emphasis on ideology and disciplined organization is antithetical to SNCC's emphasis on free expression and loose, almost nonexistent organization. One source of confusion is that SNCC people, on moral grounds, refuse to take seriously the question of Communist infiltration or its possible consequences to the success of their program. Ruth Montgomery quotes an SNCC worker as saying:

> I don't think there are any Communists on our staff, but I don't consider it relevant anyway. We feel that anyone willing to risk his life working for Negro betterment in the South ought to be allowed to work, whether he's Republican, Socialist, Democratic, or Communist.[12]

This view is in sharp contrast with that of the majority of Americans who see Communists as categorically different from other political groups because of their history of infiltration and subversion of various reform movements. People with conventional political views and radicals with strong democratic convictions single out the Communists for special opprobrium. The failure of new anarchists to share these sentiments should not be taken as a sign of pro-Communist sentiment. It is only a sign of their refusal to take seriously certain common political concerns.

The goals and principles of the new anarchists are extremely difficult to describe, partly because the movement is committed to an ideology of nonideology; they are prone to deny that they have any set program. They explain that the leaders do not lead but are, rather, instruments of oppressed groups in the society. Rather than going to oppressed people with a program, the new anarchists claim that their major effort is to help these people articulate and achieve whatever aspirations and goals they, the people themselves, may have. Despite denial of ideological commitment, several principles of the new anarchists can be discerned.

The new anarchists are not ordinary liberals sympathetic to the working class and to minority groups and interested in obtaining limited gains for these groups by conventional political means. The radical flavor of their views appears in the following statements of purpose. The first is by the editors of *Liberation,* a magazine which features contributions by new anarchists and is widely read in new anarchist circles. The second passage, from the Port Huron Statement, was formulated at the founding convention of Students for a Democratic Society.

> We do not conceive the problem of revolution or the building of a better society as one of accumulating power, whether by legislative or other methods, to 'capture the State,' and then, presumably, to transform society and human beings as well. The national, sovereign, militarized, bureaucratic State and a bureaucratized collectivist economy are themselves evils to be avoided or abolished . . . It is the transformation of society by human decision and action that we seek.[13]

Port Huron Statement:

> . . . we seek the establishment of a democracy of individual participation governed by two central aims: that the individual share in those social decisions determining the quality and direction of his life; that society be organized to encourage independence in men and provide the media for their common participation . . .[14]

A frequently recurring theme is the desire to create "communities." The concept of community is personal and moral, rather than political. The ideal community, like the anarchist utopias of old, is free from coercive, centralized power, is thoroughly equalitarian, and is ruled "from the bottom up" rather than from "the top down." This concept is similar to the idealized and romanticized version of American small towns in the nineteenth century, minus the presence of capitalism and a class system—that is, a community in which important decisions can be and are made at the local level, with the decidedly left-radical touch that people not only know and care about each other, but do so on terms of absolute equality. In some ways, this idea is quite reactionary. First, the longing for a return to a *gemeinschaft* form of social organization is the frequent basis for rightist movements and social critiques.[15] Second, there is a deeply rooted Western notion of human freedom which is antithetical to gemeinschaft society. This concept of freedom respects privacy of opinion and action, so long as such acts do not endanger the society. The right to be left alone and to remain anonymous is the source of the contrast between the freedom of urban life and the oppressive social restraints of rural or small town life.

The new anarchists perceive the impersonal, cold, and instrumental human relationships in an urban, capitalistic and industrialist society as the root of human misery. Some view racism as merely an extreme form of a far more pervasive tendency for people to treat other people as things. They are determined to help the oppressed into new forms of social organization. In their devotion to the development of communities, they reject the goal of bringing Negroes or poor whites into the business-as-usual of American society. According to this viewpoint, the means for creating communities is not that of democratic politics—which are too shallow and authoritarian. Rather, forms of community organization must be built which give the participant a sense of meaning and mastery, identity, and belonging. In this view, politics creates new values and new lives along communal lines. It is in sharp contrast to the usual view of politics as a vehicle for groups to achieve the political and economic advantages necessary to their pursuit of the conventional American dreams of individual and conjugal family acquisition of property, achievement of status, and experience of social mobility.[16]

Directly related to the new anarchists' notion of community, and equally radical, is the notion of participatory democracy.[17] In its pristine form, this idea calls for political decision making along the lines of the ideal Quaker meeting. All participants are of equal importance, and rule is by means of worked-out consensus (the "sense of the meeting") rather than by conventional parliamentary means.

Ruth Montgomery quotes an SNCC official: "All our decisions are arrived at by staff consensus, whether we stay in session a day or a week to reach agreement. . . ."[18]

From this view of participatory democracy, our conventional forms of representative democracy are a sham. Voters have only an imprecise veto over the decision makers and no real opportunity to make decisions. Crucial decisions are made by bureaucrats, technicians, and hidden elements of a power structure. Attempts by leaders to assume responsibility to speak for the people are viewed with suspicion or alarm. Staughton Lynd gives two excellent examples of this view—both of them dealing with the SNCC leader Robert Parris.[19] Parris is so disinclined towards the conventional exercise of leadership roles that he sits in the back row at meetings rather than sitting on the platform. He tries to avoid speaking; but if called upon, he rises, remains in his place, and, instead of making policy suggestions, asks provocative questions which help the people at the meeting lead themselves. Considering their orientation it is understandable that the new anarchist elements in SNCC are critical of Martin Luther King's Southern Christian Leadership Conference. They are disturbed by its reliance on mass meetings in which impoverished Negroes are led by means of "demagogic" speeches from outside leaders. In Mississippi, SNCC has been the guiding force behind the formation of the Mississippi Freedom Democratic Party. However, some new anarchists are fearful of electing an MFDP candidate to office; he might go off to Jackson or Washington and be co-opted by conventional politics. According to Lynd, Parris suggests that the candidate might refuse to take his seat and remain in his district as an expression of solidarity with his constituents.

There are two important criticisms that must be made of participatory democracy, lest the superficial attractiveness of these ideas prevent clear analysis of them. First, it raises the specter of subtle and informal means of manipulation. The skilled leader who can bring a meeting to his views by means of gentle questions from the back of the room *can* be as manipulative as the pulpit demagogue. The conversational brotherly attempt to achieve consensus may lend itself to manipulation by the most articulate and persuasive elements in the group. Opposition to their views may go unheeded for lack of skilled proponents. Formal rules and laws of parliamentary procedure certainly do not prevent oligarchies or authoritarians from wielding great influence. Yet they provide certain safeguards which are missing from an informal loosely-structured system that relies heavily on the moral character of the participants. The larger the organization and the greater its scope of responsibility, the more impractical and even dangerous the idea of participatory democracy becomes. While it may make good sense for a small neighborhood organization, it is hard to imagine how a statewide convention of the Mississippi Freedom Democratic Party could operate under the norms of participatory democracy. It seems to us safer to entrust the rights of the minority, the right of majority rule when consensus cannot be reached, and the control of cliques and manipulators to Robert's *Rules of Order* or federal or state constitutions.

The second, and perhaps more important, criticism of participatory democracy is: assuming that it is more more moral and more democratic than the conventional forms of rule-regulated democratic organization, is it so grossly inefficient as to endanger the goals of the movement? In a sense, this is the old and sticky question of means and end. For the new anarchists, participatory democracy is both means and end; for others, the forms of organization are means—vehicles—to separate ends: desegregation, job opportunities, voting rights. Could small-scale participatory democracy accomplish what King and others have achieved with the less democratic means of leader-controlled mass rallies? The question is essentially rhetorical. Even conventional forms of democratic organization are not especially efficient. All our democratic organizations from the U.S. Senate to the NAACP or SCLC have strong authoritarian or oligarchic elements built into them. As in the arena of national politics, so in most voluntary organizations, the day-to-day decision making rests with an executive director or, at best, an executive committee. The democratic mechanisms operate to set general limits on the leaders' scope and to provide a permanent and reliable source of veto against unacceptable executive action. If conventional democracy is inefficient unless leavened by oligarchy, how much more inefficient participatory democracy must be! Some elements in SNCC are strongly opposed to a central headquarters; many accept such a headquarters only if its authority over local organizations is severely limited.

Clearly the new anarchists, with sincerity and deep moral conviction, are moving towards chaotic and inefficient forms of social organization. This is not new in the history of anarchism—rather it is one of its central and distinguishing characteristics: George Woodcock, writing of the almost complete failure of anarchist movements of the past despite great strength shown at some times in some places, concludes:

> It suffered also from the weakness of its own revolutionary tactics. Anarchist action, which had the virtue of spontaneity, had also the weakness of an almost complete lack of coordination. In the minds of the more conspiratorial anarchists there doubtless existed programs for the great strategy that would finally encompass the millennial social revolution. But the history of anarchist rebellion shows only a bewildering confusion of small insurrections, individual acts of violence, and strikes which sometimes served to keep society in a state of tension but which had no lasting results.[20]

We have not even touched on the question of the ability of lay persons—especially very poorly educated and barely literate Southern Negroes—to make the actual decisions of government. Even the simple local problems of lighting and street paving seem to have a technical side which requires training and experience. Surely the more complex matters of statewide schools and roads and the construction and administration of complex budgets seem to be out of the reach of ordinary people. Obviously we believe that the possibilities of participatory democracy are limited and that the doctrine introduces a possible source of great inefficiency in the civil rights movement.

Perhaps the most important question to be asked about the new anarchists is that of the relationship between their goals—albeit somewhat unformulated ones—and the aspirations of the majority of American Negroes. We believe, partly on the basis of how Negroes have reacted to opportunities in the North and partly on the basis of intuition, that the vast majority of American Negroes are extremely conventional in their values and aspirations. We believe they have, by and large, bought the "American Dream" as a target for their aspirations and would like to use their growing political power to ensure a reality that will resemble that dream. Simply put, we believe that most Negroes want to live in nicer homes (not just free of rats, but closer to the ideal homes of television and *Life Magazine*); they would like to own more television sets, boats, cars, records, and dish washers; they would like to see their children go to integrated schools that would help them succeed (probably not to search for Truth, but, rather, like other Americans, to learn how to make good livings and obtain prestige in the community); they would like to eat out more often in nicer restaurants and go on longer vacations to more exotic places. Their dream is one of full inclusion in the mainstream of American life—the good and bad of it—rather than a creation of a new world different from, and morally superior to, anything we have known. Here again the new anarchists seem not unlike their historical forebearers:

> Linked to the failure of the anarchists as revolutionary actionists was the weakness of their practical proposals for the society that would follow their hypothetical revolution. There was much honesty in their refusal to make elaborate blueprints of the new world they hoped to create, but their disinclination to attempt specific proposals led to their producing a vague and vapid vision of an idyllic society where the instinct of mutual aid would enable men to create a variety of cooperative relationships unimaginable in the enslaved present.[21]

Since the old-fashioned anarchists were often committed to violent means, it is appropriate here to take up the question of the tactical predispositions of the new anarchists. On the question of means, as on the question of goals, they shy away from dogmatic ideological commitments. They seem for the most part to be committed to nonviolent means. Some are oriented towards a principled pacifism. Others, however, have been attracted to and have flirted with the justifiability of armed self-defense. There have been two important moves in this direction: the effort by Robert Williams to arm Negroes in Monroe, North Carolina, and, more recently and on a larger scale, the organization of the Deacons for Defense and Justice. Robert Williams, who is now in Cuba, and has been on close terms with Communist China, is well regarded by many new anarchists. In Bogalusa and Jonesboro, Louisiana, CORE, an organization with many new anarchist members, has cooperated closely with the Deacons.[22] Both Williams and the Deacons indicated that their interest in arms was of a purely defensive nature. However, for some, probably a fairly small minority, interest in violence extends beyond self-defense. The widespread admiration for revolutionary leaders and movements in the underdeveloped world, such as Castro and the Viet Cong, strongly suggests that some of the new anarchists may have views similar to more traditional revolutionary leftists.

Both the size and significance of the new anarchists are exceedingly difficult to gauge. SNCC, the most important organization in which new anarchists are active, is not a membership organization in the usual sense. Its staff organizes highly autonomous movements and organizations in various communities in the South. The problem is further complicated by the fact that by no means all, or even a majority of the people involved in SNCC activities are new anarchists. Many Southern Negroes involved in SNCC-sponsored activities seem quite conventional in their goals and aspirations. They are interested in increasing the number of Negroes registered to vote or gaining specific desegregation concessions in their local community. The only thing that can be said with any assurance is that the number of new anarchists and their positions and powers of persuasion have enabled them to affect noticeably the nature and direction of SNCC activities. This was clear in the refusal of the Mississippi Freedom Democratic Party to accept the compromise seating plan at the 1964 Democratic Convention and their general unanimity in denigrating the plan and interpreting it as a defeat. Without going into the merits and problems of the plan, which was hammered out by Hubert Humphrey and Joseph Rau of the ADA, we can state that it was not merely an attempt to prevent a Southern walkout. It gave strong symbolic recognition to the justness of the MFDP cause and, far more significant, laid an elaborate and powerful foundation for the barring of "lily-white" delegations at future conventions. The MFDP reaction was prompted by an intolerance for the ambiguities or hypocrisies (depending on one's viewpoint) of conventional politics. MFDP suffered no substantive loss, since the convention delegates merely gave symbolic assent to the Presidential and Vice-Presidential nominations and the platform chosen by President Johnson.

Outside of SNCC there are few important centers of new anarchist influence. Organizationally the most important is Students for a Democratic Society. It claims a membership of 2,000, based on 79 college campuses. Its power appears to be limited to public protests that call attention to grievances and small-scale efforts at community organization in a handful of Northern slums. In the Berkeley and New York City areas, there are a large number of people sympathetic to Students for a Democratic Society, though most are not members.

The small number of people involved in new-anarchist activity outside the SNCC efforts in the South would seem to mean their significance could be generally ignored were it not for one fact: their willingness, indeed anxiousness, to resort to unlawful means to disrupt the "business as usual" of what they regard as an evil society. We use the phrase "unlawful means" rather than "civil disobedience" advisedly. The philosophical foundations for civil disobedience by the civil rights movement in the South have been twofold: most important has been the conviction that it is moral to disobey unjust laws. The sit-ins and Freedom Rides of the early '60's were a deliberate violation of segregation laws in an effort to get the laws changed. The laws being violated were usually local or state ordinances in conflict with federal law or the decisions of the federal judiciary. In a few cases, the laws violated were not in themselves unjust, but were being used in an unjust and prejudicial manner. For instance, Southern law officials used legitimate laws dealing with blocking traffic or inciting to riot to prevent civil rights groups from exercising the right of peaceful assembly.

Civil disobedience in the North by new anarchists has followed an entirely different course. The laws violated are rarely, if ever, segregation laws. Their constitutionality rarely is in question. Nor are they generally being applied in a discriminatory fashion. Finally, unlike the lunch counter sit-inners who desired to abolish the law being violated (segregated facilities fixed by Jim Crow ordinances), the Northern law violators often had no desire to abolish the law being violated. They intended rather to use law violation only as a vehicle for the expression of protest and as means of pressuring the authorities or "society" in general. A few cases will make these points clear. The New York World's Fair stall-ins, which were proposed by new anarchist elements in the New York civil rights movement, were not designed out of objection to laws which prohibit people from interfering maliciously with the flow of traffic. Those laws are of neither doubtful morality nor doubtful legality. The announced purposes were to "call attention to grievances" and "bring pressure."

During the 1965 Selma voter registration drive, there were acts of law violation in some Northern cities. The law violators sat in or blocked the entrances to public buildings, usually federal buildings, to pressure the government to send troops to Selma. No one questioned the morality and legality of the laws which prevent people from forcibly interfering with the conduct of government business. The same analysis holds for the occupation of an administration building on the Berkeley campus of the University of California by the Free Speech Movement. Obviously, people willing to break the law can cause great public concern and difficulty for the public official no matter how small their number.

As few as twenty or thirty people who are willing to lie down in doorways or in front of cars or busses, or to pull emergency brakes on trains or subways, or to turn in false alarms, can create social chaos. It is not yet clear whether they can do any more than that. There is reason to doubt whether significant concessions can be won by such tactics. However, some have argued quite convincingly that Berkeley students won substantial concessions from the University administration. The riots, vandalism, and looting in Negro neighborhoods in the East during the summer of 1964 and in Los Angeles in 1965 were not inspired by new anarchists. However, they may indicate potential gains to be made by unlawful means. Some claim that those neighborhoods have received increased attention from local officials on the problems of police brutality, violation of building codes, unemployment, and ghetto conditions in general. In all justice, it should be said that despite our own distaste for such tactics, their effectiveness is still open to debate.

Gains by legal means—peaceful protest, political strength, legislation, court decisions—weaken both the moral and tactical arguments in favor of unlawful means. We must face the fact that the failure of legal means to bring about change in those aspects of the Negro's problems which have a searing moral impact—fantastically crowded tenements with rat-bitten children, or the denial of the vote despite legislation—both weaken the moral and tactical case for restricting the Negro movement to legal means and can serve as powerful arguments in favor of ignoring the law and questioning the value of the entire legal system. In our opinion, the achievements and clear intentions of the Johnson administration call for every possible effort to exhaust the legitimate means available before even considering illegal means. However, there are many radicals and long-suffering Negroes who do not share our inclination toward moderation.

Of course, all of this agony about the morality of lawlessness derives from an essential commitment to a system of representative democracy and the rule of law. For many of the new anarchists, that system is thoroughly rotten. They see it as a hypocritical and immoral system which ignores the main features of American life while fostering oppression of the poor and the minorities, imperialism and war-mongering abroad, and a stifling and pervasive centralism through bureaucracy that crushes individual freedom. Mario Savio, the Free Speech Movement leader and a civil rights activist, refused terms of probation that would bar him from engaging in illegal protests with these words:

> I welcome the chance to reject probation because probation imposes order on how men should act . . . . I am also, in a sense, rejecting the coercive state power which acts against the claim of individual liberty . . . Revolution is a positive duty when power is in the hands of the morally and intellectually bankrupt.[23]

AREAS OF AGREEMENT

Each of the three main branches of radicalism is distinct from the other two. Black nationalism is marked by racism; the authoritarian left is characterized by commitment to violent revolution, abolition of private property, and the creation of a one-party centralized state; the new anarchists are distinguished by a quest for gemeinschaft community, participatory democracy, and by an abhorrence of centralism and bureaucracy.

Despite these sharp differences, there are several areas of agreement. First, all share the view that American society is basically unsatisfactory and in need of changes too extreme to be brought about by gradual reforms. Second, they view the mainstream groups—King's SCLC, NAACP, liberal Democrats, etc.,—as part of the Establishment or tools of the Establishment who, while pretending to work for change, are really helping to preserve the status quo. Finally, they agree that changes in the underdeveloped world are of great relevance to the American Negro. They believe that the struggle of the American Negro is not an isolated movement in American history but, rather, is part of the broader world-wide struggle of the oppressed or nonwhite or colonial peoples. Each segment of radicals has its own device for promoting this last belief.

The nationalists call attention to the African origins of the American Negro by proposing an alliance between American Negroes and the new African states against white imperialism. The authoritarian left has a broader view that includes among the natural allies of the American Negro not only Africans, but revolutionary Communists in Latin America and Asia. Among these, some have gone so far as to suggest that what the American Negro needs is a guerilla-type national liberation war analagous to the Viet Cong operation in South Vietnam. They have offered serious proposals for the creation of an independent black nation in the Southern Black Belt by means of guerilla warfare.

The new anarchists have been less systematic and more flexible in their formulation of the relationship between the underdeveloped world and their own struggle. It is alleged that there are strong black-nationalist elements within SNCC who share many of the views of both the nationalists and the leftist authoritarians. More widespread is a general sympathy for revolutionary leaders in the underdeveloped world. However, their sympathy is oriented more towards the style than the substance of changes in the underdeveloped world. Thus SNCC enchantment with Fidel Castro is primarily a matter of admiration for his battle in the hills, his style of dress and beard, and his general disregard for the standards and opinions of the American Establishment. It does not involve any systematic endorsement of Castro or any desire to emulate the concrete changes he has wrought in Cuban life.

The most important cases of cross-fertilization thus far are certain sympathies for black nationalism among authoritarian leftists and the flirtation with the possibility of violent revolution among new anarchists. For example, in order to capitalize on the Negro revolution, some traditional leftists, such as the Trotskyites, have moved away from the position that class, not race, is the variable relevant to revolution. The Trotskyites were interested in an alliance with Malcolm X and, since his death, have been active in promoting his views in pamphlets and on records.

EFFECTS ON THE MAINSTREAM

There are many important ways in which the activities of the radicals affect the course of action and the chances for success of the mainstream of the civil rights movement. These effects are not all in a single direction. The radicals both serve and threaten the goals of the mainstreamers.

As is often the case with radical movements, they do the spade work for their more moderate competitors. In the 1930's, Communist organizers developed class consciousness and political awareness among the workers only to find that many of the people thus awakened voted for Roosevelt. In Europe, many of the workers who were awakened and stimulated by anarchists were lost to conventional trade unions and Communist or Social Democrat political parties. Similarly many Negroes, awakened by radical groups to the injustices of our society, will, in the end, support Martin Luther King and vote for liberal Democrats. Many Negroes will regard their new aspirations as more readily attainable by conventional than by radical means. The Harlem Negro who is made sensitive to police brutality by the Black Muslims or the leftist sects may decide the best way to combat police brutality is to vote for a mayoralty candidate who most strongly supports a civilian review board and other reform measures. The more successful mainstreamers are, the more the radical efforts tend to play into their hands. Some credence for this idea can be found in the sharp decline in radical party votes from 1932 to 1936.

A second way the radicals exert a positive influence on the civil rights movement is by frightening and threatening the mainstream organizations into competing with them actively. There is little doubt that the old-line Urban League and NAACP have become more effective and dynamic in order not to lose ground to the newer and more radical organizations.

Perhaps the most useful effect the radicals have comes from the fact that they "take up space on the spectrum." The existence of "extreme" groups makes the NAACP or King's Southern Christian Leadership Conference appear more moderate and reasonable than they would if there were no radical organization.[24] Consequently, they become more acceptable to conservative elements. As little as the leaders of Southern white communities may enjoy dealing with King, they would rather deal with him than with SNCC. Further they may feel that unless the mainstream groups are reasonably successful, they will lose ground to the radicals. This leads to the resigned conviction that it is better to deal with the moderates now than to face a strengthened extremism element at some future time. Simply put, the radicals tend to move the entire movement in a more radical direction.

The radicals also have some decidedly negative consequences for the mainstream. First, the public at large and even some political leaders are either incapable of, or uninterested in, carefully differentiating between various civil rights groups. Many whites perceive such incidents as the advocacy of stall-ins at the Fair as a simple matter of "those Negroes going too far." Undoubtedly resistance to Negro demands has stiffened in some communities because of disorderly and illegal demonstrations by radicals. Perhaps some of this backlash is, as radicals argue, not a change in attitude but merely an expression of a previously concealed hostility toward Negroes. Nevertheless, extreme tactics do, in some circumstances, backfire. There is little doubt that anti-Negro sentiment and the support for conservative politicians can be increased by a massive hours-long traffic jam caused by civil rights demonstrators.

The second danger the radicals pose to the mainstream is that they will provide serious competition for members and financial support. While some people who have been sensitized to the issue of police brutality by the Progressive Labor Movement will vote for a mayoralty candidate who favors a civilian review board, others may be convinced by PLM ideology. They may spend election day discouraging Negroes from voting on the grounds that elections are a fraud, and only violent revolution will solve the Negroes' problems. The loss of potentially sophisticated and effective Negro citizens to extreme radical groups is certainly tragic. One wonders what Malcolm X might have accomplished for Harlem had he chosen the road of conventional politics. Even Adam Clayton Powell, with all his shortcomings, has returned far greater rewards to his constituents than the emotional satisfaction Malcolm's audiences may have received from hearing him damn the white man.

As noted, the radical pull may benefit the mainstream groups by infusing them with new spirit and ideas. Unfortunately it may also crush them by moving the entire movement from the realm of the possible to that of the impossible—from successful reform to principled but futile protest. Frequently the refusal to compromise is a prelude to the inability to make any gains. Those who demand all or nothing run a high risk of ending up with nothing.

CONCLUSION

In the course of our discussion, we have had harsh things to say about various radical groups. Let us conclude by candidly admitting that the radicals raise two questions of enormous importance which those of us who dissent from their views will have to answer.

First, the black nationalists raise the question of where Negroes fit into the pattern of American ethnic life. They are undoubtedly right in arguing that most whites are unwilling to see thorough integration—if by integration we mean the large-scale assimilation of Negroes. They are also right in arguing that the historical force of racism and segregation is so great that, regardless of attitudes, rapid wholesale integration is impossible in any foreseeable future. We must face several facts: (1) for a long time to come most Negroes will live in neighborhoods that are predominantly Negro; (2) many Negro children will continue to go to school primarily with other Negroes; (3) for both voluntary and involuntary reasons on the level of clubs, churches, friendship cliques, and family there will be little integration. In view of these facts, neither whites nor Negroes can be expected to completely ignore race. The nationalists raise the issue of how to come to terms with this problem.

The second great issue raised by the radicals is: how radically must American society change to satisfy the just demands of the American Negro? There are powerful arguments that neither the economic nor the political system can conduct "business as usual" and still produce the changes Negroes justly demand. Negroes cannot approach equality until either the economy adjusts to the impact of technological change or the political system compensates for the failure of the economy to make such an adjustment. In other words, there must be a lot more jobs with adequate wages for Negroes or greatly improved welfare programs. The education Negroes need for economic and social advancement can come only when the present system of low quality, poorly financed, highly segregated schools is replaced by schools that are radically better. The revolutionary radicals raise the critical issue of the need for large-scale social change if the facts and consequences of racism and segregation are to begin to disappear.

Citizens who are committed to representative democracy and racial equality will be impatient and, at times, enraged by agitation for violent revolution, anarchy, or black supremacy. However, the response to radicalism must be tempered by a firm commitment to the principle that the civil liberties of everyone—even the most radical groups—must be guaranteed in a way that is consistent with public safety and national security.

More important, the response to radicalism within the Negro movement must be informed by an awareness of the challenging questions the radicals place before America:

Can the Negro achieve ethnicity without racism?

Can we achieve social revolution without violence or chaos?

Those in the mainstream have the heavy burden of providing convincing affirmative answers to these questions, with all due deliberate speed.

REFERENCES

1. See, for example, E. U. Essien-Udom, *Black Nationalism;* C. Eric Lincoln, *The Black Muslims in America;* Louis Lomax, *When the Word Is Given;* James Baldwin, *The Fire Next Time.*

2. ARNOLD ROSE, "The Negro Problem in the Context of Social Change," *The Annals of the American Academy of Political and Social Sciences,* Vol. 357, January 1965.

3. "The size of the Black Muslim membership is an organizational secret. Some estimates have ranged as high as 100,000, but informed sources say it is actually between 7,000 and 8,000." *The New York Times,* February 28, 1965, Section 4, p. 1.

4. BAYARD RUSTIN and TOM KAHN, "The Ambiguous Legacy of Malcolm X," *Dissent,* Spring 1965, pp. 188–192; Irving Howe, "New Styles in 'Leftism,'" *Dissent,* Summer 1965, pp. 295–323.

5. HOWE, *op. cit.,* p. 317.

6. See, for example, Wilson Record, *Race and Radicalism: The NAACP and the Communist Party in Conflict* (Ithaca, New York: Cornell University Press, 1964).

7. HARVEY SWADOS, "What's Left of the Left?" *The Nation,* September 20, 1965, pp. 108–114; Phillip Abbott Luce, "Why I Quit the Extreme Left," *The Saturday Evening Post,* May 8, 1965; Richard Armstrong, "The Explosive Revival of the Far Left," *The Saturday Evening Post,* May 8, 1965.

8. Armstrong, *op. cit.,* p. 30.

9. LARRY COLE, "A City of Two Tales," *The Realist,* June 1965, pp. 26–27.

10. HOWARD ZINN, *The New Abolitionists;* Calvin Trillin, "Letter from Berkeley," *The New Yorker,* March 3, 1965; Irving Howe, *op. cit.;* C. Vann Woodward, "After Watts—Where Is the Negro Revolution Headed?" *The New York Times Magazine,* August 9, 1965, pp. 24, 25, 81–84; Harry Trimborn, "New Radicalism–Groping for the Past," *Los Angeles Times,* June 20, 1965, p. G1.

11. LERONE BENNETT, JR., "SNCC: Rebels with a Cause," *Ebony,* July 1965, pp. 146–153.

12. RUTH MONTGOMERY, "Director Tells About Student Rights Group," *Los Angeles Herald-Examiner,* April 9, 1965, p. D3.

13. Quoted in Andrew Popkind, "The Politics of Avoiding Politics," *The New Republic,* March 20, 1965, p. 20.

14. TRIMBORN, *op. cit.*

15. Romantic attachment to 19th century small-town America is mentioned as a characteristic of right wingers by several contributors to Daniel Bell (ed.), *The Radical Right* (Garden City, New York: Doubleday and Co., 1963).

16. *Ebony Magazine.*

17. *Studies on the Left* has developed a regular section, "With the Movements," which serves as a channel of communication and discussion for new anarchists. See, for example: "With the Movements," and "Notes and Studies on the Left," Vol. 5, No. 2 (Spring 1965), pp. 61–92, Communications section.

18. Montgomery, *op. cit.*

19. STAUGHTON LYND, "The New Radicals and 'Participatory Democracy,'" *Dissent,* Vol. XII, No. 3, Summer 1965, pp. 324–333.

20. GEORGE WOODCOCK, *Anarchism: The History of Libertarian Ideas and Movements* (New York: Meridian Press, 1962).

21. WOODCOCK, *ibid.*

22. JACK NELSON, "Deacons Pose Growing Threat to Rights Drive," *The Los Angeles Times,* July 11, 1965, p. 78.

23. ARMSTRONG, *op. cit.*, pp. 31–32.

24. For a discussion of the contribution which SNCC and CORE make to Martin Luther King's role as a leader of the "vital center" of the civil rights movement, see: August Meier, "On the Role of Martin Luther King," *New Politics,* Vol. IV, No. 1, pp. 1–8.

Politics and Power

Edward C. Banfield
James Q. Wilson

THE NEGRO IN CITY POLITICS

In five major cities outside the South, Negroes comprise more than one fourth of the population; in two others, more than one fifth; and in five others, around one sixth. The number of Negroes in the larger central cities has been increasing rapidly. Between 1950 and 1960, the twelve largest had a net loss of more than two million whites and a net gain of nearly two million Negroes. In view of all this, one would expect to find Negroes figuring prominently in the political life of the city. They often do, but rarely because of the elective positions they hold. As Table 1 shows, remarkably few of them are elected to office.

Not only are few Negroes elected to office, but those who *are* elected generally find it necessary to be politicians first and Negroes second. If they are to stay in office, they must often soft-pedal the racial issues that are of the most concern to Negroes as Negroes. Of course,

Reprinted by permission of the publishers from Edward C. Banfield and James Q. Wilson *City Politics* (Cambridge, Mass.: Harvard University Press, 1963). Copyright 1963 by the President and Fellows of Harvard College and The Massachusetts Institute of Technology.

Mr. Banfield is Professor of Political Science, Harvard University. Mr. Wilson is Associate Professor of Government, Harvard University, and Director, the Joint Center for Urban Studies, Harvard and the Massachusett Institute of Technology.

white politicians are not indifferent to the interests—or at any rate, the votes—of Negro constituents, but to the extent that the Negro wants to be represented in the sense of "symbolized" rather than "spoken on behalf of," the white politicians are obviously unable to do it. Since the Negroes do not always represent Negroes as Negroes, and since whites can and do represent Negroes to some extent, the underrepresentation of the Negro is in some respects greater and in some respects less than the figures in Table 1 suggest.

TABLE 1. *Negro representation on city councils in selected non-Southern large cities*

CITY	TOTAL CITY COUNCIL SEATS	SEATS HELD BY NEGROES IN 1961	PERCENT OF SEATS HELD BY NEGROES	NEGROES AS PERCENT OF POPULATION, 1960
Detroit	9	1	11.1	28.9
Cleveland	33	8	24.2	28.6
St. Louis	29	6	20.7	28.6
Philadelphia	17	1	5.9	26.4
Chicago	50	6*	12.0	22.9
Cincinnati	9	0	0	21.6
New York City	25	2	8.0	14.0
Los Angeles	15	0**	0	13.5
Boston	9	0	0	9.1

* Results of preliminary elections in 1963 indicated that Chicago would add one more Negro to its council.
** Results of preliminary elections in 1963 indicated that Los Angeles would probably elect two Negroes to its council.

The anomaly of the Negro's numerical strength and political weakness can be explained largely in terms of two interrelated factors: the class structure of Negro society and the character of urban political systems. Because of these factors, much of the Negro's civic action takes place, not in the city's electoral or legislative systems, but in the courts or (more recently) in the streets. And often even this "direct action" (e.g., protest marches and mass meetings), though it occurs in the cities, has the federal rather than the city government as its ultimate target.

NEGRO CLASS STRUCTURE

The most crucial fact about Negro class structure in the larger cities is that (as compared to white) the lower class is large and economically backward. So far as we are aware, no analytical comparative studies have been published in recent years. However, the Census figures in Table 2, which compare whites and nonwhites with respect to income and education, are indicative.

Lower-class people generally are withdrawn from politics, but lower-class Negroes may be especially so. To some extent, their failure to participate can be explained by the uncertainties of their situation. Uncertainty about jobs and housing and in a good many cases fear of the police keep many Negroes on the move. It is instructive that many of the Negroes participating in the 1963 demonstrations in Birmingham, Alabama, and Greenwood, Mississippi, were unemployed and therefore immune to economic reprisals by white employers. The high rate of turnover in lower-income Negro areas makes their full political mobilization particularly difficult.

TABLE 2. *Distribution of income and education among whites and nonwhites in Chicago, 1960*

	WHITE	NONWHITES
Income of families		
Percent under $3,000 per year	9.9	28.4
Percent $10,000 per year or more	26.3	8.7
Education of persons 25 and over		
Percent with less than 1 year of high school	41.6	48.0
Percent with 4 years of college or more	6.6	3.6

Source: 1960 Census of Population, PC (1)-15C (Illinois).

More important than transiency, however, is the social disorganization which is characteristic of lower-class Negroes and which is reflected in their high rates of crime, delinquency, desertion, divorce, and illegitimacy. This is in great part the result of the weakness of the family unit. The plantation system during the period of slavery made it difficult to form stable Negro families; the continuing lack of economic opportunities since then has made it difficult for Negro men to acquire the economic self-sufficiency to become the head and breadwinner of a family. Female-centered households are common among Negroes, and the "wandering male" who is only a part-time worker and a part-time husband has contributed to the high percentage of Negro families supported by either working mothers or welfare checks or both.[1]

The cultural and economic factors which make the lower-class Negro's family life so uniquely precarious also make his sense of attachment to the community uniquely weak. The attributes which community life presupposes—education, self-respect, personal skills, a belief in the efficacy of one's own efforts, and a sense of attachment to

[1] For vivid accounts of the lower-class Negro world and the family system see E. Franklin Frazier, *The Negro Family in the United States* (Chicago: University of Chicago Press, 1939); and St. Clair Drake and Horace R. Cayton, *Black Metropolis* (New York: Harcourt, Brace, 1945), chaps. xx and xxi.

social entities larger than oneself—are often in short supply because there is no strong family unit to inculcate them. Consequently, the social institutions of the city, and especially its government, are often looked upon by Negroes as (at best) remote forces to be ignored or (at worst) hostile forces to be reckoned with.

The inability to feel himself part of a larger community may extend to the neighborhood and "the race" as well; these may be no more able to command his loyalty than is the city. In such circumstances, it is not surprising that, however much a lower-class Negro may talk of abstract racial issues, they have a good deal less meaning to him than specific material considerations—a job, a place to live, a bed in the county hospital, and help when he is in trouble with the police.

Like all people who respond to specific material inducements, the lower-class Negro is a natural potential supporter of the political machine. As we have explained, there are now few white neighborhoods where a ward leader's offers of jobs, favors, and patronage have much appeal. Among the large and relatively disadvantaged Negro lower class, however, the situation is still very much as it was among immigrant whites two generations ago. But there is one very important difference. Because most white voters have ceased to want the machine's favors and have even come to feel contempt for it, the machine is a thing of the past in most cities and the ward politician has few if any favors to offer. Not having the material wherewithal to organize lower-class Negro voters, many party organizations rely instead on generalized loyalties to party labels, on the attraction of well-known national candidates, or (in rare cases) on developing "race issues"—like allegations of "police brutality" —which are considered relevant by these voters.

Often, however, a party which has been stripped of patronage resources by the reform movement and therefore cannot offer specific material incentives will endeavor to woo the lower-class Negro vote with *general* material incentives—particularly welfare payments of various kinds. For example, Negroes are the prime beneficiaries of the program of aid to dependent children. To curtail (or even to re-examine) such programs carries the greatest risks for a party in power because Negro voters, rightly or wrongly, will interpret such actions as "anti-Negro."

There have been some efforts to organize the Negro lower classes. The most conspicuous of these is the Black Muslim movement which uses frankly nationalistic, racist, and antiwhite sentiments to instil a sense of self-respect in Negroes.[2] By persuading the Negro that he is superior to whites, the "Muslim" leaders give him a sense of his own dignity sufficient to make him behaviorally, if not economically, middle-

---

[2] See the account in E. U. Essien-Udom, *Black Nationalism* (Chicago: University of Chicago Press, 1962).

class. And often this transformation in style of life is accompanied by an improvement in the Negro's material circumstances because he becomes more strongly motivated to acquire an education, useful skills, and a stable family. The Muslim movement disavows political or civic action, however, on the grounds that it is demeaning and disadvantageous to participate in a political and civic system which is the creation of whites and which ultimately can only serve their ends. But even if the Muslims should seek to wield influence in the cities, the nature of the movement is such that its enrolled membership can never be large. The ideology on which its appeal is based is sufficiently esoteric, restrictive, and even absurd that it cannot enlist large numbers of members.

Thus the first and most important feature of Negro social structure is the predominance of a lower class lacking a strong sense of community. And a second feature is the relative inability, or unwillingness, of the middle class to identify with the lower class and to provide leadership for it. In any community, of course, it is the middle and upper classes who provide most of the civic and political leadership. But in this respect the Negro faces not only those constraints which affect any group seeking to wield influence, but an additional set which arises out of the particular nature of the Negro community.

A middle-class Negro wears a badge of color that is associated with lower-class status, and therefore cannot take for granted that the difference between him and the lower-class Negro will be appreciated. Close contact with the lower class tends to obscure the status difference which he has been at enormous pains to establish. To eat spareribs on the street would entail psychic burdens for the educated and well-to-do Negro of a kind which, it is safe to say, eating blintzes does not entail for Governor Nelson Rockefeller. At any rate, the Negro middle class conspicuously avoids contact with the lower class.[3] The Negro politician, when not a member of the lower class, tends to be drawn from among those members of the middle class who are least averse to such contact. He seldom is a member of the elite of wealth and education. Often he is a

[3] The Negro middle class, according to Essien-Udom (*ibid.*, esp. p. 304), looks upon the Negro masses with contempt and shame, and the masses have no confidence in the middle class. "Most Northern lower-class Negroes do not share in any significant way the opportunities which integration 'victories' are supposed to bring them. Northern Negroes have the right to vote where they please; yet this has not brought them nearer to the 'promised land.' They are conscious of the inequality of fortunes between them and the Negro middle class and whites in general. A great many Negroes know (and are discouraged by this awareness) that they will live and die in the Black Belt. They are beginning to resent the Negro middle-class leadership. They even feel elation when a middle-class Negro is humiliated, harassed, or actually prevented by whites in his effort to enter the white society. They are indignant and humiliated when the 'exceptional' Negro marries a white person." Essien-Udom believes that a class struggle may impend between a "semisatisfied Negro middle class and the Negro masses."

new recruit to the middle class; as a politician, his class standing is likely to be marginal.

The relatively small Negro middle class is separated from the lower by differences of interest and ethos. Whereas the lower-class Negro is concerned with "welfare" goals, the middle-class Negro is concerned with "status" goals.[4] He wants the opportunity to move into an unsegregated suburb, to send his children to an unsegregated school, to join an exclusive club, to patronize the better hotels and restaurants, to have equal opportunities in his profession (to practice in an unsegregated hospital if he is a physician, for example). Needless to say, these things that are so important to the middle-class Negro rarely enter into the life of the lower-class one at all.

In some matters there is a clear conflict of interest between the two groups. The middle-class Negro, for example, may oppose establishment of a public housing project which will bring lower-class Negroes into his neighborhood, or he may support (perhaps not in a very conspicuous way) an urban renewal project which will clear out lower-class Negroes and so "upgrade" his neighborhood.[5] Police activity which the lower-class Negro finds harassing may be vigorously supported by the middle-class Negro who wants to live in peace and quiet. Such conflicts of interest are multiplied and exacerbated by residential segregation, which forces the middle class to live in the high-density slum in close proximity to the lower class.

The Negro middle class, like the white, places a relatively high value on community-regarding goals. To many of its members the primary "community" is the racial one, not the city. The preoccupation of these Negroes with status is not simply with their individual status; it is also—and often primarily—with the status of the race. To vindicate the principle of equal rights is generally at least as important to the middle-class Negro as to win concrete benefits, especially benefits of the "welfare" kind. In Chicago, for example, "race men" opposed the building of a new county hospital in the hope that overcrowding of the old one would lead to the break-down of segregation in private hospitals. To them the most important thing was to destroy the principle of discrimination, not to provide better facilities for hospital care. Probably most of the middle class—but very little of the lower class—agreed with this view.[6]

A third important feature of Negro social structure is the fairly

[4] On this distinction, see James Q. Wilson, *Negro Politics: The Search for Leadership* (Glencoe, Ill.: Free Press, 1960), chap. viii.

[5] See Martin Meyerson and Banfield, *Politics, Planning, and the Public Interest* (Glencoe, Ill.: Free Press, 1965), p. 234.

[6] See Banfield, *Political Influence* (New York: Free Press of Glencoe, 1961), chap. ii, esp. p. 43.

large and growing number of young people who have more education than the job market enables them to use. Between 1940 and 1960 the Negro's education improved greatly. His relative income improved also, but by no means as much, and most of the improvement occurred as long ago as World War II. Table 2 indicates that although Negro-white disparities in income are great, in education they are much less.

The consequence is that there are now a great many Negroes who are, so to say, half in and half out of the middle class. Some have college degrees but can find nothing better to do than work as postmen, clerks, and the like. Others find jobs in their chosen fields—they are lawyers, professors, and journalists, for example—only to discover that their employers will not promote them. Most of these young people live in the larger cities. Having plenty of time and nothing much to lose, they become the activists in Negro civic associations. As such they are dedicated, militant, and highly articulate.

A fourth important feature of Negro social structure is the relative fewness of entrepreneurs and the consequent importance of professionals. There are very few Negro-owned businesses of any size; most of the large businesses Negroes patronize—even illegitimate ones like "policy" (a form of gambling for small amounts)—are run by whites. Few Negroes, therefore, are wealthy enough to support large-scale political undertakings. Most of the proprietors are owners of very small retail stores and service establishments. The prosperous members of the middle class are mostly professionals. Negro professionals, like white ones, often tend to be antipolitical in outlook and to come under pressure from the institutions they work for—especially schools and government agencies—to stay clear both of partisan politics and of controversy of any kind.

A fifth feature of Negro social structure is that many important individuals and institutions have a vested interest in the maintenance of discrimination and segregation. Negro churches, political organizations, voluntary associations, schools, and businesses—and therefore, of course, the individuals whose jobs and status depend upon them—benefit from discrimination both because it is their reason for being and because it frees them from the necessity of competing on equal terms with whites. Residential segregation benefits them additionally by affording economies of scale: the more that members or customers are concentrated in one place, the better the opportunities to organize or serve them. "Had it not been for segregation," a Negro alderman in Chicago was quoted as saying, "Negroes would not have been able to advance politically here. It's the same with Negro business—segregation has been a Godsend to Negro business. It's nothing new. The Poles seek out the Poles, the

Germans seek out the Germans. Why shouldn't Negroes seek out Negroes?"[7]

That Negro institutions and leaders have this vested interest does not mean, of course, that they can be depended upon to support discrimination and segregation. To do that would get them in trouble with the large sector of Negro opinion that is influenced by "race" men. As a rule, moreover, antidiscrimination and antisegregation measures take effect so slowly and incompletely as not to endanger them greatly anyway. The Negro politician or minister can support a bill for "open occupancy" secure in the knowledge that its passage (which in itself may be unlikely) will not precipitate a mass exodus from the slum to the white suburbs. The individuals and institutions with a vested interest in discrimination and segregation are seldom to be found among the most aggressive fighters for reform, but they are not likely to be open opponents of it either unless it touches them very closely.

Negro civic organizations are small in size and short on resources. This is a sixth feature of Negro social structure, and one that is to a large extent explained by the other five.

In most cities that have substantial numbers of Negroes there are only one or two permanent Negro civic associations. The National Association for the Advancement of Colored People (NAACP), a militant Negro-rights organization, has (as of 1959) 1,366 branches and about 350,000 members. The Urban League, which until a few years ago was mainly occupied in finding jobs for selected Negroes but which now concerns itself with a wide range of problems, exists in most large cities. Although staffed and led by Negroes, it is largely financed by whites.

Recently four other organizations, all utilizing a protest strategy to advance their ends, have become an important part of Negro civic affairs. One is the Congress of Racial Equality (CORE); another is the Student Nonviolent Co-ordinating Committee (SNCC). Both utilize the "sit-in" and other forms of direct protest action. A third is the Southern Christian Leadership Conference (SCLC), the organizational extension of the personality of its founder, the Rev. Martin Luther King, Jr., the leader of the Montgomery, Alabama, bus boycott and later of the Birmingham protest marches. These three groups have been primarily (although not exclusively) active in Southern cities where the targets for protest are many and obvious and where little in the way of Negro political organization exists to impede them. The fourth group is scarcely an organization at all but rather a deliberately amorphous boycott

[7] *Chicago Sun-Times,* Jan. 6, 1963, p. 36. The alderman, Kenneth E. Campbell, was described as the heir apparent to the political power of Congressman William E. Dawson.

movement led, in various Northern cities, by Negro ministers—a group which for many years has played a relatively small role in militant Negro civic action of this kind. The ministers have induced Negroes, often with surprising effectiveness, to boycott certain business firms which failed to respond to Negro demands for jobs or promotions. The movement, which began in Philadelphia, is called the "selective patronage campaign." It is a frank effort to compel businesses to re-divide the existing supply of jobs.

Lower-class Negroes play little part in most of these organizations. Nor can the middle class be said to support them very well. NAACP's membership is small (see Table 3). Moreover, of the few

TABLE 3. *NAACP membership relative to Negro population in selected cities*

CITY	NAACP MEMBER-SHIP, 1959	NAACP MEMBERS AS PERCENT OF 1960 NEGRO POPULATION
Boston	4,859	7.7
Cleveland	12,318	4.9
Detroit	16,746	3.5
St. Louis	7,234	3.4
Baltimore	8,830	2.7
San Francisco	1,583	2.1
Chicago	12,051	1.5
Los Angeles	4,328	1.3
Philadelphia	6,797	1.3

Source of membership figures: Files of national headquarters, NAACP (New York City).

Negroes who contribute money to NAACP, still fewer contribute time and effort. A large NAACP branch is doing well if it turns out 10 percent of its membership for a meeting and 2 percent for active committee work. The average member contributes only his two-dollar minimum membership fee. Because of the indifference of most members, it is usually easy for a handful of militants to dominate the activities of a branch, at least until there is a general membership meeting. Then conservatives, who often control blocs of votes through affiliation with churches, businesses, labor unions, and ward political organizations, are likely to join forces to sweep the militants out.

The older, permanent Negro civic association, like the permanent white one, tends to be immobilized in matters of importance by conflict over the concrete meaning of its goals. The newer, often *ad hoc* organizations, the memberships of which are more cohesive because they are concerned with only one issue, are usually readier to take a stand and to act; however, they suffer the disadvantage of having few allies and little money.

Negro civic associations, both permanent and *ad hoc* ones, are generally most effective (in the North) when acting as "veto groups," trying to block a measure harmful to Negro interests. They have succeeded in preventing transfers of children from one school to another, in stopping land clearance projects, and in checking mistreatment of individuals by the police. They have been least effective in initiating new policies and programs, particularly ones the importance of which is mainly symbolic or ideological and which would benefit not specifiable individuals but the "race" in general.[8]

Given all these circumstances, what is remarkable is that any effective Negro civic action occurs at all. Yet it does, and more so each year. The source of much of this activity can be found in the college-educated but underemployed young men and women who constitute in many cities the backbone of the Negro volunteer activists in the NAACP, the "selective patronage campaign," and similar movements. and the successes of this group have raised the level of expectations governing the behavior of other, more conservative Negroes, with the result that the tempo and militancy of Negro civic action as a whole increases steadily. But because of the nature of these activists, the goals sought and methods employed are often of a special kind—status rather than welfare goals, protest rather than bargaining tactics, and with middle-class rather than lower-class backing. Institutions most susceptible to such campaigns are typically those such as city agencies which have legal power over some community activity and which in turn are vulnerable to lawsuits, political pressures, and adverse public sentiment. Thus, boards of education and police departments find themselves increasingly under attack in Northern cities by militant Negroes concerned about "*de facto*" school segregation and police treatment of minorities.

Finally, it must be said that the Negro middle class has always been the beneficiary of civic action undertaken in its behalf by white liberals (often Jews) whose political ethos is markedly Anglo-Saxon Protestant. In Chicago, agitation for a state fair employment practices act was for many years led almost entirely by Jewish organizations (even though few Jews expected to benefit from such a law); the campaign for integrated public housing projects was waged largely by an *ad hoc* group of white liberals; opposition to an urban renewal project (on the grounds that it was anti-Negro) was primarily the result of efforts of a Catholic

[8] See on this James Q. Wilson, "The Strategy of Protest: Problems of Negro Civic Action," *Journal of Conflict Resolution*, September 1961, pp. 291–303.

monsignor and a few Jewish allies. In New York, where Jewish and liberal organizations are even more abundant, race relations have been even more an activity of whites. The organization which led the successful fight for various "open occupancy" laws to eliminate discrimination in private housing was created largely by Jews and (although it had several prominent Negro officers) relied on white financing and white staffs.

Many Negroes regard this assistance as a mixed blessing. No one likes to take advice or be placed in a subordinate position in a cause which he feels is peculiarly his own. But perhaps more importantly, Negroes are beginning to feel that their white allies will not go "all the way" with them in efforts (such as selective patronage campaigns and other direct action rather than legalistic programs) to attain something more than purely symbolic victories.

EFFECT OF THE POLITICAL SYSTEM

These features of the social structure set certain boundaries (so to speak) on the nature of the Negro's participation in the politics of the city. Within these boundaries, however, a considerable variety of styles of Negro politics is possible. Which style will exist in a particular city depends mainly upon the nature of that city's political system. In other words, the nature of Negro politics (within the bounds set by social structure) depends largely upon the nature of white politics.

We will amplify and illustrate this general proposition by characterizing briefly the style of Negro politics in cities whose political systems are of the following kinds: (1) ward-based,[9] machine; (2) ward-based, weak organization or factions and followings; (3) proportional representation; and (4) nonpartisan, at-large.

Ward-Based, Machine

In a city with a partisan, ward-based machine, Negroes will be organized as a sub-machine and will have as many representatives in the council as there are wards dominated by the sub-machine. The councilmen will not (at least publicly) take a "race" point of view, however, or indeed any point of view not tolerated by the leaders of the city-wide machine. Chicago is a case in point. Negroes there have long had

[9] We use the word "ward" in a broad sense here to refer to any arrangement that enables a Negro candidate to face a geographically drawn constituency that is entirely, or mainly, Negro. The ward system is in contradistinction to the at-large one, in which the candidate faces the (predominantly white) electorate of the whole city.

machine-style politics.[10] For many years the most powerful Negro boss has been Congressman William L. Dawson, who controls five all-Negro wards and therefore a large contingent of ward committeemen, aldermen, and state representatives. Control of these wards gives Dawson a safe seat in Congress (he is chairman of the House Government Operations Committee) and a place in the high councils of the Democratic National Committee.

Dawson maintains his machine in the usual way, by exchanging jobs, favors, and protection for votes. Almost every weekend he flies to Chicago to sit in a shabby ward office in the midst of the slums and to listen to all who come to him. Where the direct, material interests of his constituents are at stake, he and his organization are ready to help; they will get a sick man into the county hospital, find out why an old lady's welfare check has not arrived, defend a beleaguered homeowner against the urban renewal authority, and go to the police commissioner, and if necessary the mayor, to see to it that a case of alleged police brutality is properly investigated. Matters involving Negro rights in the abstract do not interest them, however. These concern the militants, but they are not the base upon which the machine builds.

In the realm of general principles, Dawson is virtually apolitical. He very rarely speaks in the House (although he is highly regarded by the House leadership). On occasion he has publicly opposed the "race" position on important questions and at least once he and his lieutenants packed a membership meeting of the Chicago NAACP chapter in order to unseat a militant officer. In the city council it is the Jewish alderman from the University of Chicago ward who takes the initiative in race relations. The Negro aldermen vote for the measures he introduces, but they do not fight for them.

The Dawson machine is only part of the larger one controlled by Mayor Daley. In order to maintain his sub-machine, Dawson has to depend on Daley for patronage. He and those whom he controls must therefore support the candidates slated by Daley and the legislation proposed by him. No Negro alderman connected with the organization would seriously propose any measure that had not been "cleared" with Daley, and no Democratic Negro precinct captain would fail to urge a voter to vote against a Negro and for a white if the white was the organization candidate. "Ticket splitting," a Negro ward leader explained in a newspaper interview, "weakens my force." He was quoted as

[10] For the history of Negro participation in Chicago politics, see Harold Gosnell, *The Negro Politician* (Chicago: University of Chicago Press, 1935). For an account of contemporary Negro politics there and of Congressman Dawson in particular, see Wilson, *Negro Politics;* and Wilson, "Two Negro Politicians; An Interpretation," *Midwest Journal of Political Science*, November 1960, pp. 346–369.

follows: "When I report to the central committee that 15 to 20 percent of the people in my ward split their tickets, I'm not as strong as the man with 95 percent straight ballots. The Negro gains more by voting for a party and not for a Negro candidate. Candidates on a partisan ticket should get all the votes of that party—not just the Negro ones, or the Irish ones, or those of some other group."[11]

Ward-Based, Weak Organization

In a partisan city with ward constituencies but a weak party organization (e.g., a decayed machine) or a coterie of factions and followings, as many Negroes will be elected to office as there are wards in which Negroes are in a majority, and the Negro politicians will be those who can develop personal followings or take advantage of intra-party factionalism. Manhattan is one example. Its political system does not provide Harlem politicians with sufficient patronage and other resources to build strong organizations, nor does it give city-wide politicians sufficient resources to control the Negro leaders.[12] Because of the lack of party-controlled material resources, Negro politicians in Harlem compete with personal followings (sometimes based on racial demagoguery) and with club-based factions.

Congressman Adam Clayton Powell, Jr., the principal Harlem politician, is an example of the kind of politician such a system produces. For many years the pastor of a large and fashionable church, he is entirely without ward or precinct organization. A constituent would not go to him for a job or a favor (although they might go to one of his aides in his *church*). His appeal is almost entirely personal and ideological. He is handsome, eloquent, flamboyant and—at least as he appears to his public—passionately and uncompromisingly dedicated to the cause of racial justice. This being the basis of his power, Powell is beyond the reach of party discipline. Whereas Mayor Daley and Dawson can talk to each other as two executives of the same organization and whereas Daley as head of the organization can give orders to Dawson, Mayor Wagner can do little or nothing to influence Powell.

Also in Harlem is J. Raymond Jones, a Negro politician whose stock in trade is not ideology or racism but rather his exceptional ability to survive and even prosper in the bitter factional warfare of the community. He has usually been able, by carefully timed alliances, to obtain enough patronage, favors, and nominations for elective office to

---

[11] *Chicago Sun-Times*, Jan. 6, 1963, p. 38.
[12] Elsewhere in New York City—Brooklyn, for example—there is a party machine, and Negro politics is much as it is in Chicago. See Wilson, "Two Negro Politicians: An Interpretation."

maintain a firm hold on one part of Harlem but not to dominate for long all parts of Harlem. He was almost the only Tammany leader who foresaw that Mayor Wagner was going to defeat Tammany in the 1961 primary and who joined with the mayor in time to take advantage of that victory.

The factional politics of Cleveland is somewhat similar. There, most of the eight Negro councilmen maintain followings in all-Negro neighborhoods by being good fellows, by providing the associational attractions of political clubs, and by distributing limited amounts of patronage and favors. A few, however, are race-conscious, issue-oriented leaders whose appeal cuts across neighborhood lines. If the neighborhood-based councilmen had more patronage and other resources at their disposal they would doubtless convert their followings into full-fledged machines and take the seats of the issue-oriented councilmen. By the same token, if their political resources were less, they would probably be supplanted themselves by the issue-oriented politicians. As matters stand, both lower-class and middle-class elements of the Negro community are represented in the council; for that very reason, of course, the Negro councilmen do not constitute a unified bloc.

Proportional Representation

Proportional representation deserves brief mention here (despite the fact that it is used in only one city) because it leads by a different route to a result like that just described. Under PR, a Negro candidate appeals to what is for all practical purposes an all-Negro constituency (election is at-large, but the Negro expects to attract mainly Negro votes). In a PR city, too, the candidate has no patronage or other political resources with which to build an organization; therefore he too must depend upon showmanship and racial ideology. In Cincinnati, PR produced a Negro councilman as militant as Congressman Powell (although neither as flamboyant nor as unpredictable). This, indeed, was the principle reason why it was abandoned there in 1957.[13]

Nonpartisan, At-Large

In a city with a nonpartisan, at-large system the nature of Negro politics is radically affected by the fact that the candidate must face the

[13] On Negro politics under PR in Cincinnati, see Ralph A. Straetz, *PR Politics in Cincinnati* (New York: New York University Press, 1958), esp. chap. viii. The circumstances under which PR was abandoned are described in Kenneth Gray, *A Report on City Politics in Cincinnati* (Cambridge, Mass.: Joint Center for Urban Studies, 1959, mimeo).

whole (predominantly white) electorate and must do so without benefit of a party label. Detroit is a city with a system of this kind. In order to have any chance of success, a Negro candidate for the Detroit city council must have the support of a newspaper or of some important city-wide civic associations. This means that he must be acceptable to middle-class whites. A Negro who is light-skinned, Harvard-educated, and "reasonable" on racial questions stands the best chance. Although almost 30 percent of the people of Detroit are Negroes, there is only one Negro councilman among nine.

A Negro elected under the circumstances that prevail in Detroit is in an extremely difficult position. Without a strong Negro vote he cannot hope to be re-elected, and to get a strong Negro vote he must (since he has no jobs, favors, or other material inducements to offer) be aggressive on at least some racial issues. But he must also have the support of the press and the civic associations in order to be re-elected, and he will not have this unless he is "reasonable" from the standpoint of conservative, middle-class whites. Recently, Detroit's one Negro council-man narrowly escaped being crushed between these two forces. Charges were made of police brutality. The Negro councilman introduced a measure empowering the Human Relations Commission to investigate the police department. This became an election issue. Somewhat surpris-ingly, a newspaper supported him and he was reelected. Whether he can survive many such issues is hard to say.

NEGRO POLITICS IN THE SOUTH

What we have said applies to Northern cities; the situation in the South is different. In the smaller Southern cities, Negroes have generally been denied the right to vote or to hold office, and consequently their influence in civic affairs has been negligible. This has not been the case everywhere, however. In Atlanta, where almost a third of the population is Negro, Negroes have voted for many years and they have often held the balance of power between white candidates.[14]

After the school desegregation decision of 1954, the race issue came to dominate the politics of many Southern cities and the power of the Negro increased. Negroes registered to vote in large numbers, partly because federal laws and court orders gave them protection at the polls and partly because the urbanization and industrialization of the South raised their income and educational level and made them more politi-cally conscious and assertive. Today about 25 percent of the eligible

[14] See Floyd Hunter, *Community Power Structure* (Chapel Hill: University of North Carolina Press, 1953), pp. 49–50.

Negroes in the South are registered to vote. These are heavily concentrated in the larger cities.

In these cities, Negro political associations are forming and growing at a rapid rate. In Florida, for example, where between 1944 and 1956 Negro registration rose from 5.5 percent to 37.5 percent of eligibles, many political leagues, or voters' associations, have sprung up. In some instances these began under church auspices and then soon broke away. They have developed effective tactics for identifying to the Negro voter the candidates who are preferable without at the same time running the risk of hurting the candidates' standing with their anti-Negro white constituents, and they have organized the Negro voters to make their endorsements effective at the polls.[15] Unlike the ethnic associations that have long existed in the North, these leagues do not seek "recognition" by electing their own representatives to office. That is out of the question in most places, and therefore the Southern Negro political league concentrates on trading votes for commitments from white politicians. In the nature of the case, they cannot rely on financial contributions from Negroes who expect to be elected to office or who are already in office (there are too few of them); to a considerable extent, therefore, they get them from whites who want their endorsement.

In the North the goals of lower-class and middle-class Negroes are often in conflict and the political process tends to exacerbate the conflict. In the South, by contrast, Negroes of all social classes want very much the same things—especially desegregation of schools and public accommodations, access to buses and eating places, and voting rights— and their common struggle tends to unify them. In the South, too, the issues confronting the Negro are of a kind that lend themselves well to the use of the tactics of mass protest and litigation. There is evidence that Negro civic leaders in the South are more nearly in agreement on goals and have more support from their followers than in the North.[16]

HUMAN RELATIONS AGENCIES

More and more large cities have created, as either independent agencies or as committees under the office of the mayor, public human relations organizations whose task it is to supervise the enforcement of

---

[15] H. D. Price, *The Negro and Southern Politics: A Chapter of Florida History* (New York: New York University Press, 1957), pp. 67–81.

[16] See M. Elaine Burgess, *Negro Leadership in a Southern City* (Chapel Hill: University of North Carolina Press, 1962). Compare the case histories of issues reported there with those discussed in Wilson, *Negro Politics,* which deals with a Northern city: More data will be available upon the publication by Donald R. Matthews and James W. Prothro of their large-scale study of Negro political participation and community action in the South.

civil rights ordinances and to act as fact-finding and mediation agencies. The Chicago Commission on Human Relations, established in 1943, was the first of these and it is still one of the largest. It has a staff of about thirty professional and clerical employees, and a budget of about a quarter of a million dollars a year. As of 1961, forty or so other cities in the United States had created, by ordinance, such commissions. Fifteen of these are in Illinois. Comparable commissions can be found in New York, Detroit, Philadelphia, and elsewhere. In addition, there are committees—not endowed with statutory authority—which advise mayors on race matters. Because cities in many cases do not have the constitutional authority to enact laws in this field, legislation barring discrimination in public accommodations, housing, employment, medical facilities, and such areas has often been enacted by the state; and state agencies such as New York's State Commission Against Discrimination have been created to supervise enforcement.

Indeed, so many public and private agencies have sprung up in this field that the staff members of such groups have formed a professional society, the National Association of Intergroup Relations Officials (NAIRO), and are publishing a journal.

A public human relations commission occupies a crucial but ambiguous role in the politics of race relations. On the one hand, it is a staff agency created to advise the mayor; on the other hand, it is looked to for "action" by various individuals and groups who have grievances in this field. Furthermore, it has its own conception—ingrained in the staff —of its mission to remedy certain conditions even if no one organizes a formal complaint and the mayor does not ask for advice; in such cases, the human relations agency does not act as the transmission belt which carries reports of outrages suffered from the point of grievance to the mayor, city council, or city attorney, nor does it provide the mayor with advice on what remedial policies are needed and then sit back and wait while the mayor drafts an appropriate ordinance or executive order. On the contrary, the commission is usually engaged simultaneously in stimulating protest and then proposing solutions to the mayor to eliminate the protest thus stimulated. This, of course, entails an elaborate pattern of negotiation and an organizational ability to face in several directions at once.

The very structure of Negro civic life means that a public race relations agency, if it does anything at all, must act in part as a combination of NAACP and Urban League. When Negro organizations are prevented by internal constraints from pressing for a certain goal, the commission must organize pressure of its own. When the Negro organizations *are* spontaneously exerting influence, the commission often discovers that action in the particular area is not feasible and it thus must find some way of stopping or diverting the protest activity. At the same time, the commission must maintain good relations with affected private white organizations—businesses, labor unions, hospitals, schools, and so forth—so that it can negotiate some kind of acceptable solution to a given race problem which the mayor can then ratify. In the circumstances it is hardly surprising that city human relations commissions are seldom completely successful.

Race becomes an issue in other kinds of city agencies as well, not just in those primarily charged with human relations work. In most large cities, it is an unwritten but unbreakable rule that a Negro must be appointed to certain kinds of boards and commissions—the public housing authority, the school board, the urban renewal or land clearance agency, perhaps the police commission, and so forth. The extent to which such Negro "representation" has an effect on the substance of public policy in these areas is problematical; in any case, it is sure to vary greatly from city to city. Everything depends on the terms on which the appointment is made.

In a city such as Chicago, where the Democratic party is powerful and where politics controls rewards sought by many, the mayor can appoint a Negro almost on his own terms. There are plenty of lawyers who depend on the party for business, advancement, and judicial appointments, even though they may hold no public or party office. Their service on a public commission is shaped by their expectations of future rewards and penalties and—what is equally important—by habits and attitudes acquired over years of intimate acquaintance with political leaders and deep involvement in the party's style of life.

In cities where there is no controlling party, where politics is nonpartisan or factional, and where each person must build his own career on an individual basis, Negroes may be able to dictate the terms on which they will accept appointment. Every city administration needs to legitimize its decisions; every city administration resorts, in some measure, to group representation as a way of achieving this legitimacy; but cities vary greatly in the extent to which they really depend on this sort of "front." Where the city administration lacks other sources of authority—where it has no machine and no faithful followers—it may attach a very high value indeed to the legitimacy that group representation can confer. In such a case it must seek out those representatives, including Negroes and other minorities, who have the greatest prestige as a result of their participation in *nonpolitical* activities—voluntary associations, businesses, churches, education and so forth. The price the city must pay to obtain such men, of course, is a willingness to alter substantive policies to take into account the objections and recommendations of the members of the commission.[17]

> [17] Philip Selznick makes a similar argument when he distinguishes between "formal" and "informal" co-optation in the TVA. "Formal" co-optation reflects the need to establish the legitimacy of the institution without actually sharing power (this corresponds to Negro appointments in Chicago). "Informal" co-optation refers to the need to adjust the institution to specific centers of power in the community by actually sharing power. Selznick, *TVA and the Grass Roots* (Berkeley: University of California Press, 1953), pp. 259ff.

Samuel Lubell
THE POLITICS OF RACE

MONA LISA SOUTHERNER

One intriguing feature of the public's first reaction to President Lyndon B. Johnson was the revelation of how much of our political thinking is done in symbols, to which we attach our prejudices and interests, our hopes and fears.

To loyal Kennedy supporters the new President's opening speech to Congress was assurance that "he'll hold to the liberal line." But to other voters the significant symbol was Johnson's being "a Southerner" which to them meant "He's bound to be more conservative" than Kennedy had been.

While Negroes were delighted with the President's pledge to fight for Kennedy's civil rights bill, most Southerners dismissed the pledge as "something Johnson had to say" and felt certain "he's bound to go slower" on civil rights.

The fact that he was a Southerner succeeding Kennedy, in short, gave Johnson the political equivalent of that mystifying Mona Lisa half-smile into which everyone could read his own hopes and expectations.

But if the immediate effect of Johnson's presence in the White House was to blur the conflict that had threatened to tear apart the Democratic party, this development stirred its own questions. Could the Johnson blur be institutionalized, which might usher in a new unprecedented one-party Democratic dominance? Or were the elements in conflict beyond conciliation for long? And what strategy was left for the Republicans to follow?

The early voter reaction to Johnson left little doubt that he would be able to bring at least temporary unity to the Democratic party. Throughout the South, which had been rumbling with political fury against the Kennedy brothers, there was an immediate upsurge of enthusiasm. Some Southerners were stirred with pride over having the first lifelong Southerner as President since Abraham Lincoln's assassination put another Johnson (Andrew) into the White House.

"He sounds like one of us!" exclaimed a limousine driver in Greensboro, N.C.

An airport attendant at Raleigh remarked, "When Johnson quotes from the Bible I know he's like the people I was raised with."

Other voters explained their shift to Johnson by saying "I went against Kennedy because he was a Catholic. But I'm still a Democrat."

But probably the key reason for Johnson's popularity in the South was the almost universal expectation that "he won't push as hard" as Kennedy did on civil rights. To Southerners generally Kennedy, and even more so Brother Bobby, had come to symbolize an extreme pro-Negro position. A factory foreman in Birmingham summed up the feeling of much of the South when he remarked, "That was a rotten way for Kennedy to go, but I'll be frank with you, I think Johnson will be a big improvement. He understands the South."

With this feeling, though, went a readiness to accept more of a civil rights program from Johnson than would have been taken from Kennedy. In the first few weeks after Kennedy's death, seven of every ten Southerners interviewed thought "some law has to be passed."

The feature of the bill which provoked deepest concern was the provision that would open to Negroes hotels, restaurants and other public places. In Richmond, Va., a college janitor who also owned a restaurant voiced a typical protest, "It's taking my rights and giving them to others. If they come into my place my white customers may go somewhere else. They could put me out of business."

"I'd let Johnson have it," said one Louisiana builder, "if I thought he wouldn't enforce it."

This readiness of Southerners to accept moderate civil rights legislation is not as surprising as it might seem. Actually, only a minority of Southerners, mainly in Mississippi and Alabama, believe desegregation can be halted completely. Their best hope has been to slow down the process. "We'll get it no matter who is President," was the commonly voiced feeling. "Maybe Johnson will do as well for us as anyone could."

That Southern resistance could flare up again quite quickly was made clear by the responses given me to the question: "What if Robert Kennedy is named for Vice-President with Johnson?"

More than a third of the pro-Johnson supporters declared, "I'd vote against Johnson if Bobby Kennedy runs with him."

Typifying their angry reaction were remarks like these:

"Running Bobby Kennedy would be hitting the South below the belt."

"I'll never take a chance on a Kennedy becoming President again."

"He's not for the white man."

In short, while agreement on some civil rights law seemed likely, it could hardly prove more than a shaky truce, constantly in danger of being upset. Also, as the past has shown, each new piece of civil rights legislation or court decision only sets the stage for a new, bitter struggle over enforcement.

Whoever is President is likely to find himself facing the same critical test that confronted both Kennedy and Eisenhower: Should federal toops be used to enforce integration in the South?

Either the militant Negroes or die-hard segregationists could force the President's hand—the segregationists by refusing to obey a court order, the Negroes by pressing their demands to the point of disruption.

Both Kennedy and Eisenhower suffered sharp drops in popularity in the South when they called out the troops. In the future the reaction could prove even more explosive politically. The new uncertainty is how white Northerners may react, particularly if Negro demonstrations and disturbances in the North coincide with violence in the South.

Put another way, Negro militancy seems to be transforming the civil rights struggle from what has been a North-South conflict into what could become a conflict of whites against Negroes across the whole nation.

By opening a second front in the North the Negro militants exposed themselves to the counterattack of a Southern appeal for alliance with Northern whites who might be alienated by Negro demands.

The first testing of that threat was recorded in the vote for Alabama's Governor Wallace in the 1964 presidential primaries in Maryland, Indiana and Wisconsin.

The fact that this racial struggle has become a two front war heightens the urgency for national policies that will break the racial deadlock. But the prospect of Northern white support for the Southern viewpoint could stiffen resistances to effective racial action. The deadlock that grips the Democratic party could tighten rather than ease.

The full political effects of this change may take years to register, but they clearly will add to the stresses and strains within the Democratic party. To keep the Democratic coalition from splitting will require strenuous political exertions.

These exertions will not be confined to racial actions. In fact, the more difficult it becomes to quiet racial tensions the more attention Democratic leaders are likely to give to bolstering the other ties that hold the Democratic following together.

While all the efforts that will be made cannot be foreseen, three lines of likely action can be indicated.

First, increased recognition will probably be given the Negro in the big city machines. In New York City some Democratic leaders have been making plans to turn their political clubhouses into "job agencies" for Negroes who would be employed on city projects. Other patronage favors will be extended as means of strengthening the faithful Negro Democrats against the more militant Negroes outside of the machines.

But such a strategy could backfire. In Philadelphia the new job preferences given Negroes angered even the staunchest party workers in white neighborhoods. Back in 1959 there were 33 precincts which voted 90 percent Democratic for mayor. In the 1963 mayor's election the Negro precincts in this group voted 85 percent Democratic, but the white precincts broke to only 65 percent Democratic.

A second result of the struggle to keep the Democratic coalition from flying apart is likely to be to strengthen the pressures for nominating a Catholic for Vice-President, or for President, once Johnson is out of the running. In most Northern cities the strongest resentments against Negroes are found in neighborhoods inhabited by Catholics and migrants from the South. One likely consideration in the naming of the Democratic candidates will be the reasoning that a Catholic on the ticket would cut down any potential Democratic defection among white voters over racial issues.

The risk to the Democrats, of course is that such a stratagem would keep alive the religious issue that dominated the 1960 election.

Third, heavy reliance will be placed on actions designed to strengthen the economic appeal of the Democratic party.

My own interviewing has often disclosed voters who threatened to bolt the Democratic party in racial anger, but who would reverse themselves when asked, "What if the President came out strong for medical care for older people under social security?"

Still, there is no simple formula for reconciling the economic interests of all the Democratic voting elements.

The Negroes, on the whole, constitute a powerful force for additional government spending. Many Negroes are dependent on government assistance in some form. Expanded government payrolls open new job opportunities for them. Perhaps the only way of easing the problems of the larger cities may be through liberal financial transfusions from the federal government.

One objective of the Department of Urban Affairs proposed by Kennedy was to create a claimant agency for direct grants from the federal government to the cities, bypassing the state governments. President Johnson's antipoverty program, in part at least, is another effort at accomplishing this same aim.

But other Democratic voting elements are much more divided than the Negroes on the merits of spending. These Democrats tend to favor government spending to the level where it holds up employment but are inclined to balk against spending if it means higher taxes or inflationary price rises.

The struggle over spending could also weaken the Democrats, particularly in its impact on state and local politics. During recent years state and local taxes have risen drastically as the states and cities have been forced to provide schools, hospitals and other services for a rising and shifting population.

One result is that taxpayer revolts have broken out in many communities. This political churning at the local and state levels helps explain why so many governors have been defeated for re-election in recent years.

On top of this the brunt of the racial crisis is being fought out in our cities. The financial squeeze in many localities will be screwed tighter in the hunt for extra funds to improve the schooling of Negroes and ease their other problems.

For some years to come the likely pattern of political conflict promises to be much stormier at the local and state levels than at the presidential level.

Whoever is President tends to be lifted onto a higher plane of politics, largely because of the need to preserve world peace; possibly, also, because the personality of the President is so easily projected across the national screen. But this outward façade of national unity may only conceal an ugly breakdown of national unification at the local level.

This gap between local disruption and national unity is something to be watched in the years ahead. Being nationwide in its impact, the racial crisis requires national policies which equalize the treatment of the Negro in different parts of the country. At present, however, the Democratic majority seems unable to devise a program of effective racial unification for the nation, or even to bring racial issues to a head for a decision nationally.

Perhaps the most that can be expected from a Democratic

President will be a remarkable performance in political acrobatics, in holding a party balance under seemingly impossible conditions. Often it will appear that the conflicting elements and pressures are certain to topple him. And yet it is worth remembering that the astonishing feats of the high-wire circus performer are made possible by a high-tension wire. A slack wire would be too dangerous for his turns and somersaults.

Similarly, in coalition politics tensions make possible acrobatics that would be inconceivable if pressures were slack. The party leader beset on all sides is often in a better position than if under pressure from only one direction. Conflicting pressures help define the range of bargaining that is possible. To each voting element the politician can point out that he can go only so far before he must compromise.

But if conflict exerts a tremendous cementing power, the tugging of conflicting demands could prove too violent, beyond compromise—particularly if the right Republican candidate, with the right GOP program, came along.

THE REPUBLICAN STRATEGY?

Shortly before President Kennedy's assassination, in a talk at Oberlin College, I ventured the judgment that the Republican party was on the verge of making a historic, all-out bid for the political support of the South.

Johnson's becoming President dimmed the lure of this Southern adventure. Still the forces moving the Republicans to court the South remain quite strong. These pressures are not simply those stirred by the uproar over civil rights. Long-building influences are also at work.

The basic fact is that the South has been the part of the nation where the Republicans have shown the most consistent gains in political strength since the end of World War II. Between 1950 and 1962, for example, the Republicans increased their Southern seats in Congress from two to eleven.

From 1932 through 1948 the GOP drew only a sixth to a fourth of the South's presidential vote. Eisenhower lifted this to 37 percent in 1952 and 49 percent in 1956. Nixon in 1960 drew 46 percent of the total vote cast in the eleven secession states.

The consistency of this Republican showing in the South is worth some emphasis. So strong is this consistency, in fact, that it is doubtful that the basic Republican vote in the South can be wiped out.

In 1952 Eisenhower's victory was popularly attributed to his personality and war hero fame. Yet when the election returns are analyzed precinct by precinct and county by county two striking facts emerge: First, in all three elections—1952, 1956, and 1960—the Republican vote is found in much the same counties and precincts.

Second, the voting parallels quite closely the pattern that prevails outside of the South.

It was in the cities of the South that Eisenhower and Nixon drew their strongest support. Of the South's 47 largest cities, Richard Nixon carried 30 and drew above 40 percent in the remaining 17. In all of these cities it was always the better-income neighborhoods that gave Eisenhower and Nixon their heaviest vote.

A selected group of silk stocking precincts that I have followed through every election since 1948 voted 66 percent for Nixon compared with 36 percent from a similar group of labor precincts.

In the rural counties the Eisenhower-Nixon strength was concentrated mainly in the towns, among the Main Street merchants. The farmers themselves tended to stick with the Democratic party.

In both the Southern cities and the rural countryside the Republican gains of recent years have really been a projection of the tendency toward economic voting which began with Roosevelt's New Deal. Being bound to a Democratic tradition, the South was slower to realign than the rest of the nation. Although the beginnings of this new voting cleavage on income lines show up faintly in 1944 and 1948, it did not really break through until 1952.

In this respect the historic significance of the Eisenhower victories will be found in the fact that they began the transformation of the Republican party into a truly national party with strength in every part of the country. The 1952 vote can be looked upon as the new frame for presidential voting in the South. The Republican showing will rise and fall from one election to the next but the division of voting by economic interests will persist and may even become more pronounced if the trends toward a managed economy intensify.

The 1962 balloting showed a tendency for this economic voting to be projected into state and Congressional elections. The eleven Congressional seats won by the GOP in 1962 were all districts that Eisenhower had carried.

In both Tulsa and Oklahoma City, the victorious Republican candidate for governor, Henry Bellmon, carried almost the identical precincts won by Eisenhower and Nixon. In Texas the 46 percent of the vote registered by Jack Cox represented the best showing of any Republican candidate for governor in recent Texas history. Although he fell nine percentage points below Eisenhower's showing and three percentage points under Nixon's 1960 vote, still the support for Cox flowed along in precisely the same channels that were first grooved out by Eisenhower.

A sampling of rural Texas communities shows that Cox ran nearly 10 percent stronger among the Main Street merchants than among the farmers in the countryside. Inside the Texan cities his vote showed the same scaling by income as in the 1952–1960 presidential voting.

Where Houston's well-to-do River Oaks section gave Cox 79 percent of its vote, worker precincts dropped him below 35 percent.

Of the 140 Houston precincts carried by Cox all but four voted Republican for President in 1952, 1956 and 1960. The four exceptions narrowly missed giving Nixon a majority.

In 1956 the Eisenhower-Stevenson vote broke even in precincts where homes were valued in 1950 at around $10,000. In 1962 the break-even point for Cox came in neighborhoods where the 1950 home valuation averaged $13,000.

In sum, the voting returns since 1952 reveal a considerable degree of political realignment in the South, with the old one-party loyalty giving way to a new voting division based largely on economic interest. This realignment, however, has never been completed because of the unresolved racial struggle.

In nearly every Southern state racial emotions are sufficiently powerful to constitute the balance of voting power. When these racial feelings lie quiet and bedded down, the political balance favors the Democrats. But a popular recoil against efforts to enforce integration could swing much of the South out of the Democratic fold.

In Alabama the Republican vote for U.S. Senator hit an all-time Republican high in 1962 because of the angers stirred by Kennedy's use of federal troops at the Universities of Mississippi and Alabama. The three urban counties containing Birmingham, Mobile and Montgomery voted 56 percent Republican compared with 53 percent for Nixon and 50 percent for Eisenhower. Worker precincts in Birmingham, Mobile and Montgomery that had gone for Kennedy two to one swung to give the Republicans a majority.

Even more explosive was the reaction of the black belt counties, which are most sensitive to the racial issue. In ten Alabama counties Negroes outnumber the whites but the Negroes living in these counties do not vote. These ten so-called black belt counties had given Eisenhower a third of their vote. They went 54 percent Republican in the 1962 election for senator.

When, after the Birmingham demonstrations, Democratic defection showed up in the Northern cities, some Republican strategists thought the time had come for an all-out assault upon the South. The political stage seemed set for an effort to merge into a conservative coalition all the issues symbolic of resistance to "too much government."

Johnson's becoming President bared the essential weakness in such a "Southern" strategy—its reliance on a relatively extreme sense of grievance which can wilt readily under the warming sun of moderation.

To crack the South the Republicans need to sharpen rather than blur political issues. After all, there would be little reason for a Southern Democrat to break loose from tradition unless a quite sharp difference is posed in what the Democrats and Republicans stand for.

President Johnson's first actions, however, seemed directed at blurring any sense of extremist feeling. His much-publicized efforts to turn off electric lights in the White House and to cut the Kennedy budget by a symbolic billion or two could not have been better calculated if their purpose was to lull the more conservative voters in the South.

This Republican need to sharpen issues in the South also clashes with GOP needs in many of the Northern states. The fact that so much of the Democratic following has climbed to tax-paying, middle-class status has brought into being a new, moderate-minded generation of voters, who are neither fully comfortable with all of the old Roosevelt slogans nor prepared to embrace Republicanism either. That these voters can be won over by a strategy of blurring the differences between the parties can be seen in the election of such Republican governors as Nelson Rockefeller in New York, William Scranton in Pennsylvania and George Romney in Michigan; also in the popularity of Senators like Thomas Kuchel in California, Jacob Javits in New York and Clifford Case in New Jersey.

This cleavage between the so-called "liberal" and "conservative" wings may prove too unyielding for the Republican party to make a clear-cut choice on national political strategy. Still these hesitations might be swept aside if racial antagonisms heighten.

Some "liberal" Republican strategists have urged that an all-out bid be made for the Negro vote in the major Northern cities. But this course has tended to become less and less attractive to the Republicans in view of the solidarity of the Negro Democratic vote. Negro voting solidarity, in fact, has become a major pressure pushing the Republicans toward alliance with the white South.

Consider the change in Congressional representation in the twelve largest cities in the nation. Since 1930 the northward migration of Negroes from the South has more than tripled the Negro population in these twelve cities. This has had a double impact.

First, whole sections of the inner city have been converted into a virtually solid Negro core. By 1962 five of these cities were sending Negro congressmen, all Democrats, to Washington.

Second, as more and more Negroes have moved into the central cities, white families have been pushed out. Most of these families have been Democrats. As they spread through the cities and into the suburbs they have toppled strongly Republican districts, even where Negroes do not live.

Between 1952, when the Republicans last held control of Congress, and 1962 the number of Republican congressmen from these twelve cities dropped from 22 to 8.

Six of these twelve cities—St. Louis, Baltimore, Detroit, Philadelphia, Milwaukee and Boston—are now without a single Republican congressman.

In Chicago from 1952 to 1962 the number of Republican-held seats dropped from 5 to 2, these last two being part-city and part-suburb. In New York City the number of Republican seats fell from 7 to 3; in Los Angeles from 4 districts to 1, which is partly suburban.

Largely as a result of these urban losses it has become virtually impossible for the Republicans to recapture control of Congress—unless they can pick up additional seats in the South.

Of the 259 congressional seats that the Democrats held in 1962 there were 152 which had not elected a Republican since at least 1940. Another 29 districts had been Democratic since at least 1948. Among the remaining 78 districts, 29 more could be considered "safe" seats in that they voted 60 percent Democratic or better in 1962.

This left only 49 Democratic seats, largely in the suburbs, the Western cities and the semirural Midwest, which could be considered as really contested.

To gain control of the House of Representatives, the Republicans would have to sweep all but 7 of these 49 seats, something that isn't likely to happen unless the Republicans are winning the presidency by a landslide.

The likelihood of a Republican bid for the Northern Negro vote has been reduced still further by the new tensions and strains between white and Negro Democrats in the North. The Republicans are more likely to try to win over white voters who may be alienated by Negro demands. In the spring of 1964, in fact, former Vice-President Richard Nixon hinted at such a strategy when he publicly denounced extremists among the Negro leaders and called for moderation in handling racial problems.

An appeal for racial moderation could be tied in quite easily with a strategy that sought major Republican gains in the South.

One might picture the drama of party realignment now going on as a race against time, with the South as the crucial battleground.

Johnson's presidency has given the Democrats more time to strengthen their defenses against another successful Republican onslaught in the South.

Efforts to increase Negro voting in the South can be considered part of such a strategy. The ever-widening acceptance of desegregation is another key influence making the South less vulnerable politically to Republican attack.

Against that, however, the militancy of the Southern Negro and the resistance of the extreme segregationists threaten constantly to tear apart the forces of moderation, with repercussions that reverberate into the North. If Johnson remains in office long enough the moderates may emerge triumphant in the South. But at this stage, with no racial settlement in sight, the South remains the exposed flank of the Democratic party through which it can be most effectively attacked.

THE NEGRO DILEMMA

As for the Negroes, theirs is a paradoxical political situation.

Allegiance to the Democratic party has gained Negro leaders a sympathetic audience in the White House and considerable influence with Democratic Presidents. But this same voting solidarity has been somewhat self-defeating in that it contributes to Democratic dominance in Congress, which enables the white South to retain its power to deadlock racial issues.

The Negro strategy for forcing racial change in the South has been built around executive action, on the belief that the President will intervene with troops if necessary in any showdown. But in the committees of Congress, Negro bargaining power remains weak.

As a minority in Congress the Republicans are constantly tempted to enter into coalition with some Democratic faction. In the legislative process the interests of the Negroes are likely to be traded off for Southern support on issues of importance to Republican constituencies.

This danger of too strong a commitment to one party has been recognized by many Negro leaders and scholars who, like Gunnar Myrdal, have urged Negroes to adopt a flexible strategy of dividing between both major parties. But this is not easily done. The main difficulty lies with the Negro's economic and social makeup, which makes it difficult for him to divide politically.

The contrast with the white South is significant. Among white Southerners one finds a tremendously wide range of economic interests, so wide that it has become difficult, if not impossible, to encompass them all in one party. The normal division on economic lines yields enough of a

Republican vote so that only a moderate degree of additional dissatisfaction is needed to swing some Southern states.

Among Negroes, however, one still finds comparatively little
economic differentiation. Higher income Negro neighborhoods show
more of a Republican vote than do worker areas. But, on the whole, the
new Negro middle class in the Northern cities tends to knit the Negro
more firmly to the Democratic party.

In numerical strength, government workers constitute by far the
largest single element in this middle class. The federal government
actually employs one in every eighteen Negro workers. Of 300,000
Negroes who worked for Uncle Sam in 1962, more than 1,400 held jobs
which paid over $10,000 a year. Another 34,143 held jobs paying between
$5,000 and $10,000 a year.

Perhaps as important, the sense of common interest with "business," which pulls so many other voters to the Republicans, is extremely
low among Negroes. Even among the best educated Negroes few
envision careers with a large company. The Negro financial stake in
business is quite limited.

Of the 100 Negroes rated as most influential by *Ebony* magazine
in 1963, only nine were clearly identifiable as businessmen. One, Jackie
Robinson, is vice-president of a restaurant chain; another, S. B. Fuller, is
a cosmetics manufacturer who has successfully competed in the white
market.

The seven other most influential Negro businessmen were in
insurance and savings-and-loan companies, catering primarily to Negro
customers. While Negro wealth has been growing, the few Negro
businesses of any size remain primarily life insurance companies.

In looking at other middle class elements one finds sizable
numbers of ministers and teachers, but in 1955 the annual increase of
Negro graduate engineers stood at only 150; the yearly crop of additional
doctors and lawyers was around 200.

So many bonds hold the Negro to the Democratic party that it is
extremely difficult for even an impassioned sense of racialism to sever
them. Temporary "bolts" by Negro Democrats may take place, but as of
now these are not likely to shatter the basic Democratic loyalty of the
Negro voter.

In summation two conclusions stand out:

First, for some years to come the Negro is likely to remain a
disruptive force politically, weakening the Democratic coalition.

The long-run fate of the Democratic party—the issue of survival
or slow death—hinges on whether it will be able to unify the nation
racially, which really means unifying the South with the rest of the
nation. As we have seen, the first such effort, to project the Negro labor

alliance into the South, failed. Instead the South responded with a double insurgency, an economic revolt aimed at checking the power of labor unions and government spending and a racial reaction designed to counter the influence of Negro voting in the North.

This failure to remake the South in the image of liberalism spurred the rise of a new militancy on the part of the Negro, a militancy unrestrained by the compromises of coalition politics. This militancy, in turn, transferred to the Northern Negro, now threatens to alienate the white Democratic voters in the big cities.

One of two doors can be opened to the future. Unrelenting pressures by the Negroes may force the Democrats to rise to the necessity of framing a program of racial unification for the nation, or the Democrats will fail in this effort. In that case the nation will suffer the throes and agonies that come with the slow deterioration of the majority party.

The second conclusion that arises from this analysis of the politics of race is that too heavy a reliance has been placed on the power of Negro voting. The absence of voting rights is intolerable. As the South has shown, a minimum voting representation is indispensable to avoid being disregarded completely. But it does not follow that the bargaining power of the Negro will rise proportionately with each fresh increase in Negro voting numbers.

As more and more Negroes exercise the right of suffrage, and if they continue to vote as a bloc, white voters will unite against them. If political power is to be the deciding force, enough white resistance can be expected to check Negro advances to limits acceptable to whites.

This prospect has its moral for white voters as well. Many liberals have deceived themselves with the belief that as Negroes gained political strength they would be able to demand and get better treatment. This belief encouraged the thought that time will bring into existence conditions which will render it easier to deal with these problems.

But the Negro is not strong enough to make the white man do the right thing. If we are to reconcile our racial crisis the white people will have to devise a program for racial unification which extends beyond the trials of political bargaining power and under which white and black can reconcile their interests.

Can this be done? The evidence to date testifies "No."

Bayard Rustin

FROM PROTEST TO POLITICS: THE FUTURE OF THE CIVIL RIGHTS MOVEMENT

I

The decade spanned by the 1954 Supreme Court decision on school desegregation and the Civil Rights Act of 1964 will undoubtedly be recorded as the period in which the legal foundations of racism in America were destroyed. To be sure, pockets of resistance remain; but it would be hard to quarrel with the assertion that the elaborate legal structure of segregation and discrimination, particularly in relation to public accommodations, has virtually collapsed. On the other hand, without making light of the human sacrifices involved in the direct-action tactics (sit-ins, freedom rides, and the rest) that were so instrumental to this achievement, we must recognize that in desegregating public accommodations, we affected institutions which are relatively peripheral both to the American socio-economic order and to the fundamental conditions of life of the Negro people. In a highly industrialized, 20th-century civilization, we hit Jim Crow precisely where it was most anachronistic, dispensable, and vulnerable—in hotels, lunch counters, terminals, libraries, swimming pools, and the like. For in these forms, Jim Crow does impede the flow of commerce in the broadest sense: it is a nuisance in a society on the move (and on the make). Not surprisingly, therefore, it was the most mobility-conscious and relatively liberated groups in the Negro community—lower-middle-class college students— who launched the attack that brought down this imposing but hollow structure.

The term "classical" appears especially apt for this phase of the civil rights movement. But in the few years that have passed since the first flush of sit-ins, several developments have taken place that have

Reprinted from *Commentary* by permission; Copyright © 1965 by the American Jewish Committee.

Mr. Rustin, a strategist in the civil rights movement, was a principle organizer of the 1963 March on Washington. He is Executive Director, The A. Philip Randolph Institute.

complicated matters enormously. One is the shifting focus of the movement in the South, symbolized by Birmingham; another is the spread of the revolution to the North; and the third, common to the other two, is the expansion of the movement's base in the Negro community. To attempt to disentangle these three strands is to do violence to reality. David Danzig's perceptive article, "The Meaning of Negro Strategy,"[1] correctly saw in the Birmingham events the victory of the concept of collective struggle over individual achievement as the road to Negro freedom. And Birmingham remains the unmatched symbol of grass-roots protest involving all strata of the black community. It was also in this most industrialized of Southern cities that the single-issue demands of the movement's classical stage gave way to the "package deal." No longer were Negroes satisfied with integrating lunch counters. They now sought advances in employment, housing, school intergration, police protection, and so forth.

Thus, the movement in the South began to attack areas of discrimination which were not so remote from the Northern experience as were Jim Crow lunch counters. At the same time, the interrelationship of these apparently distinct areas became increasingly evident. What is the value of winning access to public accommodations for those who lack money to use them? The minute the movement faced this question, it was compelled to expand its vision beyond race relations to economic relations, including the role of education in modern society. And what also became clear is that all these interrelated problems, by their very nature, are not soluble by private, voluntary efforts but require government action—or politics. Already Southern demonstrators had recognized that the most effective way to strike at the police brutality they suffered from was by getting rid of the local sheriff—and that meant political action, which in turn meant, and still means, political action within the Democratic party where the only meaningful primary contests in the South are fought.

And so, in Mississippi, thanks largely to the leadership of Bob Moses, a turn toward political action has been taken. More than voter registration is involved here. A conscious bid for *political power* is being made, and in the course of that effort a tactical shift is being effected: direct-action techniques are being subordinated to a strategy calling for the building of community institutions or power bases. Clearly, the implications of this shift reach far beyond Mississippi. What began as a protest movement is being challenged to translate itself into a political movement. Is this the right course? And if it is, can the transformation be accomplished?

[1] *Commentary,* February 1964.

II

The very decade which has witnessed the decline of legal Jim Crow has also seen the rise of *de facto* segregation in our most fundamental socio-economic institutions. More Negroes are unemployed today than in 1954, and the unemployment gap between the races is wider. The median income of Negroes has dropped from 57 per cent to 54 per cent of that of whites. A higher percentage of Negro workers is now concentrated in jobs vulnerable to automation than was the case ten years ago. More Negroes attend *de facto* segregated schools today than when the Supreme Court handed down its famous decision; while school integration proceeds at a snail's pace in the South, the number of Northern schools with an excessive proportion of minority youth proliferates. And behind this is the continuing growth of racial slums, spreading over our central cities and trapping Negro youth in a milieu which, whatever its legal definition, sows an unimaginable demoralization. Again, legal niceties aside, a resident of a racial ghetto lives in segregated housing, and more Negroes fall into this category than ever before.

These are the facts of life which generate frustration in the Negro community and challenge the civil rights movement. At issue, after all, is not *civil rights,* strictly speaking, but social and economic conditions. Last summer's riots were not race riots; they were outbursts of class aggression in a society where class and color definitions are converging disastrously. How can the (perhaps misnamed) civil rights movement deal with this problem?

Before trying to answer, let me first insist that the task of the movement is vastly complicated by the failure of many whites of good will to understand the nature of our problem. There is a widespread assumption that the removal of artificial racial barriers should result in the automatic integration of the Negro into all aspects of American life. This myth is fostered by facile analogies with the experience of various ethnic immigrant groups, particularly the Jews. But the analogies with the Jews do not hold for three simple but profound reasons. First, Jews have a long history as a literate people, a resource which has afforded them opportunities to advance in the academic and professional worlds, to achieve intellectual status even in the midst of economic hardship, and to evolve sustaining value systems in the context of ghetto life. Negroes, for the greater part of their presence in this country, were forbidden by law to read or write. Second, Jews have a long history of family stability, the importance of which in terms of aspiration and self-image is obvious. The Negro family structure was totally destroyed by slavery and with it the possibility of cultural transmission (the right of Negroes to marry and rear children is barely a century old). Third, Jews are white and have the *option* of relinquishing their cultural-religious identity, intermarrying, passing, etc. Negroes, or at least the overwhelming majority of them, do not have this option. There is also a fourth, vulgar reason. If the Jewish and Negro communities are not comparable in terms of education, family structure, and color, it is also true that their respective economic roles bear little resemblance.

This matter of economic role brings us to the greater problem— the fact that we are moving into an era in which the natural functioning of the market does not by itself ensure every man with will and ambition a place in the productive process. The immigrant who came to this country during the late 19th and early 20th centuries entered a society which was expanding territorially and/or economically. It was then possible to start at the bottom, as an unskilled or semi-skilled worker, and move up the ladder, acquiring new skills along the way. Especially was this true when industrial unionism was burgeoning, giving new dignity and higher wages to organized workers. Today the situation has changed. We are not expanding territorially, the western frontier is settled, labor organizing has leveled off, our rate of economic growth has been stagnant for a decade. And we are in the midst of a technological revolution which is altering the fundamental structure of the labor force, destroying unskilled and semi-skilled jobs—jobs in which Negroes are dispropor- tionately concentrated.

Whatever the pace of this technological revolution may be, the *direction* is clear: the lower rungs of the economic ladder are being lopped off. This means that an individual will no longer be able to start at the bottom and work his way up; he will have to start in the middle or on top, and hold on tight. It will not even be enough to have certain specific skills, for many skilled jobs are also vulnerable to automation. A broad educational background, permitting vocational adaptability and flexibility, seems more imperative than ever. We live in a society where, as Secretary of Labor Willard Wirtz puts it, machines have the equivalent of a high school diploma. Yet the average educational attainment of American Negroes is 8.2 years.

Negroes, of course, are not the only people being affected by these developments. It is reported that there are now 50 per cent fewer unskilled and semi-skilled jobs than there are high school dropouts. Almost one-third of the 26 million young people entering the labor market in the 1960's will be dropouts. But the percentage of Negro dropouts nationally is 57 per cent, and in New York City, among Negroes 25 years of age or over, it is 68 per cent. They are without a future.

To what extent can the kind of self-help campaign recently prescribed by Eric Hoffer in the *New York Times Magazine* cope with such a situation? I would advise those who think that self-help is the answer to familiarize themselves with the long history of such efforts in the Negro community, and to consider why so many foundered on the shoals of ghetto life. It goes without saying that any effort to combat demoralization and apathy is desirable, but we must understand that demoralization in the Negro community is largely a common-sense response to an objective reality. Negro youths have no need of statistics to perceive, fairly accurately, what their odds are in American society. Indeed, from the point of view of motivation, some of the healthiest Negro youngsters I know are juvenile delinquents: vigorously pursuing the American Dream of material acquisition and status, yet finding the conventional means of attaining it blocked off, they do not yield to defeatism but resort to illegal (and often ingenious) methods. They are not alien to American culture. They are, in Gunnar Myrdal's phrase, "exaggerated Americans." To want a Cadillac is not un-American; to push a cart in the garment center is. If Negroes are to be persuaded that the conventional path (school, work, etc.) is superior, we had better provide evidence which is now sorely lacking. It is a double cruelty to harangue Negro youth about education and training when we do not know what jobs will be available for them. When a Negro youth can reasonably foresee a future free of slums, when the prospect of gainful employment is realistic, we will see motivation and self-help in abundant enough quantities.

Meanwhile, there is an ironic similarity between the self-help advocated by many liberals and the doctrines of the Black Muslims. Professional sociologists, psychiatrists, and social workers have expressed amazement at the Muslims' success in transforming prostitutes and dope addicts into respectable citizens. But every prostitute the Muslims convert to a model of Calvinist virtue is replaced by the ghetto with two more. Dedicated as they are to maintenance of the ghetto, the Muslims are powerless to affect substantial moral reform. So too with every other group or program which is not aimed at the destruction of slums, their causes and effects. Self-help efforts, directly or indirectly, must be geared to mobilizing people into power units capable of effecting social change. That is, their goal must be genuine self-help, not merely self-improvement. Obviously, where self-improvement activities succeed in imparting to their participants a feeling of some control over their environment, those involved may find their appetites for change whetted; they may move into the political arena.

III

Let me sum up what I have thus far been trying to say: the civil rights movement is evolving from a protest movement into a full-fledged *social movement*—an evolution calling its very name into question. It is now concerned not merely with removing the barriers to full *opportunity* but with achieving the fact of *equality*. From sit-ins and freedom rides we have gone into rent strikes, boycotts, community organization, and political action. As a consequence of this natural evolution, the Negro today finds himself stymied by obstacles of far greater magnitude than the legal barriers he was attacking before: automation, urban decay, *de facto* school segregation. These are problems which, while conditioned by Jim Crow, do not vanish upon its demise. They are more deeply rooted in our socio-economic order; they are the result of the total society's failure to meet not only the Negro's needs, but human needs generally.

These propositions have won increasing recognition and acceptance, but with a curious twist. They have formed the common premise of two apparently contradictory lines of thought which simultaneously nourish and antagonize each other. On the one hand, there is the reasoning of the *New York Times* moderate who says that the problems are so enormous and complicated that Negro militancy is a futile irritation, and that the need is for "intelligent moderation." Thus, during the first New York school boycott, the *Times* editorialized that Negro demands, while abstractly just, would necessitate massive reforms, the funds for which could not realistically be anticipated; therefore the just demands were also foolish demands and would only antagonize white people. Moderates of this stripe are often correct in perceiving the difficulty or impossibility of racial progress in the context of present social and economic policies. But they accept the context as fixed. They ignore (or perhaps see all too well) the potentialities inherent in linking Negro demands to broader pressures for radical revision of existing policies. They apparently see nothing strange in the fact that in the last twenty-five years we have spent nearly a trillion dollars fighting or preparing for wars, yet throw up our hands before the need for overhauling our schools, clearing the slums, and really abolishing poverty. My quarrel with these moderates is that they do not even envision radical changes; their admonitions of moderation are, for all practical purposes, admonitions to the Negro to adjust to the status quo, and are therefore immoral.

The more effectively the moderates argue their case, the more they convince Negroes that American society will not or cannot be reorganized for full racial equality. Michael Harrington has said that a successful war on poverty might well require the expenditure of a $100 billion. Where, the Negro wonders, are the forces now in motion to compel such a commitment? If the voices of the moderates were raised in an insistence upon a reallocation of national resources at levels that could not be confused with tokenism (that is, if the moderates stopped being moderates), Negroes would have greater grounds for hope.

Meanwhile, the Negro movement cannot escape a sense of isolation.

It is precisely this sense of isolation that gives rise to the second line of thought I want to examine—the tendency within the civil rights movement which, despite its militancy, pursues what I call a "no-win" policy. Sharing with many moderates a recognition of the magnitude of the obstacles to freedom, spokesmen for this tendency survey the American scene and find no forces prepared to move toward radical solutions. From this they conclude that the only viable strategy is shock; above all, the hypocrisy of white liberals must be exposed. These spokesmen are often described as the radicals of the movement, but they are really its moralists. They seek to change white hearts—by traumatizing them. Frequently abetted by white self-flagellants, they may gleefully applaud (through not really agreeing with) Malcom X because, while they admit he has no program, they think he can frighten white people into doing the right thing. To believe this of course, you must be convinced, even if unconsciously, that at the core of the white man's heart lies a buried affection for Negroes—a proposition one may be permitted to doubt. But in any case, hearts are not relevant to the issue; neither racial affinities nor racial hostilities are rooted there. It is institutions—social, political, and economic institutions—which are the ultimate molders of collective sentiments. Let these institutions be reconstructed *today*, and let the ineluctable gradualism of history govern the formation of a new psychology.

My quarrel with the "no-win" tendency in the civil rights movement (and the reason I have so designated it) parallels my quarrel with the moderates outside the movement. As the latter lack the vision or will for fundamental change, the former lack a realistic strategy for achieving it. For such a strategy they substitute militancy. But militancy is a matter of posture and volume and not of effect.

I believe that the Negro's struggle for equality in America is essentially revolutionary. While most Negroes—in their hearts—unquestionably seek only to enjoy the fruits of American society as it now exists, their quest cannot *objectively* be satisfied within the framework of existing political and economic relations. The young Negro who would demonstrate his way into the labor market may be motivated by a thoroughly bourgeois ambition and thoroughly "capitalist" considerations, but he will end up having to favor a great expansion of the public sector of the economy. At any rate, that is the position the movement will be forced to take as it looks at the number of jobs being generated by the private economy, and if it is to remain true to the masses of Negroes.

The revolutionary character of the Negro's struggle is manifest in the fact that this struggle may have done more to democratize life for whites than for Negroes. Clearly, it was the sit-in movement of young Southern Negroes which, as it galvanized white students, banished the ugliest features of McCarthyism from the American campus and resurrected political debate. It was not until Negroes assaulted *de facto* school segregation in the urban centers that the issue of quality education for *all* children stirred into motion. Finally, it seems reasonably clear that the civil rights movement, directly and through the resurgence of social conscience it kindled, did more to initiate the war on poverty than any other single force.

It will be—it has been—argued that these by-products of the Negro struggle are not revolutionary. But the term revolutionary, as I am using it, does not connote violence; it refers to the qualitative transformation of fundamental institutions, more or less rapidly, to the point where the social and economic structure which they comprised can no longer be said to be the same. The Negro struggle has hardly run its course; and it will not stop moving until it has been utterly defeated or won substantial equality. But I fail to see how the movement can be victorious in the absence of radical programs for full employment, abolition of slums, the reconstruction of our educational system, new definitions of work and leisure. Adding up the cost of such programs, we can only conclude that we are talking about a refashioning of our political economy. It has been estimated, for example, that the price of replacing New York City's slums with public housing would be $17 billion. Again, a multi-billion dollar federal public-works program, dwarfing the currently proposed $2 billion program, is required to reabsorb unskilled and semi-skilled workers into the labor market—and this must be done if Negro workers in these categories are to be employed. "Preferential treatment" cannot help them.

I am not trying here to delineate a total program, only to suggest the scope of economic reforms which are most immediately related to the plight of the Negro community. One could speculate on their political implications—whether, for example, they do not indicate the obsolescence of state government and the superiority of regional structures as viable units of planning. Such speculations aside, it is clear that Negro needs cannot be satisfied unless we go beyond what has so far been placed on the agenda. How are these radical objectives to be achieved? The answer is simple, deceptively so: *through political power.*

There is a strong moralistic strain in the civil rights movement which would remind us that power corrupts, forgetting that the absence of power also corrupts. But this is not the view I want to debate here, for it is waning. Our problem is posed by those who accept the need for political power but do not understand the nature of the object and therefore lack sound strategies for achieving it; they tend to confuse political institutions with lunch counters.

A handful of Negroes, acting alone, could integrate a lunch counter by strategically locating their bodies so as *directly* to interrupt the operation of the proprietor's will; their numbers were relatively unimportant. In politics, however, such a confrontation is difficult because the interests involved are merely *represented*. In the execution of a political decision a direct confrontation may ensue (as when federal marshals escorted James Meredith into the University of Mississippi—to turn from an example of non-violent coercion to one of force backed up with the threat of violence). But in arriving at a political decision, numbers and organizations are crucial, especially for the economically disenfranchised. (Needless to say, I am assuming that the forms of political democracy exist in America, however imperfectly, that they are valued, and that elitist or putschist conceptions of exercising power are beyond the pale of discussion for the civil rights movement.)

Neither that movement nor the country's twenty million black people can win political power alone. We need allies. The future of the Negro struggle depends on whether the contradictions of this society can be resolved by a coalition of progressive forces which becomes the *effective* political majority in the United States. I speak of the coalition which staged the March on Washington, passed the Civil Rights Act, and laid the basis for the Johnson landslide—Negroes, trade unionists, liberals, and religious groups.

There are those who argue that a coalition strategy would force the Negro to surrender his political independence to white liberals, that he would be neutralized, deprived of his cutting edge, absorbed into the Establishment. Some who take this position urged last year that votes be withheld from the Johnson-Humphrey ticket as a demonstration of the Negro's political power. Curiously enough, these people who sought to demonstrate power through the non-exercise of it, also point to the Negro "swing vote" in crucial urban areas as the source of the Negro's independent political power. But here they are closer to being right: the urban Negro vote will grow in importance in the coming years. If there is anything positive in the spread of the ghetto, it is the potential political power base thus created, and to realize this potential is one of the most challenging and urgent tasks before the civil rights movement. If the movement can wrest leadership of the ghetto vote from the machines, it will have acquired an organized constituency such as other major groups in our society now have.

But we must also remember that the effectiveness of a swing vote depends solely on "other" votes. It derives its power from them. In that sense, it can never be "independent," but must opt for one candidate or the other, even if by default. Thus coalitions are inescapable, however tentative they may be. And this is the case in all but those few situations in which Negroes running on an independent ticket might conceivably win. "Independence," in other words, is not a value in itself. The issue is which coalition to join and how to make it responsive to your program. Necessarily there will be compromise. But the difference between expediency and morality in politics is the difference between selling out a principle and making smaller concessions to win larger ones. The leader who shrinks from this task reveals not his purity but his lack of political sense.

The task of molding a political movement out of the March on Washington coalition is not simple, but no alternatives have been advanced. We need to choose our allies on the basis of common political objectives. It has become fashionable in some no-win Negro circles to decry the white liberal as the main enemy (his hypocrisy is what sustains racism); by virtue of this reverse recitation of the reactionary's litany (liberalism leads to socialism, which leads to Communism) the Negro is left in majestic isolation, except for a tiny band of fervent white initiates. But the objective fact is that *Eastland and Goldwater* are the main enemies—they and the opponents of civil rights, of the war on poverty, of medicare, of social security, of federal aid to education, of unions, and so forth. The labor movement, despite its obvious faults, has been the largest single organized force in this country pushing for progressive social legislation. And where the Negro-labor-liberal axis is weak, as in the farm belt, it was the religious groups that were most influential in rallying support for the Civil Rights Bill.

The durability of the coalition was interestingly tested during the election. I do not believe that the Johnson landslide proved the "white backlash" to be a myth. It proved, rather, that economic interests are more fundamental than prejudice: the backlashers decided that loss of social security was, after all, too high a price to pay for a slap at the Negro. This lesson was a valuable first step in re-educating such people, and it must be kept alive, for the civil rights movement will be advanced only to the degree that social and economic welfare gets to be inextricably entangled with civil rights.

The 1964 elections marked a turning point in American politics. The Democratic landslide was not merely the result of a negative reaction to Goldwaterism; it was also the expression of a majority liberal consensus. The near unanimity with which Negro voters joined in that expression was, I am convinced, a vindication of the July 25th statement by Negro leaders calling for a strategic turn toward political action and a temporary curtailment of mass demonstrations. Despite the controversy surrounding the statement, the instinctive response it met with in the community is suggested by the fact that demonstrations were down 75 per cent as compared with the same period in 1963. But should so high a percentage of Negro voters have gone to Johnson, or should they have held back to narrow his margin of victory and thus give greater visibility to our swing vote? How has our loyalty changed things? Certainly the Negro vote had higher visibility in 1960, when a switch of only 7 per cent from the Republican column of 1956 elected President Kennedy. But the slimness of Kennedy's victory—of his "mandate"—dictated a go-slow approach on civil rights, at least until the Birmingham upheaval.

Although Johnson's popular majority was so large that he could have won without such overwhelming Negro support, that support was important from several angles. Beyond adding to Johnson's total national margin, it was specifically responsible for his victories in Virginia, Florida, Tennessee, and Arkansas. Goldwater took only those states where fewer than 45 per cent of eligible Negroes were registered. That Johnson would have won those states had Negro voting rights been enforced is a lesson not likely to be lost on a man who would have been happy with a unanimous electoral college. In any case, the 1.6 million Southern Negroes who voted have had a shattering impact on the Southern political party structure, as illustrated in the changed composition of the Southern congressional delegation. The "backlash" gave the Republicans five House seats in Alabama, one in Georgia, and one in Mississippi. But on the Democratic side, seven segregationists were defeated while all nine Southerners who voted for the Civil Rights Act were re-elected. It may be premature to predict a Southern Democratic party of Negroes and white moderates and a Republican Party of refugee racists and economic conservatives, but there certainly is a strong tendency toward such a realignment; and an additional 3.6 million Negroes of voting age in the eleven Southern states are still to be heard from. Even the *tendency* toward disintegration of the Democratic party's racist wing defines a new context for Presidential and liberal strategy in the congressional battles ahead. Thus the Negro vote (North as well as South), while not *decisive* in the Presidential race, was enormously effective. It was a dramatic element of a historic mandate which contains vast possibilities and dangers that will fundamentally affect the future course of the civil rights movement.

The liberal congressional sweep raises hope for an assault on the seniority system, Rule Twenty-two, and other citadels of Dixiecrat-Republican power. The overwhelming of this conservative coalition should also mean progress on much bottlenecked legislation of profound interest to the movement (e.g., bills by Senators Clark and Nelson on planning, manpower, and employment). Moreover, the irrelevance of the South to Johnson's victory gives the President more freedom to act than his predecessor had and more leverage to the movement to pressure for executive action in Mississippi and other racist strongholds.

None of this *guarantees* vigorous executive or legislative action, for the other side of the Johnson landslide is that it has a Gaullist quality. Goldwater's capture of the Republican party forced into the Democratic camp many disparate elements which do not belong there, Big Business being the major example. Johnson, who wants to be President "of all people," may try to keep his new coalition together by sticking close to the political center. But if he decides to do this, it is unlikely that even his political genius will be able to hold together a coalition so inherently unstable and rife with contradictions. It must come apart. Should it do so while Johnson is pursuing a centrist course, then the mandate will have been wastefully dissipated. However, if the mandate is seized upon to set fundamental changes in motion, then the basis can be laid for a new mandate, a new coalition including hitherto inert and dispossessed strata of the population.

Here is where the cutting edge of the civil rights movement can be applied. We must see to it that the reorganization of the "consensus party" proceeds along lines which will make it an effective vehicle for social reconstruction, a role it cannot play so long as it furnishes Southern racism with its national political power. (One of Barry Goldwater's few attractive ideas was that the Dixiecrats belong with him in the same party.) And nowhere has the civil rights movement's political cutting edge been more magnificently demonstrated than at Atlantic City, where the Mississippi Freedom Democratic Party not only secured recognition as a bona fide component of the national party, but in the process routed the representatives of the·most rabid racists—the white Mississippi and Alabama delegations. While I still believe that the FDP made a tactical error in spurning the compromise, there is no question that they launched a political revolution whose logic is the displacement of Dixiecrat power. They launched that revolution within a major political institution and as part of a coalitional effort.

The role of the civil rights movement in the reorganization of American political life is programmatic as well as strategic. We are challenged now to broaden our social vision, to develop functional programs with concrete objectives. We need to propose alternatives to technological unemployment, urban decay, and the rest. We need to be calling for public works and training, for national economic planning, for federal aid to education, for attractive public housing—all this on a sufficiently massive scale to make a difference. We need to protest the notion that our integration into American life, so long delayed, must now proceed in an atmosphere of competitive scarcity instead of in the security of abundance which technology makes possible. We cannot claim to have answers to all the complex problems of modern society. That is too much to ask of a movement still battling barbarism in Mississippi. But we can agitate the right questions by probing at the contradictions which still stand in the way of the "Great Society." The questions having been asked, motion must begin in the larger society, for there is a limit to what Negroes can do alone.

Appendix

The Civil Rights Acts of 1964 and 1965

A Summary of the Civil Rights Act of 1964

TITLE I—VOTING

The purpose of this section is to provide more effective enforcement of the right to vote in Federal elections (for President, Vice President, presidential electors or members of Congress) without regard to race or color. It also speeds up the procedure by which voting rights suits may be decided.

The Act:

a. requires that the same standards be applied to all individuals seeking to register and vote;

b. forbids denial of the right to vote because of some minor mistake or omission;

c. requires that only literacy tests that are written may be used as a qualification for voting; and that the tests and answers be available on request;

d. establishes that in voting rights law suits the court must presume that anyone who completed the sixth grade is literate, unless the State can prove otherwise.

In any voting suit brought by the Government charging that there is a "pattern or practice" of voting discrimination, either the Attorney General or the defendant may ask that a three-judge Federal

Reprinted from *Civil Rights Digest* (Special Bulletin, August 1964). Published by the U.S. Commission on Civil Rights, 1701 Pennsylvania Avenue, N. W., Washington, D.C.

court be appointed to hear the case. Appeals from the decisions of such a court may be taken directly to the Supreme Court.

TITLE II—PUBLIC ACCOMMODATIONS

Discrimination on the basis of race, color, religion or national origin is specifically forbidden in the following places of public accommodation:

a. hotels and motels, restaurants, lunch counters, movie houses, gasoline stations, theaters and stadiums;

b. any other establishment which offers its services to patrons of the covered establishment; for example,

—a barbershop or tavern located in a hotel, or

—a department store in which there is a restaurant: *so long as* the covered facilities either affect interstate commerce in their operations, or are supported in their discriminatory practices by State action.

In addition, discrimination is forbidden in any other place of public accommodation that is required to segregate by State or local laws.

If there are no State or local laws requiring segregation, the Federal law does not cover:

a. barbershops, beauty parlors and other service establishments unless they are located in a hotel and offer these services to hotel guests;

b. retail stores that do not serve food, or places of recreation (except as listed above) which do not serve food;

c. lodging houses, hotels or similar places which take temporary guests if they have fewer than six rooms for rent in a building occupied by the owner.

Places that are actually owned and operated as private clubs are exempted from coverage of this title except to the extent that they offer their facilities to patrons of a covered establishment, such as a country club that customarily allows guests of a hotel to use its golf course.

No person may intimidate, threaten or coerce anyone for the purpose of interfering with the rights created by this title.

The provisions of this title may be enforced in two ways:

1. By *individual action* in a civil suit filed by the persons discriminated against, or

2. By *Government action* in a civil suit filed by the Attorney General.

In public accommodations suits filed by individuals:

—the court hearing the suit may appoint a lawyer for the person bringing the complaint and exempt the complainant from the payment of certain costs;

—the court may permit the Attorney General to enter the case;

—if there is a State law or local ordinance that prohibits discrimination, the complaint must first be taken to the State or local authorities, allowing them 30 days to begin a proceeding before suit can be filed in a Federal court;

—once the case is in court, the court can postpone action until the State or local proceeding is completed;

—if there are no State or local anti-discrimination provisions, the court may refer the matter to the Community Relations Service (see Title X) so that it may seek to secure voluntary compliance within no more than 120 days.

The Attorney General may file a public accommodations suit when he believes there is a pattern or practice of resistance. As in Title I voting suits, he may request a three-judge court for this action.

In public accommodations suits brought either by individuals or the Attorney General, the court may issue temporary or permanent injunctions or restraining orders against those found to be violating the law. A person or persons failing to obey such court decrees may be punished by contempt proceedings under the jury trials provision of the law (see Title XI).

TITLE III—PUBLIC FACILITIES

The Attorney General is authorized to bring a civil suit to compel desegregation of any publicly-owned or operated facility whenever he receives a written complaint of discrimination. He must believe that the complaint merits action and must certify that the individual or individuals making the complaint are themselves unable to take the necessary legal action. State or municipally owned or operated parks, libraries and hospitals are among the facilities covered.

TITLE IV—PUBLIC EDUCATION

Under this title the U.S. Office of Education is authorized to:

a. conduct a national survey to determine the availability of equal educational opportunity;

b. provide technical assistance, upon request, to help States, political subdivisions or school districts carry out school desegregation plans;

c. arrange training institutes to prepare teachers and other school personnel to deal with desegregation problems;

d. make grants enabling school boards to employ specialists for in-service training programs.

In addition, the Attorney General is authorized to file civil suits seeking to compel desegregation of public schools, including public colleges.

Before filing such a suit the Attorney General must have received a signed complaint from a pupil or parent and must have determined that the complainant, according to standards set forth in the Act, is unable to bring the action. The Attorney General is also required to notify the school board and give it a reasonable period of time to correct the alleged condition before filing suit.

TITLE V—COMMISSION ON CIVIL RIGHTS

The life of the U.S. Commission on Civil Rights is extended until January 31, 1968. Since 1957 the Commission's functions have included investigating denials of the right to vote, studying legal developments and appraising Federal policies relating to equal protection of the laws, and making recommendations for corrective action to the President and the Congress.

Title V gives the Commission added authority to:

a. serve as a national clearinghouse for civil rights information;

b. investigate allegations of vote fraud.

Commission hearing procedures are amended to further protect the rights of individuals who may be affected by Commission proceedings.

As a national clearinghouse, the Commission will provide civil rights information in such areas as voting, housing, education, employment and the use of public facilities to Federal, State and local government agencies and officials, organizations and businesses, and the general public.

TITLE VI—FEDERALLY ASSISTED PROGRAMS

Under this title every Federal agency which provides financial assistance through grants, loans or contracts is required to eliminate discrimination on the grounds of race, color or national origin in these programs.

For example, this title would require the following:

a. hospitals constructed with Federal funds would have to serve all patients without regard to race, color or national origin;

b. elementary and secondary schools constructed, maintained and operated with Federal funds would have to admit children without regard to race, color or national origin;

c. State employment services financed by Federal funds would have to refer qualified job applicants for employment without discrimination;

d. schools for the deaf and the blind operated with Federal funds would have to serve the deaf and blind of any color;

e. colleges and universities receiving funds for their general operation or for the construction of special facilities, such as research centers, would have to admit students without discrimination;

f. construction contractors receiving funds under Federal public works programs would have to hire employees without discrimination.

Action by a Federal agency to carry out the requirements of this title may include the terminating of programs where discrimination is taking place or refusal to grant assistance to such a program.

Each agency is required to publish rules or regulations to carry out the purposes of the title. These rules and regulations are subject to the approval of the President.

Compliance actions are subject to the following conditions:

a. notice must be given of alleged failure to comply and an opportunity for a hearing must be provided;

b. in the event assistance is to be cut off, a written report must be submitted to Congress 30 days before the cut-off date;

c. compliance action may be appealed to the courts.

Social security and veteran's benefits, and other Federal benefits distributed directly to individuals are not affected by this law.

Federal assistance in the form of insurance or guaranty—for example, FHA insured loans—are not covered by this title (however, the President's Executive Order prohibiting discrimination in Federally aided housing remains in effect).

TITLE VII—EQUAL EMPLOYMENT OPPORTUNITY

This title establishes a Federal right to equal opportunity in employment. It creates an Equal Employment Opportunity Commission to assist in implementing this right.

Employers, labor unions and employment agencies are required to treat all persons without regard to their race, color, religion, sex, or national origin. This treatment must be given in all phases of employment, including hiring, promotion, firing, apprenticeship and other training programs, and job assignments.

When this title goes into full effect employers will be subject to its provisions if they have 25 or more regular employees in an industry that affects interstate commerce. Generally speaking, labor unions will be subject to the Act if they either operate a hiring hall for covered employers, or if they have 25 or more members who are employed by a covered employer. Employment agencies are also included if they regularly undertake to supply employees for a covered employer.

(Enforcement of the nondiscrimination requirements for employers and unions is postponed for one year. Employers and unions with 100 or more workers will be covered beginning July 2, 1965 and coverage will be extended each year until July 2, 1968 when employers and unions with 25 workers will be covered.)

Not covered by this title are (1) public employers, (2) bona fide private clubs, (3) educational institutions with regard to employees working in educational activities and all employment in religious educational institutions, (4) employers on or near an Indian reservation with regard to preferential treatment of Indians; and (5) religious corporations, institutions, etc., with regard to employees working in connection with religious activities.

When someone believes he has been discriminated against because of race, color, religion, sex, or national origin in any phase of job placement or employment, he may bring his complaint within 90 days to the Equal Employment Opportunity Commission or to the Attorney General.

The Commission will handle his complaint directly, unless the State where the alleged discrimination occurred has fair employment laws. If so, the person complaining must allow the State officials no more than 120 days to resolve the matter. If there is no satisfactory conclusion within this time or if the State rejects the complaint before the time is up, the complainant may then go to the Commission, which is authorized to settle valid complaints by conciliation and persuasion. Nothing said during the conciliation proceedings may be made public or used as evidence without the consent of the parties.

If the Commission fails to secure compliance within a period of no more than 60 days, the individual may take his case to a Federal court. This court may appoint an attorney and may exempt the complainant from payment of certain costs. The court, in its discretion, may allow the Attorney General to enter the case.

A worker who thinks he has been discriminated against may take his complaint directly to the Attorney General, who may bring the case before a three-judge court if he believes there is a pattern or practice of resistance to this title.

If the court in either action finds discrimination, it will order the employer, employment agency or union to take corrective action, which may include hiring or reinstating employees with or without back pay.

TITLE VIII—VOTING STATISTICS

The Secretary of Commerce is required to conduct a survey of persons of voting age by race, color, and national origin and to determine the extent to which such persons have registered and voted in such geographic areas as the Commission on Civil Rights recommends.

A similar survey must also be conducted on a nationwide basis in connection with the 1970 Census. No person questioned during such surveys may be compelled to disclose his race, color, religion or national origin and everyone must be advised of his right to refuse to give this information.

TITLE IX—INTERVENTION AND REMOVAL IN CIVIL RIGHTS CASES

The Attorney General is authorized to intervene in any Federal court action seeking relief from the denial of equal protection of the laws on account of race, color, religion or national origin. If a Federal court refuses to accept a civil rights case and sends it back to a State court, this action may be reviewed on appeal.

TITLE X—COMMUNITY RELATIONS SERVICE

A Community Relations Service is established in the Department of Commerce to provide assistance to persons or communities requiring help with civil rights problems where discriminatory practices impair constitutional rights or affect interstate commerce. The Service is authorized to cooperate with both public and private agencies, either on its own initiative or upon request from local officials or interested persons in situations where disputes threaten peaceful relations among the citizens of a community.

In addition, the Service is authorized to seek a voluntary settlement of public accommodation complaints which may be referred to it by a Federal Court. The Act directs that all activities of the Service in providing conciliation assistance shall be conducted in confidence and without publicity.

TITLE XI—MISCELLANEOUS

This title gives a right to jury trial in criminal contempt cases arising out of all sections of this Act except Title I, which retains the more limited jury trial provisions of the 1957 Civil Rights Act.

Appropriations are authorized to carry out the Act, and a separability clause provides that the rest of the Act will be unaffected if any portion is invalidated. Another section preserves existing remedies under Federal law. This title also preserves the rights of the States to legislate in the same areas covered by this Act, so long as such legislation is not inconsistent with the purposes of the Act.

A Summary of the Voting Rights Act of 1965

■ Suspends literacy tests and other devices (found to be discriminatory) as qualifications for voting in any Federal, State, local, general or primary election in the States of Alabama, Alaska, Georgia, Louisiana, Mississippi, South Carolina, Virginia and at least 26 counties in North Carolina.

■ Provides for the assignment of Federal examiners to conduct registration and observe voting in States and/or counties covered by the Act.

■ Directs the U.S. Attorney General to initiate suits immediately to test the constitutionality of poll taxes because the U.S. Congress found that the payment of such tax has been used in some areas to abridge the right to vote.

■ Extends civil and criminal protection to qualified persons seeking to vote and to those who urge or aid others to vote.

The Voting Rights Act of 1965 is the fourth bill to be enacted by the U.S. Congress since 1957 that attempts to safeguard the right of every citizen to vote, regardless of his race or color. The previous three legislative measures attempted to secure the right to vote through court cases initiated largely on a case-by-case, county-by-county basis. These cases, brought either by the U.S. Attorney General or an individual, did

Reprinted from *The Voting Rights Act of 1965* by the United States Commission on Civil Rights (CCR Special Publication, Number 4, U.S Government Printing Office, August 1965).

not adequately meet the dimensions of the problems of racial discrimination in voting.

The 1965 Act provides new tools to assure the right to vote and supplements the previous authority granted by the Civil Rights Acts of 1957, 1960 and 1964. It is intended primarily to enforce the Fifteenth Amendment to the Constitution of the United States which provides in Section 1:

> The right of citizens of the United States to vote shall not be denied or abridged by the United States or by any State on account of race, color, or previous condition of servitude.

The law has two central features:
1. Provision for suspending a variety of tests and devices that have been used to deny citizens the right to vote because of their race or color.
2. Provision for the appointment of Federal examiners to list voters in those areas where tests and devices have been suspended.

In this Act, the term "voting" includes all action necessary—from the time of registration to the actual counting of the votes—to make a vote for public or party office effective.

VOTER REQUIREMENTS OUTLAWED BY THIS ACT

No State or political subdivision (counties, municipalities and parishes) covered by the Voting Rights Act may require the use of any test or device as a prerequisite for registration or voting.

Tests or devices included in this Act are those which require:
1. A demonstration of the ability to read, write, understand or interpret any given material.
2. A demonstration of any educational achievement or knowledge of any particular subject.
3. Proof of good moral character.
4. Proof of qualifications through a procedure in which another person (such as an individual already registered) must vouch for the prospective voter.

COVERAGE

The Voting Rights Act of 1965 states that no person shall be denied the right to vote in any Federal, State or local election (including primaries) for failure to pass a test if he lives in a State or political subdivision which:

1. Maintained a test or device as a prerequisite to registration or voting as of November 1, 1964, *and*
2. Had a total voting age population of which less than 50 percent were registered or actually voted in the 1964 Presidential election.

If the above two factors are present, the State or political subdivision is automatically covered by the 1965 Act. If an entire State meets these qualifications, all of its counties come under the provisions of the Act. If only one county in a State meets them, the single county is subject to the requirements of the law.

States covered by the Act include Alabama, Alaska, Georgia, Louisiana, Mississippi, South Carolina, Virginia, and approximately 26 counties in North Carolina.

Cessation of Coverage

A State or political subdivision may be removed from coverage by filing a suit in a three-judge District Court for the District of Columbia. The State or political subdivision must convince the court that no test or device has been used for the purpose or with the effect of denying the right to vote because of race or color during the five years preceding the filing of the suit.

However, if there has been a previous court judgment against a State or political subdivision determining that tests or devices have been used to deny the right to vote, the State or political subdivision must wait five years before it can obtain an order from the District Court for the District of Columbia removing it from the coverage of the Act.

A judgment may be obtained more quickly if the Attorney General advises the court that he believes that the tests have not been used to discriminate on the basis of race or color during the five years preceding the filing of the action. He may also ask the court to reconsider its decision anytime within five years after judgment.

Changes in Voting Laws

When a State or political subdivision covered by the Act seeks to change its voting qualifications or procedures from those in effect on November 1, 1964, it must either obtain the approval of the U.S. Attorney General or initiate a Federal Court suit. If the Attorney General objects to these changes, or if they have not been submitted to him for his approval, the new laws may not be enforced until the District Court for the District of Columbia rules that the changes will not have the purpose or the effect of denying the right to vote because of the race or color of any person.

FEDERAL EXAMINERS

Once it is determined that a political subdivision is covered by the Act, the U.S. Attorney General may direct the U.S. Civil Service Commission to appoint Federal examiners to list voters if:

1. He has received twenty meritorious written complaints alleging voter discrimination, *or*
2. He believes that the appointment of examiners is necessary to enforce the guarantees of the Fifteenth Amendment.

The times, places and procedures for listing will be established by the Civil Service Commission.

Authority of the Examiners

The Federal examiners will list (that is, declare eligible and entitled to vote) those who satisfy state qualifications that have not been suspended by the Voting Rights Act. Examples of valid qualifications would be those of age and residence.

The examiners will prepare a list of qualified voters and send the list each month to State authorities who must register them—that is, place their names in the official voting records. This list must be available for public inspection. Each person on the examiner's list will be issued a certificate by the examiners as evidence of eligibility to vote in any Federal, State or local election.

No person listed by the examiner will be entitled to vote in any election unless his name has been sent to local election officials at least 45 days before that election thereby allowing the State election machinery to run without complication.

Enforcement of Action by Federal Examiners

At the request of the Attorney General the Civil Service Commission may appoint poll watchers in counties where Federal Examiners are already serving to observe whether all eligible persons are allowed to vote and whether all ballots are accurately tabulated.

If anyone who is properly listed or registered is not permitted to vote in any political subdivision where examiners are serving, a complaint may be made to the examiners of this denial within 48 hours after the polls close. If the examiner believes that the complaint has merit, he must inform the Attorney General immediately. The Attorney General may seek a district court order that provides for the casting of the ballot and suspends the election results until the vote is included in the final count.

Challenge of Listed Persons

A formal objection challenging the qualifications of a person listed by the Federal examiner may be filed (at a place to be designated by the Civil Service Commission) within ten days after the list of qualified voters has been made public and must be supported by at least two affidavits. The validity of the challenge will be determined within fifteen days after filing by a hearing officer appointed by the Civil Service Commission. The U.S. Court of Appeals may review decisions of the hearing officer.

Until the final court review is completed, any person listed by the examiner is still eligible and must be permitted to vote. If a challenge is successful, the name of the registrant will be removed from the examiner's list.

Withdrawal of Federal Examiners

Examiners may be withdrawn from a political subdivision when the names of all persons listed by the examiners have been placed in the official records and when there is no reason to believe that persons in the subdivision will be prevented from voting.

The removal may be accomplished by action of:
1. The Civil Service Commission after it receives notification from the U.S. Attorney General, *or*
2. The District Court for the District of Columbia in a suit brought by a political subdivision after the Director of the Census has determined that more than 50 percent of the nonwhite voting age population in the subdivision is registered to vote.

A political subdivision may petition the U.S. Attorney General to end listing procedures and to request that the Director of the Census conduct a survey to determine whether more than 50 percent of the nonwhite voting age population is registered.

POLL TAXES

The Act contains a Congressional finding that the right to vote has been denied or abridged by the requirement of the payment of a poll tax as a condition to voting.

The U.S. Attorney General is directed to institute suits against Alabama, Mississippi, Texas and Virginia which require the payment of poll taxes in order to determine if such taxes violate the Constitution.

While a suit is pending, or upon a finding that the poll tax is constitutional, persons registered or listed for the first time in areas covered by the Act need only pay the tax for the current year. The poll tax may be paid up to 45 days prior to an election regardless of the timeliness of the payment under State law.

VOTING SUITS

The Voting Rights Act of 1965 gives new enforcement powers to the courts in voting cases. When the court finds that there has been a denial of the right to vote in a suit brought by the U.S. Attorney General, the court must:

1. Authorize the appointment of examiners by the Civil Service Commission unless denials of the right to vote have been few in number, they have been corrected by State or local action, and there is no probability that they will reoccur.
2. Suspend the use of tests or devices in an area where it has been proved that at least one such requirement has been utilized to deny the right to vote because of race or color.

When examiners have been authorized by court order, they may be removed by an order of the authorizing court.

LANGUAGE LITERACY

If a person residing in a State where tests or devices have not been suspended has completed at least six grades in an "American-flag" school (a school in the United States or its territories), his inability to speak the English language shall not be the basis for denying him the right to vote. For example, a person who completed six grades of school in the Commonwealth of Puerto Rico but who now resides on the mainland of the United States would satisfy literacy requirements.

CRIMINAL AND CIVIL PENALTIES

Public officials or private individuals who deny persons the right to vote guaranteed by the Voting Rights Act of 1965 or anyone who attempts to or intimidates, threatens, or coerces a person from voting are subject to criminal penalties. It is also made a crime to attempt to or to intimidate, threaten or coerce anyone who urges or aids any person to vote. Criminal penalties are provided for applicants who give false information about their eligibility to vote or who accept payment to register or vote in a Federal election. The U.S. Attorney General is also authorized to bring action for injunctive relief to restrain violations of the Act.

Suggested Further Readings

An Annotated Bibliography

The popularity of various books on the race problem prompted satirist Victor Navsky, spoofing the important books of 1965, to write:

> Perhaps no subject is more worthy of attention than civil rights. But this year so many civil rights volumes have been published that I wouldn't be surprised if the white community finally decided to grant the Negro his full complement of justice in order to avoid having to read any more books about it. Of the 2,341 civil rights works out this year I suppose the one which does the least for me is "Uhuru Now," the first-person story of a daughter of the American Revolution who renounces her American citizenship and flees to Rhodesia, where she seeks happiness among the native majority.

The following list is not intended to be exhaustive nor to be a list of the "best" books. The books were selected with the general reader in mind. Most of them are relatively recent and readily available—many in paperback editions; all of them tend to be informative and analytical rather than polemical or impressionistic.

The teacher, researcher, or student with a serious interest in pursuing the topics treated in this reader will find Erwin K. Welsch's *The*

Negro in the United States: A Research Guide (Indiana University Press, 1965) absolutely indispensable. It is a well-written bibliographical guide to all aspects of the Negro's problems.

BRINK, WILLIAM J., and LOUIS HARRIS. *The Negro Revolution in America: What Negroes Want, Why and How They Are Fighting, Whom They Support, What Whites Think of Them and Their Demands* (New York: Simon and Schuster, 1964). This book is based on the pioneering large-scale surveys, done by Louis Harris and *Newsweek Magazine,* of white and Negro attitudes toward the race crisis of the sixties. There are many tables and direct quotes from respondents. The book is more valuable for the data presented than for the analysis, which tends to be superficial.

BROWN, CLAUDE. *Manchild in the Promised Land* (New York: The Macmillan Company, 1965). A detailed autobiographical account of growing up in the Harlem ghetto. One of the most compelling documents available on the meaning of segregated urban life for the lower-class Negro.

CLARK, KENNETH. *Dark Ghetto* (New York: Harper & Row, 1965). A careful, thoughtful, and, at times, angry account of the consequences of ghetto existence for the individual. The sections on education are of particular interest inasmuch as the author challenges the assumptions and motivations of those promoting a "culturally deprived" approach to the solution of the problems of youth.

CLARKE, JOHN HENRIK (Ed.). *Harlem, A Community in Transition* (New York: Citadel, 1964). An uneven collection of essays on various aspects of life in Harlem. Some of the pieces are excellent. The book as a whole yields a fascinating picture of life in the "capital" of Negro America. Especially valuable are the essays on cultural life within the Negro community—a topic not covered in most books on the Negro.

Daedalus, "The Negro American—Parts 1 and 2" (Vol. 94, No. 4, Fall 1965; Vol. 95, No. 1, Winter 1966). An extremely valuable collection of essays by such authorities as St. Clair Drake, Kenneth Clark, G. Franklin Edwards, John Hope Franklin, Daniel P. Moynihan, Thomas F. Pettigrew, Lee Rainwater, James Q. Wilson, Whitney M. Young, Jr., and others, dealing with employment, politics, religion, inter-group relations and other aspects of the contemporary situation of the American Negro and the implications of these characteristics for the future of the Negro Movement.

DAVIS, JOHN P. (Ed.). *The American Negro Reference Book* (Englewood Cliffs, N.J.: Prentice-Hall, Inc., 1966). A comprehensive collection of essays by 26 authorities on historical, demographic, economic, political, legal, educational, psychological, and artistic characteristics of Negro life in America today. The volume is sponsored by the Phelps-Stokes Fund.

DRAKE, ST. CLAIR, and HORACE R. CAYTON. *Black Metropolis: A Study of Negro Life in a Northern City* (New York: Harper Torchbooks; Harper & Row, Publishers; Revised and enlarged edition, 1962). This study of Bronzeville, the Negro area of Chicago, is the most detailed and comprehensive work on the Negro in Northern cities. Even though the research was done in the 1930's, it remains the best source of information on and analysis of urban Negro society. A good deal of the material is valid not only for Bronzeville of the thirties but also for present-day ghettos of Northern and Western cities. An outstanding feature of the book is the brilliant description and analysis of social stratification within the Negro community.

ESSIEN-UDOM, ESSIEN U. *Black Nationalism: A Search for an*

Identity in America (Chicago: University of Chicago Press, 1962). A sympathetic and thorough study of the controversial Black Muslim sect by a Nigerian scholar. The book is based on extensive participant observation and gives an insider's view of the Nation of Islam. The concluding sections of the book analyze the Muslims in terms of the Negro's need for a positive ethnic identification and deal provocatively with the whole area of integration, separatism, and problems of identity.

FRAZIER, E. FRANKLIN. *Black Bourgeoisie* (Glencoe, Ill.: Free Press, 1957). With a new preface by the author: Collier paperback, AS347, 1962. This book is at once good scholarship, fascinating reading, and highly controversial opinion. It is the assessment of the Negro middle class by the most distinguished sociologist of Negro life. While much of the criticism of the Negro middle class may seem unduly harsh, it is based on a lifetime of familiarity with this group and is worth careful consideration.

GLAZER, NATHAN, and DANIEL P. MOYNIHAN. *Beyond the Melting Pot: The Negroes, Puerto Ricans, Jews, Italians, and Irish of New York City* (Cambridge, Mass.: M.I.T. Press, 1963). A beautifully written description of ethnic life in New York City. The problems of Negroes are greatly illuminated by frequent analysis of the differences between Negroes and the other four groups considered. A sophisticated view of the relative uniqueness of the Negro community is substituted for a simple but popular view that Negroes constitute just another immigrant group in Northern cities and will easily follow the pattern of the groups that preceded them. The personal familiarity of the authors with their subject matter is evident throughout the book.

LEWIS, ANTHONY, and the New York Times. *Portrait of a Decade: The Second American Revolution* (New York: Random House, 1964). This book is based on the detailed, reliable, and thoughtful coverage of civil rights news by the *New York Times*. It covers the period from the Supreme Court decision of 1954 to 1964. The book's main value is in providing a clear picture of the major civil rights events of the period and a good sense of the cumulative effect of the events reported.

LOMAX, LOUIS E. *The Negro Revolt* (New York: Harper & Row, 1962). A journalistic account of the major groups, leaders, and events of the civil rights movement. The book begins with a section on the historical background to the civil rights movement. However, its main value is in the detailed discussion of the events of the 1950's and early sixties. The book gives a good, if somewhat simple, view of the conflict between the old-line Urban League and NAACP and the new militant movement composed of CORE, SNCC, and King's SCLC.

LUBELL, SAMUEL. *White and Black: Test of a Nation* (New York: Harper & Row, 1964). The well-known pollster and political analyst discusses American race relations in the context of the electoral process. He provides an excellent historical view of the development of the Negro vote and traces its composition and impact through the analysis of key elections. The book also features the skillful use of man-on-the-street interview material for which Lubell is so well known.

MYRDAL, GUNNAR with the assistance of Richard Sterner and Arnold Rose. *An American Dilemma: The Negro Problem and Modern Democracy*, Twentieth Anniversary Edition, (New York: Harper 1962). Two-volume McGraw-Hill paperback, 44280 and 44281. Much of the material in this massive work is now out of date. Nevertheless, this comprehensive study by the distinguished Swedish economist Gunnar Myrdal is regarded as a classic. It covers, in a systematic and scholarly fashion, every significant aspect of the Negro's problems.

PETTIGREW, THOMAS F. *A Profile of the Negro American* (Princeton, N.J.: Van Nostrand, 1964). Pettigrew has marshalled relevant literature to produce a portrait of the American Negro from the perspective of social-science studies. There are excellent summaries of facts on Negro health, intelligence, and crime. The thrust of the book is to refute as completely as possible the dogma of inherent Negro inferiority. For those who begin with a conviction of the essential equality of the races, the book provides disappointingly little in the way of new ideas or analysis. Pettigrew provides extensive bibliographical material.

ROSE, ARNOLD M. *The Negro in America* (New York: Harper & Row, 1948). A very competent condensation of Myrdal's *American Dilemma*. Rose collaborated with Myrdal on the original work and has abstracted most of its important findings and analyses.

SILBERMAN, CHARLES E. *Crisis in Black and White* (New York: Random House, 1964). Of all the recent books on race relations, this is probably the most original, creative, and provocative. It goes well beyond description and analysis—Silberman offers many thoughtful suggestions for action. While the proposals he advocates are open to dispute, most readers will appreciate the mood of action and urgency in which the book was written. Special note should be made of the lengthy discussions of Saul Alinsky-style community organization and the need for extensive preschool programs since both of these ideas have had great impact on government policy.

United States Department of Labor, Office of Policy Planning and Research. *The Negro Family: The Case for National Action* (Washington, D.C.: U.S. Government Printing Office, March 1965). Available at $.45 from U.S. Government Printing Office. Commonly known as the Moynihan Report, this brief study was prepared by former Assistant Secretary of Labor, Daniel Patrick Moynihan. Originally intended for use by government personnel only, it created such interest and controversy that it was released to the general public. The report is basically concerned with what Moynihan finds to be a shocking and steadily increasing degree of family disintegration and instability among the Negro lower class in large urban areas. The report traces both the historical causes and present-day consequences of this situation. The study is closely reasoned, well documented.

WESTIN, ALAN F. *Freedom Now! The Civil-Rights Struggle in America* (New York: Basic Books, 1964). A large and topical collection of articles and essays on the civil rights struggle. A good introduction to recent ideas and developments in this area. As with many anthologies, the pieces are of varying quality. Nevertheless, many provocative articles have been included.

WILSON, JAMES Q. *Negro Politics: The Search for Leadership* (Glencoe, Ill.: Free Press, 1960). A scholarly and perceptive study of the nature of Negro politics in Northern cities. While the book considers both the role of Negro voters and that of Negro politicians, the treatment of politicians is especially outstanding. The emphasis is on the recurring patterns of Negro-white political relations and the underlying social patterns.